# Effective TCP/IP Programming

# Effective TCP/IP Programming

## 44 Tips to Improve Your Network Programs

*Jon C. Snader*

## ADDISON–WESLEY

Boston • San Francisco • New York • Toronto • Montreal
London • Munich • Paris • Madrid
Capetown • Sidney • Tokyo • Singapore • Mexico City

Many of the designations used by manufacturers and sellers to distinguish their products are claimed as trademarks. Where those designations appear in this book, and we were aware of a trademark claim, the designations have been printed in initial capital letters or in all capitals.

UNIX is a technology trademark of X/Open Company, Ltd.

The author and publisher have taken care in the preparation of this book, but make no expressed or implied warranty of any kind and assume no responsibility for errors or omissions. No liability is assumed for incidental or consequential damages in connection with or arising out of the use of the information or programs contained herein.

The publisher offers discounts on this book when ordered in quantity for special sales. For more information, please contact:

Pearson Education Corporate Sales Division
One Lake Street
Upper Saddle River, NJ 07458
(800) 382-3419
corpsales@pearsontechgroup.com

Visit AW on the Web: www.awl.com/cseng/

*Library of Congress Cataloging-in-Publication Data*
Snader, Jon C., 1944–
    Effective TCP/IP programming : 44 tips to improve your network programs / Jon C. Snader.
        p. cm.
    Includes bibliographical references and index.
    ISBN 0-201-61589-4
    1. Internet programming.  2.  TCP/IP (Computer network protocol)  I.  Title.
    QA76.625 S63 2000
    005.7'1376—dc21                                                    00–026658

ISBN 0-201-61589-4
Text printed on recycled paper
1 2 3 4 5 6 7 8 9 10—MA—0403020100
First printing, May 2000

*For Maria*

# Contents

**Chapter 3     Building Effective and Robust Network Programs 111**

**Chapter 4     Tools and Resources                           221**

# *Preface*

## Introduction

The explosive growth of the Internet, wireless communications, and networking in general has led to a corresponding growth in the number of programmers and engineers writing networking applications. TCP/IP programming can seem seductively simple. The Application Programming Interface (API) is straightforward, and even the newest beginner can take a template for a client or server and flesh it out to a working application.

Often, however, after an initial surge of productivity, neophytes begin to bog down in details and find that their applications suffer from performance or robustness problems. Network programming is a field full of dark corners and often misunderstood details. This book sheds light into those corners and helps replace misunderstanding with an appreciation for the often subtle points of TCP/IP programming.

After finishing this book, you should have a thorough understanding of many of the trouble spots in network programming. In the text we examine many areas that seem only peripherally connected to the core knowledge that a working network programmer is expected to have. We will see, however, that by gaining an understanding of these minutiae, we also gain an appreciation for how the inner workings of the network protocols can interact with our applications. Armed with this insight, application behavior that previously seemed bewildering becomes understandable, and the solutions to problems become clear.

The organization of the text is a little unusual. We examine common problems one at a time in a series of tips. During the process of studying a particular trouble spot, we usually explore some aspect of TCP/IP programming in depth. When we finish, we will not only have identified and dealt with common problems, we will also have a fairly comprehensive understanding of how the TCP/IP protocols work and interact with our applications.

The organization of the text into tips leads to a certain disjointedness. To help guide you, Chapter 1 contains a road map that explains the material covered in each chapter and how it all hangs together. The Contents, which lists each tip, will give you a sense of the text's organization. Because the title of each tip is in the form of an imperative, we can also think of the Contents as a list of network programming precepts.

On the other hand, this organization into tips makes the text more useful as a handbook. When we run into a problem in our day-to-day work, it is easy to revisit the appropriate tip to refresh our understanding of that particular problem area. You will find that many topics are visited in more than one tip, sometimes from a slightly different viewpoint. This repetition helps solidify the concepts and makes them seem more natural.

## Readers

This text is written primarily for the advanced beginner or intermediate network programmer, but more experienced readers should find it useful as well. Although the reader is presumed to have a familiarity with networking and the basic sockets API, Chapter 1 contains a review of the elementary socket calls and uses them to build a primitive client and server. Tip 4 (Develop and Use Application Skeletons) revisits the various client and server models in more detail, so even a reader with minimal background should be able to understand and benefit from the text.

Almost all of the examples are written in the C language, so a reasonably good understanding of elementary C programming is necessary to get the full benefit from the programs in the text. In Tip 31 (Remember That All the World's Not C) we show some examples written in Perl, but no knowledge of Perl is assumed. Similarly, there are a few examples of small shell programs, but again, no previous experience with shell programming is necessary to understand them.

The examples and text attempt to be platform neutral. The examples are, with a few exceptions, intended to compile and run under any UNIX or Win32 system. Even those programmers not working on a UNIX or Windows system should have little trouble porting the examples to work on their platforms.

## Typographical Conventions

During our explorations we will build and run many small programs designed to illustrate some aspect of the problem we are examining. When we show interactive input and output, we will use the following conventions:

- Text that we type is set in **bold Courier**.
- Text that the system outputs is set in `plain Courier`.
- Comments that are not part of the actual input or output are set in *italics*.

The following is an example from Tip 9:

```
bsd: $ tcprw localhost 9000
hello
received message 1                         this is printed after a 5-second delay
                                           the server is killed here
hello again
tcprw: readline failed: Connection reset by peer (54)
bsd: $
```

Notice that we include the name of the system in the shell prompt. In the previous example, we see that `tcprw` was run on the host named bsd.

When we introduce a new API function, either our own or one from the standard system calls, we enclose it in a box. The standard system calls are enclosed in a solid box, like this:

```
#include <sys/socket.h>        /* UNIX */
#include <winsock2.h>          /* Windows */

int connect( SOCKET s, const struct sockaddr *peer, int peer_len );
```
                    Returns: 0 on success, -1 (UNIX) or nonzero (Windows) on failure

API functions that we develop are enclosed in a dashed box, like this:

```
#include "etcp.h"

SOCKET tcp_server( char *host, char *port );
```
                              Returns: a listening socket (terminates on error)

> Parenthetical remarks and material that is commonly placed in footnotes are set in smaller type and are indented like this paragraph. Often, this material can be skipped on a first reading.

Lastly, we set off URLs with angle brackets like this:

```
<http://www.freebsd.org>
```

## Source Code and Errata Availability

The source code for all the examples in this book are available electronically on the Web from `<http://www.netcom.com/~jsnader>`. Because the examples in the book were typeset directly from the program files, you can obtain and experiment with them on your own. The skeletons and library code are also available for your use.

A current list of errata is available from the same Web site.

## Rich Stevens

I am a great admirer of the "look and feel" of Rich Stevens' books. When I began this project, I wrote to Rich and asked if he would mind if I stole his layout style. Rich, with his characteristic generosity, not only replied that he had no objections, but even aided and abetted the theft by sending me a copy of the Groff macros that he used for typesetting his books.

To the extent that you find the appearance and layout of this book pleasing, we have Rich to thank. If you find something in the layout that doesn't seem right, or is not pleasing, take a look at one of Rich's books to see what I was aiming for.

## Colophon

I produced camera-ready copy for this book using James Clark's Groff package, and Rich Stevens' modified ms macros. The illustrations were prepared with gpic (including macros written by Rich Stevens and Gary Wright), the tables with gtbl, and the (limited) mathematical notation with geqn. The index was produced with the help of a set of awk scripts written by Jon Bentley and Brian Kernighan. The example code was included in the text directly from the program files with the help of Dave Hanson's loom program.

## Acknowledgments

It is customary for authors to thank their families for their help and support during the writing of a book, and now I know why. This book literally would not have been possible were it not for my wife Maria. Without her taking on an even larger share than normal of my "50 percent," there would have been no time to work on and complete this book. These words are woefully inadequate thanks for the extra chores and lonely nights that she endured.

Another extraordinarily valuable asset to a writer are the reviewers who struggle through the early drafts. The technical reviewers for this text found numerous errors, both technical and typographical, corrected my misunderstandings, suggested fresh approaches, told me things I hadn't known before, and occasionally even offered a kind word by way of encouragement. I would like to thank Chris Cleeland, Bob Gilligan (FreeGate Corp.), Peter Haverlock (Nortel Networks), S. Lee Henry (Web Publishing, Inc.), Mukesh Kacker (Sun Microsystems, Inc.), Barry Margolin (GTE Internetworking), Mike Oliver (Sun Microsystems, Inc.), Uri Raz, and Rich Stevens for their hard work and suggestions. The text is a much better work on account of it.

Finally, I would like to thank my editor, Karen Gettman, project editor, Mary Hart, production coordinator, Tyrrell Albaugh, and copy editor, Cat Ohala. They are a joy to work with and have been incredibly helpful to this first-time author.

I welcome readers' comments, suggestions, and corrections. Feel free to send me email at the address below.

Jon C. Snader

`jsnader@ix.netcom.com`

`http://www.netcom.com/~jsnader`

*Tampa, Florida*
*December 1999*

# *1*

# *Introduction*

The purpose of this book is to help the advanced beginner or intermediate network programmer make the move to journeyman, and eventually master, status. The transition to master status is largely a matter of experience and the accretion of specific, if sometimes obscure, bits of knowledge. Nothing but time and practice will provide the experience, but this book can help with the knowledge.

Network programming is a large field, of course, and there are many contenders for the choice of networking technology when we wish to enable communication between two or more machines. The possibilities range from the simple, such as serial links, to the complex, such as IBM's System Network Architecture. Today it is increasingly clear that the TCP/IP protocol suite is the technology of choice for building networks. This is driven largely by the Internet and its most popular application: the World Wide Web.

> The Web isn't really an application, of course. It's not a protocol either, although it uses both applications (Web browsers and servers) and protocols (HTTP, for example). What we mean is that the Web is the most popular user-visible application of networking technology that runs on the Internet.

Even before the advent of the Web, however, TCP/IP was a popular method of creating networks. Because it was an open standard and could interconnect machines from different vendors, it was used increasingly to build networks and network applications. By the end of the 1990s, TCP/IP had become the dominant networking technology, and it is likely to remain so for some time. Because of this, we concentrate on TCP/IP and the networks on which it runs.

If we wish to master network programming we must first absorb some of the background knowledge needed to come to a fuller understanding and appreciation of our craft. Our plan for acquiring this knowledge is to look at several common problems that beginning network programmers face. Many of these problems are the results of misconceptions about or incomplete understanding of certain facets of the TCP/IP

1

protocols and the APIs used to communicate with them. All of these problems are real. They are a constant source of confusion and the frequent subjects of questions in the networking news groups.

## A Few Conventions

The textual material and programs in this book are, with a few obvious exceptions, intended to be portable between UNIX (32 or 64 bit) and the Microsoft Win32 API. We have made no attempt to deal with 16-bit Windows applications. That said, almost all the material and many of the programs are appropriate in other environments as well.

This desire for portability has led to a few infelicities in the code examples. UNIX programmers will look askance at the notion of socket descriptors being defined as type SOCKET instead of type int for instance, and Windows programmers will notice that we are relentlessly committed to console applications. These conventions are described in Tip 4.

Similarly, we avoid, for the most part, using read and write on sockets because the Win32 API does not support these system calls on sockets. We will often speak of a read of or write to a socket, but we are speaking generically. By "read" we mean recv, recvfrom, or recvmsg; by "write" we mean send, sendto, or sendmsg. When we mean the read system call specifically, we will set it in Courier font as read, and similarly for write.

One of the hardest decisions to make was whether to include material on IPv6, the coming replacement for the current version (IPv4) of the Internet Protocol (IP). In the end, the decision was not to cover IPv6. There were many reasons for this, including

- Almost everything in this text remains true whether IPv4 or IPv6 is being used
- The differences that do appear tend to be localized in the addressing portions of the API
- This is a book based largely on the shared experiences and knowledge of journeyman network programmers and we really have no experience with IPv6 yet because implementations are just now becoming widely available

Therefore, when we speak of *IP* without qualification, we are speaking of IPv4. In those places where we do mention IPv6, we are careful to refer to it as *IPv6* explicitly.

Lastly, we refer to an 8 bit unit of data as a *byte*. It is common in the networking community to refer to such data as *octets*. The reasons for this are historical. It used to be that the size of a byte depended on the platform, and there was no agreement regarding its exact size. To avoid ambiguity, the early networking literature made the size explicit by coining the term *octet*. Today, there is universal agreement that a byte is 8 bits long [Kernighan and Pike 1999], and the use of octet seems needlessly pedantic.

> Despite this, one can still occasionally see the suggestion that bytes are 8 bits long, provoking a Usenet flame along the lines of, "Kids today! When I was a lad I worked on the Frumbaz-6, which had a byte length of 5 and a half bits. Don't tell me a byte always has 8 bits."

## Road Map to the Rest of the Book

In the rest of this chapter we review the basic sockets API and client-server architecture used when writing TCP/IP applications. This is the base on which we must build as we master our craft.

Chapter 2 discusses some basic facts and misconceptions about TCP/IP and networking. We learn, for example, the difference between a connection-oriented protocol and a connectionless one. We explore IP addressing and the often confusing subjects of subnets, *classless interdomain routing* (CIDR), and *network address translation* (NAT). We see that TCP does *not*, in fact, guarantee delivery of data, that we must be prepared for misbehavior on the part of our peers or users, and that our applications are likely to behave differently on a *wide area network* (WAN), than they do on a *local area network* (LAN).

We are reminded that TCP is a *stream* protocol, and what that means for us as programmers. Similarly, we learn that TCP does not detect loss of connectivity automatically, why this is a good thing, and what we can do about it.

We see why the sockets API should almost always be preferred to the Transport Layer Interface/X/Open Transport Interface (TLI/XTI), and why we shouldn't take the Open Systems Interconnection model (OSI) too seriously. We also see that TCP is a remarkably efficient protocol with excellent performance, and that it doesn't usually make sense to duplicate its functionality using UDP.

In Chapter 2 we also develop skeleton code for several TCP/IP application models, and use it to build a library of commonly needed functions. These skeletons and the library are important because they allow us to write applications without having to worry about the routine chores such as address conversion, connection management, and so on. Because we have these skeletons available, we are less tempted to take short-cuts, such as hard-coding addresses and port numbers, or ignoring error returns.

We use these skeletons and library repeatedly throughout the text to build test cases, example code, and even stand-alone working applications. Often we can build a special-purpose application or test case merely by adding a few lines of code to one of our skeletons.

In Chapter 3 we examine several seemingly trivial subjects in depth. For example, we start with a discussion of the TCP write operation and what it does. At first blush this seems simple: We write $n$ bytes and TCP sends them to our peer. As we shall see, however, this is often not the case. TCP has a complex set of rules for whether it can send data immediately upon the write, and if it can, how much. Understanding these rules and how they interact with our applications is essential if we are to write robust and efficient programs.

Similar considerations apply to reading data and to connection termination. We examine these operations and learn how to perform an orderly termination that ensures no data gets lost. We also examine the `connect` operation, how to time it out, and how to use it with UDP applications.

We study the use of the UNIX superserver, `inetd`, and see how its use can significantly reduce the effort needed to write a network-aware application. Similarly, we see how we can use `tcpmux` to relieve us of the necessity of worrying about assigning well-known ports to our servers. We show how `tcpmux` works and build our own version to run on systems that don't already have the facility.

We look in depth at such little understood topics as the TIME-WAIT state, the Nagle algorithm, choosing buffer sizes, and the proper use of the `SO_REUSEADDR` socket option. We see how to make our applications event driven and how we can provide individual timers for each event. We examine some common mistakes that even experienced network programmers often make, and we study some techniques we can use to increase the performance of our applications.

Finally we take a look at networking and scripting languages. By using some Perl scripts, we demonstrate how it is possible to build useful network utilities and test drivers quickly and easily.

Chapter 4 addresses two areas. First we examine several tools that are essential for every network programmer. We start with the venerable `ping` utility and show how it can be used in some elementary troubleshooting. Next we examine network sniffers in general and `tcpdump` in particular. Throughout Chapter 4 we see examples of using `tcpdump` to diagnose application problems and puzzles. We study `traceroute` and use it to explore the shape of a tiny portion of the Internet.

The `ttcp` utility (co-authored by `ping` creator Mike Muuss) is a useful tool for studying network performance and the effect that certain TCP parameters have on that performance. We use it to demonstrate some diagnostic techniques. Another public domain tool, `lsof`, is invaluable for matching up network connections with the processes that have them open. Many times, `lsof` provides information that is not otherwise available without heroic effort.

We take a long look at the `netstat` utility, and the many different types of information that it provides. We also examine system call trace facilities such as `ktrace` and `truss`.

We conclude our discussion of network diagnostic tools by building a utility to intercept and display Internet Control Messsage Protocol (ICMP) datagrams. This provides not only a useful addition to our toolbox, but also an example of the use of raw sockets.

The second part of Chapter 4 discusses resources we can use to further our knowledge and understanding of TCP/IP and networking. We look at the remarkable books by Rich Stevens, sources of networking code that we can study and learn from, the request for comments (RFC) collection available from the Internet Engineering Task Force (IETF), and the Usenet news groups.

## Client-Server Architecture

Although we speak of a *client* and a *server*, it is not always clear, in the general case, which role a particular program is playing. Often the programs are more like peers, exchanging information with neither clearly serving information to a client. With TCP/IP, though, the distinction is much clearer. The server listens for TCP connections or unsolicited UDP datagrams from a client or clients. Approaching this from the client's perspective, we can say that the client is the one who "speaks" first.

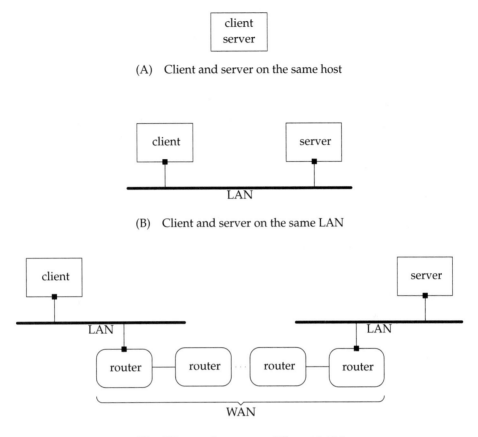

(A)   Client and server on the same host

(B)   Client and server on the same LAN

(C)   Client and server on different LANs

**Figure 1.1** Typical client-server situations

Throughout this text we consider three typical client-server situations, as shown in Figure 1.1. In the first, the client and server run on the same machine, as illustrated in Figure 1.1A. This is the simplest configuration because no physical network is involved. Output data is sent down the TCP/IP stack as usual, but instead of being placed on a network device output queue, it is looped back internally and travels back up the stack as input.

There are several advantages to this setup during development, even if the client and server eventually run on different machines. First, it is easier to judge the raw performance of the client and server applications because there is no network latency involved. Second, this method presents an idealized laboratory environment in which packets are not dropped, delayed, or delivered out of order.

At least most of the time. As we shall see in Tip 7, it is possible to stress even this environment enough to cause the loss of UDP datagrams.

Finally, development is often easier and more convenient when we debug on the same machine.

It is also possible, of course, that the client and server will run on the same machine even in a production environment. See Tip 26 for an example of this.

Our second client-server setup, illustrated in Figure 1.1B, is for the client and server to run on different machines but on the same LAN. A real network is involved here, but this environment is still nearly ideal. Packets are rarely lost and virtually never arrive out of order. This is a very common production environment, and in many cases applications are not intended to run in any other.

A common example of this type of situation is a print server. A small LAN may have only one printer for several hosts. One of the hosts (or a TCP/IP stack built into the printer) acts as a server that takes print requests from clients on the other hosts and spools the data to the printer for printing.

The third type of client-server situation involves a client and server separated by a WAN (Figure 1.1C). The WAN could be the Internet or perhaps a corporate intranet, but the point is the two applications are not on the same LAN, and IP datagrams from one to the other must pass through one or more routers.

This environment can be significantly more hostile than the first two. As the amount of traffic on the WAN increases, the router queues used to store packets temporarily until they can be forwarded begin to fill up. When the routers run out of queue space they begin to drop packets. This leads to retransmissions, which in turn leads to duplicate and out-of-order delivery of packets. These problems are not theoretical and they're not rare, as we shall see in Tip 38.

We shall have more to say about the difference between the LAN and WAN environments in Tip 12, but for now we merely note that they can behave very differently.

## Basic Sockets API Review

In this section we review the basic sockets API and use it to build rudimentary client and server applications. Although these applications are "bare-boned," they serve to illustrate the essential characteristics of a TCP client and server.

Let's start with the API calls we need for a simple client. Figure 1.2 shows the basic socket calls that are used by every client. As shown in Figure 1.2, the address of our peer is specified in a sockaddr_in structure that is passed to connect.

Generally, the first thing we must do is obtain a socket for the connection. We do this with the socket system call.

```
#include <sys/socket.h>      /* UNIX */
#include <winsock2.h>        /* Windows */

SOCKET socket( int domain, int type, int protocol );
```
Returns: Socket descriptor on success, -1 (UNIX) or INVALID_SOCKET (Windows) on failure

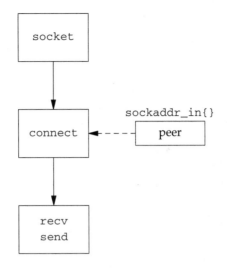

**Figure 1.2** Basic socket calls for a client

The sockets API is protocol independent and can support several different *communications domains*. The *domain* parameter is a constant that represents the desired communications domain.

The two most common domains are the `AF_INET` (or Internet) domain and the `AF_LOCAL` (or `AF_UNIX`) domain. In this text we are concerned only with the `AF_INET` domain. The `AF_LOCAL` domain is used for *interprocess communication* (IPC) on the same machine.

> It's a matter of mild controversy as to whether the *domain* constants should be AF_* or PF_*. Proponents of PF_* point to their history in now-defunct versions of the `socket` call from 4.1c/2.8/2.9BSD and to the fact that PF stands for *protocol family*. Proponents for AF_* point out that the kernel socket code matches the *domain* parameter against the AF_* constants. Because the two sets of constants are defined the same—indeed, one is often defined in terms of the other—it makes no practical difference which we use.

The *type* parameter indicates the type of socket to be created. The most common values, and the ones we use in this text, are the following:

- `SOCK_STREAM`—These sockets provide a reliable, full duplex connection-oriented byte stream. In TCP/IP, this means *TCP*.

- `SOCK_DGRAM`—These sockets provide an unreliable, best-effort datagram service. In TCP/IP, this means *UDP*.

- `SOCK_RAW`—These sockets allow access to some datagrams at the IP layer. They are for special purposes such as listening for ICMP messages.

The *protocol* field indicates which protocol should be used with the socket. With TCP/IP, this is normally specified implicitly by the socket type, and the parameter is set to zero. In some cases, such as raw sockets, there are several possible protocols, and the one desired must be specified. We see an example of this in Tip 40.

For the simplest TCP client, the only other sockets API call we need to set up a conversation with our peer is `connect`, which is used to establish the connection:

```
#include <sys/socket.h>      /* UNIX */
#include <winsock2.h>        /* Windows */

int connect( SOCKET s, const struct sockaddr *peer, int peer_len );
```
Returns: 0 on success, -1 (UNIX) or nonzero (Windows) on failure

The *s* parameter is the socket descriptor returned by the `socket` call. The *peer* parameter points to an address structure that holds the address of the desired peer and some other information. For the `AF_INET` domain, this is a `sockaddr_in` structure. We look at a simple example in a moment. The *peer_len* parameter is the size of the structure pointed to by *peer*.

Once we've set up a connection, we are ready to transfer data. Under UNIX we can simply call `read` and `write` using the socket descriptor exactly as we would a file descriptor. Unfortunately, as we've already mentioned, Windows does not overload these system calls with socket semantics, so we have to use `recv` and `send` instead. These calls are just like `read` and `write` except that they have an additional parameter:

```
#include <sys/socket.h>      /* UNIX */
#include <winsock2.h>        /* Windows */

int recv( SOCKET s, void *buf, size_t len, int flags );

int send( SOCKET s, const void *buf, size_t len, int flags );
```
Returns: number of bytes transferred on success, -1 on failure

The *s*, *buf*, and *len* parameters are the same as those for `read` and `write`. The values that the *flags* parameter can take are generally system dependent, but both UNIX and Windows support the following:

- `MSG_OOB`—When set, this flag causes urgent data to be sent or read.

- `MSG_PEEK`—This flag is used to peek at incoming data without removing it from the receive buffer. After the call, the data is still available for a subsequent read.

- `MSG_DONTROUTE`—This flag causes the kernel to bypass the normal routing function. It is generally used only by routing programs or for diagnostic purposes.

When dealing with TCP, these calls are generally all we need. For use with UDP, however, the `recvfrom` and `sendto` calls are useful. These calls are close cousins of `recv` and `send`, but they allow us to specify the destination address when sending a UDP datagram and to retrieve the source address when reading a UDP datagram:

```
#include <sys/socket.h>      /* UNIX */
#include <winsock2.h>        /* Windows */

int recvfrom( SOCKET s, void *buf, size_t len, int flags,
                struct sockaddr *from, int *fromlen );

int sendto( SOCKET s, const void *buf, size_t len, int flags,
                const struct sockaddr *to, int tolen );
```
                            Returns: number of bytes transferred on success, -1 on failure

The first four parameters—*s*, *buf*, *len*, and *flags*—are the same as they were in the `recv` and `send` calls. The *from* parameter in the `recvfrom` call points to a socket address structure in which the kernel stores the source address of an incoming datagram. The length of this address is stored in the integer pointed to by *fromlen*. Notice that *fromlen* is a *pointer* to an integer.

Similarly, the *to* parameter in the `sendto` call points to a socket address structure that contains the address of the datagram's destination. The *tolen* parameter is the length of the address structure pointed to by *to*. Notice that *tolen* is a simple integer, not a pointer.

We're now in a position to look at a simple TCP client (Figure 1.3).

*————————————————————————————— simplec.c*

```
 1 #include <sys/types.h>
 2 #include <sys/socket.h>
 3 #include <netinet/in.h>
 4 #include <arpa/inet.h>
 5 #include <stdio.h>

 6 int main( void )
 7 {
 8     struct sockaddr_in peer;
 9     int s;
10     int rc;
11     char buf[ 1 ];

12     peer.sin_family = AF_INET;
13     peer.sin_port = htons( 7500 );
14     peer.sin_addr.s_addr = inet_addr( "127.0.0.1" );

15     s = socket( AF_INET, SOCK_STREAM, 0 );
16     if ( s < 0 )
17     {
18         perror( "socket call failed" );
19         exit( 1 );
20     }
```

```
21      rc = connect( s, ( struct sockaddr * )&peer, sizeof( peer ) );
22      if ( rc )
23      {
24          perror( "connect call failed" );
25          exit( 1 );
26      }
27      rc = send( s, "1", 1, 0 );
28      if ( rc <= 0 )
29      {
30          perror( "send call failed" );
31          exit( 1 );
32      }
33      rc = recv( s, buf, 1, 0 );
34      if ( rc <= 0 )
35          perror( "recv call failed" );
36      else
37          printf( "%c\n", buf[ 0 ] );
38      exit( 0 );
39  }
```

———————————————————————————————————————————————— *simplec.c*

**Figure 1.3** A simple TCP client

We have written Figure 1.3 as a UNIX program to delay having to deal with the complications of portable code and the Windows WSAStartup logic. As we'll see in Tip 4, we can hide most of this in a header file, but we need to set up some machinery first. In the meantime, we'll just use the slightly simpler UNIX model.

**Set Up Our Peer's Address**

*12–14*    We fill the sockaddr_in structure with the server's port number (7500) and address. The 127.0.0.1 is the loopback address. It specifies that the server is on the same host as the client.

**Obtain a Socket and Connect to Our Peer**

*15–20*    We obtain a SOCK_STREAM socket. As we mentioned earlier, TCP uses this type of socket because it is a stream protocol.

*21–26*    We establish the connection with our peer by calling connect. We use this call to specify our peer's address.

**Send and Receive a Single Byte**

*27–38*    We first send the single byte 1 to our peer, then immediately read a single byte from the socket. We write the byte to stdout and terminate.

Before we can exercise our client, we need a server. The socket calls for a server are a little different, as shown in Figure 1.4.

A server must listen for client connections on its well-known port. As we see in a moment, it does this with the listen call, but first it must bind the address of the interface and well-known port to its listening socket. This is done with the bind call:

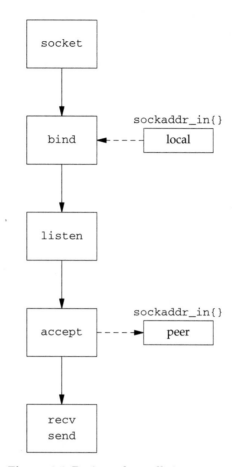

**Figure 1.4**  Basic socket calls in a server

```
#include <sys/socket.h>      /* UNIX */
#include <winsock2.h>        /* Windows */

int bind( SOCKET s, const struct sockaddr *name, int namelen );
```
Returns: 0 on success, -1 (UNIX) or SOCKET_ERROR (Windows) on error

The *s* parameter is the descriptor of the listening socket. The *name* and *namelen* parameters are used to supply the port and interface on which to listen. Usually the address is set to INADDR_ANY, indicating that a connection will be accepted on any interface. If a multihomed host wants to accept connections on only one interface, it can specify the IP address of that interface. As usual, *namelen* is the length of the sockaddr_in structure.

Once the local address is bound to the socket, we must start the socket listening for connections. This is done with the `listen` system call. This call is often misunderstood. Its only job is to mark the socket as listening. When a connection request arrives at the host, the kernel searches the list of listening sockets looking for one that matches the destination and port number in the request:

```
#include <sys/socket.h>      /* UNIX */
#include <winsock2.h>        /* Windows */

int listen( SOCKET s, int backlog );
```
                    Returns: 0 on success, -1 (UNIX) or SOCKET_ERROR (Windows) on error

The *s* parameter is the socket descriptor of the socket we wish to mark as listening. The *backlog* parameter is the maximum number of pending connections that can be outstanding. This is *not* the maximum number of connections that can be established at the given port at one time. It is the maximum number of connections or partial connections that can be queued waiting for the application to accept them (see the `accept` call described later).

Traditionally the *backlog* parameter could not be set larger than five, but modern implementations with their need to support busy applications such as Web servers have made the maximum much larger. How large is system dependent, and we must check the system documentation to find the proper value for a given machine. If we specify a number larger than the maximum, the usual action is to reduce it silently to the maximum.

The final socket call is the `accept` system call. It is used to accept a connection from the queue of completed connections. Once accepted, the connection can be used for data transfer using, for example, the `recv` and `send` calls. On success, `accept` returns a descriptor for a new socket that can be used for data transfer. This socket has the same local port as the listening socket. The local address is the interface on which the connection came in. The foreign port and address are those of the client.

Notice that *both* sockets have the same local port. This is OK because a TCP connection is completely specified by the 4-tuple consisting of the local address, local port, foreign address, and foreign port. Because (at least) the foreign address and port of the two sockets differ, the kernel is able to tell them apart:

```
#include <sys/socket.h>      /* UNIX */
#include <winsock2.h>        /* Windows */

SOCKET accept( SOCKET s, struct sockaddr *addr, int *addrlen );
```
Returns: A connected socket if OK, -1 (UNIX) or INVALID_SOCKET (Windows) on failure

The *s* parameter is the socket descriptor of the *listening* socket. As shown in Figure 1.4, `accept` returns the address of the new connection's peer in the `sockaddr_in` structure pointed to by *addr*. The kernel places the length of this structure in the integer pointed to by *addrlen*. We often don't care about our peer's address, and in this case we specify NULL for *addr* and *addrlen*.

We are now in a position to look at an elementary server (Figure 1.5). Again, this is a bare-boned program intended to show the server's structure and the basic socket calls that every server must make. As with the client code and Figure 1.2, we notice that our server follows the flow outlined in Figure 1.4 very closely.

### Fill In Address and Get a Socket

*12–20*    We fill in the sockaddr_in structure, local, with our server's well-known address and port number. We use this for the bind call. As with the client, we obtain a SOCK_STREAM socket. This is our listening socket.

### Bind Our Well-Known Port and Call `listen`

*21–32*    We bind the well-known port and address specified in local to our listening socket. We then call listen to mark the socket as a listening socket.

### Accept a Connection

*33–39*    We call accept to accept new connections. The accept call blocks until a new connection is ready and then returns a new socket for that connection.

### Transfer Data

*39–49*    We first read and print 1 byte from our client. Next, we send the single byte 2 back to our client and exit.

We can try our client and server by starting the server in one window and the client in another. Notice that it is important to start the server first or the client will fail with a "connection refused" error:

```
bsd: $ simplec
connect call failed: Connection refused
bsd: $
```

This error occurs because there was no server listening on port 7500 when the client tried to connect.

Now we start the server listening before we start the client:

```
bsd: $ simples  | bsd: $ simplec
1               | 2
bsd: $          | bsd: $
```

## Summary

In this chapter we examined a road map for the rest of the text and briefly reviewed the basic sockets API. With this behind us, we can move forward, confident that we have the necessary background to undertake the study of the subject matter to come.

*simples.c*

```
 1 #include <sys/types.h>
 2 #include <sys/socket.h>
 3 #include <netinet/in.h>
 4 #include <stdio.h>

 5 int main( void )
 6 {
 7     struct sockaddr_in local;
 8     int s;
 9     int s1;
10     int rc;
11     char buf[ 1 ];

12     local.sin_family = AF_INET;
13     local.sin_port = htons( 7500 );
14     local.sin_addr.s_addr = htonl( INADDR_ANY );
15     s = socket( AF_INET, SOCK_STREAM, 0 );
16     if ( s < 0 )
17     {
18         perror( "socket call failed" );
19         exit( 1 );
20     }
21     rc = bind( s, ( struct sockaddr * )&local, sizeof( local ) );
22     if ( rc < 0 )
23     {
24         perror( "bind call failure" );
25         exit( 1 );
26     }
27     rc = listen( s, 5 );
28     if ( rc )
29     {
30         perror( "listen call failed" );
31         exit( 1 );
32     }
33     s1 = accept( s, NULL, NULL );
34     if ( s1 < 0 )
35     {
36         perror( "accept call failed" );
37         exit( 1 );
38     }
39     rc = recv( s1, buf, 1, 0 );
40     if ( rc <= 0 )
41     {
42         perror( "recv call failed" );
43         exit( 1 );
44     }
45     printf( "%c\n", buf[ 0 ] );
46     rc = send( s1, "2", 1, 0 );
47     if ( rc <= 0 )
48         perror( "send call failed" );
49     exit( 0 );
50 }
```

*simples.c*

**Figure 1.5** A simple TCP server

# 2

# *Basics*

## Tip 1: Understand the Difference between Connected and Connectionless Protocols

One of the most fundamental notions in network programming is that of *connection-oriented* versus *connectionless* protocols. Although there is nothing intrinsically difficult about the distinction, it is a frequent cause of confusion among those new to network programming. Part of the problem is a matter of context: Obviously two computers must be "connected" in some sense if they are to communicate, so what does "connectionless communication" mean?

The answer is that *connection-oriented* and *connectionless* refer to *protocols*. That is, the terms are applied to how we transfer data over a physical medium, not to the physical medium itself. Connection-oriented and connectionless protocols can, and routinely do, share the same physical medium simultaneously.

If the distinction has nothing to do with the physical medium carrying the data, what *does* it have to do with? The essential difference is that with connectionless protocols each packet is handled independently from any other, whereas with connection-oriented protocols, state information is maintained about successive packets by the protocol implementation.

With a connectionless protocol each packet, called a *datagram*, is addressed individually and sent by the application (but see Tip 30). From the point of view of the protocol, each datagram is an independent entity that has nothing to do with any other datagram that may have been sent between the same two peers.

This is not to say that datagrams are independent from the point of view of the application. If the application implements anything more complicated than a simple request/reply protocol, in which a client sends a single request to a server and receives a single reply, then it will

15

> probably need to maintain state between the datagrams. The point is, though, that it's the application, not the protocol, maintaining the state. For an example of a connectionless server that maintains state between datagrams from its client, see Figure 3.9.

Typically this means that the client and server do not carry on an extended dialog—the client makes a request and the server sends a reply. If the client later sends another request, the protocol considers it a separate transaction, independent from the first.

It also means that the protocol is probably unreliable. That is, the network makes a best effort attempt to deliver each datagram, but there is no guarantee that it will not be lost, delayed, or delivered out of sequence.

Connection-oriented protocols, on the other hand, do maintain state between packets, and applications using them typically engage in extended dialogs. This remembered state enables the protocol to provide reliable delivery. For example, the sender can remember what data has been sent but not acknowledged, and when it was sent. If the acknowledgment is not received in some time interval, the sender can retransmit the data. The receiver can remember what data has already been received and can discard duplicate data. If a packet arrives out of order, the receiver can hold it until the packets that logically precede it arrive.

The typical connection-oriented protocol has three phases. During the first phase, a connection is established between the peers. This is followed by the data transfer phase, during which data is transfered between the peers. Finally, when the peers have finished transferring data, the connection is torn down.

The standard analogy is that using a connection-oriented protocol is like making a phone call, whereas using a connectionless protocol is like sending a letter. When we send letters to a friend, each letter is an individually addressed, self-contained entity. These letters are handled by the post office without regard to any other letters between the two correspondents. The post office does not maintain a history of previous correspondence—that is, it does not maintain state between the letters. Nor does the post office guarantee that our letters will not be lost, delayed, or delivered out of order. This corresponds to sending a datagram with a connectionless protocol.

> [Haverlock 2000] points out that a postcard is a better analogy because a misaddressed letter is returned to the sender whereas a postcard (like the typical connectionless protocol datagram) is not.

Now consider what happens when we call our friend instead of sending a letter. We initiate the call by dialing our friend's number. Our friend answers and says something like, "Hello," and we answer, "Hello, Sally. This is Harry." We chat with our friend for a while, and then we each say goodbye and hang up. This is typical of what happens in a connection-oriented protocol. During connection setup, one side contacts its peer, an initial greeting is exchanged during which parameters and options to be used in the conversation are negotiated, and the connection enters the data transfer phase.

During our phone conversation, both parties know to whom they are talking, so there is need for them to keep saying things like, "This is Harry saying something to Sally." Nor is it necessary to dial our friend's number each time before we say something—our phones are connected. Similarly, during the data transfer phase in a connection-oriented protocol, there is no need to specify our address or the address of our peer. These addresses are part of the state that the connection maintains for us. We merely send data without worrying about addressing or other protocol matters.

Just as with our phone conversation, when each side of the connection finishes transferring data, it informs its peer. When both sides have completed the transfer, they go through an orderly tear-down of the connection.

> This analogy, although useful, is not perfect. With the phone system there is an actual physical connection. Our "connection" is entirely notional—it consists only of remembered state at each end. To appreciate this point, consider what happens when a host on one side of an idle connection crashes and reboots. Is there still a connection? Certainly not from the point of view of the rebooted host. It knows nothing about the erstwhile connection. Its former peer, however, continues to believe itself to be connected because it's still maintaining state about the connection, and nothing has happened to invalidate that state.

Given the many disadvantages of connectionless protocols, one might wonder why they would ever be used. As we shall see, there are many times when using a connectionless protocol to build an application makes sense. For example, connectionless protocols can easily support one-to-many and many-to-one communications, whereas connected protocols typically require separate connections for this. Far more important, however, is that connectionless protocols are the base on which connection-oriented protocols are built. To be specific, and to return this discussion to subject of the text, let us consider the TCP/IP protocol suite. As we shall see in Tip 14, TCP/IP is based on a four-layer protocol stack, as shown in Figure 2.1.

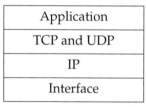

**Figure 2.1** Simplified TCP/IP protocol stack

At the bottom of the stack is the interface layer, which interfaces directly with the hardware. At the top of the stack are the applications such as telnet, `ftp`, and the other standard and user written applications. As shown in the figure, TCP and UDP are built on IP. Thus, IP is the base on which the entire TCP/IP suite is built. IP, however, provides a best effort, unreliable, connectionless service. It accepts packets from the layers above it, encapsulates them in an IP packet, and routes the packet to the correct hardware interface, which sends it on its way. Once sent, IP no longer concerns itself with the packet. Like all connectionless protocols, it remembers nothing about a packet after it has sent it.

This simplicity is also the chief strength of IP. Because it assumes nothing about the underlying physical medium, IP can run on any physical link capable of carrying packets. For example, IP runs on simple serial links, on Ethernet and Token Ring LANs, on X.25 and Asynchronous Transfer Mode (ATM) WANs, on wireless Cellular Digital

Packet Data (CDPD) networks, and on many more besides. Although these network technologies are radically different from one another, IP treats them all equally by assuming nothing about them other than that they are capable of routing packets. The implications of this are profound. Because IP can run on any network capable of carrying packets, so can the entire TCP/IP suite.

Now let's look at how TCP uses this simple connectionless service to provide a reliable connection-oriented service. Because TCP sends its packets, called *segments*, in IP datagrams, it cannot assume that they will arrive at their destination at all, let alone uncorrupted and in the proper order. To provide this reliability, TCP adds three things to the basic IP service. First, it provides a checksum of the data in the TCP segment. This helps to ensure that data that does arrive at its destination has not been corrupted by the network during transport. Second, it assigns a sequence number to each byte so that if data does arrive out of order at the destination, the receiver will be able to reassemble it into the proper order.

> TCP doesn't attach a sequence number to each byte, of course. What happens is that each TCP segment's header contains the number of the first sequenced byte in the segment. The sequence numbers of the segment's other bytes are then known by implication.

Third, TCP provides an acknowledgment-and-retransmit mechanism to ensure that every segment is eventually delivered.

The acknowledgment/retry mechanism is by far the most complicated of the three additions we are discussing, so let's examine it to see how it works.

> We are ignoring several details here. This discussion barely touches on the many subtleties of the TCP protocol and how they are used to provide a reliable and robust transport mechanism. The full details are in RFC 793 [Postel 1981b] and RFC 1122 [Braden 1989]. A more approachable exposition is given in [Stevens 1994]. RFC 813 [Clark 1982] discusses the TCP windowing and acknowledgment strategy in general terms.

Each end of a TCP connection maintains a *receive window*, which is the range of sequence numbers of data that it is prepared to accept from its peer. The lowest value, representing the left edge of the window, is the sequence number of the next expected byte. The highest value, representing the right edge of the window, is the highest numbered byte for which TCP has buffer space. The use of a receive window instead of just a next-expected-byte counter increases reliability by providing flow control. The flow control mechanism prevents TCP from overrunning the buffer space of its peer.

When a TCP segment arrives, any data with sequence numbers outside the receive window is discarded. This includes data that has been received previously (data with sequence numbers to the left of the receive window) and data for which there is no buffer space available (data with sequence numbers to the right of the receive window). If the first acceptable byte in the segment is not the next expected byte, then this segment arrived out of sequence, and most TCP implementations queue it until the missing data arrives. If the first acceptable byte in the segment is the next expected byte, then the data is made available to the application, and the sequence number of the next expected byte is updated by adding the number of acceptable bytes in the segment to it. We say that the window slides right by the number of acceptable bytes. Finally, TCP sends an ACK to its peer with the sequence number of the next byte it is expecting.

For example, in Figure 2.2A, the dashed box representing the receive window shows that the next expected byte has sequence number 4, and that TCP is willing to accept 9 bytes (4–12). Figure 2.2B shows the receive window after bytes 4, 5, 6, and 7 are received. The window has slid four sequence numbers to the right, and TCP's ACK will specify that it is expecting sequence number 8 next.

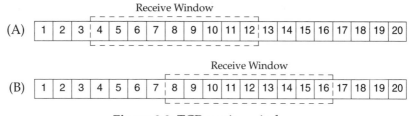

**Figure 2.2** TCP receive window

Now let's look at this same situation from the point of view of the sending TCP. In addition to a receive window, each TCP also maintains a *send window*. The send window is divided into two parts: those bytes that have been sent but not acknowledged, and those bytes that can be but have not yet been sent. Assuming that bytes 1 through 3 have already been acknowledged, the send window corresponding to the receive window in Figure 2.2A is shown in Figure 2.3A. After bytes 4 through 7 are sent, but before they are acknowledged, the send window is as shown in Figure 2.3B. TCP can still send bytes 8 through 12 without waiting for an ACK from its peer. After bytes 4 through 7 are sent, TCP starts a *retransmission timeout* (RTO) timer. If the four bytes are not acknowledged before the timer fires, TCP considers them lost, and retransmits them.

> Because many implementations don't keep track of which bytes were sent in a particular segment, it is possible that the retransmitted segment may contain more bytes than the original. For example, if bytes 8 and 9 were sent before the RTO timer fired, these implementations would retransmit bytes 4 through 9.

Note that the fact that the RTO timer fires does not mean that the original data didn't arrive at its destination. It may be that the ACK was lost or that the original segment was delayed in the network long enough that the RTO timer fired before its ACK arrived. This does not cause a problem, however, because if the original data did arrive, the retransmitted data will be outside the receiving TCP's receive window and will therefore be discarded.

When bytes 4 through 7 are acknowledged, the sending TCP discards them, and slides the send window right, as shown in Figure 2.3C.

For the application programmer, TCP provides a reliable connection-oriented protocol. For more on the meaning of reliable, see Tip 9.

UDP, on the other hand, provides the application programmer an unreliable connectionless service. In fact, UDP adds only two things to the underlying IP protocol. First, it provides an optional checksum to help detect data corruption. Although IP also has a checksum, it is only computed on the IP packet's header, and for this reason TCP and UDP also provide a checksum to protect their own headers and data. The second feature that UDP adds to IP is the notion of ports.

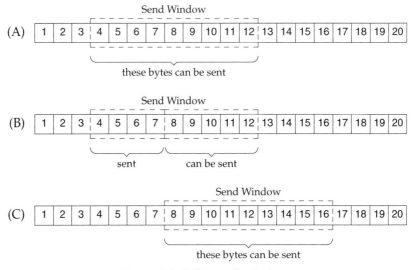

**Figure 2.3** TCP send window

IP addresses (the addresses that are usually given in the Internet standard dotted decimal notation, see Tip 2) are used to deliver an IP datagram to a particular host. When the datagram arrives at the destination host, it still needs to have its data delivered to the correct application. For example, one UDP packet may be destined for the echo service, whereas another may be destined for the time-of-day service. Ports provide a way of demultiplexing the data to the correct destination application. Each TCP and UDP socket has a port number associated with it. The application may set this port explicitly by a call to `bind`, or it may let the operating system choose one for it. When a packet arrives, the kernel searches its list of sockets for one that is associated with the protocol, addresses, and port numbers in the packet. If a match is found, the data is processed by the specified protocol (TCP or UDP in the cases we are considering) and made available to any applications that have the matching socket open.

> If more than one process or thread has the socket open, any of them can read the data, but once read the data is no longer available to the others.

Returning to our phone call/letter analogy, one can think of the network address in a TCP connection as being the phone number of the switchboard in an office, and the port number as being the extension number of the particular phone in the office that is being called. Similarly, a UDP address could be thought of as the address of an apartment building, and the port number as one of the individual mailboxes in the apartment building's lobby.

## Summary

In this tip we explored the differences between connectionless and connection-oriented protocols. We saw that unreliable connectionless datagram protocols are the base on which reliable connection-oriented protocols are built, and we briefly examined how the reliable TCP protocol is built on the unreliable IP protocol.

We also observed that with TCP the connection is entirely notional. It consists of remembered state at the end points, but there is no "physical" connection, as there is when we make a phone call.

## Tip 2:  **Understand Subnets and CIDR**

An IP (version 4) address is 32 bits long. It is customary to write them in *dotted decimal notation*, in which each of the 4 bytes is represented by a decimal number separated by dots. Thus the address 0x11345678 would be written as 17.52.86.120. Some care should be taken when writing these because many TCP/IP implementations use the standard C convention that numbers beginning with zero are octal numbers. For these systems, 17.52.86.120 is not the same as 017.52.86.120. The first is network 17 whereas the second is network 15.

### Classfull Addressing

Traditionally, IP addresses have been divided into five classes as shown in Figure 2.4. This division is called *classfull addressing*.

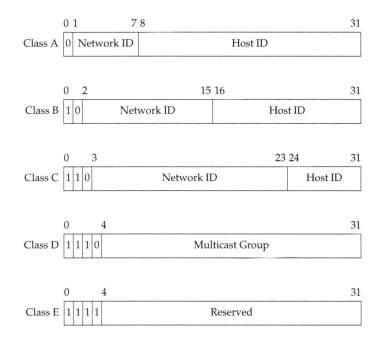

**Figure 2.4**  IP classfull addressing

Class D addresses are used for multicast addressing, and class E is reserved for future use. The remaining classes, A, B, and C, are the primary address classes used for identifying individual networks and hosts.

The class of an address is identified by the number of leading 1 bits. Class A has zero leading 1 bits, class B has one, class C has two, and so on. It is critical that the class of the address be identified because the interpretation of the remaining bits depends on the class.

The remaining bits of class A, B, and C addresses are divided into two parts. The first of these parts is the network ID, which identifies the particular network to which the address refers. After that comes the host ID, which identifies a particular host on that network.

> The class identifier bits are also considered part of the network ID. Thus, 130.50.10.200 is a class B address with the network ID 0x8232.

The reason for dividing the address space into classes is to provide flexibility without wasting addresses. For example, class A addresses are for networks with a huge number (16,777,214) of hosts.

> There are $2^{24}$ or 16,777,216 possible host IDs, but host 0 and the host ID of all ones have special meaning. The host ID of all ones is the broadcast address. IP datagrams addressed to the broadcast address are delivered to all hosts on the network. The host ID of 0 means "this host" and is used only as a source address by a host to discover its host number during start-up. For this reason, the number of hosts is always $2^n - 2$, where $n$ is the number of bits in the host ID.

Because the network ID is 7 bits, there are 128 possible class A networks.

> As with host IDs, two of these networks are reserved. Network 0 means "this network," and like host 0 is used as a source address during start-up to discover the network number. Network 127 is a network internal to the host. No datagrams addressed to network 127 should ever leave the originating host. It is often referred to as the *loopback* address, because datagrams addressed to it are "looped back" into the same host.

At the other pole are the class C networks. There are plenty of these, but each one has only 254 host IDs available. Whereas class A addresses are meant for the few networks with millions of hosts, the class C addresses are meant for the millions of networks with just a few hosts.

Figure 2.5 shows the number of possible networks and hosts, and the address ranges for each class. We count network 127 as a class A address, but it is not, of course, globally accessible.

| Class | Networks | Hosts | Address Range |
|-------|----------|-------|---------------|
| A | 127 | 16,777,214 | 0.0.0.1 to 127.255.255.255 |
| B | 16,384 | 65,534 | 128.0.0.0 to 191.255.255.255 |
| C | 2,097,252 | 254 | 192.0.0.0 to 223.255.255.255 |

**Figure 2.5** Networks, hosts, and ranges for class A, B, and C addresses

The designers of the TCP/IP protocols originally believed that networks would number in the hundreds and hosts in the thousands.

In fact, as related in [Huitema 1995], the original design had only what we now refer to as class A addresses. The division into three classes was a later fix to accommodate more than 256 networks.

As we know, the advent of the cheap and ubiquitous PC has led to explosive growth in the number of networks and hosts. The size of the Internet now far exceeds that envisioned by its designers.

This growth has brought to light some weaknesses of classfull addressing. The first problem is that the number of class A and B hosts is too large. Remember that the network ID is supposed to refer to a physical network, such as a LAN. But no one puts 65,000, let alone 16,000,000, hosts on a single physical network. Instead, large networks are partitioned into smaller segments that are connected by routers.

As a (very) simple example, consider the two network segments shown in Figure 2.6.

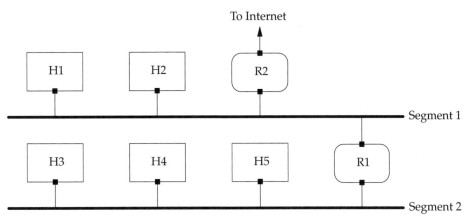

**Figure 2.6** A segmented network

If host H1 wants to communicate with host H2, it need merely map H2's IP address to its physical address using whatever method is appropriate for the underlying network, and put the IP datagram "on the wire."

Now suppose that host H1 wants to communicate with host H3. H1 cannot send an IP datagram directly to H3, even if it knows or could discover its physical address, because H1 and H3 are on separate networks—separate Ethernet cables, for example. Instead, H1 must send it indirectly through router R1. If the two segments have different network IDs, H1 need merely consult its routing table to determine that router R1 handles packets for segment 2, and send the datagram to R1 for forwarding to H3.

What are the alternatives to having separate network IDs for the two segments? With classical classfull addressing there are two possibilities. One is that H1's routing table contains an entry for each host on segment 2 that specifies R1 as the next hop for that host. This same routing table would have to reside on each host on segment 1, and similar routing tables specifying the hosts on segment 1 would have to reside on each host on segment 2. Obviously this solution does not scale well to more than a few hosts. Furthermore, the routing tables would have to be maintained by hand, and would quickly become an administrative nightmare. For these reasons, this solution is virtually never used.

The other possibility, called *proxy ARP*, is to have R1 pretend to be H3, H4, and H5 for segment 1, and H1, H2, and R2 for segment 2.

> Proxy ARP is also called *promiscuous ARP* and *the ARP hack*.

This solution works only when the underlying network uses the *Address Resolution Protocol* (ARP) to map IP addresses to physical addresses. With ARP, a host wanting to map an IP address to a physical address broadcasts a message asking the host with the desired IP address to send back its physical address. The ARP request is received by all hosts on the network, of course, but only the host with the proper IP address responds.

With proxy ARP, when H1 wants to send an IP datagram to H3, and doesn't know its physical address, it sends an ARP request asking for H3's physical address. Because H3 is on another network, it doesn't receive the ARP request, but R1, which is acting as its proxy does, and it responds with its own address. When the datagram addressed to H3 arrives, R1 forwards it to H3. To H1, it appears that H3 is on the same physical network.

As we mentioned earlier, proxy ARP works only on those networks that use ARP, and then only on fairly simple network topologies. Imagine what would happen if there were multiple routers connecting segments 1 and 2, for example.

From this discussion, it might appear that the most general solution for networks with multiple segments is to have separate network IDs for each segment, but this brings its own problems. In the first place, there are potentially many wasted IP addresses on each network. For example, if each segment of a multisegment network had its own class B address, most of the IP addresses associated with each class B network address would be wasted. Remember, there are 16,384 host addresses within each class B network address.

Second, any node that routed datagrams directly to the combined network would require a separate entry in its routing table for each segment. For our small example, this doesn't amount to much, but consider a network comprising hundreds of segments, and then consider many such networks and we see that routing tables would become huge.

> This is a larger problem than it might appear at first. Routers generally have limited memory and often place the routing tables in special-purpose memory on the interface boards. See [Huitema 1995] for some real-world examples of router failures caused by the growth of routing tables.

Notice how both problems are eliminated if there is only one network ID. None of the IP addresses are wasted permanently because we can always add another segment to make use of them if we need more hosts. Because there is only one network ID, only one routing table entry is needed to send IP datagrams to any host in the network.

## Subnetting

We would like an approach that has the small routing tables and efficient IP address space utilization of a single network ID combined with the ease of routing provided by having separate network IDs for each segment. What we want is for external hosts to see a single network, and for internal hosts to see many—one for each segment.

The mechanism that accomplishes this is called *subnetting*. The idea is surprisingly simple. Because external hosts use only the network ID portion of an IP address to make routing decisions, the allocation of host IDs can be made in any way that the system administrator finds convenient. The host ID is, in effect, a cookie with an internal structure that has no meaning outside the network.

Subnetting works by using part of the host ID to specify the segment (that is, the *subnet*) to which a host is connected, and the rest of the host ID to identify the particular host. For example, consider the class B network 190.50.0.0. We might choose to use the third byte of the address as a subnet ID and the fourth byte as the host number on that subnet. Figure 2.7A shows the address structure as seen from outside the network. The host ID is an opaque field with no apparent substructure. In Figure 2.7B, we see the address structure as seen from inside the network. Here the structure of the host ID field is revealed to comprise a subnet ID and a host number.

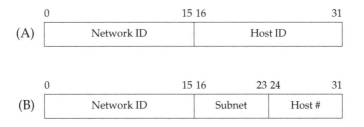

**Figure 2.7** Two views of a subnetted class B address

Although we have shown a class B address and divided the host ID field at a byte boundary, neither of these is necessary. Class A, B, and C addresses can be and are subnetted, and often the division is not made at a byte boundary. (That's not even possible for class C addresses, of course.) Associated with each subnetwork is a *subnet mask* that indicates the combined network and subnetwork parts of the address. For example, the subnet mask for Figure 2.7B would be 0xffffff00. This is often written using dotted decimal notation (255.255.255.0), but when the division is not on a byte boundary, the first form is often easier to use.

> Notice that although it's called the *subnet* mask, it actually specifies both the network and the subnetwork parts of the address—that is, everything but the host portion.

To illustrate these ideas, let us assume that the subnet ID is 10 bits and the host number is 6 bits. The subnet mask would then be 255.255.255.192 (0xfffffffc0). Figure 2.8 shows how the subnet mask is applied to the address 190.50.7.75 to obtain the network/subnetwork number of 190.50.7.64.

We can test our understanding of these concepts by verifying that the address 190.50.7.75 is for host 11 on subnet 29 of network 190.50.0.0. It is important to remember that this interpretation is known only inside the network. Outside the network, this address is interpreted as host 1867 on the network 190.50.0.0.

| | 190 | 50 | 7 | 75 |
|---|---|---|---|---|
| IP address | 10111110 | 00110010 | 00000111 | 01001011 |
| Subnet mask | 11111111 | 11111111 | 11111111 | 11000000 |
| Network/subnet | 10111110 | 00110010 | 00000111 | 01000000 |
| | 190 | 50 | 7 | 64 |

**Figure 2.8**  ANDing a subnet mask to extract the network portion of an IP address

Now let's consider how the routers in Figure 2.6 can make use of the host ID sub-structure to route datagrams within the network. For ease in identifying the subnet ID, let's assume that we have the class B network 190.50.0.0 and that the subnet mask is 255.255.255.0. This is the structure shown in Figure 2.7B.

In Figure 2.9, we have assigned the first segment from Figure 2.6 the subnet ID 1, and the second segment the subnet ID 2. We have also labeled each host interface with its IP address. Notice that the third byte of each address is the subnet to which the interface is attached. This interpretation is unknown outside the network of course.

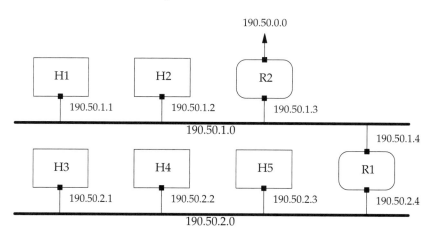

**Figure 2.9**  A network with subnets

Recalling our previous discussion, let's first see what happens when H1 wants to communicate with H3. H1 takes H3's address, 190.50.2.1, and ANDs it with the subnet mask 255.255.255.0, yielding 190.50.2.0. Because H1 is on the subnet 190.50.1.0, it knows that H3 is not directly connected, so it consults its routing table to discover that the next hop for H3 is the router R1.

> Many implementations combine these two steps by having both subnets in the routing table. When the route is looked up, IP discovers either that the target network is directly connected, or that it needs to send the datagram to an intermediate router.

H1 then maps R1's IP address to its physical address (using ARP, for example) and sends the datagram to R1. R1 looks up the destination address in its routing table, again using the subnet mask, and discovers that H3 is on the subnet connected to its 190.50.2.4 interface. Finally, R1 delivers the datagram to H3 by mapping its IP address to its physical address and sending the datagram out its 190.50.2.4 interface.

Now suppose H1 wants to send a datagram to H2. When the subnet mask is applied to H2's address (190.50.1.2) it yields 190.50.1.0, which is the same subnet as H1's. Therefore, H1 need merely map H2's IP address to its physical address and send the datagram directly to H2.

Next, let's look at what happens when a host, E, outside the network wants to send a datagram to H3. Because 190.50.2.1 is a class B address, the router at the edge of host E's network knows that H3 resides on the network 190.50.0.0. Because R2 is the gateway for this network, the datagram from host E arrives there eventually. The steps are now identical to the case in which H1 originated the datagram: R2 applies the subnet mask and extracts the subnet number 190.50.2.0, determines that the next hop is R1, and sends the datagram to R1, which delivers it to H3. Notice that host E knows nothing about the internal topology of network 190.50.0.0. It merely sends its datagram to the gateway R2. It is R2 and the other hosts inside the network that have knowledge of the subnets and the routes necessary to reach them.

An important point that we have glossed over so far is that the subnet mask is associated with an interface and therefore with a routing table entry. This means that it is possible for distinct subnets to have different subnet masks.

An example will make this clear. Suppose that our class B address 190.50.0.0 is for a university, and that each department within the university is assigned a subnet with subnet mask 255.255.255.0 (Figure 2.9 shows just a part of the larger network). The system administrator of the computer science department, which is on subnet 5, decides to have separate Ethernet segments for the students' computer lab and the rest of the department. He could try to get another subnet number from the university administration, but the students' computer lab has only a few machines, and it's not worth dedicating what amounts to a whole class C address block to it. Therefore, he would like to split his subnet between the two segments. In effect, he wants to create subnets within his subnet.

To do this he increases his subnet field to 10 bits and uses the subnet mask 255.255.255.192. The resulting address structure is shown in Figure 2.10.

| 0 | 15 16 | 25 26 | 31 |
|---|---|---|---|
| 190.50 | 0 0 0 0 0 1 0 1 X Y | Host # | |
| Network ID | Subnet ID | Host | |

**Figure 2.10**  Address structure for the 190.50.5.0 subnetwork

The upper 8 bits of the subnet ID are always 0000 0101 (5), because the rest of the network addresses the entire subnetwork as subnet 5. The X and Y bits specify which Ethernet segment within the 190.50.5.0 subnetwork is being addressed. As shown in Figure 2.11, when XY = 10, we are addressing the Ethernet in the students' lab, and when XY = 01, we are addressing the rest of the network. Part of the topology of the 190.50.5.0 subnetwork is shown in Figure 2.11.

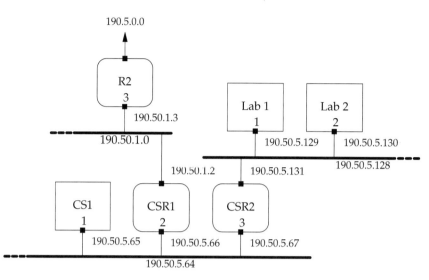

**Figure 2.11**  A subnet of a subnet

The topmost segment (subnet 190.50.1.0) of Figure 2.11 has the router R2 providing external access, as in Figure 2.9. The subnet 190.50.2.0 from Figure 2.9 is not shown. The middle segment (subnet 190.50.5.128) is the Ethernet in the students' computer lab. The bottom segment (subnet 190.50.64) is the Ethernet for the rest of the department. For clarity, the host number of each machine is the same for all of its interfaces, and is the number inside the box representing the host or router.

The subnet mask for the interfaces connecting to the 190.50.5.64 and 190.50.5.128 subnetworks is 255.255.255.192. The subnet mask for interfaces connecting to the 190.50.1.0 subnetwork is 255.255.255.0.

Notice how this situation is exactly analogous to the previous situation discussed in conjunction with Figure 2.9. Just as hosts outside the 190.50.0.0 network don't know that the third byte specifies a subnetwork, so hosts in the 190.50.0.0 network that are outside the 190.50.5.0 subnetwork don't know that the first 2 bits of the fourth byte specify a subnetwork of the 190.50.5.0 subnetwork.

Before leaving the subject of subnetworks, let's briefly consider broadcast addresses. There are four different types of broadcast addresses when subnets are being used: limited broadcast, network-directed broadcast, subnetwork-directed broadcast, and all subnetwork-directed broadcast.

### Limited Broadcast

The limited broadcast address is 255.255.255.255. It is called *limited* because datagrams using it are never forwarded by routers. They are limited to the local cable. It is used primarily during start-up, when a host does not know its IP address or subnet mask.

What happens when a host using the limited broadcast address is multihomed is implementation dependent. Many implementations send the datagram out of only one interface. Applications that need to broadcast a datagram out of multiple interfaces on such systems must query the operating system for the configured interfaces that support broadcasting.

### Network-Directed Broadcast

The network-directed broadcast address has the network ID set to the specified network, and the host ID set to all one bits. For example, the network-directed broadcast address for our 190.50.0.0 network is 190.50.255.255. Datagrams with this type of broadcast address are delivered to all hosts on the target network.

The router requirements RFC (RFC 1812) [Baker 1995], requires that routers forward directed broadcasts by default, but that they also have an option to disable this forwarding. In view of various denial-of-service attacks that can take advantage of directed broadcasts, it is likely that many routers have disabled the forwarding of these datagrams.

### Subnetwork-Directed Broadcast

A subnet-directed broadcast address specifies the network ID and the subnetwork ID. The host number portion of the address is set to all ones. Notice that it is not possible to determine whether an address is a subnetwork-directed broadcast address without knowing the subnetwork mask. For example, 190.50.1.255 would be treated as a subnetwork-directed broadcast message if the router knows that the subnetwork mask is 255.255.255.0. If a router believes the subnetwork mask is 255.255.0.0, this address is not treated as a broadcast address.

With CIDR, discussed later, this type of broadcast address is indistinguishable from a network-directed broadcast address, and RFC 1812 treats them the same.

### All Subnetwork-Directed Broadcast

This broadcast address specifies the network address, and sets the subnetwork and host portions to all ones. As with the subnetwork-directed broadcast, a knowledge of the subnetwork mask is required to distinguish this address.

Unfortunately, the use of the all subnetwork-directed broadcast address is subject to certain failure modes, and it was never implemented or deployed. With CIDR, this form is no longer used and, to quote RFC 1812, "is now relegated to the dustbin of history."

None of these broadcast addresses may be used as a source address for an IP datagram. Lastly, we should note that some early TCP/IP implementations, such as 4.2BSD, used all zero bits in the host ID field to specify the broadcast address.

## CIDR

We have seen that subnetting solves one of the problems with classfull addressing: the proliferation of routing table entries. To a lesser extent, it helps ameliorate the depletion of IP addresses by making better use of the host IDs within a given network.

The other serious problem with classfull addressing is the depletion of class B network IDs. As shown in Figure 2.5, there are less than 17,000 such network IDs available. Because most medium-size and larger organizations need more IP addresses than are provided by a class C network ID, they obtain class B network IDs.

With the depletion of class B network IDs, organizations were forced to obtain a block of class C network IDs, but this reintroduces the problem that subnetting was designed to solve: the growth of routing tables in the Internet.

Classless interdomain routing (CIDR) solves this problem by turning subnetting "inside out." Instead of making the network ID portion of an IP address longer, as in subnetting, it makes it shorter.

Let's look at how it works. An organization that needs 1,000 IP addresses would be allocated four contiguous class C network IDs that share a common prefix. For example, they might be assigned 200.10.4.0 through 200.10.7.0. The first 22 bits of these network IDs are the same and serve as the network number for the aggregated network, 200.10.4.0 in this case. As with subnetting, a network mask is used to identify the network portion of an IP address. In the case of the aggregated network described earlier, this mask would be 255.255.252.0 (`0xfffffc00`).

Unlike subnetting, this network mask does not extend the network portion of the IP address. It shortens it. For this reason, CIDR is also referred to as *supernetting*. Also unlike subnetting, the network mask is exported outside of the network. It becomes a part of every routing table entry that refers to this network.

Suppose an external router, R, wants to forward a datagram to 200.10.5.33, one of the hosts on this aggregated network. Router R goes through its routing table, each entry of which has a network mask, and compares the masked portion of 200.10.5.33 with the entry. If the router has an entry for this network, it will be 200.10.4.0 with a network mask of 255.255.252.0. When 200.10.5.33 is ANDed with this mask, the result is 200.10.4.0, which matches the network number in the entry, so the router knows the next hop for the datagram.

In cases of ambiguity, the entry with the longest match is used. For example, a router may also have an entry of the form 200.10.0.0 with a network mask of 255.255.0.0. This entry also matches 200.10.5.33, but because the match is only 16 bits long instead of the 22 bits of the first entry, the first is used.

> Situations like this can occur when an Internet service provider (ISP) "owns" all of the IP addresses with the prefix 200.10. An entry of the second type would route all datagrams with the prefix 200.10 to that ISP. The ISP may also advertise the more precise route to avoid extra hops or for some other reason.

Actually, CIDR is slightly more general than we have indicated. It is called "classless" because it does away with the notion of classes completely. Thus, each routing entry has an associated network mask that specifies the network portion of the IP address. This mask may have the effect of shortening or lengthening the network portion of the address when viewed as a classfull address, but because CIDR does away with the notion of address classes, we no longer think of the network mask as shortening or extending, but merely as specifying the network portion of the address.

In reality, the "mask" is merely a number, called the *prefix*, that specifies the length, in bits, of the network portion of the address. For example, the prefix for our aggregated network described earlier is 22, and we would write the network's address as 200.10.4.0/22, the "/22" indicating the prefix. From this point of view, classfull addressing can be thought of as a special case of CIDR with only four (or five) possible prefixes, which are encoded into the leading bits of the address.

The flexibility that CIDR provides in specifying the size of the network addresses aids in the efficient allocation of IP addresses by allowing them to be assigned in blocks tailored to the network's needs. We have already seen how CIDR can be used to aggregate several (what used to be referred to as) class C networks into a single larger network. At the other extreme, we can use it to allocate a portion of (what used to be referred to as) a class C network to a small network that needs only a few addresses. For example, an ISP could assign a small company with a single LAN the network 200.50.17.128/26, which can support up to $2^6 - 2 = 62$ hosts.

RFC 1518 [Rekhter and Li 1993], discusses address aggregation and its effects on router table sizes. It also urges that IP address prefixes (that is, the network portion of the address) be assigned in a hierarchical manner to facilitate this aggregation.

> Hierarchical address aggregation can be likened to a hierarchical file system such as those used in UNIX and Windows. Just as higher level subdirectories know about lower level subdirectories but not about the files in those lower level subdirectories, so upper level routing domains know about intermediate domains, but not about individual networks within them. For example, suppose a regional provider carries all traffic for the 200/8 prefix, and that three local ISPs having prefixes 200.1/16, 200.2/16, and 200.3/16 are connected to it. Each of these ISPs will have several customers to which parts of their address space is allocated (200.1.5/24, and so on). Routers outside the regional provider need only maintain one routing entry, that for 200/8, to reach any host within the 200/8 address range. They can make their routing decisions without knowing how the 200/8 address space is partitioned. The regional provider needs only three routing entries, one for each ISP. At the lowest level, the ISP will have a routing table entry for each of its customers. Although simplified, this example captures the essence of aggregation.

RFC 1518 is interesting reading because it demonstrates the significant gains to be had by the deployment of CIDR.

CIDR itself, and the rationale for it, are described in RFC 1519 [Fuller et al. 1993]. This RFC also contains a detailed cost/benefit analysis of CIDR and discusses some of the changes required in the interdomain routing protocols.

## Status of Subnetting and CIDR

Subnetting, as described in RFC 950 [Mogul and Postel 1985], is a Standard Protocol (Std. 5). As such, every host that runs TCP/IP is required to support it.

CIDR (RFC 1517 [Hinden 1993], RFC 1518, RFC 1519) is a Proposed Standard Protocol, and is therefore not required. Nonetheless, the use of CIDR is nearly universal in the Internet, and all new address assignments are made in accordance with it. The Internet Engineering Steering Group has selected CIDR as the short-term solution to the routing table size problem.

In the long term, both the address depletion and routing table size problems will be solved by version 6 of IP. IPv6 has a much larger address space (128 bits) and is explicitly hierarchical. The larger address space (including 64 bits for the *interface ID*) ensures that there are sufficient IP addresses for the foreseeable future. The hierarchical structure of the IPv6 address will keep routing tables reasonably sized.

### Summary

In this tip we have studied subnetting and CIDR, and seen how they are used to solve two problems with classful addressing. Subnetting helps prevent the growth of routing tables while maintaining flexible addressing. CIDR allows the efficient allocation of IP addresses and makes the hierarchical assignment of those addresses easier.

## Tip 3:  Understand Private Addresses and NAT

Before the advent of cheap and ubiquitous Internet access, it was common practice for an organization to choose any random block of IP addresses for its network. After all, the network was not and "never would be" connected to any external networks, so the choice of IP addresses was not considered an issue. Of course, things change and now the number of networks that do not have Internet connectivity are probably in the minority.

It is no longer necessary to choose an arbitrary block of IP addresses for a private network. RFC 1918 [Rekhter, Moskowitz et al. 1996] specifies three blocks of reserved IP addresses that are guaranteed never to be assigned. These address blocks are

- 10.0.0.0–10.255.255.255 (10/8 prefix)
- 172.16.0.0–172.31.255.255 (172.16/12 prefix)
- 192.168.0.0–192.168.255.255 (192.168/16 prefix)

By using one of these blocks for the network, it is possible for any host on the network to have access to any other host on the network without fear of conflicting with a globally assigned IP address. Of course, as long as the network remains unconnected to external networks, it doesn't matter what addresses are assigned, but it's just as easy to use one of the private address blocks and be protected against the day that it does become connected.

What happens if the network does become connected externally? How will a host with a private IP address be able to communicate with a host on the Internet or other external network? The most popular answer to this question is to use *network address translation*. Several types of devices support NAT, including routers, firewalls, and stand-alone NAT products. NAT works by translating between the private network addresses and one or more globally assigned IP addresses. Let's take a brief look at how this works. Most NAT devices can be configured to support three modes:

1. Static—Some or all of the hosts on the private network have their private IP address mapped to a fixed, globally assigned address.

2. Pooled—The NAT device has a pool of globally assigned IP addresses available, and it assigns one of these dynamically to a host that needs to communicate with a peer on an external network.

3. PAT—Also called *port address translation*, this method is used when there is a single globally assigned address, such as that shown in Figure 2.12. With PAT, every private address is mapped to the same external address, but the source port on the outgoing packet is changed to a unique value that is used to associate incoming packets with the private network address.

In Figure 2.12, we show a small network with three hosts using the 10/8 address block. There is also a router, labeled NAT, that has an address on the private network and an address on the Internet.

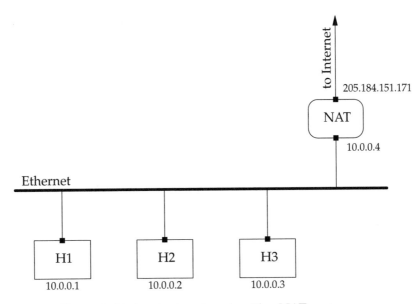

**Figure 2.12** A private network with a NAT router

Because we show only one global address associated with the NAT, let us assume for the discussion that follows that it is configured to use PAT. The static and polled cases are similar, but easier because they don't have to deal with the additional complications of translating ports as well as addresses.

Let us suppose that host H2 wants to send a TCP SYN segment to 204.71.200.69, one of the www.yahoo.com Web servers, to open a connection. In Figure 2.13A, we see the segment leaving H2 with a destination of 204.71.200.69.80 and a source of 10.0.0.2.9600.

We are using the standard convention that IP addresses written in the form A.B.C.D.P have an IP address of A.B.C.D and a port of P.

There is nothing remarkable about this except that the source address is a private network address. When this segment gets to the router, NAT must change its source address to 205.184.151.171 so that the Web server at Yahoo will know where to send its SYN/ACK and other replies. Because any Internet traffic to and from the other hosts on the private network will also have their addresses translated to 205.184.151.171, NAT must also translate the source port to a unique port number so that it can send incoming traffic on that connection to the correct host. We see that the source port of 9600 is mapped to 5555. Thus the segment that is delivered to Yahoo has a destination of 204.71.200.69.80 and a source of 205.184.151.171.5555.

As shown in Figure 2.13B, when Yahoo's reply arrives at the router, it is addressed to 205.184.151.171.5555. NAT looks up this port in its internal state table and sees that port 5555 is associated with the address 10.0.0.1.9600, and so the reply travels from the router to H2 with a source of 204.71.200.69.80 and a destination of 10.0.0.1.9600.

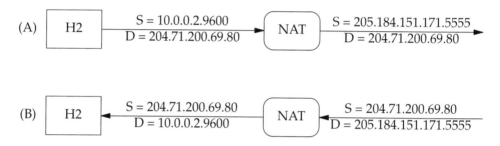

**Figure 2.13** Port address translation

Although the preceding discussion makes PAT seem straightforward, there are many subtleties that make it more complicated than it might appear. For instance, changing the source and port numbers change both the IP header checksum and the TCP segment checksum, so both of these quantities must be adjusted.

As another example of how complications can arise, consider the File Transfer Protocol (FTP) [Reynolds and Postel 1985]. When an FTP client wants to send or receive a file to or from the FTP server, it sends the server a PORT command that contains an address and port number on which it will listen for the (data) connection from the server. This means, first of all, that NAT has to recognize this TCP segment as an FTP PORT command and must translate the address and port. Furthermore, the address and port number in the PORT command are sent as an ASCII string, so changing them may also change the size of the segment. This, in turn, means that the sequence numbers (see Tip 1) change and that NAT also has to track them so that the sequence numbers in the ACK can be adjusted and so that additional segments from the host on the private network can have their sequence numbers adjusted.

Despite these complications, NAT works very well and is widely deployed. PAT, in particular, is the natural way to connect a small network to the Internet when there is only one Internet connection available.

**Summary**

In this tip we have seen how NAT makes it possible for a network to use one of the private network address blocks for internal hosts, but still be able to communicate with the Internet at large. PAT, especially, is very useful for small networks that have only a single globally accessible IP address. Unfortunately, because PAT changes source port numbers of outgoing packets, it may present problems for non-standard protocols that pass information about port numbers in the body of their messages.

## Tip 4: Develop and Use Application "Skeletons"

The majority of all TCP/IP applications fall into one of four categories:

1. A TCP server
2. A TCP client
3. A UDP server
4. A UDP client

Applications that fall into the same category generally have nearly identical "setup" code that initializes their networking aspects. For example, a TCP server must fill in a `sockaddr_in` structure with its desired address and port number, obtain a `SOCK_STREAM` socket, bind the chosen address and port number to it, set the `SO_REUSEADDR` socket option (Tip 23), call `listen`, and then be prepared to accept a connection (or connections) via `accept`.

Done correctly, each of these steps requires a check for an error return, and the address and port translation code should be prepared to accept either numeric or symbolic addresses and port numbers. Thus, every TCP server has on the order of 100 lines of nearly identical code to accomplish these tasks. One way of dealing with this is to abstract the setup code into one or more library functions, which the application can call. This is a sound strategy, and one that we will follow in this text, but sometimes the application requires a slightly different initialization sequence. When that happens, we either have to start from scratch or pull the relevant code from the library and make the necessary changes.

To deal with these cases, we build an application skeleton that has all the necessary code in it. We can then copy this skeleton into our application, make the necessary changes, and continue with the application itself. Without such a skeleton, it is tempting to take shortcuts such as hard-coding addresses into the application (Tip 29) and other dubious practices. Once we develop these skeletons, we can abstract the usual cases into a library and save the skeleton for the special cases.

As an aid to portability, we define several macros that hide some of the differences between the UNIX and Windows APIs. For example, the UNIX system call to close a socket is `close`, whereas under Windows it is `closesocket`. The UNIX version of

these macros is shown in Figure 2.14.  The Windows version is similar and is shown in
Appendix B.  Our skeletons access these macros by including the file `skel.h`.

*——————————————————————————————————————————— skel.h*

```
 1 #ifndef __SKEL_H__
 2 #define __SKEL_H__

 3 /* UNIX version */

 4 #define INIT()           ( program_name = \
 5                           strrchr( argv[ 0 ], '/' ) ) ? \
 6                           program_name++ : \
 7                           ( program_name = argv[ 0 ] )
 8 #define EXIT(s)          exit( s )
 9 #define CLOSE(s)         if ( close( s ) ) error( 1, errno, \
10                           "close failed" )
11 #define set_errno(e)     errno = ( e )
12 #define isvalidsock(s)   ( ( s ) >= 0 )

13 typedef int SOCKET;

14 #endif  /* __SKEL_H__ */
```

*——————————————————————————————————————————— skel.h*

**Figure 2.14** `skel.h`

## TCP Server Skeleton

Let's begin with a skeleton for a TCP server.  When it's completed we can start to build
our library by pulling the relevant code from the skeleton.  Figure 2.15 shows the `main`
function of our skeleton.

*——————————————————————————————————————————— tcpserver.skel*

```
 1 #include <stdio.h>
 2 #include <stdlib.h>
 3 #include <unistd.h>
 4 #include <stdarg.h>
 5 #include <string.h>
 6 #include <errno.h>
 7 #include <netdb.h>
 8 #include <fcntl.h>
 9 #include <sys/time.h>
10 #include <sys/socket.h>
11 #include <netinet/in.h>
12 #include <arpa/inet.h>
13 #include "skel.h"

14 char *program_name;

15 int main( int argc, char **argv )
16 {
17     struct sockaddr_in local;
18     struct sockaddr_in peer;
19     char *hname;
```

```
20      char *sname;
21      int peerlen;
22      SOCKET s1;
23      SOCKET s;
24      const int on = 1;

25      INIT();

26      if ( argc == 2 )
27      {
28          hname = NULL;
29          sname = argv[ 1 ];
30      }
31      else
32      {
33          hname = argv[ 1 ];
34          sname = argv[ 2 ];
35      }

36      set_address( hname, sname, &local, "tcp" );
37      s = socket( AF_INET, SOCK_STREAM, 0 );
38      if ( !isvalidsock( s ) )
39          error( 1, errno, "socket call failed" );

40      if ( setsockopt( s, SOL_SOCKET, SO_REUSEADDR, &on,
41              sizeof( on ) ) )
42          error( 1, errno, "setsockopt failed" );

43      if ( bind( s, ( struct sockaddr * ) &local,
44              sizeof( local ) ) )
45          error( 1, errno, "bind failed" );

46      if ( listen( s, NLISTEN ) )
47          error( 1, errno, "listen failed" );
48      do
49      {
50          peerlen = sizeof( peer );
51          s1 = accept( s, ( struct sockaddr * )&peer, &peerlen );
52          if ( !isvalidsock( s1 ) )
53              error( 1, errno, "accept failed" );
54          server( s1, &peer );
55          CLOSE( s1 );
56      } while ( 1 );
57      EXIT( 0 );
58 }
```

*tcpserver.skel*

**Figure 2.15** The main function of tcpserver.skel

**Includes and Globals**

*1–14*    We include header files for the standard functions that we will use.

*25*    The INIT macro performs standard initializations such as setting the global variable program_name for error, and calling WSAStartup when we are running under Microsoft Windows.

**main**

*26-35*    We expect our server to be called with either an address and port number or just a
port number. If no address is specified, INADDR_ANY is bound to the socket, thereby
accepting connections on any interface. In an actual application, there might be other
command line arguments, of course, and we would handle them here.

*36*        We call set_address to fill in the sockaddr_in structure local with the
requested address and port number. The set_address function is shown in
Figure 2.16.

*37-45*    We obtain a socket, set the SO_REUSEADDR option (Tip 23), and bind the address
and port number in local to it.

*46-47*    We call listen to inform the kernel that we are prepared to accept connections
from clients.

*48-56*    We accept connections and call server for each one. The server function can
handle the connection as part of the server process, or it can fork off a child process to
do so. In either case, the connection is closed when server returns. The unusual do-
while construction provides an easy way of having the server exit after the first connection. We need merely change the

```
while ( 1 );
```

to a

```
while ( 0 );
```

Next we look at the set_address function. We will use this same function in all
our skeletons, so it is a natural candidate for our library of common functions.

*——————————————————————— tcpserver.skel*

```
 1 static void set_address( char *hname, char *sname,
 2     struct sockaddr_in *sap, char *protocol )
 3 {
 4     struct servent *sp;
 5     struct hostent *hp;
 6     char *endptr;
 7     short port;

 8     bzero( sap, sizeof( *sap ) );
 9     sap->sin_family = AF_INET;
10     if ( hname != NULL )
11     {
12         if ( !inet_aton( hname, &sap->sin_addr ) )
13         {
14             hp = gethostbyname( hname );
15             if ( hp == NULL )
16                 error( 1, 0, "unknown host: %s\n", hname );
17             sap->sin_addr = *( struct in_addr * )hp->h_addr;
18         }
19     }
20     else
21         sap->sin_addr.s_addr = htonl( INADDR_ANY );
22     port = strtol( sname, &endptr, 0 );
```

```
23      if ( *endptr == '\0' )
24          sap->sin_port = htons( port );
25      else
26      {
27          sp = getservbyname( sname, protocol );
28          if ( sp == NULL )
29              error( 1, 0, "unknown service: %s\n", sname );
30          sap->sin_port = sp->s_port;
31      }
32  }
```
——————————————————————————————— *tcpserver.skel*

**Figure 2.16** The `set_address` function

**set_address**

*8-9*    We zero out the `sockaddr_in` structure and set the address family to `AF_INET`.

*10-19*    If *hname* is not `NULL` we first assume it is a numeric address in the standard dotted decimal notation and try to convert it using `inet_aton`. If `inet_aton` returns an error, we next try to resolve *hname* into an address by calling `gethostbyname`. If this too fails, we print a diagnostic and exit.

*20-21*    If the caller did not specify a host name or address, we set the address to `INADDR_ANY`.

*22-24*    Next, we try to convert *sname* into an integer. If this succeeds, we convert the port number into network byte order (Tip 28).

*27-30*    If the conversion of *sname* into an integer fails, we assume it is a service name and call `getservbyname` to get the port number. If the service is unknown, we print a diagnostic and exit. Notice that the port number returned by `getservbyname` is already in network byte order.

Because we will have occasion to call `set_address` directly, we record its prototype here for future reference:

```
#include "etcp.h"

void set_address( char *host, char *port,
                  struct sockaddr_in *sap, char *protocol );
```

Our final function, `error`, is shown in Figure 2.17. This is our standard diagnostic routine.

If *status* is nonzero, `error` exits after printing the diagnostic; otherwise, it returns. If *err* is nonzero, it is taken as the value of `errno` and the string corresponding to it, as well as its value, is appended to the diagnostic.

We use the `error` function continually in our examples, so we add it to our library and document its prototype as

```
#include "etcp.h"

void error( int status, int err, char *format, ... );
```

---
*tcpserver.skel*
```
 1 void error( int status, int err, char *fmt, ... )
 2 {
 3     va_list ap;
 4     va_start( ap, fmt );
 5     fprintf( stderr, "%s: ", program_name );
 6     vfprintf( stderr, fmt, ap );
 7     va_end( ap );
 8     if ( err )
 9         fprintf( stderr, ": %s (%d)\n", strerror( err ), err );
10     if ( status )
11         EXIT( status );
12 }
```
*tcpserver.skel*

---

**Figure 2.17** The `error` function

Our skeleton also includes a stub for the server function:

```
static void server( SOCKET s, struct sockaddr_in *peerp )
{
}
```

We can turn this skeleton into a simple application merely by adding some code to the server stub. For example, if we copy `tcpserver.skel` to `hello.c` and replace the stub with

```
static void server( SOCKET s, struct sockaddr_in *peerp )
{
    send( s, "hello, world\n", 13, 0 );
}
```

we obtain a network version of a famous C program. If we compile and run this and then connect to it with telnet, we get the expected results:

```
bsd: $ hello 9000 &
[1] 1163
bsd: $ telnet localhost 9000
Trying 127.0.0.1...
Connected to localhost
Escape character is '^]'.
hello, world
Connection closed by foreign host.
```

Because `tcpserver.skel` represents the normal case for a TCP server, we extract most of `main`, and turn it into a library function, called `tcp_server`, as shown in Figure 2.18. The prototype for `tcp_server` is

```
#include "etcp.h"

SOCKET tcp_server( char *host, char *port );

                              Returns: a listening socket (terminates on error)
```

The *host* parameter points to a string that is either the host's name or its IP address. Similarly, the *port* parameter points to a string that is either the symbolic service name or the ASCII port number.

From now on, we will use `tcp_server` unless we need to modify the skeleton code for a special case.

*———————————————————————————————— library/tcp_server.c*

```
 1 SOCKET tcp_server( char *hname, char *sname )
 2 {
 3     struct sockaddr_in local;
 4     SOCKET s;
 5     const int on = 1;

 6     set_address( hname, sname, &local, "tcp" );
 7     s = socket( AF_INET, SOCK_STREAM, 0 );
 8     if ( !isvalidsock( s ) )
 9         error( 1, errno, "socket call failed" );

10     if ( setsockopt( s, SOL_SOCKET, SO_REUSEADDR,
11         ( char * )&on, sizeof( on ) ) )
12         error( 1, errno, "setsockopt failed" );

13     if ( bind( s, ( struct sockaddr * ) &local,
14         sizeof( local ) ) )
15         error( 1, errno, "bind failed" );

16     if ( listen( s, NLISTEN ) )
17         error( 1, errno, "listen failed" );

18     return s;
19 }
```

*———————————————————————————————— library/tcp_server.c*

**Figure 2.18** The `tcp_server` function

## TCP Client Skeleton

Next we look at a skeleton for a TCP client application (Figure 2.19). With the exception of the `main` function and the substitution of a `client` stub for the `server` stub, it is the same as our TCP server skeleton.

*———————————————————————————————————————— tcpclient.skel*

```
 1 int main( int argc, char **argv )
 2 {
 3     struct sockaddr_in peer;
 4     SOCKET s;

 5     INIT();

 6     set_address( argv[ 1 ], argv[ 2 ], &peer, "tcp" );

 7     s = socket( AF_INET, SOCK_STREAM, 0 );
 8     if ( !isvalidsock( s ) )
 9         error( 1, errno, "socket call failed" );
```

```
10      if ( connect( s, ( struct sockaddr * )&peer,
11          sizeof( peer ) ) )
12          error( 1, errno, "connect failed" );

13      client( s, &peer );
14      EXIT( 0 );
15  }
```
————————————————————————————————————— *tcpclient.skel*

**Figure 2.19** main function from `tcpclient.skel`

**tcpclient.skel**

*6-9*    As with `tcpserver.skel`, we fill in the `sockaddr_in` structure with the requested address and port number, and obtain a socket.

*10-11*    We call `connect` to establish a connection with our peer.

*13*    When `connect` returns successfully, we call our `client` stub with the newly connected socket and the address of our peer.

We can try out this skeleton by copying it to `helloc.c`, and filling in the client stub with

```
static void client( SOCKET s, struct sockaddr_in *peerp )
{
    int rc;
    char buf[ 120 ];

    for ( ;; )
    {
        rc = recv( s, buf, sizeof( buf ), 0 );
        if ( rc <= 0 )
            break;
        write( 1, buf, rc );
    }
}
```

This client merely reads from the socket and writes to stdout until the server sends an end of file (EOF). If we connect to our hello server, we again get the expected result:

```
bsd: $ helloc localhost 9000
hello, world
bsd: $
```

We abstract the relevant portion of `tcpclient.skel` into our library, just as we did with our tcpserver skeleton. The new function, `tcp_client`, shown in Figure 2.20, has the prototype

```
#include "etcp.h"

SOCKET tcp_client( char *host, char *port );

                            Returns: a connected socket (terminates on error)
```

As with `tcp_server`, *host* is either the host name or its IP address. The *port* parameter is either the symbolic service name or its ASCII port number.

*library/tcp_client.c*

```
 1 SOCKET tcp_client( char *hname, char *sname )
 2 {
 3     struct sockaddr_in peer;
 4     SOCKET s;

 5     set_address( hname, sname, &peer, "tcp" );
 6     s = socket( AF_INET, SOCK_STREAM, 0 );
 7     if ( !isvalidsock( s ) )
 8         error( 1, errno, "socket call failed" );

 9     if ( connect( s, ( struct sockaddr * )&peer,
10         sizeof( peer ) ) )
11         error( 1, errno, "connect failed" );

12     return s;
13 }
```

*library/tcp_client.c*

**Figure 2.20** The `tcp_client` function

## UDP Server Skeleton

Our UDP server skeleton is similar to the TCP version, except that we don't need to set the `SO_REUSEADDR` socket option, and of course there is no need for the calls to `accept` and `listen` because UDP is a connectionless protocol (Tip 1). The `main` function of the skeleton is shown in Figure 2.21. The rest of the skeleton is identical to `tcpserver.skel`.

*udpserver.skel*

```
 1 int main( int argc, char **argv )
 2 {
 3     struct sockaddr_in local;
 4     char *hname;
 5     char *sname;
 6     SOCKET s;

 7     INIT();

 8     if ( argc == 2 )
 9     {
10         hname = NULL;
11         sname = argv[ 1 ];
12     }
13     else
14     {
15         hname = argv[ 1 ];
16         sname = argv[ 2 ];
17     }

18     set_address( hname, sname, &local, "udp" );
19     s = socket( AF_INET, SOCK_DGRAM, 0 );
20     if ( !isvalidsock( s ) )
21         error( 1, errno, "socket call failed" );
```

```
22    if ( bind( s, ( struct sockaddr * ) &local,
23         sizeof( local ) ) )
24       error( 1, errno, "bind failed" );

25    server( s, &local );
26    EXIT( 0 );
27 }
```
———————————————————————————————————————————————— *udpserver.skel*

**Figure 2.21** main function from udpserver.skel

**udpserver.skel**

*18*     We call set_address to fill in the sockaddr_in structure local with the address and port number at which our server will be receiving datagrams. Notice that we specify "udp" instead of "tcp".

*19-24*     We obtain a SOCK_DGRAM socket and bind the address and port in local to it.

*25*     We call our server stub to await the arrival of datagrams.

To make a UDP version of our "hello world" program, we copy the skeleton to udphello.c, and replace the server stub with

```
static void server( SOCKET s, struct sockaddr_in *localp )
{
    struct sockaddr_in peer;
    int peerlen;
    char buf[ 1 ];

    for ( ;; )
    {
        peerlen = sizeof( peer );
        if ( recvfrom( s, buf, sizeof( buf ), 0,
            ( struct sockaddr * )&peer, &peerlen ) < 0 )
            error( 1, errno, "recvfrom failed" );
        if ( sendto( s, "hello, world\n", 13, 0,
            ( struct sockaddr * )&peer, peerlen ) < 0 )
            error( 1, errno, "sendto failed" );
    }
}
```

We need to develop a UDP client skeleton (Figure 2.23) before we can try this server, so for now we just abstract the last part of main into a library function called udp_server:

```
#include "etcp.h"

SOCKET udp_server( char *host, char *port );

                                    Returns: a UDP socket bound to host on port port
```

As usual, *host* and *port* point to strings that contain the host name or IP address, and the service name or port number.

*library/udp_server*

```
 1 SOCKET udp_server( char *hname, char *sname )
 2 {
 3     SOCKET s;
 4     struct sockaddr_in local;

 5     set_address( hname, sname, &local, "udp" );
 6     s = socket( AF_INET, SOCK_DGRAM, 0 );
 7     if ( !isvalidsock( s ) )
 8         error( 1, errno, "socket call failed" );
 9     if ( bind( s, ( struct sockaddr * ) &local,
10         sizeof( local ) ) )
11         error( 1, errno, "bind failed" );
12     return s;
13 }
```

*library/udp_server*

**Figure 2.22** The `udp_server` function

## The UDP Client Skeleton

The `main` function of our UDP client skeleton does little more than fill in `peer` with the requested peer's address and port, and get a `SOCK_DGRAM` socket. The `main` function is shown in Figure 2.23. The rest of the skeleton is identical to `udpserver.skel`.

*udpclient.skel*

```
 1 int main( int argc, char **argv )
 2 {
 3     struct sockaddr_in peer;
 4     SOCKET s;

 5     INIT();

 6     set_address( argv[ 1 ], argv[ 2 ], &peer, "udp" );
 7     s = socket( AF_INET, SOCK_DGRAM, 0 );
 8     if ( !isvalidsock( s ) )
 9         error( 1, errno, "socket call failed" );

10     client( s, &peer );
11     exit( 0 );
12 }
```

*udpclient.skel*

**Figure 2.23** `main` function from `udpclient.skel`

We can try out this skeleton and test `udphello` at the same time by copying `udpclient.skel` into `udphelloc.c`, and filling in the client stub with

```
static void client( SOCKET s, struct sockaddr_in *peerp )
{
    int rc;
    int peerlen;
    char buf[ 120 ];
```

```
        peerlen = sizeof( *peerp );
        if ( sendto( s, "", 1, 0, ( struct sockaddr * )peerp,
            peerlen ) < 0 )
            error( 1, errno, "sendto failed" );
        rc = recvfrom( s, buf, sizeof( buf ), 0,
            ( struct sockaddr * )peerp, &peerlen );
        if ( rc >= 0 )
            write( 1, buf, rc );
        else
            error( 1, errno, "recvfrom failed" );

    }
```

The `client` function just sends a null byte to the server, reads the resulting datagram, writes it to stdout, and exits. Sending the null byte satisfies the `recvfrom` in udphello, which returns so that udphello can send its datagram.

When we run the two programs, we get the usual greeting:

```
bsd: $ udphello 9000 &
[1] 448
bsd: $ udphelloc localhost 9000
hello, world
bsd: $
```

As usual, we abstract the setup code from `main` into our library. Note that our library function, called `udp_client` (Figure 2.24), has a third argument that is the address of a `sockaddr_in` structure, which it will fill in with the address and port number as specified in the first two arguments:

```
#include "etcp.h"

SOCKET udp_client( char *host, char *port,
                   struct sockaddr_in *sap );

                        Returns: a UDP socket and filled in sockaddr_in structure
```

*library/udp_client.c*

```
 1 SOCKET udp_client( char *hname, char *sname,
 2     struct sockaddr_in *sap )
 3 {
 4     SOCKET s;

 5     set_address( hname, sname, sap, "udp" );
 6     s = socket( AF_INET, SOCK_DGRAM, 0 );
 7     if ( !isvalidsock( s ) )
 8         error( 1, errno, "socket call failed" );
 9     return s;
10 }
```

*library/udp_client.c*

**Figure 2.24** The `udp_client` function

**Summary**

Although this section was a long one, it illustrates how simple it can be to build up an arsenal of skeleton and library code. All of the skeletons were very similar, differing mainly in the few lines of setup code in `main`. Thus, once we wrote the first, the rest consisted of little more than copying it and making a few changes. The power of the method was illustrated by the ease with which we were then able to quickly build some elementary clients and servers merely by filling in the stub functions.

Using the skeletons to build a library of functions gives us a base from which we can easily build applications and write small test programs to exercise them. We see examples of this throughout the rest of the text.

# Tip 5:   Prefer the Sockets Interface to XTI/TLI

In the UNIX world, there are two main APIs that are used to interface to communication protocols such as TCP/IP. These are

- Berkeley sockets
- The *X/Open Transport Interface* (XTI)

The sockets interface was developed at the University of California at Berkeley for their version of the UNIX operating system. It was first widely available in 4.2BSD (1983), underwent some refinement in 4.3BSD Reno (1990), and is now provided in virtually every version of UNIX. Several other operating systems also provide a sockets API. The Winsock API, popular in the Microsoft Windows world, is derived from the BSD sockets API [WinSock Group 1997].

The XTI API is a superset of the *transport layer interface* (TLI) first provided by AT&T in UNIX System V Release 3.0 (SVR3). The TLI was designed to be protocol independent in the sense that it can support new protocols more easily. Its design was influenced heavily by the OSI protocols (Tip 14). At the time, it was widely believed that these protocols would soon replace TCP/IP, and so the interface's design is less than optimal from the point of view of a TCP/IP programmer. Even more unfortunate is the fact that although the TLI function names are very similar to those in the sockets API (except that they begin with `t_`), the semantics of the corresponding functions sometimes differ.

The lingering popularity of the interface is probably due largely to its use with the Novell Internetwork Packet Exchange/Sequenced Packet Exchange (IPX/SPX) protocols. When programs written for IPX/SPX were ported to TCP/IP, the path of least resistance was to use the same TLI interface [Kacker 1999].

Part 4 of the first volume of *UNIX Network Programming*[Stevens 1998] provides an excellent introduction to XTI and STREAMS programming. We can gain an appreciation for how much the semantics of the XTI and sockets interface differ when we realize that Stevens devotes more than 100 pages to the discussion of the XTI API.

Because of the belief that the OSI protocols would replace TCP/IP, many UNIX vendors recommended that new applications be coded using the TLI API. At least one vendor even suggested that the sockets interface would not be supported in future versions. Notice of the deaths of TCP/IP and the sockets interface turned out to be premature, of course.

The OSI protocols are essentially dead, but the TLI and its successor XTI are still available in System V-derived UNIX systems. For UNIX applications, this raises the question of whether it is better to use the sockets interface or XTI.

Before we examine the merits of each of these interfaces, it is important to realize that they *are* interfaces. For the TCP/IP application programmer, they are merely alternative ways of communicating with the TCP/IP stack. Because it is the TCP/IP stack that actually implements the communication protocols, it makes no difference to an application which API its peer is using. That is, an application using sockets can interoperate seamlessly with an application using XTI. On SVR4 systems, both interfaces are supported, and are usually implemented as libraries that interface to the same TCP/IP stack through the STREAMS subsystem.

Let's first take a look at XTI. XTI does have a place in network programming. Because of its protocol-independent design, it is possible, using TLI or XTI, to add a new protocol to a UNIX system without access to the kernel source code. The protocol designer need merely implement the transport provider as a STREAMS multiplexor, link it into the kernel, and then access it using XTI.

> How to write such STREAMS modules, as well as TLI and STREAMS programming in general, are discussed in great detail in [Rago 1993].

Notice how narrow this situation is: We must implement a protocol not already provided by the system, and we do not have access to the kernel source code.

> We must also be developing this new protocol under SVR4 or some other system that supports STREAMS and TLI/XTI, of course. Starting with Solaris 2.6, Sun provides this same functionality with the sockets API.

In addition to its advantages in the situation just described, it is sometimes argued that it is easier to write protocol-independent code using XTI/TLI [Rago 1996]. "Easier" is subjective, of course, but in Section 11.9 of *UNIX Network Programming* [Stevens 1998], Stevens uses sockets to provide a simple, protocol-independent daytime server that supports IP version 4, IP version 6, and UNIX domain sockets.

Lastly, it is sometimes argued that when both interfaces are supported, the sockets interface is layered on top of TLI/XTI, and thus TLI/XTI is more efficient. This is not correct. As stated earlier, in SVR4-based systems both interfaces are normally implemented as a set of libraries that communicate directly with the underlying STREAMS subsystem. In fact, starting with Solaris 2.6 (Solaris is Sun's version of SVR4), the socket calls are implemented in the kernel and are accessed directly through system calls.

The great advantage of the sockets interface is portability. Because a sockets interface is virtually always provided when the TLI/XTI is, maximum portability is achieved by using sockets. This is true regardless of whether our application runs only on UNIX systems because most operating systems supporting TCP/IP provide a sockets interface, and few, if any, non-UNIX systems provide TLI/XTI. For example, writing an application to be portable between UNIX and Microsoft Windows is reasonably straightforward because Windows supports Winsock, an implementation of the sockets interface.

The other advantage of sockets is that the interface is easier to use than TLI/XTI. Because they were designed as a more general interface with the OSI protocols in mind, TLI/XTI requires more work on the part of the application programmer compared with sockets. Even advocates of TLI/XTI concede that for TCP/IP applications, sockets is the preferred interface.

The following excerpt from the Solaris 2.6 Subroutine Library Introduction man page offers excellent advice on the choice of an API:

> Under all circumstances, the use of the Sockets API is recommended over the XTI and TLI APIs. If portability to other XPGV4v2 systems is a requirement, the application must use the libxnet interfaces. If portability is not required, the sockets interfaces in libsocket and libnsl are recommended over those in libxnet. Between the XTI and TLI APIs, the XTI interfaces (available with libxnet) are recommended over the TLI interfaces (available with libnsl).

### Summary

Except for very special circumstances, there is little reason to use TLI/XTI in TCP/IP programming. Sockets provide an easier, more portable interface, and there are no real differences in capabilities between the interfaces.

## Tip 6:   Remember That TCP Is a Stream Protocol

TCP is a *stream protocol*. This means that data is delivered to a recipient as a stream of bytes with no inherent notion of "message" or "message boundary." In this respect, reading TCP data is much like reading data from a serial port—one never knows how many bytes will be returned on a given call to read.

To illustrate, let us suppose that there is a TCP connection between applications on host A and host B, and that the application on host A sends messages to host B. Suppose further that host A has two messages to send, and does so by calling send twice, once for each message. It is natural to think of the two messages traveling from host A to host B as separate entities, each in its own packet as shown in Figure 2.25.

**Figure 2.25** Incorrect model of two message sends

Unfortunately, the actual transmission of the data will probably *not* follow this model. The application on host A calls send, and we imagine the data from that write traveling in a packet to host B. Actually, send usually just copies the data to the TCP/IP stack on host A and returns. TCP determines how much, if any, of the data it will send immediately. This determination is complex and depends on many factors such as the the send window (the amount of data host B is willing to receive at this point), the congestion window (an estimate of network congestion), the path maximum transmission unit (the maximum amount of data that can be sent at once along the network path between hosts A and B), and how much data is on the output queue for the connection. See Tip 15 for more on this. Figure 2.26 shows just four of the many possible ways that the data can be packetized by the TCP on host A. In Figure 2.26, $M_{1_1}$ and $M_{1_2}$ represent the first and second parts of $M_1$, and similarly for $M_{2_1}$ and $M_{2_2}$. As depicted in Figure 2.26, TCP does not necessarily send all of a message in a single packet.

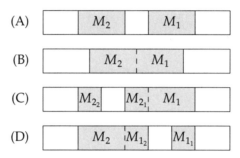

**Figure 2.26** Four possible ways to packetize two messages

Now let's look at the situation from the point of view of the application on host B. In general, the application on host B can make no assumptions about how much data TCP will have available for it on any given call to recv. When the application on host B issues its read for the first message, for instance, one of four outcomes is possible:

> Actually, there are more than four, but we're ignoring possibilities such as error and EOF conditions. Also, we are assuming that the application reads all the data that is available.

1. No data is ready for reading and the application blocks or recv returns an indication that no data is available. Exactly what happens depends on whether the socket has been marked blocking and what semantics the operating system on host B assigns to the recv system call.

2. The application gets some but not all of the data in message $M_1$. This can happen, for example, if the sending TCP packetizes the data as shown in Figure 2.26D.

3. The application gets all of the data in message $M_1$ and no more. This can happen if the data is packetized as shown in Figure 2.26A.

4. The application gets all of the data in message $M_1$ and part or all of the data in message $M_2$. This happens when the data is packetized as shown in Figure 2.26B or Figure 2.26C.

Notice that there is a timing issue here. If the application on host B does not issue the read for the first message until some time after host A has sent the second message, both messages will be available for reading. This is the same as the situation shown in Figure 2.26B. As these scenarios show, the amount of data that is ready to be read at any particular time is, in general, indeterminate.

Again, TCP is a *stream protocol* and although data is transmitted in IP packets, the amount of data in a packet is not directly related to how much data was delivered to TCP in the call to send. Furthermore, there is no reliable way for the receiving application to determine how the data was packetized, because several packets may have arrived between calls to recv.

> This can happen even if the receiving application is very responsive. For example, if a packet is lost (a very common occurrence in today's Internet, see Tip 12), and subsequent packets arrive safely, TCP holds the data from the subsequent packets until the first packet is retransmitted and received correctly. At that point, it makes *all* the data available to the application.

TCP keeps track of how many bytes it has sent and how many have been acknowledged, not how they were packetized. Some implementations, in fact, can send more or less data on a retransmission of a lost packet. This fact is sufficiently important to restate:

> **There is no such thing as a "packet" for a TCP *application*. An application with a design that depends in any way on how TCP packetizes the data needs to be rethought.**

Given that the amount of data returned in any given read is unpredictable, we must be prepared to deal with this in our applications. Often this is not a problem. It may be, for example, that we are using a Standard I/O library routine such as fgets to read the data. In this case fgets takes care of breaking the byte stream into lines for us. See Figure 3.6 for an example of this. Other times we do have to worry about message boundaries, and in these cases they must be retained at the application level.

The most simple case is fixed-length messages. For these, we need only read the fixed number of bytes in the message. Given the previous discussion, it is *not* sufficient to do a simple read such as

```
recv( s, msg, sizeof( msg ), 0 );
```

because the read may return less than sizeof( msg ) bytes (Figure 2.26D). The standard way of handling this is shown in Figure 2.27.

───────────────────────────────────────────────────────── *library/readn.c*
```
1 int readn( SOCKET fd, char *bp, size_t len)
2 {
3       int cnt;
4       int rc;

5       cnt = len;
6       while ( cnt > 0 )
7       {
8             rc = recv( fd, bp, cnt, 0 );
```

```
 9          if ( rc < 0 )                /* read error? */
10          {
11              if ( errno == EINTR )    /* interrupted? */
12                  continue;            /* restart the read */
13              return -1;               /* return error */
14          }
15          if ( rc == 0 )               /* EOF? */
16              return len - cnt;        /* return short count */
17          bp += rc;
18          cnt -= rc;
19      }
20      return len;
21  }
```
———————————————————————————————————————————————————————— *library/readn.c*

**Figure 2.27**  The `readn` function

The `readn` function is used exactly like `read`, but it doesn't return until `len` bytes have been read, an EOF is received from the peer, or an error occurs. We record its definition as

```
#include "etcp.h"

int readn( SOCKET s, char *buf, size_t len );

                               Returns: number of bytes read, or -1 on error
```

Not surprisingly, `readn` uses the same logic needed to read a specified number of bytes from serial ports and other stream-based sources for which the amount of data available at any given time is unknown. In fact, `readn` (with `int` substituted for `SOCKET` and `read` substituted for `recv`) can be, and often is, used in all these situations.

The if statement

```
if ( errno == EINTR )    /* interrupted? */
    continue;            /* restart the read */
```

at lines 11 and 12 restarts the `recv` call if it is interrupted by a signal. Some systems will restart interrupted system calls automatically, and for such systems these two lines are not needed. On the other hand, they don't hurt anything, so for maximum portability it is best to leave them in.

For applications that must support variable-length messages, there are two methods available. First, the records can be separated by an end-of-record mark. This is what happens when we use a Standard I/O routine such as `fgets` to break messages into individual lines, as described earlier. In the Standard I/O case, the newlines serve as the end-of-record marks in a natural way. In general, however, there are problems with this method. In the first place, unless the end-of-record mark is never used in the body of the message, the sending routine has to scan the message for these marks, and either escape or otherwise encode them so that they won't be mistaken for an end-of-record mark. For example, if the record separator character, RS, is chosen as the end-of-record marker, the sender must search the message body for any occurrences of the RS character and escape them, say by preceding them with a \. This means that the data has to be moved to make room for the escape character. Of course, any occurrence of the escape character also has to be escaped. Thus if we are using \ as the escape character, any occurrence of \ in the message body has to be changed to \\.

At the receiving side, the entire message must be scanned again, this time removing the escape characters and searching for (the unescaped) end-of-record marks. Because the use of end-of-record marks can require that the entire message be scanned twice, it is best to limit its use to those situations in which there is a "natural" end-of-record mark, such as the newline character used to separate records that are text lines.

The other method of handling variable records is to precede each message by a header that contains (at least) the length of the following message, as illustrated in Figure 2.28

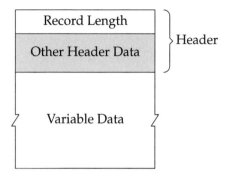

**Figure 2.28** Format of a variable record

The receiving application reads the message in two parts. First it reads the fixed-length message header, extracts the length of the variable part from the header, and then reads the variable-length part. This is illustrated in Figure 2.29 for the simple case in which the header consists of the record length only.

*library/readvrec.c*

```
 1 int readvrec( SOCKET fd, char *bp, size_t len )
 2 {
 3     u_int32_t reclen;
 4     int rc;

 5     /* Retrieve the length of the record */
 6     rc = readn( fd, ( char * )&reclen, sizeof( u_int32_t ) );
 7     if ( rc != sizeof( u_int32_t ) )
 8         return rc < 0 ? -1 : 0;
 9     reclen = ntohl( reclen );
10     if ( reclen > len )
11     {
12         /*
13          *  Not enough room for the record--
14          *  discard it and return an error.
15          */
```

```
16          while ( reclen > 0 )
17          {
18              rc = readn( fd, bp, len );
19              if ( rc != len )
20                  return rc < 0 ? -1 : 0;
21              reclen -= len;
22              if ( reclen < len )
23                  len = reclen;
24          }
25          set_errno( EMSGSIZE );
26          return -1;
27      }

28      /* Retrieve the record itself */
29      rc = readn( fd, bp, reclen );
30      if ( rc != reclen )
31          return rc < 0 ? -1 : 0;
32      return rc;
33  }
```
*——————————————————————————————————————— library/readvrec.c*

**Figure 2.29** Function to read variable records

### Read Record Size

*6-8*     The size of the record is read into `reclen`, and `readvrec` returns 0 (EOF) if `readn` does not return an integer's worth of data, or -1 if there is an error.

*9*       The size of the record is converted from network to host byte order. See Tip 28 for more on this.

### Check If Record Will Fit

*10-27*   The caller's buffer size is checked to verify that it is large enough to hold the entire record. If there is not enough room in the buffer, the record is discarded by successively reading `len`-size pieces into the buffer. After discarding the record, `errno` is set to `EMSGSIZE` and `readvrec` returns -1.

### Read the Record

*29-32*   Finally, the record itself is read. `readvrec` returns -1, 0, or `reclen` to the caller depending on whether `readn` returns an error, a short count, or success.

Since `readvrec` is a useful function, which we will use in other tips, we record its definition as

```
#include "etcp.h"

int readvrec( SOCKET s, char *buf, size_t len );

                                   Returns: number of bytes read, or -1 on error
```

Figure 2.30 shows a simple server that reads variable-length records from a TCP connection using `readvrec`, and writes them to stdout.

*vrs.c*

```
 1 #include "etcp.h"

 2 int main( int argc, char **argv )
 3 {
 4     struct sockaddr_in peer;
 5     SOCKET s;
 6     SOCKET s1;
 7     int peerlen = sizeof( peer );
 8     int n;
 9     char buf[ 10 ];

10     INIT();
11     if ( argc == 2 )
12         s = tcp_server( NULL, argv[ 1 ] );
13     else
14         s = tcp_server( argv[ 1 ], argv[ 2 ] );
15     s1 = accept( s, ( struct sockaddr * )&peer, &peerlen );
16     if ( !isvalidsock( s1 ) )
17         error( 1, errno, "accept failed" );
18     for ( ;; )
19     {
20         n = readvrec( s1, buf, sizeof( buf ) );
21         if ( n < 0 )
22             error( 0, errno, "readvrec returned error" );
23         else if ( n == 0 )
24             error( 1, 0, "client disconnected\n" );
25         else
26             write( 1, buf, n );
27     }
28     EXIT( 0 );          /* not reached */
29 }
```

*vrs.c*

**Figure 2.30** vrs—a server demonstrating the use of readvrec

*10–17*    The server is initialized and accepts a single connection.

*20–24*    readvrec is called to read the next variable record. If there is an error, a diagnostic is printed and the next record is read. If readvrec returns an EOF, a message is printed and the server exits.

*26*    The record is written to stdout.

Figure 2.31 shows the corresponding client that reads messages from its standard input, attaches the length of the message, and sends it to the server.

**Define Packet Structure**

*6–10*    We define the packet structure that holds the message and its length when we call send. The u_int32_t data type is an unsigned 32-bit integer. Because Windows does not define this data type, there is a typedef for it in the Windows version of skel.h.

> There is another potential problem with this example of which we should be aware. We are assuming that the compiler will pack the data in the structure without any padding exactly as we specified. Because the second element is an array of bytes, this assumption is valid on most

```
                                                                                    vrc.c
 1 #include "etcp.h"

 2 int main( int argc, char **argv )
 3 {
 4     SOCKET s;
 5     int n;
 6     struct
 7     {
 8         u_int32_t reclen;
 9         char buf[ 128 ];
10     } packet;

11     INIT();
12     s = tcp_client( argv[ 1 ], argv[ 2 ] );
13     while ( fgets( packet.buf, sizeof( packet.buf ), stdin )
14         != NULL )
15     {
16         n = strlen( packet.buf );
17         packet.reclen = htonl( n );
18         if ( send( s, ( char * )&packet,
19             n + sizeof( packet.reclen ), 0 ) < 0 )
20             error( 1, errno, "send failure" );
21     }
22     EXIT( 0 );
23 }
                                                                                    vrc.c
```

**Figure 2.31** vrc—a client that sends variable-length messages

systems, but we should be alert for problems with assumptions about how compilers pack data in structures. We revisit this problem in Tip 24, where we discuss other means of sending two or more distinct pieces of data at once.

### Connect, Read, and Send Lines

*12*      The client connects to the server by calling tcp_client.

*13–21*     fgets is called to read a line from stdin, and places it in the buf field of the message packet. The line's length is determined by a call to strlen, and this value, after being converted to network byte order, is placed in the reclen field of the message packet. Finally, send is called to send the packet to the server.

For another way of sending messages of two or more parts, see Tip 24.

We test these programs by starting the server vrs on sparc, and then the client vrc on bsd. The runs are shown side by side so we can see the input to the client and the corresponding output of the server. We've also wrapped the error message on line 4:

```
bsd: $ vrc sparc 8050    sparc: $ vrs 8050
123                      123
123456789                123456789
1234567890               vrs: readvrec returned error:
                             Message too long (97)
12                       12
^C                       vrs: client disconnected
```

Because the server's buffer is 10 bytes, `readvrec` returns an error when we send the 11 characters 1, . . . , 0, <LF>.

## Summary

One of the most common errors that beginning network programmers make is to fail to understand that TCP delivers a byte stream that has no concept of record boundaries. We can summarize this important fact by saying that TCP has no user-visible notion of "packet." It merely delivers a stream of bytes, and we cannot predict reliably how many will be returned on a particular read. In this tip we explored several strategies that our applications can use to deal with this fact.

# Tip 7:   Don't Underestimate the Performance of TCP

Because TCP is a complex protocol that adds reliability and flow control to the basic IP datagram service, whereas UDP merely adds a checksum, it might seem that UDP would be an order of magnitude or more faster than TCP. Because of this presumption, many application programmers believe that they must use UDP to get acceptable performance. There are situations when UDP is considerably faster than TCP, but this is not always the case. As we shall see, TCP can sometimes perform substantially better than UDP.

As usual with network programming, the performance of any protocol depends on the network, the application, the loading, and other factors including, of course, the implementation quality. The only sure way of knowing which protocol and algorithms will perform optimally is to test them under the same conditions in which the application is expected to run. This is not always practical, of course, but often we can get a good idea of how things will perform by using our skeletons to build simple programs that simulate our expected network traffic.

Before we look at building some test cases, let us consider for a moment why and under what conditions UDP can be expected to perform substantially better than TCP. First, because TCP is more complex, there is more processing to do than with UDP.

> [Stevens 1996] reports that the 4.4BSD implementation of TCP contains approximately 4,500 lines of C code compared with approximately 800 for UDP. The normal code path for both protocols is considerably shorter, of course, but the numbers do give an indication of the relative code complexity.

In general, though, the CPU processing for both protocols is dominated by data copying and checksumming (Tip 26), so we don't expect to see much difference here. Indeed, in [Partridge 1993] Jacobson describes an experimental version of TCP in which the normal receive segment code path is only 30 (RISC) machine instructions long (excluding checksumming and copying the data to the user's buffer, which are done together).

The next thing we notice is that to provide reliability, the receiving TCP must send ACKs back to the sending TCP. This adds to the processing that each side must do, but not as much as we might expect. In the first place, the receiving side can piggyback the

ACK onto any data that it has to send back to its peer. Many TCP implementations, in fact, delay sending the ACK for a few milliseconds in case the application on its side generates a reply to the incoming segment. Second, TCP does not necessarily generate an ACK for each segment. Most TCP implementations ACK only every other segment under normal conditions.

> RFC 1122 [Braden 1989], the host requirements RFC, recommends delaying ACKs for up to 0.5 seconds, as long as every second segment is ACKed.

The other major difference between TCP and UDP is that TCP is a connection-oriented protocol (Tip 1), and so must deal with connection setup and tear down. Connection establishment requires the exchange of three segments in the normal case. Connection tear down normally requires four segments, but all except the last of these can often be combined with data-bearing segments.

Let us assume that the time for connection tear down is mostly absorbed into the data exchange, and concentrate on what happens during connection setup. As Figure 2.32 shows, the client begins the setup by sending a SYN (synchronization) segment to the server. This segment specifies the first sequence number that the client will use for its data as well as certain other connection parameters such as the *maximum segment size* (MSS) that it is willing to accept, and the size of its initial receive window. The server responds with its own SYN segment that also contains an ACK of the client's SYN. Finally, the client ACKs the server's SYN, completing connection establishment. At this point the client, for example, can send its first data segment.

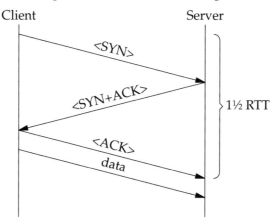

**Figure 2.32** Connection setup

In the figure, RTT represents one *round-trip time*—the time it takes for a packet to travel from one host to its peer and back. As we see, connection establishment takes one and one half round trip times.

If the connection between the client and server is long lived (for example, if a large amount of data is transfered between the client and server), the one and one half RTT is amortized across all the data transfers, and does not significantly affect the performance. If, however, we have a simple transaction in which the client sends a single request, to which the server responds, then connection setup time becomes a significant portion of the time for the entire transaction. Thus, we expect that UDP performs best against TCP exactly when the application involves short request/reply sessions, and that TCP performs best against UDP when the connection is long lived and involves the transfer of significant amounts of data.

To test the relative performance of TCP and UDP, and to give an example of building small test programs, we write a set of simple servers and clients. Our intent is not to provide a comprehensive benchmark, but rather to see how well the two protocols perform in a bulk data transfer. That is, we are interested in the relative performance of the protocols in moving a large amount of data from one application to another. The FTP protocol is a familiar example of bulk data transfer.

## A UDP Source and Sink

For UDP, the client sends any number of datagrams, which the server reads, counts, and discards. The client is shown in Figure 2.33.

```
                                                              ──────── udpsource.c
 1 #include "etcp.h"
 2 int main( int argc, char **argv )
 3 {
 4     struct sockaddr_in peer;
 5     SOCKET s;
 6     int rc;
 7     int datagrams;
 8     int dgramsz = 1440;
 9     char buf[ 1440 ];

10     INIT();
11     datagrams = atoi( argv[ 2 ] );
12     if ( argc > 3 )
13         dgramsz = atoi( argv[ 3 ] );
14     s = udp_client( argv[ 1 ], "9000", &peer );
15     while ( datagrams-- > 0 )
16     {
17         rc = sendto( s, buf, dgramsz, 0,
18             ( struct sockaddr * )&peer, sizeof( peer ) );
19         if ( rc <= 0 )
20             error( 0, errno, "sendto failed" );
21     }
22     sendto( s, "", 0, 0,
23         ( struct sockaddr * )&peer, sizeof( peer ) );
24     EXIT( 0 );
25 }
                                                              ──────── udpsource.c
```

**Figure 2.33** UDP client that sends any number of datagrams

*10–14*    The number of datagrams to send, and optionally the datagram size, is read from the command line, and a UDP socket is established with the address of the requested server in `peer`. Despite Tip 29, the port is hard-coded as 9000.

*15–21*    The requested number of datagrams is sent to the server.

*22–23*    A final 0-byte datagram is sent to the server. This serves as an EOF indicator for the server.

The server, presented in Figure 2.34, is even simpler.

——————————————————————————————— *udpsink.c*
```
 1 #include "etcp.h"
 2 int main( int argc, char **argv )
 3 {
 4     SOCKET s;
 5     int rc;
 6     int datagrams = 0;
 7     int rcvbufsz = 5000 * 1440;
 8     char buf[ 1440 ];

 9     INIT();
10     s = udp_server( NULL, "9000" );
11     setsockopt( s, SOL_SOCKET, SO_RCVBUF,
12         ( char * )&rcvbufsz, sizeof( int ) );
13     for( ;; )
14     {
15         rc = recv( s, buf, sizeof( buf ), 0 );
16         if ( rc <= 0 )
17             break;
18         datagrams++;
19     }
20     error( 0, 0, "%d datagrams received\n", datagrams );
21     EXIT( 0 );
22 }
```
——————————————————————————————— *udpsink.c*

**Figure 2.34**  A datagram sink

*10*       The server is set to receive datagrams on port 9000 from any interface.

*11–12*    The receive buffer is set large enough to hold 5,000 1,440-byte datagrams.

> Although we set the buffer size to 7,200,000 bytes, there is no guarantee that the operating system will actually allocate that much. Our host, bsd, actually set the buffer size to 41,600 bytes. This explains the loss of datagrams that we see later.

*13–19*    The datagrams are read and counted until an empty datagram is received or an error occurs.

*20*       The number of datagrams received is written to stderr.

## A TCP Source and Sink

As explained in Tip 32, we get better performance from TCP when the socket send and receive buffers are sized correctly. Thus we want to set the sizes of the server's socket receive buffer and the client's socket send buffer.

Because our `tcp_server` and `tcp_client` functions use the default socket buffer sizes, we start with our TCP client and server skeletons from Tip 4. Because TCP needs to know the buffer sizes during connection setup, we must set the sizes before calling listen in the server or connect in the client. This is the reason we can't use tcp_server and tcp_client: the calls to listen and connect have already been made when they return. We start with the client in Figure 2.35.

*tcpsource.c*

```
 1 int main( int argc, char **argv )
 2 {
 3     struct sockaddr_in peer;
 4     char *buf;
 5     SOCKET s;
 6     int c;
 7     int blks = 5000;
 8     int sndbufsz = 32 * 1024;
 9     int sndsz = 1440;   /* default ethernet mss */
10     INIT();
11     opterr = 0;
12     while ( ( c = getopt( argc, argv, "s:b:c:" ) ) != EOF )
13     {
14         switch ( c )
15         {
16             case 's' :
17                 sndsz = atoi( optarg );
18                 break;

19             case 'b' :
20                 sndbufsz = atoi( optarg );
21                 break;

22             case 'c' :
23                 blks = atoi( optarg );
24                 break;

25             case '?' :
26                 error( 1, 0, "illegal option: %c\n", c );
27         }
28     }
29     if ( argc <= optind )
30         error( 1, 0, "missing host name\n" );

31     if ( ( buf = malloc( sndsz ) ) == NULL )
32         error( 1, 0, "malloc failed\n" );
33     set_address( argv[ optind ], "9000", &peer, "tcp" );
34     s = socket( AF_INET, SOCK_STREAM, 0 );
35     if ( !isvalidsock( s ) )
36         error( 1, errno, "socket call failed" );

37     if ( setsockopt( s, SOL_SOCKET, SO_SNDBUF,
38         ( char * )&sndbufsz, sizeof( sndbufsz ) ) )
39         error( 1, errno, "setsockopt SO_SNDBUF failed" );

40     if ( connect( s, ( struct sockaddr * )&peer,
41         sizeof( peer ) ) )
42         error( 1, errno, "connect failed" );

43     while( blks-- > 0 )
44         send( s, buf, sndsz, 0 );
```

```
45      EXIT( 0 );
46 }
```

tcpsource.c

**Figure 2.35** `main` function of a TCP client that acts as a source

**`main`**

*12-30*    We call `getopt` repeatedly to read and process the command line arguments. Because we will use this program again later, we build in extra configurability. The command line options allow us to set the size of the socket send buffer, the amount of data to send in each write, and the total number of writes to make.

*31-42*    This is our standard TCP server setup code except that we have added a call to `setsockopt` to set the send buffer size, and have `malloced` a buffer for the requested amount of data to send in each write. Note that we needn't initialize the buffer pointed to by `buf` because we don't care what data we send.

*43-44*    We call `send` the requested number of times.

The `main` function of the server, shown in Figure 2.36, is our standard TCP server skeleton with the addition of a call to `getopt` to obtain the socket receive buffer size, and a call to `setsockopt` to set it.

tcpsink.c

```
 1 int main( int argc, char **argv )
 2 {
 3      struct sockaddr_in local;
 4      struct sockaddr_in peer;
 5      int peerlen;
 6      SOCKET s1;
 7      SOCKET s;
 8      int c;
 9      int rcvbufsz = 32 * 1024;
10      const int on = 1;

11      INIT();
12      opterr = 0;
13      while ( ( c = getopt( argc, argv, "b:" ) ) != EOF )
14      {
15          switch ( c )
16          {

17              case 'b' :
18                  rcvbufsz = atoi( optarg );
19                  break;

20              case '?' :
21                  error( 1, 0, "illegal option: %c\n", c );
22          }
23      }

24      set_address( NULL, "9000", &local, "tcp" );
25      s = socket( AF_INET, SOCK_STREAM, 0 );
26      if ( !isvalidsock( s ) )
27          error( 1, errno, "socket call failed" );
```

```
28     if ( setsockopt( s, SOL_SOCKET, SO_REUSEADDR,
29         ( char * )&on, sizeof( on ) ) )
30         error( 1, errno, "setsockopt SO_REUSEADDR failed" );
31     if ( setsockopt( s, SOL_SOCKET, SO_RCVBUF,
32         ( char * )&rcvbufsz, sizeof( rcvbufsz ) ) )
33         error( 1, errno, "setsockopt SO_RCVBUF failed" );
34     if ( bind( s, ( struct sockaddr * ) &local,
35         sizeof( local ) ) )
36         error( 1, errno, "bind failed" );
37     listen( s, 5 );
38     do
39     {
40         peerlen = sizeof( peer );
41         s1 = accept( s, ( struct sockaddr * )&peer, &peerlen );
42         if ( !isvalidsock( s1 ) )
43             error( 1, errno, "accept failed" );
44         server( s1, rcvbufsz );
45         CLOSE( s1 );
46     } while ( 0 );
47     EXIT( 0 );
48 }
```
———————————————————————————————————————————— *tcpsink.c*

**Figure 2.36** `main` function of a TCP server that acts as a sink

The `server` function merely reads and counts data until an EOF (Tip 16) arrives or an error occurs. It allocates a buffer equal to the socket receive buffer size in an attempt to read as much data at once as possible. The `server` function is shown in Figure 2.37.

———————————————————————————————————————————— *tcpsink.c*
```
 1 static void server( SOCKET s, int rcvbufsz )
 2 {
 3     char *buf;
 4     int rc;
 5     int bytes = 0;
 6     if ( ( buf = malloc( rcvbufsz ) ) == NULL )
 7         error( 1, 0, "malloc failed\n" );
 8     for ( ;; )
 9     {
10         rc = recv( s, buf, rcvbufsz, 0 );
11         if ( rc <= 0 )
12             break;
13         bytes += rc;
14     }
15     error( 0, 0, "%d bytes received\n", bytes );
16 }
```
———————————————————————————————————————————— *tcpsink.c*

**Figure 2.37** The `server` function

To help us gauge the relative performance of TCP and UDP in a bulk transfer, we run the client from bsd with the server running on various hosts. The hosts bsd and

localhost are the same, of course, but as we shall see, the results are dramatically different. We run the client and server on the same host to get an idea of how TCP and UDP
perform without the influence of a network. In both cases, UDP datagrams or TCP segments are encapsulated in IP datagrams and sent to the loopback interface, lo0, which
loops them back to the IP input routine as shown in Figure 2.38.

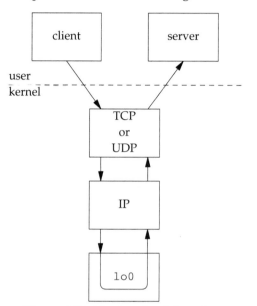

**Figure 2.38** The loopback interface

First we run each test 50 times with a datagram (UDP) or write (TCP) size of 1,440 bytes.
The size 1,440 was chosen because it is close to the largest segment size that TCP will
send over an Ethernet LAN.

> This number comes from the fact that an Ethernet frame can carry at most 1,500 data bytes.
> The IP and TCP headers each require 20 bytes, leaving 1,460 bytes. We reserve another 20
> bytes for TCP options. On bsd, TCP sends 12 bytes of options, so its actual maximum segment
> send size is 1,448 bytes.

Figure 2.39 summarizes the results averaged over the 50 runs. In the table, three time
measurements are given for each protocol. Clock time is the elapsed time between
starting the client and its finishing. User time is the time that the application spent executing in user space. System time is the time that the application spent executing in the
kernel. The MB/Sec column is the total number of bytes sent divided by the clock time.
The Drops column under UDP is the average number of datagrams dropped by each
run of the test.

The first thing we notice is that TCP performs significantly better when the server is
localhost than it does when the server is bsd. This is not the case for UDP, for which
there is no significant difference in performance. To understand why TCP performs so
much better when the client is directed at localhost, we invoke netstat (Tip 38) with
the -i option. The two relevant lines of output (with extraneous information removed)

| Server | TCP | | | | UDP | | | | |
|---|---|---|---|---|---|---|---|---|---|
| | **Clock** | **User** | **System** | **MB/Sec** | **Clock** | **User** | **System** | **MB/Sec** | **Drops** |
| bsd | 2.88 | 0.0292 | 1.4198 | 2.5 | 1.9618 | 0.0316 | 1.1934 | 3.67 | 336 |
| localhost | 0.9558 | 0.0096 | 0.6316 | 7.53 | 1.9748 | 0.031 | 1.1906 | 3.646 | 272 |
| sparc | 7.1882 | 0.016 | 1.6226 | 1.002 | 5.8284 | 0.0564 | 0.844 | 1.235 | 440 |

**Figure 2.39** Comparison of TCP and UDP performance (1,440 bytes)

are

```
Name   Mtu     Network        Address
ed0    1500    172.30         bsd
lo0    16384   127            localhost
```

We see that the MTU for bsd is 1,500, whereas for localhost it is 16,384.

> This behavior is an artifact of the implementation of BSD-derived TCPs. It does not happen under Solaris, for example. When the route to bsd is first built, the routing code assumes it is on the LAN because the network portion of its IP address is the same as that of the Ethernet's interface. It is not until the route is used the first time that TCP discovers it is on the same host and switches to the loopback interface. By that time, however, the route metrics, including the MTU, have already been set to that of the LAN's interface.

This means that when we are sending to localhost, TCP can send up to 16,384-byte segments (or $16,384 - 20 - 20 - 12 = 16,332$ bytes of data). When sending to bsd, however, the total number of data bytes is 1,448, as discussed earlier. These larger segments mean that fewer segments are sent, which means that there is less processing and less overhead from the headers that IP and TCP added to each segment of data. We can see the difference that this makes: The results for localhost are three times faster than those for bsd.

The second thing we notice about these results is that TCP is approximately twice as fast as UDP on localhost. Again, this is because TCP can combine several of the 1,440-byte writes into a single segment, whereas UDP sends each 1440-byte datagram separately.

Finally, we notice that on the LAN, UDP is approximately 20 percent faster than TCP, but that UDP lost a significant number of datagrams. This loss, which happened even when we were running both server and client on the same machine, was the result of running out of buffer space. Although sending 5,000 datagrams as fast as we can could be called pathological, it is worth remembering these results and what they imply: With UDP there is *no* guarantee that any particular datagram will arrive safely, even if we are running both applications on the same machine.

The results for localhost versus bsd suggest that relative performance is also affected by the size of the datagram that we send. For example, if we rerun our tests with 300-byte writes (TCP) and 300-byte datagrams (UDP), we see in Figure 2.40 that TCP outperforms UDP on both the local machine and on the LAN.

The important point about these examples is that it is wrong to make a priori assumptions about the relative performance of TCP and UDP. Changing the conditions, even in seemingly small ways, can dramatically change the performance figures. The

| Server | TCP | | | | UDP | | | | |
|--------|-------|-------|--------|--------|-------|-------|--------|--------|-------|
|        | Clock | User  | System | MB/Sec | Clock | User  | System | MB/Sec | Drops |
| bsd    | 1.059 | 0.0124| 0.445  | 1.416  | 1.6324| 0.0324| 0.9998 | .919   | 212   |
| sparc  | 1.5552| 0.0084| 1.2442 | .965   | 1.9118| 0.0278| 1.4352 | .785   | 306   |

**Figure 2.40** Comparison of TCP and UDP performance (300 bytes)

best way to make an informed choice about which protocol to use is to benchmark our application with each and see how they perform (but see Tip 8). When that's not practical, we can write small test cases, as we did earlier to get an idea of the relative performance.

As a practical matter, modern TCP implementations are "as fast as they need to be." The fact is, TCP can easily run at "wire speed" on 100MB FDDI networks, and some recent experiments have achieved near-gigabit speeds on PC hardware [Gallatin et al. 1999].

> On July 29, 1999, researchers at Duke University obtained gigabit speeds with a DEC/Compaq Alpha-based XP1000 workstation and a Myrinet gigabit-per-second network. The researchers used the standard FreeBSD 4.0 TCP/IP stack modified for zero-copy sockets. The same experiment obtained more than 800 Mb/s on a PII 450 MHz PC using an older version of the Myrinet network. Details are available at <http://www.cs.duke.edu/ari/trapeze>.

### Summary

We have seen that UDP does not necessarily provide better performance than TCP. Many factors can influence the relative performance of the two protocols, and we should always benchmark our applications to see how they perform with each of the protocols.

## Tip 8:  Avoid Reinventing TCP

As we saw in Tip 7, UDP can perform significantly better than TCP in simple request/reply applications. This leads us to consider using UDP as the underlying protocol for such transaction-based applications. The UDP protocol, however, is unreliable, so the application must provide the reliability itself.

At a minimum, this means that the application must worry about datagrams that get lost or corrupted by the network. Many beginning network programmers believe that this is a remote possibility in a LAN setting, and that they can therefore effectively ignore the chances of it happening. As we saw in Tip 7, however, it is easy to lose datagrams even if we are sending them to an application on the same host. Thus, the requirement to protect the application against lost datagrams can never be ignored.

If our application is going to run on a WAN, the possibility also exists that the datagrams may arrive out of order. This can happen any time there is more than one path from sender to receiver.

In view of the previous discussion, any reasonably robust UDP application must provide for (1) retransmitting a request for which a reply is not received within a reasonable time, and (2) ensuring that replies are matched correctly to requests.

The first of these requirements is met by starting a timer, called a *retransmission time-out* (RTO) timer, when each request is sent. If the timer expires before the reply is received, then the request must be resent. We will consider some efficient ways of doing this in Tip 20. The second requirement is easily implemented by attaching a sequence number to each request and having the server return it with its reply.

If our application is going to run on the Internet, a fixed-length RTO will not work well because the RTT between two hosts can vary significantly over even short time intervals. Thus, we want to adjust the value of the RTO timer as network conditions vary. Furthermore, if the RTO timer does expire, then we should probably increase it for the retransmission, because it's likely that the old value was too small. This leads us to consider some sort of exponential backoff for the RTO when retransmissions are necessary.

Next, if our application is going to use more than just a simple request/reply protocol, for which the client sends a request and then waits for a reply before sending any additional datagrams, or if the server's reply can consist of multiple datagrams, we need to provide some sort of flow control. For example, if the server is a personnel database application, and the client's request is "send me the name and address of each employee in engineering," the reply could comprise multiple records, each sent as a separate datagram. Without flow control, the multiple datagrams in the server's reply could overrun the client's buffers. The sliding window flow control that TCP uses (counting datagrams rather than bytes) is a common method of doing this.

Finally, if our application involves the transfer of more than a few datagrams in succession, we need to worry about congestion control. An application that injects datagrams into the network without regard for congestion control can easily cause severe throughput degradation for all network users, and can even cause network failure.

When we survey all the steps that an application must take to make a UDP-based protocol reliable, we see that we have largely reinvented TCP. Sometimes this is unavoidable. There are, after all, simple transaction-based applications for which the overhead of TCP connection setup and tear down would approach, or even exceed, the time required to send and receive the actual data.

> An everyday example of this is the *Domain Name System* (DNS), which is used to map a domain name to its IP address. For example, when we enter the name www.rfc-editor.org in our Web browser, a DNS client in the browser sends a UDP datagram to a DNS server requesting the IP address associated with the name. The server responds with a UDP datagram containing the appropriate IP address of 128.9.160.27. DNS is discussed further in Tip 29.

Nevertheless, we should evaluate carefully each application to assess the wisdom of doing so. If an application requires the reliability of TCP, it is possible that TCP is the best solution.

In the first place, it is unlikely that TCP functionality duplicated in a user application will be as efficient as the real thing. This is partly because TCP implementations are the results of substantial experience and research. Over the years, TCP has evolved in response to often subtle observations about its functioning in a variety of circumstances and networks, including the Internet.

It is also because TCP almost always executes in kernel context. To see why this can affect performance, let us imagine what happens when the RTO timer of our application expires. First the kernel must wake up the application, requiring a context switch to user space. The application must then resend the data. This requires another context switch back to the kernel, which must copy the datagram from user space into the kernel. The kernel determines the correct route for the datagram, moves it to the appropriate network interface, and returns to the application, requiring another context switch. The application must arrange to set the RTO timer again, so another context switch to the kernel is necessary.

Now consider what happens when TCP's RTO timer expires. The kernel already has a stored copy of the data, so it is not necessary to recopy it from user space. Furthermore, no context switches are required. TCP merely resends the data. Most of the work here involves moving the data from the kernel's buffer to the network interface. There is no need to do routing calculations because TCP has cached this information.

Another reason to avoid implementing TCP functionality at the user level concerns what happens when a server's reply is lost. Because the client does not receive the reply, it times out and resends the request. This means that the server processes the request again, which may be undesirable. Consider a client that requests a server to transfer funds from one banking account to another, for example. With TCP, the retry logic is not in the application, so the server does not see the request a second time.

> We're leaving aside, here, the possibility of a network failure, or of one of the hosts crashing. See Tip 9 for more on this.

Transaction-processing applications and some of the problems involved with using TCP or UDP to implement them are discussed in RFC 955 [Braden 1985]. In it, Braden argues for the need for a protocol that lies between the connectionless but unreliable UDP and the reliable but connection-oriented TCP protocols. The considerations in this RFC led Braden to propose *TCP Extensions for Transactions* (T/TCP), which we discuss next.

One way of having the reliability of TCP while still avoiding the cost of connection establishment is to use T/TCP. This is an extension to TCP that achieves transaction performance comparable with UDP by (usually) dispensing with the three-way handshake that TCP uses for connection establishment, and by shortening the TIME-WAIT phase (Tip 22) of connection tear down.

The rationale for T/TCP, and the concepts necessary for its implementation are described in RFC 1379 [Braden 1992a]. RFC 1644 [Braden 1994] contains a functional specification for T/TCP as well as a discussion of some implementation issues. [Stevens 1996] discusses T/TCP, its performance relative to UDP, changes in the sockets API to support it, and its implementation in the 4.4BSD TCP/IP stack.

Unfortunately, T/TCP is not widely available, although it is implemented in FreeBSD and there are patches available for the Linux 2.0.32 kernel and for SunOS 4.1.3.

Rich Stevens maintains a T/TCP home page that contains links to these and other T/TCP resources at <http://www.kohala.com/start/ttcp.html>.

## Summary

We have examined the steps required to build a reliable protocol on top of UDP. Although there are some applications, such as DNS, that do this, we saw that doing it correctly requires us to largely reinvent TCP. Because our UDP-based protocol is unlikely to be as efficient as TCP, it seldom makes sense to do this.

We also briefly examined T/TCP, an extended TCP that is optimized for transaction-based applications. Although T/TCP solves many of the problems with using TCP for transactions, it is not widely available.

## Tip 9: Realize That TCP Is a Reliable Protocol, Not an Infallible Protocol

As we have discussed many times, TCP is a reliable protocol. This is sometimes expressed as "TCP guarantees delivery of the data it sends." This formulation, although common, is exceedingly unfortunate.

First of all, even a moment's thought makes it clear that it couldn't be true. Suppose, for example, that we disconnect a host from the network in the middle of a data transfer. No amount of effort on TCP's part is going to get the remaining data delivered. Network outages do occur, hosts do crash, and users do turn off their machines while TCP connections are still active. These events and others like them can all render TCP unable to deliver data that it has accepted from an application.

More important, however, is the subtle effect that the notion of TCP's "guaranteed delivery" has on the mind of the unwary network programmer. No one really believes, of course, that TCP has some magical power that invariably causes data to arrive safely at its destination. Rather, the belief in TCP's guaranteed delivery manifests itself in the attitude that there is no need to program defensively or to consider failure modes because, after all, *TCP guarantees delivery.*

### Reliability—What It Is, What It Isn't

Before we consider the sorts of failure modes that can occur with TCP, let us be clear on what TCP reliability entails. If TCP doesn't guarantee to deliver all the data that we commit to it, what *does* it guarantee? The first question is: Guarantee to whom? Figure 2.41 shows data flowing from application A down through the TCP/IP stack on application A's host, through several intermediate routers, up through the TCP/IP stack on application B's host, and finally to application B. When a TCP segment leaves the TCP layer of application A's host, it is encapsulated in an IP datagram for transmission to its peer host. The route it travels may take it through many routers, but as shown in Figure 2.41, these routers don't have a TCP layer—they merely forward IP datagrams.

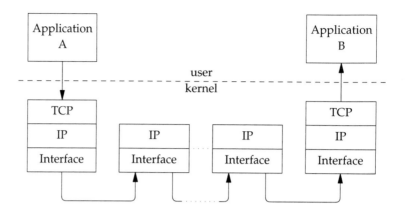

**Figure 2.41**  Network with intermediate routers

Some "routers" may, in fact, be general-purpose computers that do have a full TCP/IP stack, but in these cases their routing function does not involve the TCP or application layers.

Because we know that IP is an unreliable protocol, it should be clear that the first place in the data path that it makes sense to talk about a guarantee is at the TCP layer in application B's host. When a segment does arrive at the TCP layer on application B's host, the only thing we know for sure is that the segment has arrived. It may be corrupted, it may be duplicate data, it may be out of order, or it may be unacceptable for some other reason. Notice that the sending TCP can make no guarantees about segments that arrive at the receiver's TCP.

The receiving TCP, however, is prepared to make a guarantee to the sending TCP, and that is that any data that it ACKs and all the data that came before it has been received correctly *at the TCP layer*, and the sending TCP may safely discard its copy of the data. This does *not* mean that the data has been delivered to the application or that it ever will be. The receiving host could crash immediately after ACKing the data but before it was read by the application, for example. It is worth considering this point further: The only notification of data receipt that TCP provides to the sender is this ACK. The sending application has no way of telling from TCP alone whether its data was actually received by its peer application. As we note later, this represents a possible TCP failure mode of which application writers should be aware.

The other place that it makes sense to talk about a guarantee is at application B. As we've seen, there can be no guarantee that all data sent by application A will arrive. What TCP does guarantee to application B is that all data that does arrive will be in order and uncorrupted.

The data is guaranteed uncorrupted to the extent that the Internet checksum is able to detect errors. Because this checksum is the 16-bit ones-complement sum of byte pairs, it detects an error burst of 15 bits or less [Plummer 1978]. Under the assumption of uniformly distributed data, the TCP checksum accepts a corrupted segment with a probability of no more than $1/(2^{16} - 1)$. [Stone et al. 1998] shows, however, that over real data such as that found in typical

TCP segments, the Internet checksum failure rate can be substantially higher under some circumstances.

## Failure Modes

We have already seen one TCP failure mode presented earlier: the possibility that data ACKed by TCP does not, in fact, reach its destination application. Like most of the failure modes that we will discuss, this is a relatively rare event, and even when it happens, the effects can be benign. The important point is for the network programmer to be aware of the possibility, and to build in protection when this or any other failure mode can have undesirable consequences. What we are trying to avoid is the attitude that TCP will take care of everything for us so there is no need to worry about the robustness of our application protocol.

For the failure mode discussed earlier, the solution is evident. If it is important to an application to know for sure that its peer received a particular message, then the peer must inform the sender of that fact. Often, this acknowledgment is implicit. For example, if a client asks a server for some data, and the server responds, that response implicitly acknowledges the receipt of the original request. See Tip 19 for one possible way of handling explicit server acknowledgments.

The harder question is what does the client do if the server does not acknowledge receipt? This is highly dependent on the particular application, of course, and there is probably not a general solution. We should notice, however, that it is not always acceptable merely to resend the request: As we discussed in Tip 8, we wouldn't want to request a transfer of funds from a bank account twice. Database systems use a three-phase commit protocol to handle this type of problem, and some applications may have to employ a similar strategy to ensure that operations are performed "at most once." One example of this is the *concurrency, commitment, and recovery* (CCR) services provided as part of the common application service elements (CASE) in the application layer of the OSI reference stack. [Jain and Agrawala 1993] discusses the CCR protocol and how it works.

TCP is an end-to-end protocol, meaning that it concerns itself with providing a reliable transport mechanism between peers. It is important to realize, however, that the "end points" are the peer TCP layers, *not* the peer applications. Applications that require an end-to-end acknowledgment must provide it themselves.

Let us examine some other "common" failure modes. As long as the two peers remain connected, TCP guarantees to deliver the data in order and uncorrupted. It is only when that connectivity is interrupted that failure occurs. What sorts of events can cause such an interruption? There are three ways for this to happen:

1. A permanent or temporary network outage can occur.
2. Our peer application can crash.
3. The host on which our peer application is running can crash.

As we shall see, each of these events manifests itself in a different way at the sending application.

## Network Outage

Network outages can occur for several reasons, ranging from the loss of a router or backbone link to someone tripping over a local Ethernet cable and knocking it loose. Losses that occur away from the end points are generally temporary because the routing protocols are designed to discover and route around trouble spots.

By *endpoint* we mean the LAN or host on which one of the applications resides.

When a problem occurs at an end point, there is generally no alternative path, so the problem is apt to persist until it's repaired.

Unless an intermediate router sends an ICMP message indicating that the destination network or host is unreachable, neither the applications nor their TCP/IP stacks will be immediately aware of an outage (Tip 10). In this case, the sender eventually times out and resends any segments that have not been acknowledged. This continues until the sending TCP gives up, drops the connection, and reports an error. In the traditional BSD stack, this occurs after the segment has been retransmitted 12 times (approximately 9 minutes). If a read is pending, the read returns an error condition, and errno is set to ETIMEDOUT. If a read is not pending, the next write fails, either with a SIGPIPE signal or an error of EPIPE if the signal is ignored or caught.

If an intermediate router is unable to forward an IP datagram containing the segment, it sends the originating host an ICMP message indicating that either the destination network or the host is unreachable. In this case, some implementations return ENETUNREACH or EHOSTUNREACH as the error.

## Peer Crashes

Next, let's look at what happens if our peer application crashes or otherwise terminates. The first thing to realize is that from the point of view of our application, our peer crashing is indistinguishable from our peer calling close (or closesocket in the case of a Windows application) and exit. In both cases, our peer's TCP sends a FIN to our TCP. The FIN serves as an EOF indicating that the side sending it has no more data to send. It does *not* (necessarily) mean that the side sending it has exited or even that it is unwilling to *receive* more data. See Tip 16 for more on this. How, if at all, our application is notified of the receipt of the FIN depends on what it is doing when the FIN arrives. To illustrate the various things that can happen, we build a small TCP client that reads a line from stdin, sends it to a server, reads the server's reply, and writes it to stdout. Figure 2.42 shows this client.

*8-9*    We initialize our application as a TCP client and connect to the server and port specified on the command line.

*10-15*    We read lines from stdin and send them to the server until we get an EOF on stdin.

*16-20*    After sending data to the server, we read a line of reply. The readline function reads a single line by reading data from the socket until it finds a newline character. The readline function is shown in Figure 2.55 of Tip 11. If the call to readline fails or returns an EOF (Tip 16), we output a diagnostic and quit.

*22*    Otherwise, we write the reply to stdout.

```
 1 #include "etcp.h"
 2 int main( int argc, char **argv )
 3 {
 4     SOCKET s;
 5     int rc;
 6     int len;
 7     char buf[ 120 ];
 8
 9     INIT();
 9     s = tcp_client( argv[ 1 ], argv[ 2 ] );
10     while ( fgets( buf, sizeof( buf ), stdin ) != NULL )
11     {
12         len = strlen( buf );
13         rc = send( s, buf, len, 0 );
14         if ( rc < 0 )
15             error( 1, errno, "send failed" );
16         rc = readline( s, buf, sizeof( buf ) );
17         if ( rc < 0 )
18             error( 1, errno, "readline failed" );
19         else if ( rc == 0 )
20             error( 1, 0, "server terminated\n" );
21         else
22             fputs( buf, stdout );
23     }
24     EXIT( 0 );
25 }
```

**Figure 2.42** A TCP client that reads and writes lines

To exercise this client, we write a server that merely loops reading lines from the client and returning messages that indicate how many lines it has received. To simulate processing latency at the server, we sleep for 5 seconds between receiving a message and sending a reply. The server is shown in Figure 2.43.

```
 1 #include "etcp.h"
 2 int main( int argc, char **argv )
 3 {
 4     SOCKET s;
 5     SOCKET s1;
 6     int rc;
 7     int len;
 8     int counter = 1;
 9     char buf[ 120 ];
10     INIT();
11     s = tcp_server( NULL, argv[ 1 ] );
12     s1 = accept( s, NULL, NULL );
13     if ( !isvalidsock( s1 ) )
14         error( 1, errno, "accept failed" );
15     while ( ( rc = readline( s1, buf, sizeof( buf ) ) ) > 0 )
16     {
17         sleep( 5 );
```

```
18              len = sprintf( buf, "received message %d\n", counter++ );
19              rc = send( s1, buf, len, 0 );
20              if ( rc < 0 )
21                  error( 1, errno, "send failed" );
22          }
23      EXIT( 0 );
24  }
```
──────────────────────────────────────────────────────────────── *count.c*

**Figure 2.43** A server that counts messages


To see what can happen when a server crashes, we first start our server and client in
different windows on bsd:

```
bsd: $ tcprw localhost 9000
hello
received message 1                          this is printed after a 5-second delay
                                            the server is killed here

hello again
tcprw: readline failed: Connection reset by peer (54)
bsd: $
```

We send one message to the server, and after 5 seconds we get the expected reply. At
this point, we kill the server process, simulating a crash. On the client side, nothing
happens. That is because the client is blocked in the call to `fgets`, and TCP has no way
of notifying the client that it has received an EOF (the FIN) from the other side. If nothing else happens, the client remains blocked in the call to `fgets` forever and never
learns that its peer has terminated.

Next, we type another line at the client. The client immediately fails, telling us the
server's host has reset the connection. What happened is that when the client returned
from the `fgets`, it was still unaware of the EOF from the server. Because it is perfectly
legal for an application to send data after receiving a FIN, the client's TCP stack tried to
send the second line to the server. When TCP received the data, it responded with an
RST (the reset) because the connection no longer existed; the server had terminated.
When the client calls `readline`, the kernel returns an `ECONNRESET` error informing the
client that a reset was received. Figure 2.44 shows the time line for these events.

Now let us see what happens when the server crashes before it has finished processing a request and replied. Once again, we start the server and client in different windows on bsd:

```
bsd: $ tcprw localhost 9000
hello
                                            the server is killed here
tcprw: server terminated
bsd: $
```

We send a line to the server and then terminate the server before it wakes up from the
call to `sleep`. This simulates the server crashing before it has finished processing the

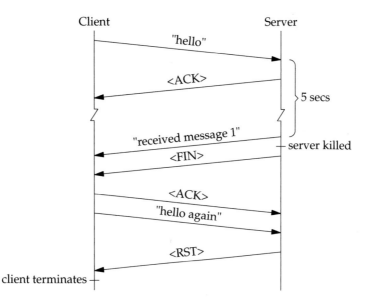

**Figure 2.44** Time line of a server crash

request. This time, the client gets an immediate error indicating that the server has terminated. In this example, the client is blocked in the call to `readline` when the FIN is received, and TCP is able to notify the client immediately by having `readline` return an EOF. The time line for these events are shown in Figure 2.45.

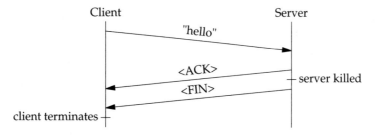

**Figure 2.45** Server crash with client read pending

A third type of error can occur if we ignore the connection reset error and continue to send data. To simulate this, we change the `error` call following the `readline` to output a diagnostic, but not quit. To do this, we change line 17 of Figure 2.42 to

```
error( 0, errno, "readline failed" );
```

Now we rerun the first test:

```
bsd: $ tcprw localhost 9000
hello
received message 1
```
                                                                *the server is killed here*
```
hello again
tcprw: readline failed: Connection reset by peer (54)
```
                                                        *the client ignores the last line, but*
                                                        *the connection is dropped by TCP*
```
hello for the last time
Broken pipe
bsd: $
```
                                                        *client terminated by* SIGPIPE *signal*

When we type the second line, the client immediately reports the same error (connection reset by peer) as before, but does not terminate. Instead, it makes another call to fgets to retrieve more input to send to the server. When we type the third line, our client immediately terminates and the shell tells us that we were terminated with a SIGPIPE signal. In this case, the second send elicits an RST, as before, but we ignore it. After this RST is received, however, TCP drops the connection, so when we try to send the third line, it immediately terminates the client with the SIGPIPE signal. The time line for this case is the same as in Figure 2.44. The difference is that the client is terminated when it tries to write rather than after it tries to read.

Well-designed applications don't generally ignore error conditions, of course, but this failure mode can also occur in perfectly robust applications. Consider an application that performs two or more consecutive writes without an intervening read. FTP is a common example. If the application's peer crashes, its TCP sends a FIN. Because the application is only sending and not receiving, it is not notified of the FIN. The next segment that the application sends elicits an RST from its peer. Again, the application is not notified of the RST, because it does not have a pending read. On the second write after the crash of its peer, the application receives a SIGPIPE signal, or, if the signal is caught or ignored, gets an EPIPE error.

This behavior is very common among applications that do multiple writes with no read, and its implications should be understood. It is only after the *second* write to a terminated peer that the application gets notified. Because the first write causes the connection to be reset, all the data from that write is lost.

Other behaviors are possible, depending on timing. For example, if we rerun the first example with the server running on sparc and the client on bsd, we get

```
bsd: $ tcprw sparc 9000
hello
received message 1
```
                                                        *this is printed after a 5-second delay*
                                                        *the server is killed here*
```
hello again
tcprw: server terminated
bsd: $
```

This time, the client detects the EOF that was generated when the server terminated. The RST is still generated as a result of sending the second line, but because of the latency of the LAN, the client is able to call readline and discover that the server has terminated before the RST is received at bsd. If we insert

```
sleep( 1 );
```

between lines 14 and 15 of Figure 2.42 to simulate client processing or system load, we get the same results as when we ran both client and server on the same host.

### Peer's Host Crashes

The final failure mode we want to examine is a crash of our peer's host. This is different from a crash of our peer because our peer's TCP is unable to inform our application through a FIN that its peer is no longer running.

Until our peer's host is rebooted, this error looks just like a network outage: Our peer's TCP no longer responds. As with a network outage, our application's TCP continues to retransmit the unacknowledged segments. Eventually, if our peer's host is not rebooted, it gives up and returns an ETIMEDOUT error to our application.

What happens if our peer's host is rebooted before our TCP gives up and drops the connection? In this case, one of our retransmitted segments arrives at our peer's newly rebooted host, which has no record of the connection. In this case, the TCP specification [Postel 1981b] calls for the receiving host to return an RST to the sending host. This causes the sending host to drop the connection, and the application sees either an ECONNRESET error (if it has a read pending) or the next write results in a SIGPIPE signal or an EPIPE error.

### Summary

In this tip we examined the notion of TCP's reliability. We saw that there is no such thing as "guaranteed delivery," and that TCP is, in fact, subject to several types of failure. None of these failure modes need be fatal, but we must be prepared to deal with them.

## Tip 10: Remember That TCP/IP Is Not Polled

Network programmers who are new to the TCP/IP protocol suite but who have experience with other networking technologies are often puzzled or even dismayed to discover that TCP does not provide an application with immediate notification of connection loss. Some have even concluded that this makes TCP unsuitable for general-purpose application-to-application communications. In this tip we examine why TCP does not provide this notification, the advantages and disadvantages of not doing so, and what the application programmer must do to detect loss of connectivity.

As we saw in Tip 9, network outages or system crashes can render peer applications unable to communicate with each other without either application being immediately aware of the fact. An application that is sending data to its peer may not discover the loss of connectivity until TCP has exhausted its retries. This can take considerable time—approximately 9 minutes for BSD-derived systems. If the application is not sending data, it may never discover the loss. It may be, for example, that the application is a server that is waiting for its peer to make its next request. Because the client is unable to communicate with the server, the next request never comes, and even when the client's TCP gives up and drops the connection, causing the client to terminate, the server is unaware of this.

Other communication protocols, such as SNA and X.25, do provide applications with notification when connectivity is lost. Let us consider for a moment how they do this. Anything more complicated then a simple direct point-to-point dedicated link must use some sort of polling protocol to test continually for the presence of its peer. This may take the form of explicit "do you have anything to send me?" messages such as those used in poll-select protocols, or they may take the form of background quiescent frames that continually monitor the health of a virtual circuit. In any event, the capability does not come for free. It exacts a cost in network bandwidth. Each of these polling messages consumes network resources that could otherwise be used to carry "payload" data.

Obviously, the cost in available network bandwidth is one reason for TCP not to provide immediate notification of connectivity loss. Most applications have no need for immediate notification, and so they shouldn't have to pay for it with decreased bandwidth. Applications that do need to know in a timely manner when their peers become unreachable, can implement their own mechanism for discovering the loss, as shown later.

There is also a philosophical objection to having this notification built into the TCP/IP suite. One of the fundamental principals used in the design of TCP/IP is the end-to-end argument [Saltzer et al. 1984], which when applied to networks, states (roughly) that all the intelligence should be as close as possible to the end points of a connection, and that the network itself should be relatively dumb. This is why, for example, TCP handles error control itself, rather than depending on the network to provide it. As we saw in Tip 1, IP (and TCP, which is built on top of it) assumes very little about the underlying network. When applied to monitoring connectivity between peer applications, this principle means that the applications should provide the ability when it is needed, rather than having it provided to all applications, whether it is needed or not. [Huitema 1995] provides an interesting discussion of the end-to-end argument and its application to the Internet.

The most important reason for not having TCP provide immediate notification of connectivity loss, however, has to do with one of its major design goals: the ability to maintain communications in the face of network disruptions. TCP is the result of research sponsored by the Department of Defense to provide a networking protocol that can maintain reliable computer communications even when confronted with the major network disruptions associated with war or natural disasters. Often, network outages are only momentary, or the routers can find another path for the connection. By allowing for temporary losses of connectivity, TCP is often able to cope with an outage without the end applications even being aware of it.

A disadvantage of forcing applications to implement connection monitoring is that code must now be built into each application (that needs it), and that naive implementations may waste bandwidth or indulge in other behavior that has detrimental effects for the network and its other users. Even here, however, one can argue that by doing the monitoring in the application, it can be fine-tuned to meet the needs of the application and to work with the application protocol as seamlessly as possible.

## Keep-Alives

TCP does, in fact, have a mechanism, called *keep-alives*, for detecting dead connections, but as we shall see it is often not useful to applications. When an application enables the keep-alive mechanism, TCP sends a special segment to its peer when the connection has been idle for a certain interval. If the peer host is reachable and the peer application is still running, the peer TCP responds with an ACK. In this case, the TCP sending the keep-alive resets the idle time to zero, and the application receives no notification that the exchange took place.

If the peer host is reachable but the peer application is not running, the peer TCP responds with an RST, and the TCP sending the keep-alive drops the connection and returns an ECONNRESET error to the application. This is normally the result of the peer host crashing and being rebooted, because, as discussed in Tip 9, if the peer application merely terminated or crashed, the peer TCP would have sent a FIN.

If the peer host does not respond with either an ACK or an RST, the TCP sending the keep-alive continues to send keep-alive probes until it decides that its peer is unreachable or has crashed. At that point it drops the connection and informs the application with an ETIMEDOUT or, if a router has returned an ICMP host or network unreachable error, with an EHOSTUNREACH or ENETUNREACH error.

The first problem with keep-alives for applications that need immediate notification of connectivity loss is the time intervals involved. RFC 1122 [Braden 1989] requires that if a TCP implements keep-alives, it must have a default idle time of at least 2 hours before it starts sending keep-alive probes. Then, because the ACK from its peer is not delivered reliably, it must send repeated probes before abandoning the connection. The 4.4BSD implementation sends nine probes spaced 75 seconds apart before dropping the connection.

> This is an implementation detail. RFC 1122 does not specify how many or how often probes should be sent before dropping the connection, only that an implementation must not interpret the lack of a response to any single probe as an indication of a dead connection.

This means that BSD-derived implementations using the default values take 2 hours, 11 minutes, 15 seconds to discover that connectivity has been lost. This value makes more sense when we realize that keep-alives are intended to release the resources held by defunct connections. Such connections can come about, for example, when a client connects to a server and the client's host crashes. Without the keep-alive mechanism, the server waits forever for the client's next request, because it never receives a FIN.

> This situation is increasingly common due to users of PC-based systems merely turning off the computer or its modem instead of shutting down applications correctly.

Some implementations allow one or both time intervals to be changed, but this is almost always on a systemwide basis. That is, the change affects *all* TCP connections on the system. This is the main reason that keep-alives are not really useful as a connection monitoring mechanism: The default time periods are too long, and if the default is changed, they are no longer useful for their original purpose of cleaning up long-dead connections.

There is a new POSIX socket option, `TCP_KEEPALIVE`, which does allow the time-out interval to be specified on a per-connection basis, but it is not widely implemented.

The other problem with keep-alives is that they don't merely detect dead connections, they drop them. This may or may not be what the application wants.

## Heartbeats

The problems with using keep-alives to monitor connectivity are easily solved by implementing a similar mechanism in the application. The best method of doing this depends on the application, and it is here that we see the flexibility that providing this mechanism in the application provides. As examples, let us consider two extreme cases:

1. A client and server that exchange several different types of messages, each having a header that identifies the message type.

2. An application that provides data to its peer as a byte stream with no inherent notion of record or message.

The first case is relatively easy. We introduce a new message type, `MSG_HEARTBEAT`, that one side can send to another. On receipt of the `MSG_HEARBEAT` message, the application merely returns the message to its peer. As we shall see, this allows us great latitude. One or both sides of the connection can monitor it for connectivity, with only one side actually sending the heartbeat.

First we look at the header file that is used by both client and server (Figure 2.46).

──────────────────────────────────────────────────────────────── *heartbeat.h*

```
 1 #ifndef __HEARTBEAT_H__
 2 #define __HEARTBEAT_H__

 3 #define MSG_TYPE1       1       /* application specific msg */
 4 #define MSG_TYPE2       2       /* another one */
 5 #define MSG_HEARTBEAT   3       /* heartbeat message */

 6 typedef struct                  /* message structure */
 7 {
 8     u_int32_t type;             /* MSG_TYPE1, ... */
 9     char data[ 2000 ];
10 } msg_t;

11 #define T1              60      /* idle time before heartbeat */
12 #define T2              10      /* time to wait for response */

13 #endif  /* __HEARTBEAT_H__ */
```
──────────────────────────────────────────────────────────────── *heartbeat.h*

**Figure 2.46** The heartbeat header file

*3–5*    These manifest constants define the various message types that the client and server exchange. Only the `MSG_HEARTBEAT` message is meaningful in the example.

*6–10*    This typedef defines the structure of the messages passed between the client and the server. Again, only the `type` field is used in the example. A real application would customize this structure to fit its needs. See the remarks discussing Figure 2.31 for the meaning of `u_int32_t` and the dangers of making assumptions about the packing of structures.

*11*    This constant defines the amount of time that the connection can be idle before the client sends a heartbeat to its peer. We have arbitrarily chosen 60 seconds, but a real application would have to choose a value based on its needs and on the type of network.

*12*    The other timer value is the amount of time that the client waits for a response to its heartbeat message.

Next, we show the client side (Figure 2.47), which initiates the heartbeat. This choice is completely arbitrary and we could have just as easily chosen the server as the initiator.

*—————————————————————————————— hb_client.c*

```
 1 #include "etcp.h"
 2 #include "heartbeat.h"

 3 int main( int argc, char **argv )
 4 {
 5     fd_set allfd;
 6     fd_set readfd;
 7     msg_t msg;
 8     struct timeval tv;
 9     SOCKET s;
10     int rc;
11     int heartbeats = 0;
12     int cnt = sizeof( msg );

13     INIT();
14     s = tcp_client( argv[ 1 ], argv[ 2 ] );
15     FD_ZERO( &allfd );
16     FD_SET( s, &allfd );
17     tv.tv_sec = T1;
18     tv.tv_usec = 0;
19     for ( ;; )
20     {
21         readfd = allfd;
22         rc = select( s + 1, &readfd, NULL, NULL, &tv );
23         if ( rc < 0 )
24             error( 1, errno, "select failure" );
25         if ( rc == 0 )        /* timed out */
26         {
27             if ( ++heartbeats > 3 )
28                 error( 1, 0, "connection dead\n" );
29             error( 0, 0, "sending heartbeat #%d\n", heartbeats );
30             msg.type = htonl( MSG_HEARTBEAT );
31             rc = send( s, ( char * )&msg, sizeof( msg ), 0 );
32             if ( rc < 0 )
33                 error( 1, errno, "send failure" );
34             tv.tv_sec = T2;
```

```
35              continue;
36          }
37          if ( !FD_ISSET( s, &readfd ) )
38              error( 1, 0, "select returned invalid socket\n" );
39          rc = recv( s, ( char * )&msg + sizeof( msg ) - cnt,
40              cnt, 0 );
41          if ( rc == 0 )
42              error( 1, 0, "server terminated\n" );
43          if ( rc < 0 )
44              error( 1, errno, "recv failure" );
45          heartbeats = 0;
46          tv.tv_sec = T1;
47          cnt -= rc;                          /* in-line readn */
48          if ( cnt > 0 )
49              continue;
50          cnt = sizeof( msg );

51          /* process message */
52      }
53 }
```
───────────────────────────────────────────────────────────── *hb_client.c*

**Figure 2.47** A message-based client with a heartbeat

### Initialization

*13–14*     We perform our standard initialization and connect to the server at the host and port specified on the command line.

*15–16*     We set up the select mask for our connect socket.

*17–18*     We initialize our timer to T1 seconds. If we don't receive a message within T1 seconds, `select` returns with a timer expiration.

*21–22*     We set the read select mask and then block in the call to `select` until we have data on the socket or until the timer expires.

### Handle Timeout

*27–28*     If we have sent more than three consecutive heartbeats without an answer, we declare the connection dead. In this example, we merely quit, but a real application could take whatever steps it deemed appropriate.

*29–33*     If we haven't yet exhausted our heartbeat probes, we send our peer a heartbeat.

*34–35*     We set the timer to T2 seconds. If we don't receive a message from our peer within this amount of time, we either send another heartbeat or declare the connection dead depending on the value of `heartbeats`.

### Process Message

*37–38*     If `select` returns any socket other than the one connected to our peer, we quit with a fatal error.

*39–40*     We call `recv` to read up to one message. These lines and the code below that housekeeps `cnt` are essentially an in-line version of `readn`. We can't call `readn` directly because it could block indefinitely disabling our heartbeat timing.

*41–44*     If we get either an EOF or a read error, we output a diagnostic and quit.

*45–46*     Because we have just heard from our peer, we set the heartbeat count back to zero and reset the timer for T1 seconds.

*47-50*    This code completes the in-line `readn`. We decrement `cnt` by the amount of data just read. If there is more data to be read, we continue at the call to `select`. Otherwise, we reset `cnt` for a full message and finish processing the message we have just read.

Figure 2.48 shows the server for our example. We have chosen to have the server monitor the connection also, but that is not strictly necessary.

```
                                                              ———— hb_server.c
 1 #include "etcp.h"
 2 #include "heartbeat.h"

 3 int main( int argc, char **argv )
 4 {
 5     fd_set allfd;
 6     fd_set readfd;
 7     msg_t msg;
 8     struct timeval tv;
 9     SOCKET s;
10     SOCKET s1;
11     int rc;
12     int missed_heartbeats = 0;
13     int cnt = sizeof( msg );

14     INIT();
15     s = tcp_server( NULL, argv[ 1 ] );
16     s1 = accept( s, NULL, NULL );
17     if ( !isvalidsock( s1 ) )
18         error( 1, errno, "accept failed" );
19     tv.tv_sec = T1 + T2;
20     tv.tv_usec = 0;
21     FD_ZERO( &allfd );
22     FD_SET( s1, &allfd );
23     for ( ;; )
24     {
25         readfd = allfd;
26         rc = select( s1 + 1, &readfd, NULL, NULL, &tv );
27         if ( rc < 0 )
28             error( 1, errno, "select failure" );
29         if ( rc == 0 )        /* timed out */
30         {
31             if ( ++missed_heartbeats > 3 )
32                 error( 1, 0, "connection dead\n" );
33             error( 0, 0, "missed heartbeat #%d\n",
34                 missed_heartbeats );
35             tv.tv_sec = T2;
36             continue;
37         }
38         if ( !FD_ISSET( s1, &readfd ) )
39             error( 1, 0, "select returned invalid socket\n" );
40         rc = recv( s1, ( char * )&msg + sizeof( msg ) - cnt,
41             cnt, 0 );
42         if ( rc == 0 )
43             error( 1, 0, "client terminated\n" );
44         if ( rc < 0 )
45             error( 1, errno, "recv failure" );
```

```
46          missed_heartbeats = 0;
47          tv.tv_sec = T1 + T2;
48          cnt -= rc;                  /* in-line readn */
49          if ( cnt > 0 )
50              continue;
51          cnt = sizeof( msg );
52          switch ( ntohl( msg.type ) )
53          {
54              case MSG_TYPE1 :
55                  /* process type1 message */
56                  break;

57              case MSG_TYPE2 :
58                  /* process type2 message */
59                  break;

60              case MSG_HEARTBEAT :
61                  rc = send( s1, ( char * )&msg, sizeof( msg ), 0 );
62                  if ( rc < 0 )
63                      error( 1, errno, "send failure" );
64                  break;

65              default :
66                  error( 1, 0, "unknown message type (%d)\n",
67                      ntohl( msg.type ) );
68          }
69      }
70      EXIT( 0 );
71  }
```
*———————————————————————————————————————— hb_server.c*

**Figure 2.48** A message-based server with a heartbeat

**Initialization**

*14–18*     We perform our standard initializations and accept a connection from our peer.

*19–20*     We set our initial timer value to T1 + T2 seconds. Because our peer sends a hearbeat after T1 seconds of inactivity, we allow a little extra time by increasing our timeout value by T2 seconds.

*21–22*     Next, we initialize our select mask for readability on the socket connected to our peer.

*25–28*     We call `select` and deal with any error returns.

**Handle Timeout**

*31–32*     If we have missed more than three consecutive heartbeats, we declare the connection dead and quit. As with the client, the server could take any other appropriate action at this point.

*35*     The timer is reset to T2 seconds. By now, the client should be sending us heartbeats every T2 seconds, and we time out after that amount of time so that we can count the missed heartbeats.

**Process Message**

*38–39*     We make the same invalid socket check that we did in the client.

*40–41*    As with the client, we make an in-line call to `readn`.

*42–45*    If `recv` returns an EOF or error, we output a diagnostic and quit.

*46–47*    Because we have just received a message from our peer, we know that the connection is still alive, so we reset our missed heartbeat count to zero and our timer value to T1 + T2 seconds.

*48–51*    This code, which is identical to that in the client, completes the in-line `readn`.

*60–64*    If this is a heartbeat message, we return it to our peer. When our peer receives this message, both sides know that the connection is still alive.

To test these programs, we run `hb_server` on sparc and `hb_client` on bsd. After `hb_client` has connected to `hb_server`, we disconnect sparc from the network. The outputs from server and client are shown side by side:

```
sparc: $ hb_server 9000            bsd: $ hb_client sparc 9000
hb_server: missed heartbeat #1     hb_client: sending heartbeat #1
hb_server: missed heartbeat #2     hb_client: sending heartbeat #2
hb_server: missed heartbeat #3     hb_client: sending heartbeat #3
hb_server: connection dead         hb_client: connection dead
sparc: $                           bsd: $
```

## Another Example

The model that we used in the last example does not work very well when one side sends the other a stream of data that has no inherent message or record boundaries. The problem is that if we send a heartbeat, it just appears among the other data and therefore would have to be checked for explicitly and perhaps even escaped as we discussed in Tip 6. To avoid these complications, we take a completely different tack.

The idea with this method is to use a separate connection for the hearbeats. It may seem strange to use one connection to monitor another, but remember that we are trying to detect either the crash of our peer's host or a partitioning of the network. If one of these events occurs, either both connections are affected or neither is. There are several ways of approaching this problem. One natural way is to use a separate thread to control the heartbeat function. Another way is to use the general timing mechanism that we will develop in Tip 20. However, for simplicity and to avoid worrying about the differences between the Win32 thread API and the UNIX pthreads API, we modify the select code that we used in the previous example.

The new versions of the client and server are very similar to the originals. The major differences are in the select logic, which must now handle two sockets, and in the additional logic to set up the extra connection. After the client connects to the server, it sends the server a port number on which it listens for the heartbeat connection from the server. This arrangement is similar to what the FTP server does when it establishes a data connection back to the client.

> This may cause a problem if NAT (Tip 3) is being used to translate private network addresses to a public one. Unlike the case with FTP, the NAT software does not know to change this port number to a remapped port. In this case, it's probably easiest to dedicate a second "well-known" port to the application.

We start with the initialization and connection logic of the client in Figure 2.49.

─────────────────────────────────────────────────────────── *hb_client2.c*

```
 1 #include "etcp.h"
 2 #include "heartbeat.h"

 3 int main( int argc, char **argv )
 4 {
 5     fd_set allfd;
 6     fd_set readfd;
 7     char msg[ 1024 ];
 8     struct timeval tv;
 9     struct sockaddr_in hblisten;
10     SOCKET sdata;
11     SOCKET shb;
12     SOCKET slisten;
13     int rc;
14     int hblistenlen = sizeof( hblisten );
15     int heartbeats = 0;
16     int maxfd1;
17     char hbmsg[ 1 ];

18     INIT();
19     slisten = tcp_server( NULL, "0" );
20     rc = getsockname( slisten, ( struct sockaddr * )&hblisten,
21         &hblistenlen );
22     if ( rc )
23         error( 1, errno, "getsockname failure" );
24     sdata = tcp_client( argv[ 1 ], argv[ 2 ] );
25     rc = send( sdata, ( char * )&hblisten.sin_port,
26         sizeof( hblisten.sin_port ), 0 );
27     if ( rc < 0 )
28         error( 1, errno, "send failure sending port" );
29     shb = accept( slisten, NULL, NULL );
30     if ( !isvalidsock( shb ) )
31         error( 1, errno, "accept failure" );
32     FD_ZERO( &allfd );
33     FD_SET( sdata, &allfd );
34     FD_SET( shb, &allfd );
35     maxfd1 = ( sdata > shb ? sdata: shb ) + 1;
36     tv.tv_sec = T1;
37     tv.tv_usec = 0;
```

─────────────────────────────────────────────────────────── *hb_client2.c*

**Figure 2.49**  Client initialization and connection logic

### Initialization and Connection

*19-23*    We first call tcp_server with a port number of 0. This causes the kernel to allocate an ephemeral port (Tip 18) for us. We then call getsockname to find out what port number the kernel chose. We do this so that there is only one well-known port associated with the server.

*24-28*    The next step is to connect to the server and send it the port number to which it should connect for the heartbeat connection.

*29-31*    The call to `accept` blocks until the server establishes the heartbeat connection with us. In a production-quality program we might want to put a timer around this call to prevent it from hanging if the server never makes the heartbeat connection. We could also check that the host making the heartbeat connection is, in fact, the server to which we connected in line 24.

*32-37*    We initialize the select masks and timer.

The rest of the client is shown in Figure 2.50. Here we see the message and heartbeat processing.

*――――――――――――――――――――――――――――― hb_client2.c*
```
38    for ( ;; )
39    {
40        readfd = allfd;
41        rc = select( maxfd1, &readfd, NULL, NULL, &tv );
42        if ( rc < 0 )
43            error( 1, errno, "select failure" );
44        if ( rc == 0 )        /* timed out */
45        {
46            if ( ++heartbeats > 3 )
47                error( 1, 0, "connection dead\n" );
48            error( 0, 0, "sending heartbeat #%d\n", heartbeats );
49            rc = send( shb, "", 1, 0 );
50            if ( rc < 0 )
51                error( 1, errno, "send failure" );
52            tv.tv_sec = T2;
53            continue;
54        }
55        if ( FD_ISSET( shb, &readfd ) )
56        {
57            rc = recv( shb, hbmsg, 1, 0 );
58            if ( rc == 0 )
59                error( 1, 0, "server terminated (shb)\n" );
60            if ( rc < 0 )
61                error( 1, errno, "bad recv on shb" );
62        }
63        if ( FD_ISSET( sdata, &readfd ) )
64        {
65            rc = recv( sdata, msg, sizeof( msg ), 0 );
66            if ( rc == 0 )
67                error( 1, 0, "server terminated (sdata)\n" );
68            if ( rc < 0 )
69                error( 1, errno, "recv failure" );

70            /* process data */
71        }
72        heartbeats = 0;
73        tv.tv_sec = T1;
74    }
75 }
```
*――――――――――――――――――――――――――――― hb_client2.c*

**Figure 2.50** Client message processing

**Process Data and Heartbeats**

*40–43*     We call `select` and handle any errors it returns.

*44–54*     The timeout processing is identical to that of Figure 2.47 except that we send the heartbeat on the `shb` socket.

*55–62*     If data is ready on the `shb` socket, we read the heartbeat byte but don't do anything with it.

*63–71*     If data is ready on the `sdata` socket, we read as much data as we can and process it. Note that because we are no longer dealing with fixed-size messages, we read all the data that is available up to our buffer size. If there is less data than the buffer can hold, the call to `recv` returns whatever is available, but won't block. If there is more data than the buffer can hold, the socket is still readable, so the next call to `select` returns immediately and we can process the next buffer of data then.

*72–73*     Because we have just heard from our peer, we reset `heartbeats` and the timer.

Finally, we examine the server code for this example (Figure 2.51). Like the client, it is nearly identical to the original server (Figure 2.48) with the exception of the code to connect and handle multiple sockets.

```
                                                                      ─── hb_server2.c
 1 #include "etcp.h"
 2 #include "heartbeat.h"

 3 int main( int argc, char **argv )
 4 {
 5     fd_set allfd;
 6     fd_set readfd;
 7     char msg[ 1024 ];
 8     struct sockaddr_in peer;
 9     struct timeval tv;
10     SOCKET s;
11     SOCKET sdata;
12     SOCKET shb;
13     int rc;
14     int maxfd1;
15     int missed_heartbeats = 0;
16     int peerlen = sizeof( peer );
17     char hbmsg[ 1 ];

18     INIT();
19     s = tcp_server( NULL, argv[ 1 ] );
20     sdata = accept( s, ( struct sockaddr * )&peer,
21         &peerlen );
22     if ( !isvalidsock( sdata ) )
23         error( 1, errno, "accept failed" );
24     rc = readn( sdata, ( char * )&peer.sin_port,
25         sizeof( peer.sin_port ) );
26     if ( rc < 0 )
27         error( 1, errno, "error reading port number" );
28     shb = socket( PF_INET, SOCK_STREAM, 0 );
29     if ( !isvalidsock( shb ) )
30         error( 1, errno, "shb socket failure" );
31     rc = connect( shb, ( struct sockaddr * )&peer, peerlen );
```

```
32      if ( rc )
33          error( 1, errno, "shb connect error" );
34      tv.tv_sec = T1 + T2;
35      tv.tv_usec = 0;
36      FD_ZERO( &allfd );
37      FD_SET( sdata, &allfd );
38      FD_SET( shb, &allfd );
39      maxfd1 = ( sdata > shb ? sdata : shb ) + 1;
```
———————————————————————————————— *hb_server2.c*

**Figure 2.51** Server initialization and connection

### Initialization and Connection

*19–23*     We listen for and accept the data connection from the client. Notice that we also retrieve the client's address in `peer` so that we can make the heartbeat connection.

*24–27*     Next, we read the port number on which the client is listening for the heartbeat connection. We read this directly into the `peer` structure. There is no need to worry about calling `htons` or `ntohs` because the port is already in network byte order, and that is how we must store it in `peer`.

*28–33*     After getting our `shb` socket, we make the heartbeat connection.

*34–39*     We initialize the timer and select masks.

We conclude this example by looking at the remainder of the server code in Figure 2.52.

———————————————————————————————— *hb_server2.c*
```
40      for ( ;; )
41      {
42          readfd = allfd;
43          rc = select( maxfd1, &readfd, NULL, NULL, &tv );
44          if ( rc < 0 )
45              error( 1, errno, "select failure" );
46          if ( rc == 0 )         /* timed out */
47          {
48              if ( ++missed_heartbeats > 3 )
49                  error( 1, 0, "connection dead\n" );
50              error( 0, 0, "missed heartbeat #%d\n",
51                  missed_heartbeats );
52              tv.tv_sec = T2;
53              continue;
54          }
55          if ( FD_ISSET( shb, &readfd ) )
56          {
57              rc = recv( shb, hbmsg, 1, 0 );
58              if ( rc == 0 )
59                  error( 1, 0, "client terminated\n" );
60              if ( rc < 0 )
61                  error( 1, errno, "shb recv failure" );
62              rc = send( shb, hbmsg, 1, 0 );
63              if ( rc < 0 )
64                  error( 1, errno, "shb send failure" );
65          }
```

```
66              if ( FD_ISSET( sdata, &readfd ) )
67              {
68                  rc = recv( sdata, msg, sizeof( msg ), 0 );
69                  if ( rc == 0 )
70                      error( 1, 0, "client terminated\n" );
71                  if ( rc < 0 )
72                      error( 1, errno, "recv failure" );

73                  /* process data */
74              }

75              missed_heartbeats = 0;
76              tv.tv_sec = T1 + T2;
77          }
78      EXIT( 0 );
79 }
```
───────────────────────────────────────────────────────── *hb_server2.c*

**Figure 2.52** Server message processing

*42–45*    As with the client, we call `select` and deal with any errors.

*46–53*    The timeout processing is unchanged from our first server in Figure 2.48.

*55–65*    If the `shb` socket is readable, we read the single-byte heartbeat from the socket and return it to the client.

*66–74*    If there is data on the data connection, we read and process it, checking for errors and EOF.

*75–76*    Because we have just heard from our peer, we know the connection is still alive, so we reset the missed heartbeat counter and the timer.

When we run this client and server, and then simulate a network outage by disconnecting one of the hosts from the network, we get the same results as we did for `hb_server` and `hb_client`.

## Summary

We have seen that although TCP does not provide a method for informing applications of loss of connectivity in a timely manner, it is easy to build this into the applications themselves. We explored two different models for providing a heartbeat function. Although this might seem like overkill, neither model is best in all cases.

The first example considered heartbeats when the applications exchange messages that contain a field identifying the message type. This method has the advantage of simplicity: We merely add another message type for the heartbeat.

The second example examined the case when the applications exchanged a stream of data with no inherent message boundaries and with no associated type field. A series of keystrokes is one example of this type of data transfer. In this case, we used a separate connection to send and receive the heartbeats. This same method could be used when the applications exchange messages of course, but it is more complicated than just adding a heartbeat message type.

Section 21.5 of
*UNIX Network Programming* [Stevens 1998] develops another method of providing heartbeats using TCP urgent data. Again, this demonstrates the flexibility that is available to the application programmer when implementing the heartbeat function.

Finally, we should realize that although this discussion has concentrated on TCP, the same principals apply to UDP. Consider a server that broadcasts messages to several clients on a LAN, or perhaps multicasts them to clients over a WAN. Because there is no connection, the clients are unaware of a server crash, a server host crash, or a network outage. Either of the two methods that we examined for providing TCP heartbeats can be modified for use with UDP.

If the datagrams contain a type field, the server need merely define a heartbeat datagram type and send it if there has been no other messages for some time interval. Likewise, it could broadcast heartbeat datagrams to a separate port, to which the clients would also listen.

## Tip 11: Be Prepared for Rude Behavior from a Peer

Often when writing network applications, there is a temptation to dismiss the likelihood of some particular event as so remote that it is not worth dealing with in the application. In this regard, we should keep the following excerpt from the host requirements RFC (RFC 1122 [Braden 1989], page 12) in mind:

> Software should be written to deal with every conceivable error, no matter how unlikely; sooner or later a packet will come in with that particular combination of errors and attributes, and unless the software is prepared, chaos can ensue. In general, it is best to assume that the network is filled with malevolent entities that will send in packets designed to have the worst possible effect. This assumption will lead to suitable protective design, although the most serious problems in the Internet have been caused by unenvisaged mechanisms triggered by low-probability events; mere human malice would never have taken so devious a course!

Today, this advice is even more apropos than when it was written. There are now many more TCP implementations, and some of them are broken in serious ways. Likewise, the number of engineers writing network applications is increasing, and many of these engineers lack the experience of the previous generation of network programmers.

Probably the largest factor, however, is the rise in popularity with the general population of PCs connected to the Internet. In the past, users could be counted on to have a certain amount of technical expertise, and to understand the consequences of actions such as turning off their computers without exiting a networked application. This is no longer the case.

As a result, it is vitally important that we program defensively and try to anticipate every action that our peer may take, no matter how unlikely. We have already touched on this in Tip 9, when we discussed TCP failure modes, and in Tip 10, when we discussed detecting loss of connectivity. In this tip we examine some of the things that our peers can do to cause mischief. The overriding rule is to not assume that our peer will follow the application protocol, even if we implemented both sides of the protocol.

## Checking for Client Termination

For example, let us assume that a client signals that it is done making requests by sending the server the string "quit" on a line by itself. Let's further assume that the server reads lines of input using the `readline` function (shown later in Figure 2.55), which we first saw in Tip 9. What happens if the client crashes or is terminated before it sends the quit command? The client's TCP sends a FIN to its peer TCP and the server's read returns an EOF. That's easy to detect, of course, but the point is that the server must detect it. It's easy to assume that the client will do what it's supposed to, and write code like

```
for ( ;; )
{
    if ( readline( s, buf, sizeof( buf ) ) < 0 )
        error( 1, errno, "readline failure" );
    if ( strcmp( buf, "quit\n" ) == 0 )
        /* do client termination functions */
    else
        /* process request */
}
```

Although this looks superficially correct, it fails, possibly by repeatedly processing the last request, if the client terminates without sending the quit command.

Next, assume that we see the problem with the previous code fragment (or find it the hard way) and alter our code to check explicitly for the EOF:

```
for ( ;; )
{
    rc = readline( s, buf, sizeof( buf ) );
    if ( rc < 0 )
        error( 1, errno, "readline failure" );
    if ( rc == 0 || strcmp( buf, "quit\n" ) == 0 )
        /* do client termination functions */
    else
        /* process request */
}
```

This code is still not correct because it fails to consider what happens if the client's host crashes before the client sends the quit command or terminates. This is the point when it's easy to make a bad decision even if we see the problem. Checking for a crash of the client's host requires setting a timer around the `readline` call, and that requires about twice as much code if we want to do some sort of end-of-client processing. Faced with adding all this code, we think, "Well, how likely is it that the client's host will crash, anyway?"

The problem is that the client's host doesn't have to crash. If it's a PC, the user could simply turn it off without terminating the application—the client could be executing in a window that is minimized or hidden under another, for example, making it easy to forget that it's still running. There are other possibilities as well. If the network connection between the applications involves a modem at the client's host (as most Internet connections do today), the user could simply turn off the modem, or there could be noise on the phone line that causes the modem to drop the connection. All of these cases are indistinguishable from the client's host crashing as far as the server is concerned.

> In some circumstances it may be possible to recover from modem problems by redialing (recall that TCP can recover from temporary network outages), but often the IP addresses of both sides of the telco link are assigned dynamically by the ISP when the connection is made. In these cases, it is unlikely that the same addresses will be assigned, and therefore the client will be unable to revive the connection.

It is not necessary to implement a heartbeat, as we did in Tip 10, to detect the loss of the client. We need only put a timer around the read operation so that if the client makes no requests for some time period, the server can assume the client is gone. This is what many FTP servers do: If the client doesn't make any requests for some time interval, the server aborts the connection. This is easily done with either an explicit timer or by using the `select` timer, as we did in the heartbeat examples.

If our concern is just that the server not hang forever, then we can use keep-alives to abort the connection after the keep-alive timer interval passes. Figure 2.53 shows a simple TCP server that accepts a connection from a client, reads from the socket, and writes the result to stdout. To prevent this server from hanging forever, we enabled keep-alives with a call to `setsockopt`. The fourth argument to `setsockopt` must point to a nonzero integer to enable keep-alives, or to a zero integer to disable them.

We start this server on bsd, and use telnet on another system to connect to it. After we connect and send "hello" to ensure that the connection is established, we disconnect the other system from the network. The output from the server is as follows:

```
bsd: $ keep 9000
hello
                                        Other system disconnected from network
                                        ...
                                        2 hours, 11 minutes, 15 seconds later
keep: recv failure: Operation timed out (60)
bsd: $
```

As expected, the TCP on bsd drops the connection and returns an `ETIMEDOUT` error to the server. At that point, the server terminates and all its resources are released.

## Checking for Valid Input

It's a commonplace principle in programming of any sort that we shouldn't assume that an application will receive only the type of data it was designed to process. The failure to heed this principle is another example of failing to program defensively, and we expect that professional programmers building commercial-quality software will, in fact, follow it. It is surprising, therefore, how often this principle is ignored. In [Miller et al. 1995], researchers generated random input and fed it to a large collection of the

```
                                                                                ── keep.c
 1 #include "etcp.h"
 2 int main( int argc, char **argv )
 3 {
 4      SOCKET s;
 5      SOCKET s1;
 6      int on = 1;
 7      int rc;
 8      char buf[ 128 ];

 9      INIT();
10      s = tcp_server( NULL, argv[ 1 ] );
11      s1 = accept( s, NULL, NULL );
12      if ( !isvalidsock( s1 ) )
13          error( 1, errno, "accept failure\n" );
14      if ( setsockopt( s1, SOL_SOCKET, SO_KEEPALIVE,
15          ( char * )&on, sizeof( on ) ) )
16          error( 1, errno, "setsockopt failure" );
17      for ( ;; )
18      {
19          rc = readline( s1, buf, sizeof( buf ) );
20          if ( rc == 0 )
21              error( 1, 0, "peer disconnected\n" );
22          if ( rc < 0 )
23              error( 1, errno, "recv failure" );
24          write( 1, buf, rc );
25      }
26 }
                                                                                ── keep.c
```

**Figure 2.53** Server using keep-alives

standard UNIX utility programs from several vendors. They were able to crash (with a core dump) or hang (with an infinite loop) between 6 and 43 percent of the utilities (depending on which vendor's software they were testing) just by feeding them this random data. The seven commercial systems tested had an average failure rate of 23 percent.

The lesson is clear: If these results can be obtained with mature software that is generally considered to be "industrial strength," then we must program defensively and always be on the alert for places in our own applications where unexpected input can cause unintended results. Let us examine for a moment some of the ways that unexpected data can cause problems.

Two of the most common causes of application crashes are buffer overflows and runaway pointers. Indeed, in the study just cited these two errors resulted in a large percentage of the failures. One might think that buffer overflows would be rare in network programs because we must always specify a buffer size in our calls to the read functions (read, recv, recvfrom, readv, and readmsg), but as we shall see, it is easy to make this mistake. Indeed, see the remarks concerning line 42 of shutdownc.c in Tip 16 for an actual example.

To see how this might come about, let us develop the readline function that we first used in Tip 9. Our goal is to write a function that reads a single newline terminated line from a socket into a buffer pointed to by `bufptr`, and then null terminate it. The definition for `readline` is:

```
#include "etcp.h"

int readline( SOCKET s, char *buf, size_t len );

                                Returns: number of bytes read or -1 on error
```

One approach that we can reject immediately is something along the lines of

```
while ( recv( fd, &c, 1, 0 ) == 1 )
{
    *bufptr++ = c;
    if ( c == '\n' )
        break;
}
/* check for errors, null terminate, etc. */
```

In the first place, making repeated calls to `recv` is very inefficient because it requires two context switches at every call.

> On the other hand, we must sometimes write code like this—see the `readcrlf` function in Figure 3.13.

More important, however, is that no check is made for buffer overflow.

To see how this same error can occur in a more reasonable implementation, consider the fragment

```
static char *bp;
static int cnt = 0;
static char b[ 1500 ];
char c;

for ( ;; )
{
    if ( cnt-- <= 0 )
    {
        cnt = recv( fd, b, sizeof( b ), 0 );
        if ( cnt < 0 )
            return -1;
        if ( cnt == 0 )
            return 0;
        bp = b;
    }
    c = *bp++;
    *bufptr++ = c;
    if ( c == '\n' )
    {
        *bufptr = '\0';
        break;
    }
}
```

This implementation avoids the inefficiency of the first fragment by reading a large block of data into an intermediate buffer and then moving bytes one by one into the final buffer while checking for the newline. Notice, though, that it suffers from the same error as the first fragment. No check is made for overflowing the buffer pointed to by `bufptr`. Although we might not write a general-purpose line-reading function like this, it is easy to imagine this code, error and all, being embedded in-line in some larger function.

Now let's try a real implementation (Figure 2.54).

*readline.c*

```
 1 int readline( SOCKET fd, char *bufptr, size_t len )
 2 {
 3     char *bufx = bufptr;
 4     static char *bp;
 5     static int cnt = 0;
 6     static char b[ 1500 ];
 7     char c;

 8     while ( len-- > 0 )
 9     {
10         if ( cnt-- <= 0 )
11         {
12             cnt = recv( fd, b, sizeof( b ), 0 );
13             if ( cnt < 0 )
14                 return -1;
15             if ( cnt == 0 )
16                 return 0;
17             bp = b;
18         }
19         c = *bp++;
20         *bufptr++ = c;
21         if ( c == '\n' )
22         {
23             *bufptr = '\0';
24             return bufptr - bufx;
25         }
26     }
27     set_errno( EMSGSIZE );
28     return -1;
29 }
```

*readline.c*

**Figure 2.54** An incorrect implementation of `readline`

At first glance, this implementation appears correct. We pass in the size of our buffer to `readline`, and the outer loop makes sure that we don't exceed that size. If we do, we set `errno` to `EMSGSIZE` and return −1.

To see the problem with this code, imagine that we make the call

```
rc = readline( s, buffer, 10 );
```

and that we read the line

```
123456789<nl>
```

from the socket. When we load the newline into c, len is zero, indicating that this is the last byte we can accept. At line 20 we store the newline in the buffer and advance bufptr past the end of the buffer. The problem occurs at line 23, where we store the 0 byte *outside* the buffer.

Notice that there is a similar error involving the inner loop. To see it, imagine that we enter the readline function with cnt equal to zero, and that recv returns 1 byte. What happens next? We might describe this as a buffer underflow error.

This example shows how easy it is to make buffer overflow errors, even when we think we have checked for them. Figure 2.55 shows the final, correct version of readline.

*────────────────────────────────────────────────────────── readline.c*
```
 1 int readline( SOCKET fd, char *bufptr, size_t len )
 2 {
 3     char *bufx = bufptr;
 4     static char *bp;
 5     static int cnt = 0;
 6     static char b[ 1500 ];
 7     char c;

 8     while ( --len > 0 )
 9     {
10         if ( --cnt <= 0 )
11         {
12             cnt = recv( fd, b, sizeof( b ), 0 );
13             if ( cnt < 0 )
14             {
15                 if ( errno == EINTR )
16                 {
17                     len++;         /* the while will decrement */
18                     continue;
19                 }
20                 return -1;
21             }
22             if ( cnt == 0 )
23                 return 0;
24             bp = b;
25         }
26         c = *bp++;
27         *bufptr++ = c;
28         if ( c == '\n' )
29         {
30             *bufptr = '\0';
31             return bufptr - bufx;
32         }
33     }
34     set_errno( EMSGSIZE );
35     return -1;
36 }
```
*────────────────────────────────────────────────────────── readline.c*

**Figure 2.55** Final version of readline

The only differences between this version and the last is that we predecrement the counters `len` and `cnt`, and that we check for and ignore an `EINTR` error on the call to `recv`. By predecrementing `len`, we ensure that there is always room for the 0 byte. Similarly, by predecrementing `cnt`, we ensure that we don't try to read data from an empty buffer.

## Summary

We must always be prepared for unexpected actions and data from our users and peers. In this tip we examined two instances of rude behavior on the part of our peer. First, we saw that we can't rely entirely on our peer to tell us when it has finished sending us data. Second, we saw the importance of checking for valid input, and developed a robust `readline` function along the way.

## Tip 12: Don't Assume That a Successful LAN Strategy Will Scale to a WAN

Many network applications are developed and tested on a LAN or even on a single machine. This has the advantages of being simple, convenient, and inexpensive, but it can also mask problems.

Despite the losses that we were able to induce in Tip 7, LANs provide an environment in which IP datagrams are almost never lost or delayed, and are virtually never delivered out of order. Because LANs provide such an ideal environment, we shouldn't assume that an application that runs successfully on a LAN will scale well to a WAN or the Internet. There are two types of problems that can occur:

1. Performance on the WAN may not be satisfactory because of the extra latency introduced by the WAN.

2. Incorrect code that worked on the LAN might fail on the WAN.

Problems of the first sort usually mean that the application's design should be rethought.

### Performance Problem Example

As an example of this type of problem, we change our `hb_server` (Figure 2.48) and `hb_client` (Figure 2.47) programs by setting T1 to 2 seconds and T2 to 1 second (see Figure 2.46). This causes a heartbeat to be sent every 2 seconds, and if no reply is received within 3 seconds, the application terminates.

First, we try these programs on a LAN. After running for almost 7 hours, the server reported a loss of one heartbeat 36 times, and the loss of two heartbeats once. The client reported having to send a second heartbeat 11 of 12,139 times. Both the client and server ran until the client was terminated manually. These results are typical for a LAN. Except for occasional small delays, the messages were delivered in a timely fashion.

Next, we run these two programs over the Internet. After a little more than 12 minutes, the client sends three heartbeats without an answer and terminates. The client's output, part of which is shown here, gives us a good idea of how things went:

```
sparc: $ hb_client 205.184.151.171 9000
hb_client: sending heartbeat #1
hb_client: sending heartbeat #2
hb_client: sending heartbeat #3
hb_client: sending heartbeat #1
hb_client: sending heartbeat #2
hb_client: sending heartbeat #1
                                        Many lines deleted
hb_client: sending heartbeat #1
hb_client: sending heartbeat #2
hb_client: sending heartbeat #1
hb_client: sending heartbeat #2
hb_client: sending heartbeat #3
hb_client: connection dead              Terminates 1 second after last heartbeat
sparc: $
```

This time the client sent its first heartbeat 251 times, but had to send a second 247 times. That is, it almost never received a reply to its first heartbeat in time. The client needed to send a third heartbeat ten times.

The server also showed dramatically degraded performance. It timed out waiting for its first heartbeat 247 times, its second heartbeat five times, and its third heartbeat once.

This example shows how an application that performs well on a LAN can have marked performance problems on a WAN.

## Masked Error Example

As an example of the second sort of problem, consider a TCP-based telemetry application in which a server receives a packet of measurements every second from a remote sensing device. These packets contain either two or three integer values. A naive implementation of the server might have an event loop like the following:

```
int pkt[ 3 ];
for (;;)
{
        rc = recv( s, ( char * )pkt, sizeof( pkt ), 0 );
        if ( rc != sizeof( int ) * 2 && rc != sizeof( int ) * 3 )
                /* log error and quit */
        else
                /* process rc / sizeof( int ) values */
}
```

We know from Tip 6 that this code is incorrect, but let's try a simple simulation. We write a server, as shown in Figure 2.56, that implements a loop like the one just presented.

―――――――――――――――――――――――――――――――――――― *telemetrys.c*
```
 1 #include "etcp.h"
 2 #define TWOINTS      ( sizeof( int ) * 2 )
 3 #define THREEINTS    ( sizeof( int ) * 3 )
 4 int main( int argc, char **argv )
 5 {
 6     SOCKET s;
 7     SOCKET s1;
 8     int rc;
 9     int i = 1;
10     int pkt[ 3 ];
11     INIT();
12     s = tcp_server( NULL, argv[ 1 ] );
13     s1 = accept( s, NULL, NULL );
14     if ( !isvalidsock( s1 ) )
15         error( 1, errno, "accept failure" );
16     for ( ;; )
17     {
18         rc = recv( s1, ( char * )pkt, sizeof( pkt ), 0 );
19         if ( rc != TWOINTS && rc != THREEINTS )
20             error( 1, 0, "recv returned %d\n", rc );
21         printf( "Packet %d has %ld values in %d bytes\n",
22             i++, ntohl( pkt[ 0 ] ), rc );
23     }
24 }
```
―――――――――――――――――――――――――――――――――――― *telemetrys.c*

**Figure 2.56** Simulation of a telemetry server

*11-15*    These lines implement our standard initialization and accept sequences.

*16-23*    This loop receives data repeatedly from the client. If we don't get exactly `sizeof( int ) * 2` or `sizeof( int ) * 3` bytes on each read, we log an error and quit. Otherwise, we convert the first integer to host byte order (Tip 28) and print it and the number of bytes read to stdout. We will see later (Figure 2.57) that the client places the number of values it is sending in this packet in the first integer. This is intended to help us see what is happening in the simulation, and is not a "size of message" header as discussed in Tip 6.

To test this server, we also write a client to send a packet of integers every second, simulating the remote sensing device. The client is shown in Figure 2.57.

―――――――――――――――――――――――――――――――――――― *telemetryc.c*
```
 1 #include "etcp.h"
 2 int main( int argc, char **argv )
 3 {
 4     SOCKET s;
 5     int rc;
 6     int i;
 7     int pkt[ 3 ];
```

```
 8      INIT();
 9      s = tcp_client( argv[ 1 ], argv[ 2 ] );
10      for ( i = 2;; i = 5 - i )
11      {
12          pkt[ 0 ] = htonl( i );
13          rc = send( s, ( char * )pkt, i * sizeof( int ), 0 );
14          if ( rc < 0 )
15              error( 1, errno, "send failure" );
16          sleep( 1 );
17      }
18 }
```
———————————————————————————————————————————————— *telemetryc.c*

**Figure 2.57** Telemetry client simulation

*8–9*    We initialize and connect to the server.

*10–17*    Every second we send a packet of either two or three integers to the server. As discussed earlier, we use the number of integers we are sending (converted to network byte order) as the first value.

To run our simulation, we start the server on bsd and the client on sparc. The output from the server is as follows:

```
bsd: $ telemetrys 9000
Packet 1 has 2 values in 8 bytes
Packet 2 has 3 values in 12 bytes
```
                                                   *Many lines deleted*
```
Packet 22104 has 3 values in 12 bytes
Packet 22105 has 2 values in 8 bytes
```
                                                   *Client terminated after*
                                                   *6 hrs., 8 mins., 25 secs.*
```
telemetrys: recv returned 0
bsd: $
```

Although the server has an obvious error, it ran flawlessly on the LAN for more than 6 hours, at which time we ended the simulation by terminating the client manually.

> The output from the simulation was checked with an awk script to verify that each read returned the correct number of bytes.

When we run this server over the Internet, however, the results are much different. Again we run the client on sparc and the server on bsd, but we route the data over the Internet by pointing the client at the address of an interface on bsd that is connected to the Internet. As we see from the last few lines printed by the server, there was a fatal error after 15 minutes:

```
Packet 893 has 2 values in 8 bytes
Packet 894 has 3 values in 12 bytes
Packet 895 has 2 values in 12 bytes
Packet 896 has -268436204 values in 8 bytes
Packet 897 has 2 values in 12 bytes
Packet 898 has -268436204 values in 8 bytes
```

```
Packet 899 has 2 values in 12 bytes
Packet 900 has -268436204 values in 12 bytes
telemetrys: recv returned 4
bsd: $
```

The problem occurs when processing packet 895, where we should have read 8 bytes, but read 12 instead. Figure 2.58 shows what happened.

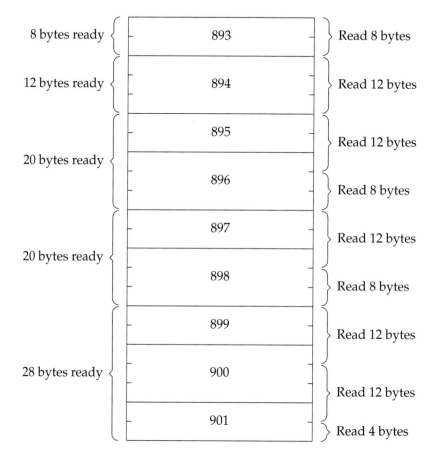

**Figure 2.58** A fatal error

The numbers on the left show how many bytes the server's TCP had available to be read. The numbers on the right show how many were actually read. We see that packets 893 and 894 are delivered and read as expected. When telemetrys calls recv to read packet 895, there are 20 bytes available to be read.

> A network trace taken with tcpdump (Tip 34) shows TCP segments from both hosts were being lost at this point. This was probably because network congestion caused intermediate routers to drop packets. Before packet 895 can be delivered, telemetryc has packet 896 ready, and they are delivered together.

Packet 895 was 8 bytes but because packet 896 was also available, packet 895 and the first integer from packet 896 were read. That's why the output from `telemetrys` shows that 12 bytes were read but that packet 895 had only two integers. The next read returns the second two integers from packet 896, and `telemetrys` prints garbage for the number of values because `telemetryc` did not initialize the second value.

As shown in Figure 2.58, this happens again with packets 897 and 898, and then on the next read there are 28 bytes available. Now `telemetrys` reads packet 899 and the first value from packet 900, the rest of packet 900 and the first value from packet 901, and the last value in packet 901. This last read returns only 4 bytes, causing the test at line 19 of `telemetrys` to fail, ending the simulation.

Unfortunately, something much worse happens earlier in the simulation:

```
Packet 31 has 2 values in 8 bytes
Packet 32 has 3 values in 12 bytes
Packet 33 has 2 values in 12 bytes
Packet 34 has -268436204 values in 8 bytes
Packet 35 has 2 values in 8 bytes
Packet 36 has 3 values in 12 bytes
```

Just 33 seconds into the simulation, there is an undetected error. As shown in Figure 2.59, when `telemetrys` does the read for packet 33, there are 20 bytes available and so 12 bytes are read instead of 8. This means that a packet with two values is mistaken for a packet with three, and then that a packet with three values is mistaken for a packet with two. Notice that with packet 35, `telemetrys` is back in sync and the error goes undetected.

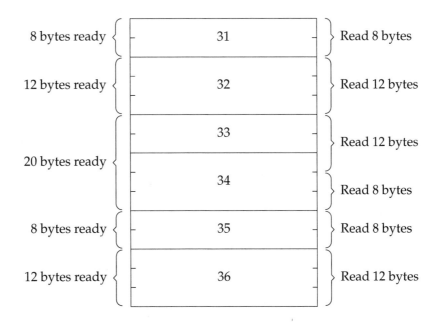

**Figure 2.59** An undetected error

## Summary

The near-ideal environment supplied by a LAN can mask performance problems and even errors with our network applications. We should never assume that an application that runs successfully on a LAN will continue to do so on a WAN.

The increased latency of a WAN can cause an application with satisfactory performance on a LAN to demonstrate unsatisfactory performance on the WAN. This can sometimes require that the design of the application be changed.

Congestion on busy WANs, especially the Internet, can cause data to be delivered in unexpected quantities and at unexpected times. This requires that we be especially vigilant in avoiding any assumptions about how much data will arrive at any given time, and about the rates at which it will arrive.

Although we have concentrated on TCP applications in this tip, our results apply with even greater force to UDP, because it does not have the advantage of reliability to mitigate the rigors of the WAN environment.

# Tip 13: Learn How the Protocols Work

In [Stevens 1998], Stevens remarks that the majority of network programming problems have nothing to do with programming and APIs, but rather arise from a lack of understanding of the underlying network protocols. This observation is frequently borne out by the questions asked in the networking news groups (Tip 44). For example, anyone can discover how to disable the Nagle algorithm (Tip 24) by consulting the on-line documentation on either a UNIX or Windows machine, but unless we understand TCP's flow control and the Nagle algorithm's role in it, we will have no idea when it is wise to do so and when it is not.

Similarly, the lack of immediate notification of loss of connectivity, as discussed in Tip 10, may seem perverse until we understand the reasons for it. Once we do understand the reasons, it is a simple matter to arrange a heartbeat probe at whatever interval makes sense for our application.

There are several ways to acquire an understanding of the protocols, and many of them are discussed in Chapter 4, but it is worth listing some here as well. The primary source for information on the TCP/IP suite are the RFCs. Although the RFCs cover a broad spectrum of subjects with varying degrees of seriousness, all of the TCP/IP protocol suite specifications are published as RFCs. The RFCs are the official definitive source about how the TCP/IP protocols are *supposed* to work. The RFCs and their index are available through the RFC editor's home page at

```
<http://www.rfc-editor.org>.
```

See Tip 43 for other ways of obtaining copies of the RFCs.

Because the RFCs are the work of many authors, there is a large range in their clarity. Additionally, some topics are discussed in a series of RFCs, and it is not always easy to get a complete picture.

Fortunately, there are additional sources of information about the protocols that are easier for the beginner to use. We will examine two such sources here, and defer discussion of other resources until Chapter 4.

[Comer 1995] examines the TCP/IP protocol suite from the point of view of the RFCs. That is, Comer examines the major protocols and describes how they are supposed to function as specified in the RFCs. For this reason, some have described his book as taking a theoretical approach to the TCP/IP protocols, as opposed to the more practical approach taken by Stevens [Stevens 1994, Stevens 1996].

Comer's book is an excellent, clearly written introduction to the TCP/IP protocols that contains frequent pointers to the RFCs. These pointers facilitate additional study and present an organized view of the RFCs.

[Stevens 1994, Stevens 1996] examines the TCP/IP protocol suite from an implementation point of view. That is, the books look at how the major TCP/IP implementations *actually* work in practice. This is accomplished mainly by capturing the live protocol data with `tcpdump` (Tip 34) and using it and time lines, such as Figure 2.32, drawn from them to watch the protocol in action. This, along with detailed diagrams of packet formats and small test programs designed to expose some aspect of the protocol under discussion, make the protocol come alive in a way that a mere description could not.

Although these books look at the TCP/IP protocols from different perspectives, we shouldn't assume that one approach is better than the other and that therefore one book is better than the other. Which book we should use at any given time depends on our needs at the moment. The books are, in fact, complementary, and any serious network programmer has a copy of each.

### Summary

In this tip we discussed the importance of understanding how the protocols work. We noted that the RFCs contain the official specifications for TCP/IP, and recommended the books of Comer and Stevens for further discussions of the protocols and their functioning.

## Tip 14: Don't Take the OSI Seven-Layer Reference Model Too Seriously

Because the design and implementation of networking protocols is such a large and difficult task, it is usually simplified by partitioning it into smaller, easier to understand pieces. The traditional way of doing this is to divide the tasks into layers. Each layer provides services for the layers above it and uses the services of the layers below it.

For example, in Figure 2.1, our simplified TCP/IP protocol stack, we see that the IP layer provides a service, namely datagram delivery, to the TCP and UDP layer. To provide this service, IP makes use of the services of the interface layer to put the datagrams on the physical medium.

## The OSI Model

Probably the best known example of network protocol layering is the International Standards Organization (ISO) Reference Model of Open Systems Interconnection.

> Many people have the mistaken belief that the OSI model introduced the notions of layering, virtualizing, and other fundamental networking concepts. In fact, these ideas were widely known and in use by the early ARPANET researchers who developed the TCP/IP suite well before the introduction of the OSI model. For an interesting perspective on this, see RFC 871 [Padlipsky 1982].

Because this model has seven layers, as shown in Figure 2.60, it is often referred to as the OSI 7-layer model.

| 7 | Application |
|---|---|
| 6 | Presentation |
| 5 | Session |
| 4 | Transport |
| 3 | Network |
| 2 | Data Link |
| 1 | Physical |

**Figure 2.60** The OSI 7-Layer reference model

As we mentioned earlier, layer $N$ provides *services* for layer $N + 1$ using the services of layer $N - 1$. In addition, each layer can communicate only with its immediate neighbors, above and below. This communication takes place through a well-defined *interface* between adjacent layers, so that in principle a layer could be replaced by another layer providing the same services without affecting the other layers at all. Corresponding layers in communicating stacks exchange data (over the network) by means of a *protocol*.

Because these layers are frequently referenced in networking literature, it is worthwhile to give a brief description of the services that each layer provides.

1. *Physical*—This layer deals with the hardware. It specifies electrical and timing characteristics of the interface, how bits are placed on the medium, physical framing, and even the size and shape of the connectors.

2. *Data link*—The data link layer is the software interface to the physical layer. Its job is to provide a "reliable wire" for the network layer. It includes the "device drivers" that the network layer uses to talk to the physical devices, but also deals with issues such as framing data for the link, checksums to detect corruption, and mediating access to the underlying physical medium. The common

interface between the network and data link layers is the mechanism that allows device independence.

3. *Network*—The network layer deals with delivering packets between nodes. It is responsible for such things as addressing and route calculation, fragmentation and reassembly, and congestion and flow control.

4. *Transport*—The transport layer deals with reliable end-to-end communication between peers. It compensates for the unreliability of the lower layers by dealing with errors caused by corruption, lost packets, and out-of-order packets. It may also provide flow control and congestion avoidance.

5. *Session*—The transport layer provides a full duplex reliable communication stream between peers. The session layer builds on this to provide additional services to the applications such as session establishment and release (for example, login, logout), dialog control (for example, emulating a half duplex terminal), synchronization (for example, checkpointing large file transfers), and otherwise adding structure to the simple reliable layer 4 stream.

6. *Presentation*—The presentation layer deals with data translation. This layer handles conversion between data representations (for example, ASCII to EBCDIC), and compression.

7. *Application*—The application layer consists of the user programs that make use of the other six layers to deliver data. Familiar examples from the TCP/IP world are telnet, `ftp`, mail clients, and Web browsers.

The official description of the OSI 7-layer model is given in [International Standards Organization 1984], but it merely describes, in general terms, what each layer should do. Detailed descriptions of the services provided by and the protocols used in the individual layers are left to various other ISO documents. A reasonably detailed explanation of the model and its various layers as well as pointers to the relevant ISO documents can be found in [Jain and Agrawala 1993].

Although the OSI model is useful as a framework for discussing network architectures and implementations, it should not be considered a blueprint for implementing networking architectures. Nor should the fact that the model places some function in layer $N$ be taken to mean that layer $N$ is the only, or even the best, place for that function. One criticism of the model is, in fact, that the placement of functions within the layers is arbitrary and not always obvious.

The fact is that the OSI model suffers from a variety of defects, and although some implementations were finally produced, the OSI protocols are essentially dead today. Indeed, one of the problems with the model was that it was designed (by committee) without the benefit of an implementation. Contrast this with the development of the TCP/IP suite for which the standards were based on and benefited from the results of experimental implementations.

Another problem with the OSI model is its extraordinary complexity and inherent inefficiency. Some functions are performed in several layers. Error detection and correction, for example, are performed in most of the layers.

As Tanenbaum points out [Tanenbaum 1996], one of the most serious defects with the model is that it suffers from a "communications mentality." This is reflected both in the terminology, which differs from the normal networking usage, and in the specification of the interface primitives used between the layers, which is more appropriate for telephone systems than for computers.

Finally, the choice of seven layers appears to have been chosen more for political than for technical reasons. Indeed, the session and presentation layers rarely appear in any actual network implementations.

## The TCP/IP Model

Let's contrast the OSI model with that used by TCP/IP. It is important to understand that the TCP/IP model merely documents the design of the TCP/IP protocol suite, and that it was not meant to serve as reference model the way the OSI model was. For this reason, one does not see it used as the basis for the design of new network architectures. Nonetheless, it is instructive to compare it with the OSI model and to see how the TCP/IP layers map onto the OSI model. If nothing else, it serves to remind us that the OSI model is not the "one true way."

As we see in Figure 2.61, the TCP/IP protocol stack comprises four layers. The application layer performs all of the chores assigned to the application, presentation, and session layers in the OSI model. The transport layer is similar to the corresponding layer in the OSI model in that it deals with end-to-end communications. The transport layer defines the TCP and UDP protocols. The Internet layer defines the IP, ICMP, and IGMP protocols. It corresponds to the network layer in the OSI model.

| OSI Model | TCP/IP Stack | |
| --- | --- | --- |
| Application | Application | telnet, ftp, etc. |
| Presentation | | |
| Session | | |
| Transport | Transport | TCP, UDP |
| Network | Internet | IP, ICMP, IGMP |
| Data Link | Interface | |
| Physical | | |

**Figure 2.61** Comparison of the OSI model and TCP/IP stack

We are already familiar with IP. ICMP is the *Internet Control Message Protocol* that is used to communicate control and error information between systems. For example, "host unreachable" messages are carried as ICMP messages, as are the echo request and reply messages that the ping utility uses. IGMP is the *Internet Group Management Protocol* that hosts use to keep multicast routers informed about local multicast group membership. Although ICMP and

> IGMP messages are carried in IP datagrams, they are considered an integral part of IP and are not viewed as higher level protocols.

Finally, the interface layer deals with the interface between the host computer and the underlying network hardware. It corresponds roughly to the link and physical layers in the OSI model. The interface layer is not really described in the TCP/IP architecture except to say that it handles the interface to the network hardware in a system-dependent way.

Before we leave the subject of layers in the TCP/IP protocol stack, let us examine the communication between peer layers in end-to-end networking. Figure 2.62 shows two TCP/IP stacks communicating through several intermediate routers.

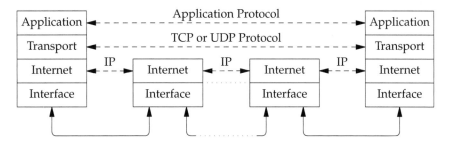

**Figure 2.62** Peer-to-peer communication

Although we know that data from an application on one stack flows down the stack, across the network, and up the peer's stack to the peer application, each layer in the stack acts as if it were carrying on a conversion directly with its peer layer. For example, if the application is FTP, the FTP client "talks" directly to the FTP server without worrying about the workings of TCP, IP, or the physical network involved.

This same thing is true for each of the layers. For example, if TCP is the transport layer, it carries on a conversation with its peer TCP and does not worry about what protocols or networks are being used to carry that conversation. The ideal is that when layer $N$ sends a message, its peer layer $N$ receives exactly the same message, and whatever manipulation of the data was performed by lower layers is undone before the message reaches the peer layer.

This last point requires some explanation. When we examine Figure 2.62, we see that the transport layer is the lowest end-to-end layer. It is the lowest layer that carries on a conversation directly between the two end points. The Internet layer, on the other hand, carries on a conversation with the router or system at the "next hop."

> We are assuming, for this discussion, that there are intermediate routers, so that for a system at one of the end points, the "next hop" is not the final destination.

Because intermediate systems may change certain fields, such as the *time to live* (TTL) field, in the IP header, the Internet layer at the destination end point may not see exactly the same message that the Internet layer at the source end point sent.

This point serves to sharpen the distinction between the Internet and transport layers. The Internet layer is concerned with getting messages to the next hop, and it carries on its conversation with this next hop's Internet layer, not the Internet layer at the end point. The transport layer on the other hand, carries on its conversation directly with the transport layer of the end point, and is unaware of intermediate systems.

## Summary

In this tip we compared and contrasted the OSI and TCP/IP models. We saw that the OSI 7-layer model is a useful descriptive tool, but that implementations based on it have had limited success

# 3

# *Building Effective and Robust Network Programs*

## Tip 15: Understand the TCP Write Operation

This tip and the next discuss certain aspects of the write and read operations in TCP/IP programming. We focus not on the specific API, nor on the details of the system calls themselves, but rather on certain semantic issues involving the write and read operations.

We have already seen in Tip 6 that there is not a one-to-one correspondence between calls to write and segments sent by TCP. In this tip we explore this subject a little further. Although the exact interaction between a write call and TCP/IP is system dependent, the protocol specifications are specific enough that we can draw general conclusions by looking at a particular implementation. Therefore, to be specific we describe the traditional BSD implementation. This is widely considered the reference implementation, and the source code for it is readily available.

> The source code for the original 4.4BSD-lite2 implementation is available from Walnut Creek CDROM (<http://www.cdrom.com>). An excellent exegesis, complete with the source code, is given in [Wright and Stevens 1995].

### The Write Operation from the Application's Perspective

When a user program makes a write call on a TCP connection, the first thing that happens is that the data is copied from the user's buffer into the kernel. From this point on, what happens depends on the state of the connection. TCP might decide to send all, some, or none of the data. We take a closer look at this decision in a moment, but first let's look at the write's action from the point of view of the user application.

It is tempting to imagine that when a write of $n$ bytes returns the value $n$, that $n$ bytes have, in fact, been sent to our peer, and perhaps even acknowledged. Unfortunately, this is not correct. TCP sends as much data as it can (perhaps none) and then immediately returns with a value of *n*. The application cannot determine how much of the data has been sent or if its peer has acknowledged it.

In general, writes do not block unless the TCP send buffer fills up. This means that writes almost always return promptly, and that when they do, there are no guarantees about the disposition of the data that was written. As we discussed in Tip 9, this has implications for the reliable transfer of data.

From the application's point of view, the data has been written, so TCP's "guaranteed delivery" ensures that it arrives at the peer. In actuality, some or all of the data from the write may still be queued for transmission when the write returns, so if either the host or the peer application should crash at this point, that data will be lost.

> If the *sending* application crashes, TCP continues to try to deliver the data to its peer.

Another important point of which we should be aware is the handling of errors that occur on a write call. When we write data to a disk, and `write` returns without an error, we know that the write was successful and that we no longer need be concerned with the disposition of the data that we wrote.

> This isn't really true, of course. Usually the data is sitting in a kernel buffer waiting to be flushed to disk, and it is certainly possible to lose this data if the system should crash before the data is written. The point is, though, that once the `write` returns, that is the last indication we get as to whether a problem occurred. We are inclined to think of data being lost before it's flushed as an unavoidable but unlikely event such as the disk itself crashing.

With TCP, however, it is unusual to get an error return from the write. Because the write can return before data is actually sent, the common errors are usually returned through the next operation, as we saw in Tip 9. Because the next operation is very often a read, it is common to say that write errors are returned through the read. Write operations return only errors that are obvious at the time of the write call. These include errors such as

- The socket descriptor is invalid.
- The file descriptor does not point to a socket (in the case of `send` and its siblings).
- The socket specified in the call does not exist or is not connected.
- The buffer address parameter specifies an illegal address.

Most of these errors result from incorrect code, and we should rarely encounter them after the development stage of the program. The exception to this is the `EPIPE` error (or `SIGPIPE` signal) that can occur when a connection is reset by its peer. The conditions under which this can happen were discussed when we looked at peer application crashes in Tip 9.

We can sum up these considerations by saying that, when applied to a TCP connection, the write operation is best understood as an action that copies the data to the send queue and notifies TCP that there is new data on the queue. We take up what TCP does as a result of this notification next, but we should consider it essentially asynchronous to the write itself.

### The Write Operation from TCP's Perspective

As we discussed earlier, the write operation is responsible for moving data from the application's write buffer into the kernel, and for notifying TCP that there is new data from the application for it to process. Now let's examine some of the criteria that TCP uses in deciding whether it can send any of the newly arrived data immediately, and if so, how much. Our intent is not to provide a complete explanation of how the TCP send logic works, but to come to an appreciation for some of the factors that influence that logic. In this way we will better understand the behavior that we observe in our applications.

One of the principal goals of TCP's send policy is to make as efficient use of the available bandwidth as possible. To achieve this, TCP prefers to send data in MSS-size chunks.

> During connection establishment, each side of a TCP connection can specify the MSS that it is willing to receive. Its peer must honor this by not sending more than an MSS-size segment. The MSS is derived from the MTU, as discussed in Tip 7

At the same time, it can't overrun its peer's buffers. As we saw in Tip 1, this is controlled by TCP's send window.

If these were the only considerations, the send policy would be simple: Immediately send all available data in MSS-size segments up to the maximum allowed by the send window. Unfortunately, there are other, competing, considerations.

First, there is the extremely important matter of congestion control. If TCP were to suddenly inject a large number of segments into the network, router buffer space could become exhausted, resulting in dropped datagrams. This results in retransmissions, which congest the network further. In the extreme case, the network becomes so congested that few or no datagrams are delivered, and we say that the network has suffered *congestive collapse*. To help avoid congestion, TCP does not suddenly send several segments on an idle connection all at once. Instead, it starts with a single segment and increases the number of unacknowledged segments in the network until a steady state is reached.

> We can visualize the problem by imagining a room with several people in which someone yells "Fire!" Everyone rushes to the door at the same time, and a logjam results with few or no people getting through. If, on the other hand, people walk through the door single file, there is no congestion and everyone gets out.

TCP uses two algorithms to prevent congestion. Both use another window, called the *congestion window*, to control congestion. The maximum amount of data that TCP sends at any moment is the minimum of the send and congestion windows. Notice that these two windows are responsible for different aspects of flow control. The send window, imposed by our peer's TCP, prevents us from overrunning our peer's buffers. The congestion window, imposed by our TCP, prevents us from overrunning the network's capacity. By limiting our data transmissions to the minimum of the two windows, we ensure that both types of flow control are honored.

The first congestion control algorithm, called *slow start*, "slowly" increases the rate at which segments are injected into the network up to a threshold.

> Slowly is in quotes because the increase is actually exponential. During slow start the congestion window is opened by one segment for every ACK. Starting with 1 segment, this yields the sequence $1, 2, 4, 8, \cdots$ segments for the congestion window size.

When the size of the congestion window reaches the threshold, called the *slow start threshold*, slow start is over, and another algorithm, *congestion avoidance*, takes over. During congestion avoidance, the connection is assumed to have reached steady state, and the network is probed continually for any additional bandwidth that may become available. During the congestion avoidance phase, the congestion window is opened linearly—at most one segment per round trip time.

For the TCP send policy, the congestion window can potentially prevent the sending of data that would otherwise be allowed. If congestion occurs (as indicated by a lost segment), or if the network has been idle for a while, the congestion window is decreased, perhaps to one segment. Depending on how much data is already queued and how much data the application is trying to send, this may prevent some or all of the data from being transmitted.

The definitive source for information on the congestion avoidance algorithms is [Jacobson 1988], which first proposed them. This paper is very readable and gives the results of several experiments that demonstrate the marked improvement in network performance when these algorithms are in place. [Stevens 1994] includes a detailed explanation of the algorithms and output from LAN traces that shows them at work. Today, these algorithms are a required part of any conformant TCP implementation (RFC 1122; [Braden 1989]).

> For all their power, the implementation of these algorithms is very simple—two state variables and a few lines of code. The details can be found in [Wright and Stevens 1995].

Another factor affecting the TCP send policy is the Nagle algorithm. This algorithm, first proposed in RFC 896 [Nagle 1984], specifies that there can be no more than one unacknowledged "small" segment outstanding at any given time. By "small segment," we mean a segment less than the MSS. The intent of the Nagle algorithm is to prevent TCP from flooding the network with a series of small segments. Rather, TCP saves small amounts of data until it receives the ACK for the previous small segment, and then sends all the data at once. As we shall see in Tip 24, the Nagle algorithm can have substantial effects on the efficiency of an application if we don't allow for it.

If our application is writing data in small chunks, the effect of the Nagle algorithm is obvious. Let's suppose, for example, that we have an idle connection, that the send and congestion windows are large, and that we perform two small back-to-back writes. The data from the first write is sent immediately because the windows allow it and the Nagle algorithm doesn't prevent transmission because there is no unacknowledged data (the connection is idle). When the data from the second write arrives at TCP, however, it is not sent even though there is room in the send and congestion windows. This is because there is already an unacknowledged small segment outstanding, and therefore the Nagle algorithm requires that the data be queued until the ACK from the previous segment arrives.

The Nagle algorithm is usually implemented by requiring that a small segment not be sent if there is any unacknowledged data outstanding. This is the procedure recommended by RFC 1122. BSD-derived implementations, as well as many others, bend this rule a little to allow sending a final small segment for a large write on an idle connection. For example, if the MSS of an idle connection is 1,460 bytes, and an application writes 1,600 bytes, then—the send and congestion windows allowing—TCP will send a 1,460-byte segment followed by a 140-byte segment without waiting for any ACKs. A strict interpretation of the Nagle algorithm would require holding the 140 bytes until either the previous 1,460 bytes were acknowledged or until the application writes enough new data to fill a full-size segment.

The Nagle algorithm is actually one half of a set of algorithms referred to as *silly window syndrome* (SWS) avoidance. SWS avoidance seeks to prevent the sending of small amounts of data. SWS and how it can significantly degrade performance is discussed in RFC 813 [Clark 1982]. As we've seen, the Nagle algorithm is a form of SWS avoidance for the sender. SWS avoidance also requires effort on the part of the receiver, namely that the receiver not advertise small windows.

Recall that the send window is an estimate of the amount of buffer space available at our peer. Our peer announces the current amount of available buffer space by including a *window update* in every segment that it sends. The receiver-side SWS avoidance consists of not announcing small increases in buffer space.

An example will make this clear. Suppose that our peer has 14,600 bytes of buffer space available and the MSS is 1,460 bytes. Let us further suppose that our peer application is sluggish and that it reads 100 bytes at a time. After we send ten segments to our peer, the send window is filled and we have to stop sending data. Now our peer application reads 100 bytes, so there are 100 bytes of additional room in the receive buffer. If our peer advertised that additional 100 bytes, then we would eventually send a small segment of 100 bytes because TCP will override the Nagle algorithm if it is unable to send a small segment in a reasonable amount of time. Furthermore, it's easy to see that we would keep sending 100-byte packets because each time our peer reads 100 bytes, it would issue a window update announcing another 100 bytes of buffer space.

Receiver-side SWS avoidance works by not issuing a window update unless there is a "significant increase" in buffer space. RFC 1122 defines "significant" as an increase of either a full-size segment or an increase greater than half the size of the maximum window. BSD-derived implementations require an increase of two full-size segments or one half of the maximum window.

It might seem as if receiver-side SWS avoidance is unnecessary (because sender-side SWS prevents the transmission of small segments), but it provides protection against TCP/IP stacks that do not implement the Nagle algorithm properly, and for those connections for which the Nagle algorithm has been disabled (see Tip 24). RFC 1122 requires that a conformant TCP implement both sides of SWS avoidance.

Armed with all of this information, we are now in a position to outline the send policy of a BSD-derived TCP. The policy of other implementations may vary in some of the details, but are substantially the same.

Whenever the TCP output routine is called, it calculates the amount of data it can send as the minimum of the amount of data in the send buffer, the send window size, the congestion window size, and the MSS. Data is transmitted if any of the following are true:

1. We can send a full MSS-size segment.
2. The connection is idle and we can empty the send buffer.
3. The Nagle algorithm is disabled and we can empty the send buffer.
4. There is urgent data to send.
5. We have a small segment that we have been unable to send for "a while."

> When TCP has a small segment that can't be sent, it starts a timer for the same amount of time that it would wait for an ACK before retransmitting if it had sent it (subject to the constraint that it be between 5 and 60 seconds). That is, the timer is set to the RTO. If this timer, called the *persist timer*, expires, TCP transmits the segment subject only to the send and congestion window constraints. Even if our peer is advertising a window of 0 bytes, TCP still tries to send 1 byte. This is to prevent a lost window update from resulting in a deadlock.

6. Our peer's receive window is at least half open.
7. We need to retransmit a segment.
8. We need to send an ACK for data from our peer.
9. We need to issue a window update.

### Summary

In this tip we examined the TCP write operation in detail. We saw that, from an application's point of view, the best way to think of a write is as an operation that copies data from user space into the kernel's send buffer, and then returns. When TCP actually transmits the data, and how much of it is transmitted at once depends on the state of the connection, and is, in general, not predictable by the application.

We examined the BSD TCP send policy and saw how the amount of buffer space available at our peer (as indicated by the send window), an estimate of network congestion (as indicated by the congestion window), the amount of data available to send, SWS avoidance, and the TCP retransmit strategy all play a role in whether data can be sent.

## Tip 16: Understand the TCP Orderly Release Operation

As we have seen, a TCP connection has three phases:

1. A connection set up phase
2. A data transfer phase
3. A connection tear-down phase

This tip is concerned with the transition between the data transfer and connection tear-down phases. Specifically, we are interested in how we know our peer has finished the data transfer phase and is ready to tear down the connection, and how we can communicate the same to our peer.

As we shall see, it is perfectly normal for one side to finish sending data and signal its peer of that fact, while still receiving data. This is possible because TCP connections are full duplex, and the flow of data in one direction is independent of the flow in the other direction.

For example, a client might connect to a server, make a series of queries, and then close its half of the connection to signal the server that it is through making queries. The server may have to do substantial processing, or even contact other servers to answer the client, so it may still have data to send to the client even though the client has stopped sending data to it. Furthermore, the server may respond with an arbitrary amount of data, so the client may not be able to "count bytes" to know when the server is done. Therefore, the server can use the same strategy as the client, and close its half of the connection to signal the client that it is through responding.

When the answer to the client's last query is sent, and the server has closed its side of the connection telling the client that it has finished replying, the connection can complete the tear-down phase. Notice what has happened here: Both the client and the server have used the closing of their side of the connection as a natural way of signaling their peer that they've finished sending data. They have, in effect, sent an EOF.

## The `shutdown` Call

How does an application close only half of the connection? It can't just terminate or close the socket, because there may still be data coming from its peer. Instead, the sockets API provides the `shutdown` interface. The `shutdown` call is used just like a `close` call except that there is an additional parameter to indicate which side or sides of the connection should be closed:

```
#include <sys/socket.h>      /* UNIX */
#include <winsock.h>         /* Windows */

int shutdown( int s, int how )      /* UNIX */
int shutdown( SOCKET s, int how )   /* Windows */
```

Returns: 0 on success, -1 (UNIX) or SOCKET_ERROR (Windows) on error

Unfortunately, there are semantic and API differences between the UNIX and Winsock implementations of `shutdown`. The traditional `shutdown` implementation just used numbers for the *how* parameter. Both POSIX and Winsock give them symbolic names, but these names are different. Figure 3.1 gives the values, names, and meanings of *how*.

The difference in names for the values of *how* are easily compensated for by defining one set in terms of the other in a header file or merely by using the numeric values. More serious, however, are the semantic differences between the implementations. Let's take a look at what each of the three actions do.

*how* = 0 The receive side of the connection is closed. Both implementations mark the socket as unable to receive anymore data, and return an EOF if the

| how | | | Action |
|---|---|---|---|
| Numeric | POSIX | Winsock | |
| 0 | SHUT_RD | SD_RECEIVE | The receive side of the connection is closed. |
| 1 | SHUT_WR | SD_SEND | The send side of the connection is closed. |
| 2 | SHUT_RDWR | SD_BOTH | Both sides are closed. |

**Figure 3.1** Values of the shutdown *how* parameter

application issues any further reads, but the response to data already queued for the application at the time of the shutdown, or the receipt of new data from the peer, is markedly different. UNIX flushes the input queue, thereby disposing of any data that the application has not yet read. If new data arrives, TCP ACKs but then silently discards it because the application is no longer able to receive data. Winsock, on the other hand, resets the connection if data is queued or if new data arrives. For this reason, some authors (see [Quinn and Shute 1996] for example) consider the use of

```
shutdown( s, 0 );
```

unsafe under Winsock.

*how* = 1  The send side of the connection is closed. The socket is marked as unable to send any additional data, and any subsequent attempts to issue a write operation on the socket results in an error. After any data in the send buffer is sent, TCP sends a FIN to its peer, telling it that there is no more data coming. This is called a *half close*. This is the most common use of shutdown, and both implementations have the same semantics for it.

*how* = 2  Both sides of the connection are closed. The action is as if shutdown were called twice, once with *how* set to zero, and once with *how* set to one. Although one might think that

```
shutdown( s, 2 );
```

is equivalent to close or closesocket, this is not the case, as explained later. There should usually be no reason to call shutdown with *how* set to two, but [Quinn and Shute 1996] reports that in some Winsock implementations, closesocket does not function correctly unless shutdown is called with *how* = 2 first. Under Winsock, calling shutdown with *how* set to two has the same problem that calling it with *how* set to zero does—the connection may be reset.

There are important differences between closing a socket and calling shutdown. In the first place, shutdown does not actually "close" the socket, even if it is called with *how* set to two. That is, the socket and its resources (except perhaps the receive buffer when *how* is zero or two) are not released. Also, notice that when shutdown is called, it affects all processes that have the socket open. A call to shutdown with *how* set to one, for example, renders *all* holders of the socket unable to write to it. If a call to `close` or `closesocket` is made instead, other holders of the socket are still able to use it as if nothing had happened.

This last fact can often be used to our advantage. By calling `shutdown` with *how* = 1, we can ensure that our peer receives an EOF, regardless of whether other processes have the socket open. Calling `close` or `closesocket` does not guarantee this because the FIN is not be sent to our peer until the reference count of the socket is decremented to zero. That is, until all processes have closed the socket.

Finally, we should mention that although we are concerned with TCP in this tip, `shutdown` can also be used with UDP. Because there is no connection to close, the utility of calling `shutdown` with *how* set to one or two is questionable, but it can be useful to call it with *how* set to zero to prevent the receipt of datagrams on a particular UDP port.

## Orderly Release

Now that we have examined the `shutdown` call, let's see how it can be used in the *orderly release* of a connection. The purpose of an orderly release is to ensure that both sides receive all the data from their peers before the connection is torn down.

> The term *orderly release* is related to but should not be confused with the XTI (Tip 5) `t_sndrel` command, which is often referred to as an orderly release to distinguish it from the *abortive release*, `t_snddis`. The `t_sndrel` command performs the same functions as the sockets interface's `shutdown` command. Both commands are used to invoke an orderly release of a connection.

Merely closing the connection is not enough in some cases because data from the other side can be stranded. Recall that when an application closes a connection, any data not already delivered to it is discarded.

To help us experiment with the orderly release process, we write a client that sends data to a server, and then reads and prints any replies from the server. We show this client in Figure 3.2. Our client reads stdin to get the data to send to the server. When `fgets` returns `NULL` indicating EOF, the client begins the connection tear-down. The `-c` command line switch controls how the client tears down the connection. If `-c` is not specified, `shutdownc` calls `shutdown` to close the write side of the connection. If `-c` is specified, `shutdownc` calls `CLOSE`, sleeps for 5 seconds, and then exits.

*——————————————————————————————— shutdownc.c*

```
 1 #include "etcp.h"
 2 int main( int argc, char **argv )
 3 {
 4     SOCKET s;
 5     fd_set readmask;
 6     fd_set allreads;
 7     int rc;
 8     int len;
 9     int c;
10     int closeit = FALSE;
11     int err = FALSE;
```

```
12        char lin[ 1024 ];
13        char lout[ 1024 ];

14        INIT();
15        opterr = FALSE;
16        while ( ( c = getopt( argc, argv, "c" ) ) != EOF )
17        {
18            switch( c )
19            {
20                case 'c' :
21                    closeit = TRUE;
22                    break;

23                case '?' :
24                    err = TRUE;
25            }
26        }
27        if ( err || argc - optind != 2 )
28            error( 1, 0, "usage: %s [-c] host port\n",
29                program_name );
30        s = tcp_client( argv[ optind ], argv[ optind + 1 ] );
31        FD_ZERO( &allreads );
32        FD_SET( 0, &allreads );
33        FD_SET( s, &allreads );
34        for ( ;; )
35        {
36            readmask = allreads;
37            rc = select( s + 1, &readmask, NULL, NULL, NULL );
38            if ( rc <= 0 )
39                error( 1, errno, "bad select return (%d)", rc );
40            if ( FD_ISSET( s, &readmask ) )
41            {
42                rc = recv( s, lin, sizeof( lin ) - 1, 0 );
43                if ( rc < 0 )
44                    error( 1, errno, "recv error" );
45                if ( rc == 0 )
46                    error( 1, 0, "server disconnected\n" );
47                lin[ rc ] = '\0';
48                if ( fputs( lin, stdout ) )
49                    error( 1, errno, "fputs failed" );
50            }
51            if ( FD_ISSET( 0, &readmask ) )
52            {
53                if ( fgets( lout, sizeof( lout ), stdin ) == NULL )
54                {
55                    FD_CLR( 0, &allreads );
56                    if ( closeit )
57                    {
58                        CLOSE( s );
59                        sleep( 5 );
60                        EXIT( 0 );
61                    }
62                    else if ( shutdown( s, 1 ) )
63                        error( 1, errno, "shutdown failed" );
64                }
```

```
65              else
66              {
67                  len = strlen( lout );
68                  rc = send( s, lout, len, 0 );
69                  if ( rc < 0 )
70                      error( 1, errno, "send error" );
71              }
72          } .
73      }
74  }
```
———————————————————————————————————————— *shutdownc.c*

**Figure 3.2** Client for experimenting with orderly release

### Initialization

*14-30*    We perform our normal TCP client initialization, and check the command line switch for -c.

### Process Data

*40-50*    If the TCP socket becomes readable, we attempt to read as much data as possible up to the size of the buffer. If we get an EOF or error, we terminate; otherwise, we write whatever data we received to stdout.

> Note the sizeof( lin ) - 1 in the recv call on line 42. Despite the exhortations in Tip 11 about avoiding buffer overflows, the original version of this code specified sizeof( lin ), which caused a failure when the
>
> lin[ rc ] = '\0';
>
> at line 47 overflowed the buffer.

*53-64*    If we get an EOF on stdin, we either call shutdown or CLOSE, depending on the setting of the -c switch.

*65-71*    Otherwise, we write the data from stdin to the server.

We could use the system-supplied echo service to experiment with this client, but to see what errors occur and to introduce an optional latency, we provide our own version of a TCP echo server. There is nothing at all remarkable about tcpecho.c except that it takes an optional command line argument, which, if present, causes the program to sleep for the specified number of seconds between reading and echoing each block of data (Figure 3.3).

First, we run shutdownc with the -c switch so that it closes the socket when it gets an EOF on stdin. We set tcpecho to delay 4 seconds before echoing the data that it reads:

```
bsd: $ tcpecho 9000 4 &
[1] 3836
bsd: $ shutdownc -c localhost 9000
data1                                   These three lines were
data2                                   entered one after another
^D                                      as quickly as possible.
tcpecho: send failed: Broken pipe (32)  4 seconds after "data1" sent
```

*——————————————————————————— tcpecho.c*

```
 1 #include "etcp.h"

 2 int main( int argc, char **argv )
 3 {
 4      SOCKET s;
 5      SOCKET s1;
 6      char buf[ 1024 ];
 7      int rc;
 8      int nap = 0;

 9      INIT();
10      if ( argc == 3 )
11          nap = atoi( argv[ 2 ] );
12      s = tcp_server( NULL, argv[ 1 ] );
13      s1 = accept( s, NULL, NULL );
14      if ( !isvalidsock( s1 ) )
15          error( 1, errno, "accept failed" );
16      signal( SIGPIPE, SIG_IGN ); /* report sigpipe to us */
17      for ( ;; )
18      {
19          rc = recv( s1, buf, sizeof( buf ), 0 );
20          if ( rc == 0 )
21              error( 1, 0, "client disconnected\n" );
22          if ( rc < 0 )
23              error( 1, errno, "recv failed" );
24          if ( nap )
25              sleep( nap );
26          rc = send( s1, buf, rc, 0 );
27          if ( rc < 0 )
28              error( 1, errno, "send failed" );
29      }
30 }
```

*——————————————————————————— tcpecho.c*

**Figure 3.3** TCP echo server

Next, we type the two lines "data1" and "data2" followed immediately by <CNTRL-D>, which sends an EOF to shutdownc, causing it to close the socket. Notice that neither line is echoed back to us. The error message from tcpecho tells us what happened: When the server returned from the sleep call and attempted to echo the "data1" line, it got an RST back because the client had already closed the connection.

> As explained in Tip 9, it is actually the write of the second line ("data2") that returns the error. Also notice that this is one of the cases when an error is returned by the write call instead of through the read. See Tip 15 for more on this.

The important point is that although our client signaled the server that it was through sending data, it dropped the connection before the server was able to complete its processing, and data was lost. The left half of Figure 3.4 shows the exchange of TCP segments.

Next we repeat the experiment, but we invoke `shutdownc` without the `-c` switch:

```
bsd: $ tcpecho 9000 4 &
[1] 3845
bsd: $ shutdownc localhost 9000
data1
data2
^D
data1                                          4 seconds after "data1" sent
data2                                          4 seconds after "data1" received
tcpecho: client disconnected
shutdownc: server disconnected
```

This time, things work correctly. When `shutdownc` sees the EOF on stdin, it calls `shutdown`, signaling `tcpecho` that it is through sending data, but it continues to read data from the connection. When `tcpecho` sees the EOF from the client, it closes the connection, causing its TCP to send any remaining data that it has queued along with a FIN. When the client receives the EOF, it knows that it has received all data from the server, so it terminates.

Notice that the server can't tell which action (`shutdown` or `close`) the client took until it tries to write and either gets an error or the EOF. As shown in Figure 3.4, the exchanges are identical up until the point that `shutdownc`'s TCP responds to the segment containing the echoed "data1."

There is a final point that deserves mention because it is a frequent cause of confusion. We have seen several times in our example code that when TCP receives a FIN from its peer, it signals the application of this fact by returning from a read operation with a return value of 0. We see examples of this on line 45 of Figure 3.2 and line 20 of Figure 3.3, where the EOF condition is checked for explicitly by asking if `recv` returned 0. The confusion most often happens in cases similar to that in Figure 3.2, when a `select` call is involved. When an application's peer closes the write side of its connection by either closing or shutting it down or by terminating, `select` returns with a read event for the socket. If the application does not check for the EOF condition, it may try to process a zero-length segment or it may loop continually between the read and `select`.

A frequent topic in the networking news groups is the complaint that "although `select` indicates that there is data to be read, when I do the actual read, there is no data available." What is happening here, of course, is that the peer has closed (at least) the write side of the connection, and the "read event" is really TCP sending the application an EOF from its peer.

## Summary

We have examined the TCP `shutdown` system call and contrasted it with the `close` call. We saw that we can close either the read, write, or both sides of a connection with `shutdown`, and that it affects the reference count of a socket differently than `close` does.

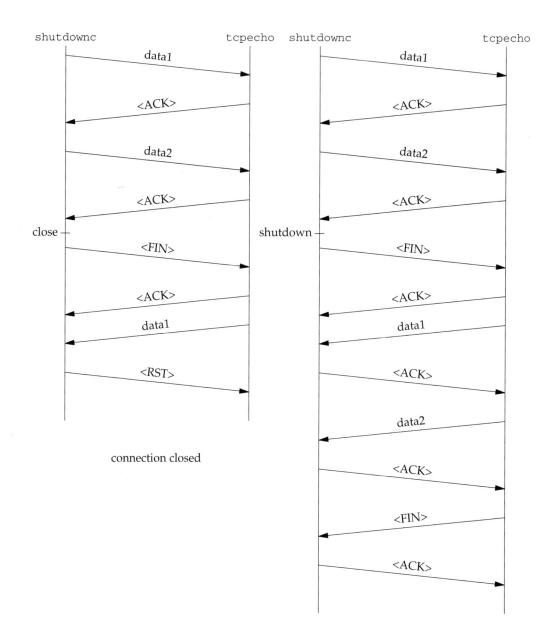

**Figure 3.4** `close` versus `shutdown`

Next we showed how `shutdown` can be used to invoke an orderly release of a connection. The orderly release is a procedure to tear down a connection while ensuring that no data gets lost.

## Tip 17: Consider Letting `inetd` Launch Your Application

When running on UNIX and certain other systems, the Internet superserver, `inetd`, provides an easy way to make applications network aware with very little work. At the same time, having a single process listen for incoming connections or UDP datagrams helps to conserve system resources.

Typically, `inetd` supports at least the TCP and UDP protocols, and may support others as well. We consider the use of `inetd` with TCP and UDP only. The behavior of `inetd` differs markedly depending on whether it is listening for TCP connections or UDP datagrams.

### TCP Servers

For TCP servers, `inetd` listens for a connection request on the application's well-known port; accepts the connection; maps the connection onto stdin, stdout, and stderr; and starts the appropriate server. When the server runs, it takes its input from stdin, and writes its output to either stdout or stderr. That is, the connection to the peer is available on file descriptors 0, 1, and 2. Unless specifically directed to do otherwise in the `inetd` configuration file (`/etc/inetd.conf`), `inetd` then listens for additional connections to the well-known port. If such a connection arrives, another instance of the server is started, regardless of whether the first has terminated. This is illustrated in Figure 3.5. Note that the server need not concern itself with the possibility of serving multiple clients. It merely performs its function for the single client at the other end of the connection and then terminates. Other clients are served by additional instances of the server.

Using `inetd` is often an attractive strategy because it relieves us of the necessity of managing the TCP connection or UDP setup ourselves, and enables us to write the application more or less as if it were an ordinary filter. A simple, if not particularly interesting, example of this is shown in Figure 3.6.

There are a number of points to make about this program:

1. There is no reference to TCP or networking in the program's code. This does not mean that we can't make socket-related calls (`getpeername`, `[gs]etsockopt`, and so on), only that we don't always need to. Nor are we restricted to using `read` and `write`. We can use `send`, `recv`, `sendto`, and `recvfrom` just as if `inetd` were not being used.

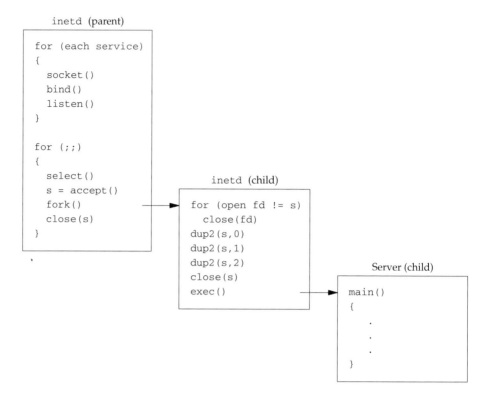

**Figure 3.5** Action of `inetd` when starting a TCP server

```
 1 #include <stdio.h>

 2 void main( void )
 3 {
 4     int cnt = 0;
 5     char line[ 1024 ];

 6     /*
 7      * We have to explicitly set line buffering since the stdio
 8      * routines will not see the socket as a terminal device.
 9      */
10     setvbuf( stdout, NULL, _IOLBF, 0 );
11     while ( fgets( line, sizeof( line ), stdin ) != NULL )
12         printf( "%3i: %s", ++cnt, line );
13 }
```

**Figure 3.6** `rlnumd`—a line-numbering program

2. We had to set line buffering explicitly. This is because the standard I/O library sets line buffering automatically only if it senses that it is writing to a terminal. Standard I/O does this to provide immediate feedback for interactive applications.

3. The standard I/O library handles the parsing of the input stream into records, as we discussed in Tip 6.

4. We are tacitly assuming that lines will be no longer than 1,023 bytes. Lines with more than 1,023 bytes will have numbers interpolated after every 1,023 bytes.

> This fact, which was pointed out by [Oliver 2000], is another example of how easy it is to miss buffering errors. We discussed this at some length in Tip 11.

5. Even though this is a trivial application, many of the "real" TCP/IP applications such as rlogin, telnet, and ftp use this same technique.

The program in Figure 3.6 can function as either a "normal" filter or as a remote line-numbering service. To set up a remote line-numbering service, we need only choose a port number, add an entry in /etc/services with the service name and port number, and add an entry in /etc/inetd.conf that describes the service and where to find the executable for it. For example, if we call our service rlnum, implement it with the server rlnumd and assign it to port 8000, we would add the line

```
rlnum             8000/tcp #remote line-numbering service
```

to /etc/services and the line

```
rlnum stream tcp nowait jcs /usr/home/jcs/rlnumd rlnumd
```

to /etc/inetd.conf. The line in the /etc/services file merely says that the service rlnum uses TCP on port 8000. The meanings of the fields in the /etc/inetd.conf are as follows:

1. The service name as listed in /etc/services. This is the "name" of the well-known port to which clients connect when using this server. In our example, the service name is rlnum.

2. The socket type that the server uses. This is stream for TCP servers, and dgram for UDP servers. Because our example is a TCP server, we specified stream.

3. The protocol used by the server. This is either tcp or udp . For our example, we specified tcp.

4. The wait/nowait flag. This is *always* wait for UDP servers, and is almost always nowait for TCP servers. When nowait is specified, inetd resumes listening for additional connections on the server's well-known port immediately. If wait is specified, inetd does nothing further with the socket until the server terminates. At that point, it resumes listening for connections (stream-based servers)

or the arrival of datagrams (datagram-based servers). If wait is specified for a stream-based server, `inetd` does not call `accept` for the connection, but passes the listening socket to the server, which must then accept at least one connection before terminating. As [Kacker 1998] points out, specifying wait for a TCP application is a powerful but little understood option. Here are some possible applications for the wait option on a TCP connection:

- As a restart device for unreliable network daemon processes. As long as the daemon runs correctly, it accepts connections from its clients, but if the daemon should crash for some reason, the next connection attempt causes `inetd` to restart it.

- As a way of ensuring that only one client can use the server at a time

- As a way to control a load-driven multithreaded/multiprocess application. With this model, the initial process is started by `inetd`, and then it manages the load dynamically by spawning children or threads on an as-needed basis. As the load decreases, children or threads are reaped, and finally, when the parent becomes idle, it terminates, releasing all resources and returning control of the listening socket to `inetd`.

In our example, we specified `nowait` as is normally done for TCP servers.

5. The user name under which to run the server. This name must be in `/etc/passwd`. Most of the standard servers in `/etc/inetd.conf` specify `root` as the user name, but servers can be run under any user name. We chose to run our rlnum server as user `jcs`.

6. The full pathname of the server's executable. Because `rlnumd` is in user `jcs`'s home directory, we specified `/usr/home/jcs/rlnumd`.

7. Up to five arguments (starting with `argv[0]`) that will be passed to the server. Because our server takes no arguments, we specified only `argv[0]`.

To try our new service, we force `inetd` to reread its configuration file (by sending it a `SIGHUP` signal in most implementations) and connect to it with telnet:

```
bsd: $ telnet localhost rlnum
Trying 127.0.0.1...
Connected to localhost
Escape character is '^]'.
hello
  1: hello
world
  2: world
^]
telnet> quit
Connection closed.
bsd: $
```

## UDP Servers

Because UDP is a connectionless protocol (see Tip 1), there is no connection for inetd to listen for. Instead, inetd directs the operating system (via the select system call) to notify it when there is a datagram to be read on the UDP server's well-known port. When the notification arrives, inetd maps the socket onto stdin, stdout, and stderr, and starts the UDP server. Unlike the normal nowait case of TCP servers, inetd takes no further action on the well-known port until the server that it started terminates. At that point, it again directs the operating system to notify it when a datagram arrives at the well-known port. The server must read at least one message from the socket before exiting so that inetd doesn't see the same message and fork and exec again, causing an endless loop.

An example of a simple inetd launched UDP server that echoes its input along with its process ID is shown in Figure 3.7.

```
                                                                    udpecho1.c
 1 #include "etcp.h"
 2 int main( int argc, char **argv )
 3 {
 4      struct sockaddr_in peer;
 5      int rc;
 6      int len;
 7      int pidsz;
 8      char buf[ 120 ];

 9      pidsz = sprintf( buf, "%d: ", getpid() );
10      len = sizeof( peer );
11      rc = recvfrom( 0, buf + pidsz, sizeof( buf ) - pidsz, 0,
12          ( struct sockaddr * )&peer, &len );
13      if ( rc <= 0 )
14          exit( 1 );
15      sendto( 1, buf, rc + pidsz, 0,
16          ( struct sockaddr * )&peer, len );
17      exit( 0 );
18 }
                                                                    udpecho1.c
```

**Figure 3.7** A simple request/reply UDP server

**udpecho1**

9        We obtain the server's process ID (PID) from the operating system, convert it to ASCII, and place it at the beginning of the I/O buffer.

10–14    We read the datagram from the client into the buffer after the server's PID.

15–17    We return the datagram along with the server's PID to the client, and the server exits.

To experiment with this server, we use the simple UDP client, shown in Figure 3.8, that reads requests from stdin, sends them to the server, and writes the reply to stdout.

*—————————————————————————————————————————————— udpclient.c*

```
 1 #include "etcp.h"
 2 int main( int argc, char **argv )
 3 {
 4     struct sockaddr_in peer;
 5     SOCKET s;
 6     int rc = 0;
 7     int len;
 8     char buf[ 120 ];

 9     INIT();
10     s = udp_client( argv[ 1 ], argv[ 2 ], &peer );
11     while ( fgets( buf, sizeof( buf ), stdin ) != NULL )
12     {
13         rc = sendto( s, buf, strlen( buf ), 0,
14             ( struct sockaddr * )&peer, sizeof( peer ) );
15         if ( rc < 0 )
16             error( 1, errno, "sendto failed" );
17         len = sizeof( peer );
18         rc = recvfrom( s, buf, sizeof( buf ) - 1, 0,
19             ( struct sockaddr * )&peer, &len );
20         if ( rc < 0 )
21             error( 1, errno, "recvfrom failed" );
22         buf[ rc ] = '\0';
23         fputs( buf, stdout );
24     }
25     EXIT( 0 );
26 }
```

*—————————————————————————————————————————————— udpclient.c*

**Figure 3.8** A simple UDP client

**udpclient**

*10*    We call udp_client to fill peer with our peer's address and to obtain a UDP socket.

*11–16*    We read a line from stdin and send it as a UDP datagram to the host and port specified on the command line.

*17–21*    We call recvfrom to read the server's reply, and quit if there is an error.

*22–23*    We null terminate the reply and write it to stdout.

There are two points to make about udpclient:

1. Our client assumes that it always receives a reply from the server. As discussed in Tip 1, there is no guarantee that the datagram from the server will actually arrive. Because udpclient is an interactive program, we can always abort it and start over if the call to recvfrom hangs. In a noninteractive client, however, we would have to set a timer on recvfrom to protect against lost datagrams.

   > We don't have to worry about this with udpecho1, because we know there is a datagram ready to be read (or inetd wouldn't have started the server). In our next server

(Figure 3.9), lost datagrams are a concern, so we do put a timer around the call to recvfrom.

2. For use with udpecho1, we don't need to receive the sender's address and port because we already have it. Thus lines 18 and 19 could be replaced with

```
rc = recvfrom( s, buf, sizeof( buf ) - 1, 0, NULL, NULL );
```

As shown in the next example, however, the client sometimes needs the address from which the server sends its reply, so our UDP client always retrieves it.

To test this server we add the line

```
udpecho dgram udp wait jcs /usr/home/jcs/udpechod udpechod
```

to /etc/inetd.conf, and the line

```
udpecho        8001/udp
```

to /etc/services on bsd. Then we rename udpecho1 as udpechod, and signal inetd to reread its configuration file. When we run udpclient from sparc, we get

```
sparc: $ udpclient bsd udpecho
one
28685: one
two
28686: two
three
28687: three
^C
sparc: $
```

This output illustrates an important point about typical UDP servers: They don't usually carry on a dialog with the client. That is, they receive a single request and respond with a single reply. In the case of UDP servers launched by inetd, the typical action is to receive a request, respond, and then exit. They have to exit as soon as possible because inetd does not listen for other requests on the server's well-known port until it detects that the server has terminated.

In the previous output, we see that even though udpclient is acting as if it were carrying on a dialog with udpecho1, it is really invoking another instance of the server for each message that it sends. This is obviously inefficient, but more importantly it means that the server is not maintaining state between messages from the client. That doesn't matter for udpecho1 because each message is essentially a separate transaction, but this isn't true for all servers. One way to solve this problem is for the server to accept a message from the client (to prevent an infinite loop), connect to the client, thus obtaining a new (ephemeral) port, fork off a child process, and terminate. The child process then carries on the dialog with the client.

> There are other possibilities as well. For example, the server could keep track of several individual clients by itself. By accepting datagrams from more than one client, a server can amortize its start-up costs over several clients by not exiting until it has been idle for some period of time. This method has the advantage of making the clients a little simpler, at the cost of more complexity for the server.

To see how this works, we change udpecho1, as shown in Figure 3.9.

```
                                                                    ———— udpecho2.c
 1 #include "etcp.h"
 2 int main( int argc, char **argv )
 3 {
 4     struct sockaddr_in peer;
 5     int s;
 6     int rc;
 7     int len;
 8     int pidsz;
 9     char buf[ 120 ];

10     pidsz = sprintf( buf, "%d: ", getpid() );
11     len = sizeof( peer );
12     rc = recvfrom( 0, buf + pidsz, sizeof( buf ) - pidsz,
13         0, ( struct sockaddr * )&peer, &len );
14     if ( rc < 0 )
15         exit( 1 );

16     s = socket( AF_INET, SOCK_DGRAM, 0 );
17     if ( s < 0 )
18         exit( 1 );
19     if ( connect( s, ( struct sockaddr * )&peer, len ) < 0 )
20         exit( 1 );
21     if ( fork() != 0 )                    /* error or parent? */
22         exit( 0 );

23     /* child process */

24     while ( strncmp( buf + pidsz, "done", 4 ) != 0 )
25     {
26         if ( write( s, buf, rc + pidsz ) < 0 )
27             break;
28         pidsz = sprintf( buf, "%d: ", getpid() );
29         alarm( 30 );
30         rc = read( s, buf + pidsz, sizeof( buf ) - pidsz );
31         alarm( 0 );
32         if ( rc < 0 )
33             break;
34     }
35     exit( 0 );
36 }
                                                                    ———— udpecho2.c
```

**Figure 3.9** Another version of udpechod

**udpecho2**

*10-15*    We get the process's PID, put it in the buffer, and receive the first message, just as we did in udpecho1.

*16-20*    We get a new socket and connect it to the client using the address in peer that was filled in by the call to recvfrom.

*21-22*    The parent forks and exits. At this point, inetd is free to listen for additional messages on the server's well-known port. The important point here is that the child is using a *new* port number that was bound to the socket s as a result of the call to `connect`.

*24-35*     We next send the client's first message back to it with the parent's PID prepended. We continue to receive messages from the client, prepend the child's PID, and echo it back to the client until we obtain a message that starts with "done." At that point the server terminates. The alarm around the read on line 30 is to prevent a client that terminates without sending "done" from causing `udpecho2` to hang forever. Because we didn't set a signal handler for `SIGALRM`, UNIX terminates the program if the alarm goes off.

When we rename our new version of the server to `udpechod`, and run it, we get

```
sparc: $ udpclient bsd udpecho
one
28743: one
two
28744: two
three
28744: three
done
^C
sparc: $
```

This time we see that the first message has the PID of the parent (the server launched by `inetd`), and the others have the same PID—that of the child. We can see now why `udpclient` always retrieves its peer's address: It needs to discover the new port number (and possibly the new IP address in the case of multihomed servers) for subsequent messages. It is only the first `recvfrom` that must do this, of course, but for simplicity we don't make a special case of the first call.

## Summary

In this tip we have seen how we can significantly reduce the effort needed to make an application network capable. The `inetd` daemon takes care of listening for connections or datagrams; mapping the socket onto stdin, stdout, and stderr; and starting the application. Thereafter, the application can merely read or write to stdin, stdout, and stderr without worrying about or even knowing that it is talking to the network. We examined a simple example of a filter that had no network code at all, yet worked perfectly well as a remote service when started by `inetd`.

We also examined a UDP server that can carry on an extended dialog with its client. This required the server to obtain a new socket and port number, and then fork off a child process before exiting.

## Tip 18: Consider Letting `tcpmux` "Assign" Your Server's Well-known Port

One of the problems facing the designer of a server is what number to use for the well-known port. The Internet Assigned Numbers Authority (IANA) divides the available port numbers into three groups: the "official" well-known ports, the registered port numbers, and the dynamic or private ports.

> We have been using the term *well-known port* in the generic sense of a server's access port number. Strictly speaking, the well-known ports are those controlled by the IANA.

The well-known port numbers are those between 0 and 1023. They are controlled by the IANA. The registered port numbers are those between 1024 and 49151. The IANA does not control these port numbers, but they do register and list them as a service to the networking community. The dynamic or private ports are those between 49152 and 65535. These port numbers are supposed to be used for the ephemeral ports, but many systems don't follow this convention. BSD-derived systems, for example, have traditionally used the range 1024 to 5000 for the ephemeral ports. A complete list of the latest IANA assignments of well-known and registered ports is available at `<http://www.isi.edu/in-notes/iana/assignments/port-numbers>`.

One option is for the server designer to obtain a registered port number from the IANA.

> A request for a well-known or registered port number assignment can be made online at `<http://www.isi.edu/cgi-bin/iana/port-number.pl>`.

This does not prevent others from using it, of course, and sooner or later two servers using the same port end up running on the same machine. One common method of dealing with this is to have a default port number, but have a command line option to change it.

Another solution, less used but more flexible, is to use the TCP Port Service Multiplexor (TCPMUX) facility of `inetd` (Tip 17). The TCPMUX facility is described in RFC 1078 [Lotter 1988]. TCPMUX listens on port 1 for TCP connections. A client connects to TCPMUX and sends it the name of the service that it wants to start followed by a carriage return and linefeed (<CR><LF>). The server, or optionally TCPMUX, sends the client a single character indicating a positive (+) or negative (-) acknowledgment, followed by an optional explanatory message, followed by <CR><LF>. These service names, which are not case sensitive, are also in the `inetd.conf` file, but they begin with the string `tcpmux/` to distinguish them from normal service names. If the service name begins with a + character, TCPMUX sends the positive acknowledgment instead of the server. That allows servers, such as `rlnumd` (Figure 3.6), that were not written with the TCPMUX protocol in mind to still make use of TCPMUX.

For example, if we wanted to run our remote line-numbering service from Tip 17 as a TCPMUX server, we would add the line

```
tcpmux/+rlnumd stream tcp nowait jcs /usr/home/jcs/rlnumd rlnumd
```

to `/etc/inetd.conf`. We can try this by signaling `inetd` to reread its configuration file and then using telnet, specifying the TCPMUX service:

```
bsd: $ telnet localhost tcpmux
Trying 127.0.0.1...
Connected to localhost
Escape character is '^]'.
```

```
rlnumd
+Go
hello
  1: hello
world
  2: world
^]
telnet> quit
Connection closed.
bsd: $
```

One problem with TCPMUX is that it is not supported by all operating systems, or even all UNIX operating systems. Fortunately, the TCPMUX protocol is simple enough that we can write our own version easily. Because TCPMUX must do pretty much the same things as inetd (with the exception of monitoring several sockets), our version also helps to solidify the ideas behind the working of inetd. We start with the defines, global variables, and main function (Figure 3.10).

─────────────────────────────────────────────────────── *tcpmux.c*

```
 1 #include "etcp.h"

 2 #define MAXARGS     10        /* maximum arguments to server */
 3 #define MAXLINE     256       /* maximum line size in tcpmux.conf */
 4 #define NSERVTAB    10        /* number of service_table entries */
 5 #define CONFIG      "tcpmux.conf"

 6 typedef struct
 7 {
 8     int flag;
 9     char *service;
10     char *path;
11     char *args[ MAXARGS + 1 ];
12 } servtab_t;

13 int ls;                        /* socket to listen on */
14 servtab_t service_table[ NSERVTAB + 1 ];

15 int main( int argc, char **argv )
16 {
17     struct sockaddr_in peer;
18     int s;
19     int peerlen;

20     /* Initialize and start the tcpmux server */

21     INIT();
22     parsetab();
23     switch ( argc )
24     {
25         case 1:    /* default everything */
26             ls = tcp_server( NULL, "tcpmux" );
27             break;

28         case 2:    /* specify interface, default port */
29             ls = tcp_server( argv[ 1 ], "tcpmux" );
30             break;
```

```
31          case 3:     /* specify everything */
32              ls = tcp_server( argv[ 1 ], argv[ 2 ] );
33              break;

34          default:
35              error( 1, 0, "usage: %s [ interface [ port ] ]\n",
36                  program_name );
37      }
38      daemon( 0, 0 );
39      signal( SIGCHLD, reaper );

40      /* Accept connections to tcpmux port */

41      for ( ;; )
42      {
43          peerlen = sizeof( peer );
44          s = accept( ls, ( struct sockaddr * )&peer, &peerlen );
45          if ( s < 0 )
46              continue;
47          start_server( s );
48          CLOSE( s );
49      }
50  }
```
———————————————————————————————————————————————————————— *tcpmux.c*

**Figure 3.10** tcpmux—defines, globals, and main function

**main**

*6-12*    The servtab_t object defines the entries in service_table. The flag field is set to TRUE if tcpmux instead of the server should send the positive acknowledgment.

*22*    We begin by calling parsetab to read and parse tcpmux.conf, and to build service_table. The parsetab routine is shown later in Figure 3.12.

*23-37*    Our version of tcpmux allows the user to specify the interface or port on which it will listen. This code initializes the server with whatever parameters the user specified, and uses the defaults for the others.

*38*    We call the daemon function to put tcpmux in the background and disassociate it from the terminal.

*39*    We install a signal handler for the SIGCHLD signal. This is to prevent the servers that we start from becoming zombies (and tying up system resources) when they terminate.

> In some systems, the signal function provides an interface to the older "unreliable signal" semantics. For these systems the sigaction function should be used to provide reliable signal semantics. A common strategy is to provide our own signal function written in terms of sigaction. We show such an implementation in Appendix A.

*41-49*    This loop accepts connections to tcpmux, and calls start_server, which forks and execs the server requested. The start_server function is shown in Figure 3.11. When start_server returns, the socket is closed because the parent process has no further use for it.

Next we look at the start_server function. This is the routine that does most of the work in tcpmux.

*tcpmux.c*

```
 1 static void start_server( int s )
 2 {
 3     char line[ MAXLINE ];
 4     servtab_t *stp;
 5     int rc;
 6     static char err1[] = "-unable to read service name\r\n";
 7     static char err2[] = "-unknown service\r\n";
 8     static char err3[] = "-unable to start service\r\n";
 9     static char ok[] = "+OK\r\n";

10     rc = fork();
11     if ( rc < 0 )        /* fork error */
12     {
13         write( s, err3, sizeof( err3 ) - 1 );
14         return;
15     }
16     if ( rc != 0 )       /* parent */
17         return;

18     /* child process */

19     CLOSE( ls );         /* close listening socket */

20     alarm( 10 );
21     rc = readcrlf( s, line, sizeof( line ) );
22     alarm( 0 );
23     if ( rc <= 0 )
24     {
25         write( s, err1, sizeof( err1 ) - 1 );
26         EXIT( 1 );
27     }

28     for ( stp = service_table; stp->service; stp++ )
29         if ( strcasecmp( line, stp->service ) == 0 )
30             break;
31     if ( !stp->service )
32     {
33         write( s, err2, sizeof( err2 ) - 1 );
34         EXIT( 1 );
35     }

36     if ( stp->flag )
37         if ( write( s, ok, sizeof( ok ) - 1 ) < 0 )
38             EXIT( 1 );
39     dup2( s, 0 );
40     dup2( s, 1 );
41     dup2( s, 2 );
42     CLOSE( s );
43     execv( stp->path, stp->args );
44     write( 1, err3, sizeof( err3 ) - 1 );
45     EXIT( 1 );
46 }
```

*tcpmux.c*

**Figure 3.11** The `start_server` function

**start_server**

*10-17*    First we fork to create a child process that is identical to its parent. If the fork fails, we write an error message to the client and return (because the fork failed, there is no child process—we are returning to `main` in the parent process). If the fork succeeds and this is the parent process, we merely return.

*19-27*    In the child process, we close the listening socket and read the service that the client wants to start from the connected socket. We place an alarm around the read so that we terminate if the client never sends the service name. If `readcrlf` returns an error, we send an error message to the client and exit. The `readcrlf` function is shown later in Figure 3.13.

*28-35*    We search `service_table` for the name of the requested service. If we don't find it, we write an error message to the client and exit.

*36-38*    If the service name begins with a +, we send the client a positive acknowledgment. Otherwise, we let the server send it.

*39-45*    We `dup` the socket onto stdin, stdout, and stderr, and then close the original socket. Finally we call `execv` to replace our process image with the server's. After the `execv` call, the child process is the server that the client requested. If `execv` returns, we inform the client that we were unable to start the requested service and exit.

The `parsetab` routine is shown in Figure 3.12. It performs a simple but tedious parsing of the `tcpmux.conf` file. The format of the file is

```
service_name path arguments ...
```

```
                                                                          tcpmux.c
 1 static void parsetab( void )
 2 {
 3     FILE *fp;
 4     servtab_t *stp = service_table;
 5     char *cp;
 6     int i;
 7     int lineno;
 8     char line[ MAXLINE ];

 9     fp = fopen( CONFIG, "r" );
10     if ( fp == NULL )
11         error( 1, errno, "unable to open %s", CONFIG );
12     lineno = 0;
13     while ( fgets( line, sizeof( line ), fp ) != NULL )
14     {
15         lineno++;
16         if ( line[ strlen( line ) - 1 ] != '\n' )
17             error( 1, 0, "line %d is too long\n", lineno );
18         if ( stp >= service_table + NSERVTAB )
19             error( 1, 0, "too many entries in tcpmux.conf\n" );
20         cp = strchr( line, '#' );
21         if ( cp != NULL )
22             *cp = '\0';
23         cp = strtok( line, " \t\n" );
24         if ( cp == NULL )
25             continue;
```

```
26          if ( *cp == '+' )
27          {
28              stp->flag = TRUE;
29              cp++;
30              if ( *cp == '\0' || strchr( " \t\n", *cp ) != NULL )
31                  error( 1, 0, "line %d: white space after '+'\n",
32                      lineno );
33          }
34          stp->service = strdup( cp );
35          if ( stp->service == NULL )
36              error( 1, 0, "out of memory\n" );
37          cp = strtok( NULL, " \t\n" );
38          if ( cp == NULL )
39              error( 1, 0, "line %d: missing path name (%s)\n",
40                  lineno, stp->service );
41          stp->path = strdup( cp );
42          if ( stp->path == NULL )
43              error( 1, 0, "out of memory\n" );
44          for ( i = 0; i < MAXARGS; i++ )
45          {
46              cp = strtok( NULL, " \t\n" );
47              if ( cp == NULL )
48                  break;
49              stp->args[ i ] = strdup( cp );
50              if ( stp->args[ i ] == NULL )
51                  error( 1, 0, "out of memory\n" );
52          }
53          if ( i >= MAXARGS && strtok( NULL, " \t\n" ) != NULL )
54              error( 1, 0, "line %d: too many arguments (%s)\n",
55                  lineno, stp->service );
56          stp->args[ i ] = NULL;
57          stp++;
58      }
59      stp->service = NULL;
60      fclose ( fp );
61 }
```
———————————————————————————————————————————————————— *tcpmux.c*

**Figure 3.12** The `parsetab` function

The `readcrlf` function, shown in Figure 3.13, reads 1 byte at a time from its input. Although this is inefficient, it ensures that we read only the first line of data from the client. All data after the first line is destined for the server that we are starting, and if we did a buffered read and the client sent more than the first line, it is possible that some of the server's data would be read by `tcpmux` and lost.

Notice that `readcrlf` accepts a line that is terminated by a newline only. This is in accordance with the Robustness Principle [Postel 1981a], which states: "Be liberal in what you accept, and conservative in what you send." In either case, the <CR><LF> or <LF> is eliminated.

Our `readcrlf` function has the familiar definition shared by `read`, `readline`, `readn`, and `readvrec`:

```
#include "etcp.h"

int readcrlf( SOCKET s, char *buf, size_t len );

                              Returns: number of bytes read or -1 on error
```

*———————————————————————————————————— library/readcrlf.c*
```
 1 int readcrlf( SOCKET s, char *buf, size_t len )
 2 {
 3     char *bufx = buf;
 4     int rc;
 5     char c;
 6     char lastc = 0;

 7     while ( len > 0 )
 8     {
 9         if ( ( rc = recv( s, &c, 1, 0 ) ) != 1 )
10         {
11             /*
12              *  If we were interrupted, keep going,
13              *  otherwise, return EOF or the error.
14              */
15             if ( rc < 0 && errno == EINTR )
16                 continue;
17             return rc;
18         }
19         if ( c == '\n' )
20         {
21             if ( lastc == '\r' )
22                 buf--;
23             *buf = '\0';                /* don't include <CR><LF> */
24             return buf - bufx;
25         }
26         *buf++ = c;
27         lastc = c;
28         len--;
29     }
30     set_errno( EMSGSIZE );
31     return -1;
32 }
```
*———————————————————————————————————— library/readcrlf.c*

**Figure 3.13** The readcrlf function

Finally, we look at the reaper function (Figure 3.14). When a server that tcpmux has started terminates, UNIX sends a SIGCHLD signal to the parent (tcpmux). This causes reaper to be called, which in turn calls waitpid to retrieve the status of any children that have terminated. This is necessary in UNIX because a child process can return a status to its parent on termination (the argument to exit, for example).

Some UNIX systems can return other information as well. BSD-derived systems, for example, can return a summary of the resources used by the terminating process and its children. All UNIX systems return at least an indication of whether the process terminated because it called `exit` and what the exit status was if so, or whether the process was terminated by a signal and what signal it was if so.

Until the parent collects this status by calling `wait` or `waitpid`, UNIX must retain the portion of the child's resources that contains the termination status information. Children that have terminated but whose parents have not yet collected the status information are said to be *defunct* or *zombie processes*.

———————————————————————————————————— *tcpmux.c*

```
1 void reaper( int sig )
2 {
3     int waitstatus;

4     while ( waitpid( -1, &waitstatus, WNOHANG ) > 0 )
5                 {;}
6 }
```

———————————————————————————————————— *tcpmux.c*

**Figure 3.14** The `reaper` function

We can try out our `tcpmux` by creating a `tcpmux.conf` file with the line

```
+rlnum /usr/home/jcs/rlnumd rlnumd
```

in it. Then we start `tcpmux` on sparc, which doesn't support the `tcpmux` service, and telnet to it from bsd:

```
sparc: # tcpmux
bsd: $ telnet sparc tcpmux
Trying 10.9.200.201...
Connected to sparc.
Escape character is '^]'.
rlnum
+OK
hello
  1: hello
world
  2: world
^]
telnet> quit
Connection closed.
bsd: $
```

## Summary

The TCPMUX service, which is available on many systems, helps solve the problem of assigning a well-known port to a server. We implemented our own version of a `tcpmux` daemon, so that systems that don't have a native version can make use of its services.

## Tip 19: Consider Using Two TCP Connections

In many applications it is convenient to let different processes or threads handle the reading and writing of TCP connections. This is a particularly common practice in the UNIX community, where it is traditional to fork off a child process to handle the writing (say) of a TTY connection, while the parent process handles the reading.

The typical situation is shown in Figure 3.15, which depicts a terminal emulator. The parent process spends most of its time blocked on a read of the TTY connection. When data becomes available on the TTY connection, it reads the data and writes it to the screen, perhaps performing some reformatting. The child process spends most of its time blocked on a read of the keyboard. When data from the keyboard becomes available, the child process does whatever key mapping is appropriate and writes the data to the TTY connection.

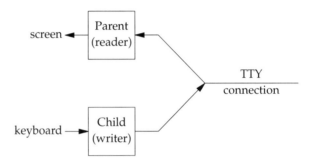

**Figure 3.15** Two processes servicing a TTY connection

This is an attractive strategy because it automatically handles the multiplexing of the keyboard and TTY input, and because it separates the keyboard mapping and screen reformatting logic into different modules, providing a conceptually simpler program than one that has the code intermixed. Indeed, before the introduction of the `select` mechanism, this technique was the only practical means of handling multiple inputs.

### A One-Connection Architecture

Notice that nothing changes if we replace "TTY connection" with "TCP connection" in Figure 3.15. Thus the same technique can be, and often is, used for handling network connections as well. Also notice that using two threads instead of two processes does not really change the situation shown in the figure either, so the same method can be used in threaded environments too.

There is one complication however. With a TTY connection, any errors that occur on the write operation are returned from the `write` call itself, whereas with TCP, errors are most likely to be returned with the read operation as we discussed in Tip 15. In the multiprocess case, it is difficult for the reading process to notify the writing process of the error. In particular, if the peer application terminates, only the reader process is notified, and it must in turn inform the writer process.

Let's change our point of view a little and imagine that we have an application that accepts messages from and sends messages to an external system over a TCP connection. Messages are sent and received asynchronously—that is, not all inbound messages generate a response, and not all outbound messages are in response to an inbound message. If we further assume that messages have to be reformatted when entering or leaving the application, it makes sense to use a multiprocess application such as that shown in Figure 3.16.

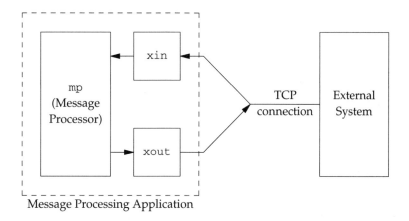

Message Processing Application

**Figure 3.16** Messaging application with one TCP connection

In the figure, the `xin` process reads data from the external system, accumulates it into messages, reformats as necessary, and passes the reformatted message on to the main message-handling process. Similarly, the `xout` process reformats outbound messages to the format required by the external system and writes the data to the TCP connection. The main process, `mp`, processes the reformatted inbound messages and generates the outbound messages. We leave the IPC mechanism among the three processes composing the application unspecified, but it could be pipes, shared memory, message queues, or any of several other types. See [Stevens 1999] for a thorough treatment of the possibilities. A real-world example of this sort of application might be a gateway that transfers messages between a system that communicates via TCP and a system using some other protocol.

If we extend this example to include other external systems with different message-formatting requirements, we see how powerful this method can be. Each external host has its own set of communication processes to handle its messages, which makes the system conceptually simpler, allows changes to be made for one external host without affecting the others, and allows the system to be easily configured for a given set of external hosts merely by starting the required communication processes for each host.

We do, however, have the problem to which we alluded earlier: The writer process has no way of receiving error messages from its writes. Furthermore, it may be that the application must be certain that the external system actually received the message, and must therefore implement some sort of positive acknowledgment, as discussed in Tip 9. This means that either a separate communication channel must be established between `xin` and `xout` or that `xin` must send error indications and ACKs to `mp`, which must in turn send them to `xout`. Both of these options complicate all of the processes involved in the exchange.

We could, of course, abandon the multiprocess architecture and fold everything into a single process, perhaps using `select` to handle the multiplexing. This means, however, that we must sacrifice the flexibility and conceptual simplicity that we discussed previously.

In the rest of this tip we look at an alternative architecture that maintains the flexibility of Figure 3.16, but allows each communication process to handle its TCP connection completely.

### A Two-Connection Architecture

Although `xin` and `xout` share the TCP connection with the external system in Figure 3.16, it is difficult for them to share information about the status of the connection with each other. Furthermore, `xin` and `xout` treat the connection as if it were simplex—that is, as if data were flowing in only one direction. They must do this so that `xout` doesn't "steal" input from `xin` and so that `xin` doesn't corrupt the data that `xout` sends. These facts lead to the problems that we discussed earlier.

The solution to these problems is to maintain two connections with the external system, one each for `xin` and `xout`. With this change, our system architecture becomes that depicted in Figure 3.17.

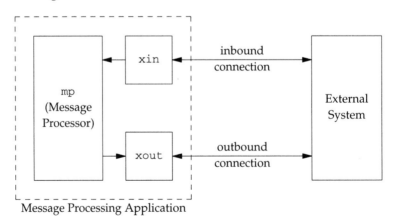

Message Processing Application

**Figure 3.17**  Messaging application with two TCP connections

If our system does not require application-level ACKs, this architecture's main benefit is to `xout`, which now has a direct way of learning about errors and EOFs from its peer. On the other hand, `xout` must now be a little more complicated because it must have a read pending to collect these events. Fortunately, this is easily done using the `select` system call.

To try this out, we write a simple `xout` process that reads data from stdin and writes it to a TCP connection. Our program, shown in Figure 3.18, uses `select` to keep a read pending on the connection, even though the only input it expects is an EOF or error indication.

```
                                                                       ─ xout1.c
 1 #include "etcp.h"

 2 int main( int argc, char **argv )
 3 {
 4      fd_set allreads;
 5      fd_set readmask;
 6      SOCKET s;
 7      int rc;
 8      char buf[ 128 ];

 9      INIT();
10      s = tcp_client( argv[ 1 ], argv[ 2 ] );
11      FD_ZERO( &allreads );
12      FD_SET( s, &allreads );
13      FD_SET( 0, &allreads );
14      for ( ;; )
15      {
16          readmask = allreads;
17          rc = select( s + 1, &readmask, NULL, NULL, NULL );
18          if ( rc <= 0 )
19              error( 1, rc ? errno : 0, "select returned %d", rc );

20          if ( FD_ISSET( 0, &readmask ) )
21          {
22              rc = read( 0, buf, sizeof( buf ) - 1 );
23              if ( rc < 0 )
24                  error( 1, errno, "read failure" );
25              if ( send( s, buf, rc, 0 ) < 0 )
26                  error( 1, errno, "send failure" );
27          }

28          if ( FD_ISSET( s, &readmask ) )
29          {
30              rc = recv( s, buf, sizeof( buf ) - 1, 0 );
31              if ( rc == 0 )
32                  error( 1, 0, "server disconnected\n" );
33              else if ( rc < 0 )
34                  error( 1, errno, "recv failure" );
35              else
36              {
37                  buf[ rc ] = '\0';
38                  error( 1, 0, "unexpected input [%s]\n", buf );
39              }
40          }
41      }
42 }
                                                                       ─ xout1.c
```

**Figure 3.18** A "writer" that reads only for errors and EOF

### Initialization

*9–13*    We perform our usual initialization, call `tcp_client` to establish a connection, and set up to select on either stdin or the TCP connection we just established.

### Handle Stdin Events

*20–27*    If we get input on stdin, we send it to our peer over the TCP connection.

### Handle Socket Events

*28–40*    If we get a read event on the socket, we check for an EOF or error. We shouldn't get any data from the connection, so we output a diagnostic and terminate if we do.

We can demonstrate xout1 by using our `keep` program from Figure 2.53 as the external system, and a simple shell script as the message processor (mp in Figure 3.17). The shell script simply echos the word "message" and a count to stdout every second:

```
MSGNO=1
while true
do
    echo message $MSGNO
    sleep 1
    MSGNO=`expr $MSGNO + 1`
done
```

Notice that in this case xout1 is using a pipe as the IPC mechanism. This means that as it stands, xout1 is not portable to the Windows environment because the `select` call works only for sockets under Windows. We could have used TCP or UDP for the IPC, but this would have required a more elaborate program for our message processor.

To try out xout1, we first start our external system, keep, in one window, and our message processor and xout1 in another:

```
bsd: $ keep 9000                        bsd: $ mp | xout1 localhost 9000
message 1
message 2
message 3
message 4
^C        "External System" terminated   xout1: server disconnected
bsd: $                                   Broken pipe
                                         bsd: $
```

The "Broken pipe" message is from the mp script. When xout1 terminates, the pipeline between it and the script is closed. When the script tries to write its next line, the write fails and the script terminates with the Broken pipe error.

A more interesting situation occurs if ACKs are required between the external system and the message-processing application. In this case, both xin and xout need to be changed (assuming we want ACKs in both directions—if we are only concerned about messages *to* the external system, we need not bother changing xin). We develop an example writer (xout) process. The reader process is similar.

Our new writer process must solve the same types of problems as our heartbeat functions from Tip 10. After we send a message, we must receive an ACK from our peer before a timer expires. If the timer fires, we must initiate some sort of error recovery. In our example, we merely terminate.

Our strategy for the new writer, xout2, is not to accept any additional messages from stdin until the last message that we sent over the TCP connection is acknowledged by the external system. A more sophisticated approach using the general timing mechanism described in Tip 20 is also possible, and we examine such an implementation later, but for many applications the simple approach that we take here is adequate. We show xout2 in Figure 3.19.

─────────────────────────────────────────────────────── *xout2.c*

```
 1 #include "etcp.h"

 2 #define ACK     0x6      /* an ACK character */

 3 int main( int argc, char **argv )
 4 {
 5     fd_set allreads;
 6     fd_set readmask;
 7     fd_set sockonly;
 8     struct timeval tv;
 9     struct timeval *tvp = NULL;
10     SOCKET s;
11     int rc;
12     char buf[ 128 ];
13     const static struct timeval T0 = { 2, 0 };

14     INIT();
15     s = tcp_client( argv[ 1 ], argv[ 2 ] );
16     FD_ZERO( &allreads );
17     FD_SET( s, &allreads );
18     sockonly = allreads;
19     FD_SET( 0, &allreads );
20     readmask = allreads;
21     for ( ;; )
22     {
23         rc = select( s + 1, &readmask, NULL, NULL, tvp );
24         if ( rc < 0 )
25             error( 1, errno, "select failure" );
26         if ( rc == 0 )
27             error( 1, 0, "message timed out\n" );

28         if ( FD_ISSET( s, &readmask ) )
29         {
30             rc = recv( s, buf, sizeof( buf ), 0 );
31             if ( rc == 0 )
32                 error( 1, 0, "server disconnected\n" );
33             else if ( rc < 0 )
34                 error( 1, errno, "recv failure" );
35             else if ( rc != 1 || buf[ 0 ] != ACK )
36                 error( 1, 0, "unexpected input [%c]\n", buf[ 0 ] );
37             tvp = NULL;                /* turn timer off */
38             readmask = allreads;    /* and stdin on */
39         }
```

```
40              if ( FD_ISSET( 0, &readmask ) )
41              {
42                  rc = read( 0, buf, sizeof( buf ) );
43                  if ( rc < 0 )
44                      error( 1, errno, "read failure" );
45                  if ( send( s, buf, rc, 0 ) < 0 )
46                      error( 1, errno, "send failure" );
47                  tv = T0;                    /* reset timer */
48                  tvp = &tv;                  /* turn timer on */
49                  readmask = sockonly;    /* and stdin off */
50              }
51          }
52  }
```
──────────────────────────────────────────────────────── *xout2.c*

**Figure 3.19**  A "writer" that processes ACKs

### Initialization

*14–15*    This is our standard initialization for a TCP client.

*16–20*    We set up two `select` masks—one that accepts events from stdin and the TCP socket, and one that accepts only events from the socket. We use the second mask, `sockonly`, after we send data to the TCP connection so that we do not read any additional data from stdin until we receive the acknowledgment from the external system.

### Handle Timer Events

*26–27*    If the `select` call times out, we did not get the acknowledgment in time, so we output a diagnostic and terminate.

### Handle Socket Events

*28–39*    When we receive a read event from the socket, we check to see whether it is an error or an EOF and terminate if so, just as in Figure 3.18. If we received data, we check to make sure that it's a single character, and that the character is an ACK. If we pass this test, the last message is being acknowledged, so we turn off the timer by setting `tvp` to `NULL`, and we allow input from stdin again by setting `readmask` to check for both stdin and the socket.

### Handle Stdin Events

*40–46*    When we get a stdin event, we check for an error or EOF as usual. If the `read` was successful, we write the data to the TCP connection.

*47–50*    Because we have just written data to the external host, we are expecting an ACK back. We set and start our timer by setting `tv` and pointing `tvp` at it. Finally, we inhibit stdin events by setting `readmask` to `sockonly` so that `select` recognizes events from the TCP connection only.

We can try out `xout2` by adding the two lines

```
if ( send( s1, "\006", 1, 0 ) < 0 )          /* \006 == ACK */
    error( 1, errno, "send failure" );
```

just before the write on line 24 of `keep.c` (Figure 2.53). If we test this as we did `xout1`, we get the same results except that `xout2` terminates if it doesn't receive an ACK from its peer.

We revisit this example one more time in Tip 21, where we use a general timing mechanism that allows us to process stdin requests at any time rather than inhibiting them while we are waiting for an ACK from our peer.

## Summary

In this tip we explored the idea of using two connections between peer applications. We saw that this allows us to monitor the status of a connection even if the reading and writing of the connection is performed in different processes.

## Tip 20: Consider Making Your Applications Event Driven (1)

In this tip and the next, we examine the idea of using event-driven techniques for our TCP/IP programming. As part of this examination, we develop a general-purpose timing mechanism that allows us to specify that an event should take place after a certain interval, and have that event take place asynchronously at the appointed time. We study the implementation of our timer mechanism in this tip, and then apply it in Tip 21, where we revisit our two-connection architecture from Tip 19.

The difference between an event-driven application and one that is not is nicely illustrated by our two applications `hb_client2` (Figure 2.49, Figure 2.50) and `tcprw` (Figure 2.42). In `tcprw`, the flow of control is sequential: First a line is read from stdin and is sent to our peer, and then a reply is received from our peer and is written to stdout. Notice that we are unable to receive from our peer while we are waiting for input from stdin. As we have seen, this means that we may miss the fact that our peer has terminated and sent us an EOF. Similarly, while we are waiting for a response from our peer, we are unable to read any additional data from stdin. This means that the application can be unresponsive from the user's point of view, and again, that we can hang if our peer's host crashes before our peer application can respond.

Contrast this with `hb_client2`, in which at any time we can receive data on either connection, or have a timeout. None of these "events" has to wait for any of the others—that's why we describe it as *event driven*.

Notice that it would be easy to extend `hb_client2` to deal with more connections or inputs. It is the `select` mechanism that makes this possible. It allows us to block on several events at once and to return when *any* of them are ready. Under UNIX, this mechanism, or its SysV sibling `poll`, is the only effective way of doing this in a non-threaded environment.

> Until recently, the conventional wisdom was that portability concerns dictated that we prefer `select` to `poll` because Winsock and virtually all modern UNIX systems support `select`, whereas `poll` is most often found in SysV implementations. However, some large server applications (such as Web servers) that support many simultaneous connections are using the `poll` mechanism because it scales better to a large numbers of descriptors. This is because `select` is limited to a fixed number of descriptors. This limit is often 1,024, but can be smaller. On the FreeBSD-based bsd, for example, it is 256 by default. Changing the default

requires rebuilding the kernel, which is inconvenient but usually possible. But even rebuilding the kernel merely increases the limit, it does not eliminate it. The `poll` mechanism, on the other hand, has no fixed limit on the number of descriptors that it can handle.

Another consideration is efficiency. The typical implementation of `select` can be very inefficient when there is a large number of descriptors. See [Banga and Mogul 1998] for more on this. (This paper also offers another example of the dangers of extrapolating the results of tests done on a LAN to the expected performance on a WAN, as we discussed in Tip 12.) This performance problem can be particularly acute when we are waiting for only a few events on a large number of descriptors—that is, when the first argument, *maxfd*, is large, but only a few descriptors were registered with `FD_SET`. This is because the kernel must check *each* possible descriptor $(0 \cdots maxfd)$ to see whether the application wants to wait on an event for it. The `poll` call uses an array of descriptors to tell the kernel which events the application is interested in, so this problem does not occur.

Although the use of `select` or `poll` allows us to multiplex several I/O events easily, it is more difficult to handle multiple timers because the calls provide only a single timeout value. To solve this problem, and thereby provide a more flexible environment for event-driven programs, we develop a variation of the `select` routine called `tselect`. Although the `timeout` and `untimeout` calls associated with `tselect` are modeled after the UNIX kernel timer routines of the same name, they are implemented in user space and depend on `select` to provide the I/O multiplexing and the timer.

As we indicated earlier, there are three calls associated with the `tselect` function. First, there is `tselect` itself, which is used just like `select` to multiplex I/O events. The only difference is that `tselect` has no *timeout* parameter (the fifth parameter to `select`). Rather, all timer events are specified with the `timeout` call, by which the user specifies how long the timer should run and what action should be taken when it expires. The `untimeout` call is used to cancel a timer before it expires.

We summarize the three calls here:

```
#include "etcp.h"

int tselect( int maxfd, fd_set *rdmask, fd_set *wrmask,
             fd_set *exmask );

                  Returns: number of ready events, 0 if no remaining events, -1 on error

unsigned int timeout( void ( *handler )( void * ), void *arg, int ms );

                          Returns: timer ID to be used in the untimeout call

void untimeout( unsigned int timerid );
```

When a timer associated with a `timeout` call expires, the function specified by the *handler* parameter is called with the argument specified in the *arg* parameter. Thus, to arrange for the function `retransmit` to be called in 1.5 seconds with the integer argument *sock*, we would first make the call

```
timeout( retransmit, ( void * )sock, 1500 );
```

followed later by a call to `tselect`. The expiration time, *ms*, is specified in milliseconds, but we must realize that the granularity of the system clock is apt to be coarser than this. A typical value for a UNIX system is 10 ms, so we wouldn't expect our timer to be more accurate than that.

We look at some examples using `tselect` later, but first let's examine its implementation. The definition of the `tevent_t` structure and the global declarations are given in Figure 3.20.

```
                                                              lib/tselect.c
 1 #include "etcp.h"

 2 #define NTIMERS 25

 3 typedef struct tevent_t tevent_t;
 4 struct tevent_t
 5 {
 6     tevent_t *next;
 7     struct timeval tv;
 8     void ( *func )( void * );
 9     void *arg;
10     unsigned int id;
11 };

12 static tevent_t *active = NULL;      /* active timers */
13 static tevent_t *free_list = NULL;   /* inactive timers */
                                                              lib/tselect.c
```

**Figure 3.20** Global data for `tselect`

### Declarations

2    The `NTIMERS` define specifies how many timers we should allocate at a time. Initially, there are no timers, so the first call to `timeout` causes `NTIMERS` timers to be allocated. If these timers are all in use and another call to `timeout` is made, an additional `NTIMERS` is allocated.

3-11    Each active timer is represented by an instance of the `tevent_t` structure. These structures are linked together with the `next` field. We use the `tv` field to hold the time that the timer expires. The `func` and `arg` fields are used for the timer handler function that gets called when the timer expires. Finally, we put the ID of each active timer in the `id` field.

12    The active timers are linked together in order of expiration time on the active timer list. The (module) global variable `active` points to the first timer on the list.

13    Timers that are not currently active are linked together on a free list. When the `timeout` routine needs a new timer, it pops one off the free list. The `free_list` (module) global points to the top of the free list.

Next, we look at the `timeout` and timer allocation routines (Figure 3.21).

### allocate_timer

4-13    The `allocate_timer` routine is called by `timeout` to allocate a free timer. If the free list is empty, we allocate enough memory for `NTIMERS` `tevent_t` structures from the heap and link them together.

*———————————————————————————————— lib/tselect.c*

```
 1 static tevent_t *allocate_timer( void )
 2 {
 3     tevent_t *tp;
 4     if ( free_list == NULL )     /* need new block of timers? */
 5     {
 6         free_list = malloc( NTIMERS * sizeof( tevent_t ) );
 7         if ( free_list == NULL )
 8             error( 1, 0, "couldn't allocate timers\n" );
 9         for ( tp = free_list;
10               tp < free_list + NTIMERS - 1; tp++ )
11             tp->next = tp + 1;
12         tp->next = NULL;
13     }
14     tp = free_list;              /* allocate first free */
15     free_list = tp->next;        /* and pop it off list */
16     return tp;
17 }
18 unsigned int timeout( void ( *func )( void * ), void *arg, int ms )
19 {
20     tevent_t *tp;
21     tevent_t *tcur;
22     tevent_t **tprev;
23     static unsigned int id = 1;          /* timer ID */
24     tp = allocate_timer();
25     tp->func = func;
26     tp->arg = arg;
27     if ( gettimeofday( &tp->tv, NULL ) < 0 )
28         error( 1, errno, "timeout: gettimeofday failure" );
29     tp->tv.tv_usec += ms * 1000;
30     if ( tp->tv.tv_usec > 1000000 )
31     {
32         tp->tv.tv_sec += tp->tv.tv_usec / 1000000;
33         tp->tv.tv_usec %= 1000000;
34     }
35     for ( tprev = &active, tcur = active;
36           tcur && !timercmp( &tp->tv, &tcur->tv, < ); /* XXX */
37           tprev = &tcur->next, tcur = tcur->next )
38     { ; }
39     *tprev = tp;
40     tp->next = tcur;
41     tp->id = id++;                        /* set ID for this timer */
42     return tp->id;
43 }
```

*———————————————————————————————— lib/tselect.c*

**Figure 3.21** The `timeout` and `allocate_timer` routines

*14–16*     We pop the first timer off the free list and return it to the caller.

**timeout**

*24–26*     We allocate a timer and fill in the `func` and `arg` fields from the parameters passed to us.

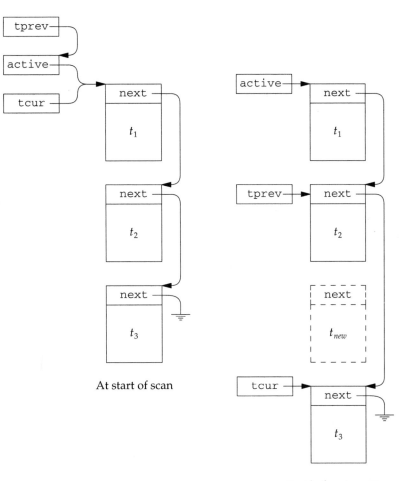

At start of scan

Just before insertion

**Figure 3.22** Active timer list before and after scanning for the insertion point

27–34      We calculate the time for the timer to expire by adding the *ms* parameter to the current time. We store the result in the `tv` field.

35–38      We search down the list of active timers until we find the proper place for this timer. The "proper place" is the position where the expiration time of all the timers before it is less than or equal to its expiration time, and all the timers after it have a greater expiration time. Figure 3.22 illustrates this and shows the use of the `tcur` and `tprev` variables during the scan. In Figure 3.22, we are inserting into the list a new timer that expires at $t_{new}$ with $t_0 \leq t_1 \leq t_{new} < t_2$. The dashed box labeled $t_{new}$ shows the position in the list where the new timer will be inserted. The somewhat convoluted use of the `timercmp` macro in line 36 is because the version defined in `winsock2.h` is broken and does not support the '>=' operator.

*39–42*    We insert the new timer in its proper place, assign it a timer ID, and return that ID to the caller. We return an ID rather than, say, the address of the `tevent_t` structure to avoid race conditions. When a timer expires, the `tevent_t` structure is returned to the head of the free list. If a new timer is allocated, it uses this structure. If the application now tries to cancel the first timer and we used the address of the structure, the second timer would be canceled instead. By using the ID, we avoid this problem.

The timer ID that we returned at the end of Figure 3.21 is used by the `untimeout` function shown in Figure 3.23

————————————————————————————————————— *lib/tselect.c*

```
 1 void untimeout( unsigned int id )
 2 {
 3      tevent_t **tprev;
 4      tevent_t *tcur;
 5
 6      for ( tprev = &active, tcur = active;
 7            tcur && id != tcur->id;
 8            tprev = &tcur->next, tcur = tcur->next )
 9      { ; }
10      if ( tcur == NULL )
11      {
12          error( 0, 0,
13              "untimeout called for non-existent timer (%d)\n", id );
14          return;
15      }
16      *tprev = tcur->next;
17      tcur->next = free_list;
18      free_list = tcur;
18 }
```

————————————————————————————————————— *lib/tselect.c*

**Figure 3.23** The `untimeout` function

### Find Timer

*5–8*    We scan the active timer list looking for a timer with an ID that matches `id`. This loop is similar to the one in `timeout` (Figure 3.21).

*9–14*    If the timer that we are trying to cancel is not there, we output a diagnostic and return.

### Cancel Timer

*15–17*    We cancel the timer by unlinking the `tevent_t` structure from the active list and returning it to the free list.

The final function in our set of timer routines is `tselect` itself (Figure 3.24).

————————————————————————————————————— *lib/tselect.c*

```
 1 int tselect( int maxp1, fd_set *re, fd_set *we, fd_set *ee )
 2 {
 3      fd_set rmask;
 4      fd_set wmask;
 5      fd_set emask;
```

```
 6        struct timeval now;
 7        struct timeval tv;
 8        struct timeval *tvp;
 9        tevent_t *tp;
10        int n;
11    if ( re )
12        rmask = *re;
13    if ( we )
14        wmask = *we;
15    if ( ee )
16        emask = *ee;
17    for ( ;; )
18    {
19        if ( gettimeofday( &now, NULL ) < 0 )
20            error( 1, errno, "tselect: gettimeofday failure" );
21        while ( active && !timercmp( &now, &active->tv, < ) )
22        {
23            active->func( active->arg );
24            tp = active;
25            active = active->next;
26            tp->next = free_list;
27            free_list = tp;
28        }
29        if ( active )
30        {
31            tv.tv_sec = active->tv.tv_sec - now.tv_sec;;
32            tv.tv_usec = active->tv.tv_usec - now.tv_usec;
33            if ( tv.tv_usec < 0 )
34            {
35                tv.tv_usec += 1000000;
36                tv.tv_sec--;
37            }
38            tvp = &tv;
39        }
40        else if ( re == NULL && we == NULL && ee == NULL )
41            return 0;
42        else
43            tvp = NULL;
44        n = select( maxp1, re, we, ee, tvp );
45        if ( n < 0 )
46            return -1;
47        if ( n > 0 )
48            return n;
49        if ( re )
50            *re = rmask;
51        if ( we )
52            *we = wmask;
53        if ( ee )
54            *ee = emask;
55    }
56 }
```

*— lib/tselect.c*

**Figure 3.24** The `tselect` function

### Save Event Masks

*11-16*    Because a single call to `tselect` may generate several calls to `select`, we save the event masks that we pass to `select`.

### Dispatch Timer Events

*19-28*    Although the first `tevent_t` structure on the active list has an expiration time that is less than or equal to the current time, we call the handler for that timer, pop the structure off the active list, and return it to the free list. As in Figure 3.21, the peculiar invocation of `timercmp` is required by the broken version of `timercmp` found on some systems.

### Calculate Time of Next Event

*29-39*    If there are still timers on the active list, we calculate the delta between the current time and the expiration of the timer. This value is passed to `select`.

*40-41*    If there are no additional timers *and* there are no I/O events to be waited for, `tselect` returns. Notice that we return 0, indicating that there are no events pending. This meaning differs from a zero return from `select`.

*42-43*    If there are no more timer events, but there are I/O events, we set `tvp` to NULL to tell `select` that it shouldn't time out.

### Call `select`

*44-48*    We call `select` to wait on an event. If `select` returns an error, we return it to the application. If `select` returns a positive value, indicating that one or more I/O events are ready, we return the number of events to the application. Because we called `select` with pointers to the application's event masks, they will already be set.

*49-54*    If `select` returned 0, then one or more timer events are ready. Because `select` will have zeroed the events in the application's event masks, we restore them before continuing at the top of the for loop, where we dispatch the timers.

We used a straightforward linear search for the insertion and deletion of timers. Although this is fine for a small or moderate number of timers, it does not scale well to a large number of timers because insertion and deletion are $O(n)$ ($n$ timers) operations (dispatching of timer events is an $O(1)$ operation). Other possible implementations are heaps [Sedgewick 1998], which are $O(\log n)$ for insertion, deletion, and dispatch, or hashed timing wheels [Varghese and Lauck 1997], which can be as efficient as $O(1)$ for all three operations.

Notice that there is nothing in `tselect` that requires that we have a pending I/O event, so it is possible to use it strictly as a timing mechanism. This has two advantages over using `sleep`:

1. Under UNIX, the `sleep` mechanism is fairly coarse grained. The sleep interval must be an integral number of seconds. The Windows version of sleep does not have this restriction, and many UNIX implementations have other timer mechanisms that are finer grained, but these are not universally available. We would like to have a fine-grained timer mechanism that works across a large number of

platforms. For this reason, it is common in UNIX to use the `select` call as a fine-grained timer.

2. Using `sleep` or a plain `select` for multiple timers is difficult to manage because of the bookkeeping required. The advantage of `tselect` is that it does this bookkeeping for us.

Unfortunately, using `tselect` as a timer does not work as well under Windows. The Winsock API specification [WinSock Group 1997], refers to using `select` for a timer as "inexcusably lame." One might wonder where the lameness lies when a system call does not perform according to its published specification, but we should nevertheless adhere to this recommendation. We can still use the `tselect` routines under Windows, we just shouldn't use them without an I/O event specified.

## Summary

In this tip we discussed the advantages of making our applications event driven. We also developed a generalized timer facility that provides an unlimited number of timers.

## Tip 21: Consider Making Your Applications Event Driven (2)

This tip continues the discussion from Tip 20. We shall demonstrate our `tselect` routines in an application, and examine some additional aspects of event-driven programming. For our demonstration, we revisit the two-connection architecture from Tip 19.

If we look again at `xout2` (Figure 3.19), we see that it is not event driven. Once we have written a message to our peer, we accept no additional input from stdin until we have received the ACK for that message. The reason for this is to prevent a new message from resetting the timer. If we were to restart the timer for a subsequent message before the first message was acknowledged, we would have no way of knowing if the first message did not get ACKed.

The problem, of course, is that `xout2` has only one timer and therefore cannot time more than a single message at once. By using `tselect`, we are able to multiplex several timers onto the single timer provided by `select`.

To set a context for what is to follow, let us imagine that the external system from Tip 19 is some sort of gateway that forwards our messages to a third system using an unreliable protocol. It might, for example, send datagrams into a radio-based network. Let's further assume that the gateway itself provides no indication of whether the message was delivered successfully. It merely forwards the message and returns to us any ACK that it receives from the third system.

To provide a modicum of reliability, our new writer module, `xout3`, resends a message one time if it doesn't receive an ACK within a given time interval. If the message is still not acknowledged after the retry, `xout3` logs that fact and drops the message. To associate ACKs with the message it is ACKing, `xout3` includes a cookie with each message. The final recipient of the message returns the cookie with its ACK. We begin by looking at the declaration section of xout3 in Figure 3.25.

*xout3.c*

```
 1 #define ACK          0x6     /* an ACK character */
 2 #define MRSZ         128     /* max unacknowledged messages */
 3 #define T1           3000    /* wait 3 secs for first ACK */
 4 #define T2           5000    /* and 5 seconds for second ACK */
 5 #define ACKSZ        ( sizeof( u_int32_t ) + 1 )

 6 typedef struct              /* data packet */
 7 {
 8     u_int32_t len;          /* length of cookie and data */
 9     u_int32_t cookie;       /* message ID */
10     char buf[ 128 ];        /* message */
11 } packet_t;

12 typedef struct              /* message record */
13 {
14     packet_t pkt;           /* pointer to saved msg */
15     int id;                 /* timer id */
16 } msgrec_t;

17 static msgrec_t mr[ MRSZ ];
18 static SOCKET s;
```

*xout3.c*

**Figure 3.25** xout3 declarations

**Declarations**

5       The cookie that we attach to each message is actually a 32-bit message number. An ACK from our peer is defined to be an ASCII ACK character followed by the cookie of the message that is being ACKed. Therefore, we define ACKSZ as the size of the cookie plus one.

6-11    The packet_t structure defines the packet that we send to our peer. Because our messages can be of varying length, we include the length of each message in the packet. Our peer can use this field to break the data stream into records, as we discussed in Tip 6. The len field is the size of the message itself and the attached cookie. See the discussion following Figure 2.31 for some cautionary words concerning the packing of members in a structure.

12-16   The msgrec_t structure contains the packet_t structure that we send to our peer. We keep the packet in the msgrec_t structure in case we need to resend it. The id field is the ID of the timer that is serving as the RTO timer for the message.

17      Each unacknowledged message has an associated msgrec_t structure. These structures are kept in the mr array.

Next we look at the main function of xout3 (Figure 3.26).

**Initialization**

11-15   Just as with xout2 we connect to our peer and initialize our tselect event masks for stdin and the socket returned by tcp_client.

*16–17*    We mark each `msgrec_t` entry available by setting the packet length to -1.

*18–25*    We call `tselect` exactly as we would `select` except that there is no timer parameter. If `tselect` returns an error or 0, we output a diagnostic and terminate. Unlike `select`, a zero return from `tselect` is unexpected because timeout events are handled internally.

### Handle Socket Input

*26–32*    When we get a read event for the socket, we are expecting an ACK. As we discussed in Tip 6, we can't just call `recv` asking for ACKSZ bytes, because that much data may not yet be available. Nor can we call a function such as `readn` that doesn't return until the specified number of bytes are received because that would destroy the event-driven nature of our application—no other event could be processed until the `readn` returned. Therefore, we post a read for as much data as needed to complete the ACK that we are currently reading. The variable `cnt` contains that number of bytes that we have already read, so `ACKSZ - cnt` is the amount of data needed to complete the ACK.

*33–35*    If the total data we have read is less than ACKSZ, we loop back to `tselect` to wait for more data or some other event. If the current `recv` has finished reading a complete ACK, we reset `cnt` to zero for the next ACK (no bytes of the next ACK have been read yet).

*36–40*    Next, in accordance with Tip 11, we perform a sanity check on our data. If the message is not a valid ACK, we output a diagnostic and continue. It might be wiser to terminate here because this error indicates that our peer is sending us unexpected data.

*41–42*    Finally, we copy the cookie out of the ACK, call `findmsgrec` to get the pointer to the `msgrec_t` structure associated with this message, and use it to cancel the timer and free the `msgrec_t` structure. The `findmsgrec` and `freemsgrec` functions are shown in Figure 3.27.

### Handle Stdin Input

*51–57*    When `tselect` returns a read event on stdin, we allocate a `msgrec_t` entry and read the message into our data packet. We assign the message ID from our consecutive message counter, `msgid`, and store it in the `cookie` field of the packet. Note that we don't have to call `htonl` because our peer does not examine the cookie, but merely returns it to us unaltered. Finally, we set the total length of the message and cookie into the message packet. This time, we do call `htonl` because our peer uses this field to read the rest of the message (see Tip 28).

*58–61*    We send the completed packet to our peer, and start the RTO timer with a call to `timeout`.

```
                                                              ──── xout3.c
1 int main( int argc, char **argv )
2 {
3     fd_set allreads;
4     fd_set readmask;
5     msgrec_t *mp;
6     int rc;
7     int mid;
8     int cnt = 0;
```

```
 9      u_int32_t msgid = 0;
10      char ack[ ACKSZ ];

11      INIT();
12      s = tcp_client( argv[ 1 ], argv[ 2 ] );
13      FD_ZERO( &allreads );
14      FD_SET( s, &allreads );
15      FD_SET( 0, &allreads );
16      for ( mp = mr; mp < mr + MRSZ; mp++ )
17          mp->pkt.len = -1;
18      for ( ;; )
19      {
20          readmask = allreads;
21          rc = tselect( s + 1, &readmask, NULL, NULL );
22          if ( rc < 0 )
23              error( 1, errno, "tselect failure" );
24          if ( rc == 0 )
25              error( 1, 0, "tselect returned with no events\n" );

26          if ( FD_ISSET( s, &readmask ) )
27          {
28              rc = recv( s, ack + cnt, ACKSZ - cnt, 0 );
29              if ( rc == 0 )
30                  error( 1, 0, "server disconnected\n" );
31              else if ( rc < 0 )
32                  error( 1, errno, "recv failure" );
33              if ( ( cnt += rc ) < ACKSZ )/* have whole msg? */
34                  continue;                /* no, wait for more */
35              cnt = 0;                     /* new msg next time */
36              if ( ack[ 0 ] != ACK )
37              {
38                  error( 0, 0, "warning: illegal ACK msg\n" );
39                  continue;
40              }
41              memcpy( &mid, ack + 1, sizeof( u_int32_t ) );
42              mp = findmsgrec( mid );
43              if ( mp != NULL )
44              {
45                  untimeout( mp->id );     /* cancel timer */
46                  freemsgrec( mp );        /* delete saved msg */
47              }
48          }

49          if ( FD_ISSET( 0, &readmask ) )
50          {
51              mp = getfreerec();
52              rc = read( 0, mp->pkt.buf, sizeof( mp->pkt.buf ) );
53              if ( rc < 0 )
54                  error( 1, errno, "read failure" );
55              mp->pkt.buf[ rc ] = '\0';
56              mp->pkt.cookie = msgid++;
57              mp->pkt.len = htonl( sizeof( u_int32_t ) + rc );
58              if ( send( s, &mp->pkt,
59                  2 * sizeof( u_int32_t ) + rc, 0 ) < 0 )
60                  error( 1, errno, "send failure" );
```

```
61                         mp->id = timeout( ( tofunc_t )lost_ACK, mp, T1 );
62               }
63          }
64 }
```
*———————————————————————————————————————— xout3.c*

**Figure 3.26** xout3 main function

The rest of xout3 is shown in Figure 3.27.

*———————————————————————————————————————— xout3.c*
```
 1 msgrec_t *getfreerec( void )
 2 {
 3     msgrec_t *mp;

 4     for ( mp = mr; mp < mr + MRSZ; mp++ )
 5         if ( mp->pkt.len == -1 )    /* record free? */
 6             return mp;
 7     error( 1, 0, "getfreerec: out of message records\n" );
 8     return NULL;         /* quiet compiler warnings */
 9 }
10 msgrec_t *findmsgrec( u_int32_t mid )
11 {
12     msgrec_t *mp;

13     for ( mp = mr; mp < mr + MRSZ; mp++ )
14         if ( mp->pkt.len != -1 && mp->pkt.cookie == mid )
15             return mp;
16     error( 0, 0, "findmsgrec: no message for ACK %d\n", mid );
17     return NULL;
18 }
19 void freemsgrec( msgrec_t *mp )
20 {
21     if ( mp->pkt.len == -1 )
22         error( 1, 0, "freemsgrec: message record already free\n" );
23     mp->pkt.len = -1;
24 }
25 static void drop( msgrec_t *mp )
26 {
27     error( 0, 0, "Dropping msg:   %s", mp->pkt.buf );
28     freemsgrec( mp );
29 }
30 static void lost_ACK( msgrec_t *mp )
31 {
32     error( 0, 0, "Retrying msg:   %s", mp->pkt.buf );
33     if ( send( s, &mp->pkt,
34          sizeof( u_int32_t ) + ntohl( mp->pkt.len ), 0 ) < 0 )
35         error( 1, errno, "lost_ACK: send failure" );
36     mp->id = timeout( ( tofunc_t )drop, mp, T2 );
37 }
```
*———————————————————————————————————————— xout3.c*

**Figure 3.27** xout3 support functions

### getfreerec

*1–9*    This routine finds an unused entry in the `mr` array. We do a simple-minded linear scan of the array until we find an entry with a packet length of -1, indicating that the entry is free. If the `mr` array was large, we could maintain a free list like we did for the `tevent_t` records in Figure 3.21.

### findmsgrec

*10–18*    This routine is nearly identical to `getfreerec` except that we search for a record with the specified message ID.

### freemsgrec

*19–24*    After checking to make sure that this entry is not already free, we set the message packet length to -1, marking the entry as free.

### drop

*25–29*    This function is called when the second send of a message is not acknowledged (see `lost_ACK`). We log a diagnostic and drop the message by calling `freemsgrec`.

### lost_ACK

*30–37*    This function is called when the first send of a message is unacknowledged. We resend the message, and start a new RTO timer specifying `drop` as the function to call if the timer expires.

To test `xout3`, we write a server application that drops messages randomly. We call our server `extsys` (for external system) and show it in Figure 3.28.

```
                                                                    extsys.c
 1 #include "etcp.h"

 2 #define COOKIESZ    4    /* set by our peer */

 3 int main( int argc, char **argv )
 4 {
 5     SOCKET s;
 6     SOCKET s1;
 7     int rc;
 8     char buf[ 128 ];

 9     INIT();
10     s = tcp_server( NULL, argv[ 1 ] );
11     s1 = accept( s, NULL, NULL );
12     if ( !isvalidsock( s1 ) )
13         error( 1, errno, "accept failure" );
14     srand( 127 );
15     for ( ;; )
16     {
17         rc = readvrec( s1, buf, sizeof( buf ) );
18         if ( rc == 0 )
19             error( 1, 0, "peer disconnected\n" );
20         if ( rc < 0 )
21             error( 1, errno, "recv failure" );
```

```
22          if ( rand() % 100 < 33 )
23              continue;
24          write( 1, buf + COOKIESZ, rc - COOKIESZ );
25          memmove( buf + 1, buf, COOKIESZ );
26          buf[ 0 ] = '\006';
27          if ( send( s1, buf, 1 + COOKIESZ, 0 ) < 0 )
28              error( 1, errno, "send failure" );
29      }
30  }
```
———————————————————————————————————————————— *extsys.c*

**Figure 3.28** An "external system"

### Initialization

*9–14*     We perform our usual server initialization chores and call `srand` to seed the random number generator.

> The standard C runtime library function, `rand`, although quick and easy, has several undesirable properties. Although it is fine for our demonstration of `xout3`, a serious simulation would use a more sophisticated random number generator. See [Knuth 1998] for details.

*17–21*     We use our `readvrec` function to read the variable-length record from `xout3`.

*22–23*     We randomly drop approximately one third of the messages we receive.

*24–28*     If we don't drop the message, we write it to stdout, move the cookie down one position in the input buffer, add the ACK character, and return the ACK to our peer.

We test `xout3` by starting `extsys` in one window, and using the pipeline from Tip 20 in another (Figure 3.29).

```
bsd $ mp | xout3 localhost 9000    bsd $ extsys 9000
xout3: Retrying msg:    message 3   message 1
xout3: Retrying msg:    message 4   message 2
xout3: Retrying msg:    message 5   message 3
xout3: Dropping msg:    message 4   message 6
xout3: Dropping msg:    message 5   message 7
xout3: Retrying msg:    message 11  message 8
xout3: Retrying msg:    message 14  message 9
xout3: Dropping msg:    message 11  message 10
xout3: Retrying msg:    message 16  message 12
xout3: Retrying msg:    message 17  message 13
xout3: Dropping msg:    message 14  message 15
xout3: Retrying msg:    message 19  message 18
xout3: Retrying msg:    message 20  message 17
xout3: Dropping msg:    message 16  message 21
xout3: server disconnected          message 20
Broken pipe                         message 23
bsd $                               ^C          Server terminated
                                    bsd $
```

**Figure 3.29** `xout3` demonstration

We can make a few observations about `xout3`:

1. In-order delivery of messages is not guaranteed. Indeed, as we saw with messages 17 and 20 in Figure 3.29, a retried message can arrive out of order.

2. We could enable multiple retries of a message by adding a retry count to the `msgrec_t` structure, and having `lost_ACK` resend the message until the retries were exhausted.

3. We could easily modify `xout3` to use UDP instead of TCP. This would be a first step in providing a reliable UDP (but see Tip 8).

4. For an application that handles more than a few sockets with `tselect`, it would make sense to abstract the in-line `readn` code into a separate function. Such a function might accept as input a structure containing `cnt`, a pointer to the input buffer (or the buffer itself), and the address of a function to call when a complete message has been read.

5. As an example, `xout3` may seem a little forced, especially in the context of Tip 19, but it does illustrate a solution to a type of problem that occurs frequently in real-world applications.

## Summary

This tip and the last examined event-driven programming and how to use `select` to respond to events as they happen. In Tip 20, we developed the `tselect` function, which allows us to multiplex multiple timers onto the single `select` timer. This function and the supporting `timeout` and `untimeout` functions allow us to time multiple events with a minimum of housekeeping.

In the current tip, we used the `tselect` routine to improve an example from Tip 19. By using `tselect` we were able to provide individual retransmission timers for messages sent to an unreliable end point through the gateway server `xout3`.

## Tip 22: Don't Use TIME-WAIT Assassination to Close a Connection

In this tip we look at the TCP TIME-WAIT state, what functions it serves in TCP, and why we shouldn't try to defeat it. Because the TIME-WAIT state is buried in the details of the TCP state machine, many network programmers are only dimly aware of its existence and have no real understanding of its purpose and importance. Indeed, it is possible to write TCP/IP applications without ever hearing about the TIME-WAIT state, but a working knowledge of it is essential if we are to understand seemingly strange behavior in our applications (see Tip 23, for example) and avoid practices that have unforeseen consequences.

We begin by examining what the TIME-WAIT state is and how it fits into the evolution of a TCP connection. Next we examine the purpose of the TIME-WAIT state and why it's important. Finally we examine why and how some programmers try to defeat it, and we point to a tip that shows the correct way to accomplish the same thing.

## What It Is

The TIME-WAIT state comes into play during connection tear-down. Recall from Tip 7 that tearing down a TCP connection normally requires the exchange of four segments, as illustrated in Figure 3.30.

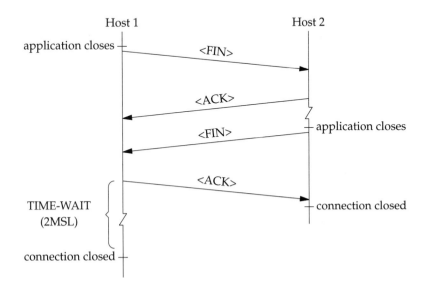

**Figure 3.30** Connection tear-down

Figure 3.30 shows a connection between applications on host 1 and host 2. The application on host 1 closes its side of the connection, causing TCP to send a FIN to host 2. Host 2 ACKs this FIN, and delivers the FIN to the application as an EOF (assuming the application has a read pending—see Tip 16). Sometime later, the application on host 2 closes its side of the connection, causing a FIN to be sent to host 1, which replies with an ACK.

At this point, host 2 closes the connection and releases its resources. From the point of view of host 2, the connection no longer exists. Host 1, however, does not close the connection, but instead enters the TIME-WAIT state and remains there for two maximum segment lifetimes (2MSL).

> The maximum segment lifetime (MSL) is the maximum amount of time that a segment can remain in the network before being discarded. Each IP datagram has a *TTL* field that is decremented each time the datagram is forwarded by a router. When the *TTL* field becomes zero, the datagram is discarded. Although, officially, the units of the *TTL* field are *seconds*, the field is almost universally treated as a simple hop count by routers. RFC 1812 [Baker 1995] discusses this and the reasons for it.

After waiting for the 2MSL, host 1 also closes the connection and releases its resources.

We should be aware of three points about the TIME-WAIT state.

1. Normally, only one side—the side doing the active close—enters the TIME-WAIT state.

    > By *active close* we mean the side that sends the first FIN. The other side is said to do a *passive close*. It is also possible to have a *simultaneous close*, in which both sides close at the same time, with their FINs crossing in the network. In this case, both applications are deemed to have done an active close, and both enter the TIME-WAIT state.

2. RFC 793 [Postel 1981b] defines the MSL to be 2 minutes. With this definition, a connection remains in the TIME-WAIT state for 4 minutes. This value is widely ignored in practice, however. BSD-derived systems, for example, use a value of 30 seconds for the MSL, so that TIME-WAIT lasts for a minute. Other values between 30 seconds and 2 minutes are also common.

3. If any segments arrive while the connection is in the TIME-WAIT state, the 2MSL timer is restarted. We'll see the why this happens when we discuss the reasons for the TIME-WAIT state next.

### Why It's There

The TIME-WAIT state serves two purposes:

1. It maintains the connection state in case the final ACK, which is sent by the side doing the active close, is lost, causing the other side to resend its FIN.

2. It provides time for any "stray segments" from the connection to drain from the network.

Let's examine each of these in turn. When the side doing the active close is ready to ACK the other side's FIN, we know that all data transmitted so far by either side has been received. It is possible, however, for this final ACK to be lost. If that happens, the side doing the passive close times out and retransmits its FIN (because it didn't receive an ACK for its final sequence number).

Now consider what would happen if the side doing the active close had not gone into TIME-WAIT but had merely closed the connection. When the retransmitted FIN arrived, TCP would no longer have a record of the connection, and would therefore respond with an RST (a reset), generating an error condition for its peer instead of an orderly termination. But because the side that sends the last ACK *is* in the TIME-WAIT state and still has a record of the connection, it is able to respond correctly to a retransmitted FIN from its peer.

This explains why the 2MSL timer is restarted when a segment arrives while a connection is in the TIME-WAIT state. If the final ACK is lost and the peer retransmits its FIN, the side in TIME-WAIT again ACKs the FIN, and it restarts the timer in case this ACK is also lost.

The other purpose of the TIME-WAIT state is more important. Because IP datagrams can be lost or delayed in a WAN, TCP uses its positive-acknowledgment mechanism to retransmit segments that are not ACKed by its peer in a timely manner (Tip 1). If a datagram is merely delayed but not lost, or if the ACK for it is lost, the retransmission of the data can arrive after the original data is received. TCP deals with this by noticing that the sequence numbers of the delayed data are outside the current receive window and discards them.

Now consider what happens if the delayed or retransmitted segment arrives after the connection is closed. Normally, this is not a problem because TCP merely discards the data and responds with an RST. When the RST arrives at the host originating the delayed segment, it too is discarded because that host no longer has a record of the connection either. If, however, a new connection was established between the same two hosts with the same port numbers, then the stray segment would look as if it belonged to that connection. If any of the sequence numbers of the data in the stray segment happened to fall in the current receive window for the new connection, that data would be accepted and would consequently corrupt the new connection.

The TIME-WAIT state prevents this by ensuring that the old socket pair (the two IP addresses and their corresponding port numbers) are not reused until all segments from the old connection have drained from the network. Thus we see that the TIME-WAIT state plays an important role in providing TCP's reliability. Without it, TCP could not promise to deliver the data "in order and uncorrupted," as we discussed in Tip 9.

## TIME-WAIT Assassination

Unfortunately, it is possible to terminate the TIME-WAIT state prematurely. This is referred to as *TIME-WAIT assassination*. This can happen either "by accident" or on purpose.

First, let's see how it can happen by accident. RFC 793 specifies that when a connection is in the TIME-WAIT state and receives an RST, it should immediately close the connection. Suppose we have a connection in TIME-WAIT and an old duplicate segment arrives that is unacceptable to TCP (the sequence number is outside the current receive window, say). TCP responds with an ACK indicating what sequence number it is expecting (the one after its peer's FIN). The peer, however, no longer has a record of the connection, and therefore responds to the ACK with an RST. When this RST arrives back at the host with the connection in the TIME-WAIT state, it causes the connection to be closed immediately—the TIME-WAIT state is assassinated.

This possibility is described in RFC 1337 [Braden 1992b], which also discusses the hazards associated with TIME-WAIT assassination. These hazards affect any reincarnation of the old connection (that is, a connection with the same socket pair), and include the erroneous acceptance of old data, the desynchronization of the connection resulting in an infinite ACK loop, and the erroneous termination of the new connection.

Fortunately, this possibility is easily prevented by changing TCP to ignore RSTs in the TIME-WAIT state. Although recommended by RFC 1337, this change has not been officially adopted, but is nevertheless implemented in some stacks.

The other way for TIME-WAIT assassination to occur is on purpose. By using the SO_LINGER socket option, as discussed next, it is possible for the programmer to force an immediate close of a connection even if the application is doing the active close. This dubious practice is sometimes recommended as a way to get a server out of the TIME-WAIT state so that it can be restarted after a crash or termination. The details of this problem, and a much better solution to it, are discussed in Tip 23. Robust applications should *never* interfere with the TIME-WAIT state—it's an important part of TCP's reliability mechanism.

Normally, when an application closes a connection, the `close` or `closesocket` call returns immediately even if there is still data in the send buffer waiting to be transmitted. TCP still tries to deliver the unsent data, of course, but the application does not know whether it succeeded. To prevent this problem, we can set the `SO_LINGER` socket option. To do this, we fill in a `linger` structure and call `setsockopt` with `SO_LINGER`.

In most UNIX systems, the linger structure is defined in the header file `/usr/include/sys/socket.h`. In Windows systems it is defined in `winsock.h` or `winsock2.h`. In either case, it has the form

```
struct linger {
    int l_onoff          /* option on/off */
    int l_linger;        /* linger time */
};
```

If the `l_onoff` member is zero, the linger option is turned off and the behavior is identical to the default action—the `close` or `closesocket` call returns immediately and the kernel continues to try to deliver any unsent data. If `l_onoff` is nonzero, the behavior depends on the value of `l_linger`. If `l_linger` is nonzero, it is taken as a time interval that the kernel will linger, waiting for any pending data to be sent and acknowledged. That is, `close` or `closesocket` does not return until either all data is delivered or until the time interval expires.

If there is still undelivered data when the linger timer expires, `close` or `closesocket` returns `EWOULDBLOCK` and any undelivered data may be lost. If the data is delivered, then both calls return 0.

> Unfortunately, the meaning of the `l_linger` member is implementation dependent. Under Windows and some UNIX implementations it is the number of seconds to linger when closing the socket. On BSD-derived systems, it is the number of timer ticks to linger (even though the documentation says it's in seconds).

We should be aware that when using the `SO_LINGER` option in this way, we are ensuring only that the data was delivered to our peer *TCP*. It does *not* guarantee that the data was read by our peer application. A better way of accomplishing this is to use the orderly shutdown procedure described in Tip 16.

Finally, if the `l_linger` member is zero, the connection is aborted. That is, an RST is sent to the peer and the connection is closed immediately without going through the TIME-WAIT state. This is the purposeful TIME-WAIT assassination that we mentioned earlier. As we also mentioned, this is a dangerous practice that should never be used in a normal application.

**Summary**

In this tip we examined the often misunderstood TIME-WAIT state. We saw that the TIME-WAIT state is an important part of TCP's reliability, and that efforts to defeat it are ill-advised. We saw that the TIME-WAIT state can be terminated prematurely by certain "natural" network events, and that it can also be terminated under program control by using the SO_LINGER socket option.

## Tip 23: Servers Should Set the **SO_REUSEADDR** Option

One of the most frequently asked questions in the networking news groups is: "If my server crashes or is terminated, and I try to restart it, I get the error 'Address already in use.' After a few minutes, I am able to restart the server. How can I cause my server to restart immediately?" To illustrate the problem, let's write a naive echo server that has this problem (Figure 3.31).

*———— badserver.c*

```
 1 #include "etcp.h"

 2 int main( int argc, char **argv )
 3 {
 4     struct sockaddr_in local;
 5     SOCKET s;
 6     SOCKET s1;
 7     int rc;
 8     char buf[ 1024 ];

 9     INIT();
10     s = socket( PF_INET, SOCK_STREAM, 0 );
11     if ( !isvalidsock( s ) )
12         error( 1, errno, "Could not allocate socket" );
13     bzero( &local, sizeof( local ) );
14     local.sin_family = AF_INET;
15     local.sin_port = htons( 9000 );
16     local.sin_addr.s_addr = htonl( INADDR_ANY );
17     if ( bind( s, ( struct sockaddr * )&local,
18         sizeof( local ) ) < 0 )
19         error( 1, errno, "Could not bind socket" );
20     if ( listen( s, NLISTEN ) < 0 )
21         error( 1, errno, "listen failed" );
22     s1 = accept( s, NULL, NULL );
23     if ( !isvalidsock( s1 ) )
24         error( 1, errno, "accept failed" );
25     for ( ;; )
26     {
27         rc = recv( s1, buf, sizeof( buf ), 0 );
28         if ( rc < 0 )
29             error( 1, errno, "recv failed" );
```

```
30            if ( rc == 0 )
31                error( 1, 0, "Client disconnected\n" );
32            rc = send( s1, buf, rc, 0 );
33            if ( rc < 0 )
34                error( 1, errno, "send failed" );
35        }
36 }
```
*────── badserver.c*

**Figure 3.31** A naive echo server

At first glance, other than the hard-coded port number, this server appears reasonable. In fact, if we run it in one window and connect to it with telnet in another, we get the expected results (Figure 3.32; we have removed the telnet connection messages from the output in this tip)

```
bsd $ badserver                          bsd $ telnet localhost 9000
badserver: Client disconnected           hello
bsd $ badserver                          hello
badserver: Client disconnected           ^]
bsd $                                     telnet> quit          Client terminated
                                         Connection closed.
                                                               Server restarted
                                         bsd $ telnet localhost 9000
                                         world
                                         world
                                         ^]
                                         telnet> quit          Client terminated
                                         Connection closed.
                                         bsd $
```

**Figure 3.32** Client terminates

After verifying that the server is working, we terminate the client by escaping into telnet command mode and quitting. Notice that when we immediately repeat this experiment, we get the same results. That is, badserver restarts without a problem.

Now let's rerun this experiment, but this time we terminate the server. When we try to restart the server, we get the "Address already in use" error (we wrapped the error diagnostic onto the next line). The difference is that in the second experiment we terminated the server rather than the (telnet) client (Figure 3.33).

```
bsd $ badserver                          bsd $ telnet localhost 9000
^C                    Server terminated  hello again
bsd $ badserver                          hello again
badserver: Could not bind socket:        Connection closed by foreign host.
Address already in use (48)              bsd $
bsd $
```

**Figure 3.33** Server terminates

To see what's happening with these two examples, we need to understand two things:

1. The TCP TIME-WAIT state
2. That TCP connections are completely specified by the 4-tuple (*local address, local port, foreign address, foreign port*).

Recall from Tip 22 that the side of a TCP connection that does the active close (sends the first FIN) enters the TIME-WAIT state and remains in it for 2MSL. This fact provides the first clue to the behavior that we saw with our examples: When the client does the active close, we are able to restart both sides of the connection without incident, but when the server does the active close, we cannot restart it. TCP is not allowing our server to restart because the previous connection is still in the TIME-WAIT state.

If our server restarts and a client connects, however, we would have a new connection, perhaps not even with the same remote host. As we noted earlier, a TCP connection is completely specified by the local and remote addresses and port numbers, so even if a client from the same remote host connected to our server, there would still be no problem unless it used the same port number as the previous connection.

> Even if the client is from the same remote host and uses the same port number there *may* not be a problem. The traditional BSD implementation allows the connection as long as the sequence number of the SYN from the client is greater than the last sequence number from the connection in the TIME-WAIT state.

Given these facts, we may be puzzled that TCP returns an error when we try to restart the server. The problem does not really lie with TCP, which requires only that the 4-tuple be unique, but with the sockets API, which requires two calls to specify the 4-tuple completely. At the time of the bind call, it is unknown whether connect will be called next, and if it is, whether it will specify a unique connection or try to reuse one that already exists. Torek [Torek 1994], among others, has proposed replacing bind, connect, and listen with a single function that provides the functionality of all three, making it possible for TCP to detect attempts to specify a 4-tuple that is already in use without rejecting attempts to restart a server that has terminated or crashed, leaving a connection in the TIME-WAIT state. Unfortunately, Torek's elegant solution was not adopted.

Fortunately, there is an easy solution to this problem. We can instruct TCP to allow us to bind a port that is already in use by first setting the SO_REUSEADDR socket option. To try this out, we change our badserver application by adding the line

```
const int on = 1;
```

between lines 7 and 8, and the lines

```
if ( setsockopt( s, SOL_SOCKET, SO_REUSEADDR, &on,
    sizeof( on ) ) )
    error( 1, errno, "setsockopt failed" );
```

between lines 12 and 13 of badserver.c (Figure 3.31). Notice that it is important that we make the setsockopt call *before* the call to bind. If we call this new server goodserver and rerun the experiment in Figure 3.33, we get the result in Figure 3.34.

| | |
|---|---|
| bsd $ **goodserver** | bsd $ **telnet localhost 9000** |
| ^C              *Server terminated* | **hello once again** |
| bsd $ **goodserver** | hello once again |
| | Connection closed by foreign host. |
| |                          *Server restarted* |
| | bsd $ **telnet localhost 9000** |
| | **hello one last time** |
| | hello one last time |

**Figure 3.34** Server using SO_REUSEADDR terminates

This time we are able to restart our server without having to wait for the previous connection's TIME-WAIT state to expire. For this reason, we should *always* set SO_REUSEADDR in our servers. Notice that our skeleton code and the library function tcp_server do this for us automatically.

Some people, including, unfortunately, some who write books, believe that setting SO_REUSEADDR is dangerous because it will allow the creation of identical TCP 4-tuples and thus lead to failure. This is not true. For example, if we try to create two identical listening sockets, TCP rejects the bind, even if we specify SO_REUSEADDR:

```
bsd $ goodserver &
[1] 1883
bsd $ goodserver
goodserver: Could not bind socket: Address already in use (48)
bsd $
```

Similarly, if we bind the same local address and port to two different clients using SO_REUSEADDR, the bind succeeds for the second client, but if we then try to connect the second client to the same remote host and port as the first, TCP rejects the connection.

To reiterate, there is no reason not to set SO_REUSEADDR in a server, and doing so prevents the problem of not being able to restart the server immediately if it should fail or otherwise do the active close.

> Stevens [Stevens 1998], points out that there is a small security risk associated with SO_REUSEADDR. If a server binds the wildcard address, INADDR_ANY, as is most often the case, another server could set SO_REUSEADDR, bind the same port but a more specific address, and thus "steal" connections from the first server. This is a particular problem with the network file system (NFS), even on UNIX systems, because NFS binds a nonrestricted port, 2049, on which to listen. Notice, though, that this risk exists not because NFS sets SO_REUSEADDR, but because the other server can. In other words, this risk exists regardless of whether we set SO_REUSEADDR in our server, and so is not a reason to fear setting it.

We should also note that SO_REUSEADDR has other uses. For example, suppose that a server runs on a multihomed host and needs to know which interface a client is specifying as its destination address. With TCP this is easy because the server need merely call `getsockname` as each connection is established, but unless the TCP/IP implementation supports the `IP_RECVDSTADDR` socket option, there is no way for a UDP server to discover this. The UDP server can solve this problem by specifying `SO_REUSEADDR` and binding its well-known port to the specific interfaces it cares about, and to the wildcard address, `INADDR_ANY`, for those that it doesn't. The server then knows which destination address the client is specifying by which socket the datagram arrives on.

A similar scheme is sometimes used by TCP (or UDP) servers that want to provide different versions of a service depending on which address the client specifies. For example, let's suppose that we want to use our home-grown version of `tcpmux` (Tip 18) to provide one set of services when a client connects to a certain interface, 198.200.200.1 say, and another set if the client connects to any other interface. To do this, we start an instance of `tcpmux` with the special set of services on interface 198.200.200.1 and another instance, with the standard set of services, specifying the wildcard address, `INADDR_ANY`. Because our `tcpmux` server sets the `SO_REUSEADDR` option, TCP allows us to bind port 1 the second time, even though the second bind specifies the wildcard address.

Finally, `SO_REUSEADDR` is used on systems that support multicasting to allow several applications to listen for incoming multicast datagrams at the same time. Details on this use can be found in [Stevens 1998].

### Summary

In this tip we examined the `SO_REUSEADDR` socket option, and saw how setting it allows us to restart a server having a previous incarnation in the TIME-WAIT state. We observed that servers should always set this option, and that there is no security risk in doing so.

## Tip 24: When Possible, Use One Large Write Instead of Multiple Small Writes

There are two reasons for the suggestion in the title of this tip. The first is obvious, and we have discussed it before: Each call to one of the write functions (`write`, `send`, and so on) requires at least two context switches, a relatively expensive operation. On the other hand, except for rampant abuse, such as writing a single byte at a time, multiple writes probably won't add excessive overhead to our applications. Thus, the admonition to avoid the extra system calls is more a matter of good engineering practice than an urgent performance concern.

There is, however, a much more pressing reason to avoid multiple small writes: the effects of the Nagle algorithm. We discussed the Nagle algorithm briefly in Tip 15, but now we want to examine it, and its interaction with our applications, in depth. As we shall see, failure to take the Nagle algorithm into account can have a dramatic negative effect on some applications.

Unfortunately, the Nagle algorithm, like the TIME-WAIT state, is poorly understood by many network programmers, and as with the TIME-WAIT state, this lack of understanding often leads to an incorrect solution to the problems associated with the algorithm. Let's begin by examining the reason for the algorithm. Then we'll look at when and how it can be disabled, and finally, we will see how to deal with it in an effective way that provides good application performance without adverse effects on the network.

The Nagle algorithm was first proposed in 1984 by John Nagle (RFC 896 [Nagle 1984]) in response to performance problems with telnet and similar programs. The problem is that these programs typically send each keystroke in a separate segment, resulting in a series of "tinygrams" being introduced into the network. It is easy to see why this can be a problem. First of all, because the minimum TCP segment (with no data) is 40 bytes, sending 1 byte per segment results in a 4,000 percent overhead. But more important is that the number of packets in the network increases, causing congestion, which can lead to retransmissions that cause more congestion. In extreme cases, there are several copies of each segment in the network, and throughput slows to a fraction of its normal rate.

We say a connection is idle if there is no unacknowledged data outstanding (our peer has ACKed all the data that we have sent). As originally conceived, the Nagle algorithm prevented the problems described previously by not transmitting any new data from the application unless the connection was idle. This prevented a connection from having more than one small segment outstanding at once.

The procedure specified in RFC 1122 [Braden 1989] relaxes this a little by allowing data to be sent if there is enough for a full segment. That is, if we can send at least MSS bytes of data, then do so even if the connection is not idle. Notice that this maintains the Nagle condition: Each connection can have at most one small segment outstanding at a time.

Many implementations bend this rule a bit by interpreting the Nagle algorithm on a per-send, rather than on a per-segment, basis. To see the difference, assume that the MSS is 1,460 bytes, that an application does a write of 1,600 bytes, that the send and congestion windows are at least 2,000 bytes, and that the connection is idle. An implementation that interprets the Nagle algorithm on a per-segment basis sends 1,460 bytes and then waits for an ACK before sending the remaining 140 bytes—the Nagle algorithm is applied each time a segment is sent. An implementation that interprets the Nagle algorithm on a per-send basis would send the 1,460-byte segment followed immediately by the short 140-byte segment—the algorithm is applied only when the application delivers new data to TCP for transmission.

By itself, the Nagle algorithm works well. It prevents applications from flooding the network with tinygrams, and in most cases performs at least as well as a TCP that doesn't implement it.

> Imagine, for example, an application that delivers a byte to TCP every 200 ms. If the RTT for the connection is 1 second, a TCP without the Nagle algorithm will send five segments a second with a 4,000 percent overhead. With Nagle, the first byte is sent immediately, and the next 4 bytes that arrive from the user are held until the ACK for the first segment arrives. At that

point the 4 bytes are sent together. Thus only two segments are sent instead of five, reducing the overhead to 1,600 percent while maintaining the same data rate of 5 bytes per second.

Unfortunately, the Nagle algorithm can interact badly with another, later, feature of TCP—the delayed ACK.

When a segment arrives from its peer, TCP delays sending the ACK in the hope that the application makes some response to the data just received so that the ACK can be piggybacked onto the new data. The traditional value for this delay (from the BSD implementation) is 200 ms.

> RFC 1122 is silent on how long the delay should be except to say that it must not be longer than 500 ms. It also recommends that at least every other segment be ACKed.

Like the Nagle algorithm, delayed ACKs serve to reduce the number of segments that get transmitted.

Let's see how these two mechanisms interact in a typical request/response session. In Figure 3.35, a client sends a short request to a server, waits for the response, and then makes another request.

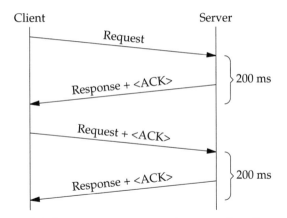

**Figure 3.35** Single-segment response/request data flow

Notice that Nagle does not come into play here because the client does not send another segment until the response, along with the ACK of the first request, is received. On the server side, the delayed ACK gives the server time to respond, and as a result each request/response pair takes only two segments. If $RTT$ is the round-trip time for a segment, and $T_p$ is the time it takes the server to process the request and respond (in milliseconds), then each request/response pair takes $RTT + T_p$ milliseconds.

Now suppose the client sends its request as two separate writes. A frequent reason for this is that the request has a header followed by some data. For example, a client sending variable-length requests to a server might first send the length of the request followed by the actual request.

> We saw an example of this sort of thing in Figure 2.31, but there we took care to send the length and data as a single segment.

Figure 3.36 shows the data flow.

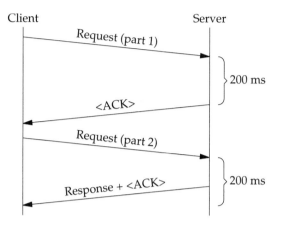

**Figure 3.36** Nagle and delayed ACK algorithms interacting

This time, the two algorithms interact in a way that doubles the number of segments sent for each request/response pair and also introduces significant delay.

The data from the first part of the request is sent immediately, but the Nagle algorithm prevents the second part from being sent. When the server application receives the first part of the request, it can't respond because it does not yet have the entire request. This means that the delayed ACK timer has to run out before the ACK for the first part is generated. In effect, the Nagle and delayed ACK algorithms have blocked each other: The Nagle algorithm prevents the transmission of the second part of the request until the first part is ACKed, and the delayed ACK algorithm prevents the sending of the ACK until the timer expires because the server is waiting for the second part. Each request/response pair now takes four segments and $2 \times RTT + T_p + 200$ ms. A consequence of this is that no more than five request/response pairs can be processed per second even if we completely disregard the server processing and round trip times.

> For many systems, this discussion is a simplification. BSD-derived systems, for example, check all connections for a delayed ACK every 200 ms, and send the ACK at that time regardless of the actual delay. This means that the actual delay can be between 0 and 200 ms, and that we would therefore expect the average delay to be 100 ms. Often, however, the delay can still be 200 ms due to "phase effects," in which delays after the first are terminated by the next clock tick 200 ms later. The first response, in effect, synchronizes the responses with the clock ticks. See [Minshall et al. 1999] for a very nice example of this.

If we examine this last example, we see that the problem was that the client was doing a sequence of write, write, read operations. Any such sequence triggers the interaction between the Nagle and delayed ACK algorithms, and should therefore be avoided. More generally, an application doing small writes will experience this problem anytime its peer does not respond immediately.

Let us imagine, for example, a data-gathering application that sends a single integer to a server every 50 ms. If the server does not reply to these messages, but merely logs them for later analysis, we see the same interaction. The client sends one integer, is blocked by Nagle and the delayed ACK algorithms for (say) 200 ms, and thereafter sends four integers every 200 ms.

## Disabling the Nagle Algorithm

Because the server in our last example merely logged the data it received, the interaction between the Nagle and delayed ACK algorithms did no harm, and in fact reduced the number of packets by a factor of four. Suppose, however, that the client is sending the server a series of temperature readings, and that the server must respond within 100 ms if these readings go outside a critical range. The 200 ms latency induced by the interaction of the two algorithms is no longer benign, and we would like to eliminate it.

Fortunately, RFC 1122 requires that there be a method of disabling the Nagle algorithm. Our example of the temperature-monitoring client is one instance of when this is necessary. A less dramatic but more realistic example is the X Window system that runs on UNIX. Because X uses TCP to communicate between the display (server) and application (client) portions of the system, the X server must deliver input (such as mouse movements) to the X client without the delay imposed by the Nagle algorithm.

With the sockets API, the Nagle algorithm is disabled by the TCP_NODELAY socket option. Setting this option on disables the Nagle algorithm:

```
const int on = 1;

setsockopt( s, IPPROTO_TCP, TCP_NODELAY, &on, sizeof( on ) );
```

Just because we *can* turn the Nagle algorithm off, doesn't mean that we *should* turn it off. The number of applications that have legitimate reasons for disabling it is far less than the number that do. What happens with distressing regularity is that a programmer stumbles into the classic Nagle/delayed ACK interaction by doing a series of small writes instead of one large write to deliver a message to the peer application. The programmer then notices that the application's performance is much poorer than it should be and asks for help. Someone invariably says, "Oh, that's because of the Nagle algorithm. Just turn it off." Sure enough, when the Nagle algorithm is disabled, the performance problems largely disappear. Unfortunately, the performance gain is at the expense of increased tinygrams in the network. If enough applications do this, or worse yet if Nagle were disabled by default, as some have suggested, network congestion would increase and perhaps even lead to collapse in extreme situations.

## Gathering Writes

As we have seen, there are some applications that must disable the Nagle algorithm, but the majority of applications that do, do so because of performance problems caused by sending logically connected data in a series of small writes. There are many ways of coalescing data so that it can be written together. We could, in the extreme case, copy the various pieces of data into a single buffer before writing it, but as explained in Tip 26, this should be the method of last resort. Sometimes, with a little planning, we can arrange to have the data stored together as we did in Figure 2.31. Often, however, the data resides in two or more noncontiguous buffers, and we would like an efficient way to write it all at once.

Fortunately, the UNIX and Winsock environments each provide a way of doing this. Unfortunately, they each provide a slightly different way. Under UNIX, the `writev` and corresponding `readv` calls are available. With `writev`, we specify a list of buffers from which the data to be written is gathered. This solves our problem neatly: We can arrange for data held in more than one buffer to be written at the same time and therefore avoid the interaction of the Nagle and delayed ACK algorithms.

```
# include <sys/uio.h>

ssize_t writev( int fd, const struct iovec *iov, int cnt );

ssize_t readv( int fd, const struct iovec *iov, int cnt );
```
                                             Returns: bytes transferred or -1 on error

The *iov* parameter is a pointer to an array of `iovec` structures that point to the buffers and specify their lengths:

```
struct iovec {
    char *iov_base;     /* Base address. */
    size_t iov_len;     /* Length. */
};
```

> The previous definition was taken from the FreeBSD system. Many systems are now defining the base address pointer as
>
>     void *iov_base;     /* Base address. */

The third parameter, *cnt*, is the number of `iovec` structures in the array (in other words, the number of distinct buffers).

The `writev` and `readv` calls are a general interface. They can be used with any type of file descriptor, not just sockets.

To see how this works, let's rewrite the variable record client from Figure 2.31 using `writev` (Figure 3.37).

────────────────────────────────────────────────────────────────────── *vrcv.c*
```
 1 #include "etcp.h"
 2 #include <sys/uio.h>

 3 int main( int argc, char **argv )
 4 {
 5     SOCKET s;
 6     int n;
 7     char buf[ 128 ];
 8     struct iovec iov[ 2 ];

 9     INIT();
10     s = tcp_client( argv[ 1 ], argv[ 2 ] );
11     iov[ 0 ].iov_base = ( char * )&n;
12     iov[ 0 ].iov_len = sizeof( n );
```

```
13        iov[ 1 ].iov_base = buf;
14        while ( fgets( buf, sizeof( buf ), stdin ) != NULL )
15        {
16            iov[ 1 ].iov_len = strlen( buf );
17            n = htonl( iov[ 1 ].iov_len );
18            if ( writev( s, iov, 2 ) < 0 )
19                error( 1, errno, "writev failure" );
20        }
21        EXIT( 0 );
22   }
```
———————————————————————————————————————————— *vrcv.c*

**Figure 3.37** A client that sends variable-length messages using `writev`

### Initialization

9-13    After performing our usual client initialization, we set up the iov array. Because the prototype for `writev` specifies `const` for the structures pointed to by the *iov* parameter, we are guaranteed that the `iov` array will not be changed by `writev`, and that we can therefore set most of the fields outside the while loop.

### Event Loop

14-20    We call `fgets` to read a line of input, calculate its length, and set this length in our `iov` array. We also convert the length to network byte order and put it in n.

If we start our vrs server from Tip 6, and run vrcv, we get the same results as before.

Under Winsock, we have a different but similar interface:

```
#include <winsock2.h>

int WSAAPI WSAsend( SOCKET s, LPWSABUF buf, DWORD cnt,
        LPDWORD sent, DWORD flags, LPWSAOVERLAPPED ovl,
        LPWSAOVERLAPPED_COMPLETION_ROUTINE func );
```

Returns: 0 if successful, SOCKET_ERROR otherwise

The last two arguments are for use with overlapped I/O and can be ignored for our purposes. We should set them both to NULL. The *buf* parameter points to an array of WSABUF structures, which play a roll similar to that of the `iovec` structures used with `writev`:

```
typedef struct _WSABUF {
    u_long      len;      /* the length of the buffer */
    char FAR *  buf;      /* the pointer to the buffer */
} WSABUF, FAR * LPWSABUF;
```

The *sent* parameter is a pointer to a DWORD that contains the number of bytes sent if the call succeeds. The *flags* parameter is similar to the *flags* field used with `send`.

We can use WSASend to make a Winsock version of our variable-length message client (Figure 3.38).

—————————————————————————————————————————————————— *vrcvw.c*

```
 1 #include "etcp.h"

 2 int main( int argc, char **argv )
 3 {
 4     SOCKET s;
 5     int n;
 6     char buf[ 128 ];
 7     WSABUF wbuf[ 2 ];
 8     DWORD sent;

 9     INIT();
10     s = tcp_client( argv[ 1 ], argv[ 2 ] );
11     wbuf[ 0 ].buf = ( char * )&n;
12     wbuf[ 0 ].len = sizeof( n );
13     wbuf[ 1 ].buf = buf;
14     while ( fgets( buf, sizeof( buf ), stdin ) != NULL )
15     {
16         wbuf[ 1 ].len = strlen( buf );
17         n = htonl( wbuf[ 1 ].len );
18         if ( WSASend( s, wbuf, 2, &sent, 0, NULL, NULL ) < 0 )
19             error( 1, errno, "WSASend failure" );
20     }
21     EXIT( 0 );
22 }
```

—————————————————————————————————————————————————— *vrcvw.c*

**Figure 3.38** A Winsock version of `vrcv`

As we see, except for a different gathering write call, the Winsock version is identical to the UNIX version.

### Summary

In this tip we examined the Nagle algorithm and its interaction with the delayed ACK algorithm. We saw that applications that perform several small writes instead of a large single write are apt to experience significant performance degradation.

Because the Nagle algorithm helps prevent a very real problem—the flooding of the network with tinygrams—it should not be disabled to solve the performance problems of applications that make several small writes. Rather, the applications should arrange to write all logically connected data at once. We examined a convenient method of doing this: the `writev` call under UNIX and the `WSASend` call under Winsock.

## Tip 25: Understand How to Time Out a `connect` Call

As we discussed in Tip 7, the normal TCP connection establishment procedure involves the exchange of three segments (called the *three-way handshake*). As shown in Figure 3.39, the procedure is initiated by a `connect` call from the client, and ends when the server receives the ACK of its SYN.

Other exchanges, such as simultaneous connects in which the initial SYN segments cross in the network, are possible, of course, but the vast majority of connection establishments take the form shown in Figure 3.39.

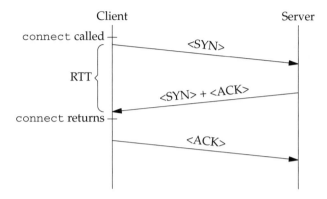

**Figure 3.39** Normal three-way handshake

In the normal case of a blocking socket, connect does not return until the ACK from the client's SYN arrives. Because this is at least one RTT, and could be longer if there is network congestion or the host being contacted is not up, it is often useful to be able to abort connect. TCP eventually aborts the connect call itself, of course, but the default time (75 seconds is a typical value) for this may be longer than we want to wait. Some implementations, such as Solaris, provide socket options to control the connect abort timeout, but unfortunately these options are not available in all systems.

## Using Alarm

There are two methods for timing out a connect call. The easiest way is simply to set an alarm around the call. Suppose, for example, we want to wait no longer than 5 seconds for connect to complete. To do this, we modify our tcpclient.skel (Figure 2.19) by adding a simple signal handler and modifying the main function as shown here:

```
void alarm_hndlr( int sig )
{
    return;
}

int main( int argc, char **argv )
{
    ...
    signal( SIGALRM, alarm_hndlr );
    alarm( 5 );
    rc = connect( s, ( struct sockaddr * )&peer, sizeof( peer ) );
    alarm( 0 );
```

```
        if ( rc < 0 )
        {
            if ( errno == EINTR )
                error( 1, 0, "connect timed out\n" );
        ...
    }
```

If we rename our skeleton `connectto`, and try to connect to a busy Web site such as Yahoo, we get the expected results:

```
bsd: $ connectto yahoo.com daytime
connectto: connect timed out                    5 seconds later
bsd: $
```

Although this solution is easy, there are several potential problems with it. Let's discuss some of these problems, and then look at another method that, although more complicated, avoids these difficulties.

First, our sample code assumes the alarm timer is not in use by any other part of the program, and that there is no other signal handler set for it. If the timer is already running, our code resets it, canceling the old timer. To be robust, we would have to save and restore the amount of time left on the current timer (returned by the `alarm` call), and also save and restore the current handler for the `SIGALRM` signal (returned by the `signal` call). To do this correctly, we should also retrieve the amount of time used while waiting for `connect`, and subtract it from the time remaining for the original timer.

Next, in the interest of simplicity, we merely terminated our client if `connect` times out, but we might want to take some other action. We should be aware, however, that we cannot restart `connect`. That's because the socket is still bound as a result of the first `connect`, and an attempt to restart `connect` results in an "Address already in use" error. If we want to retry `connect`, perhaps after a suitable delay, we should first close and then reopen the socket by calling `close` (or `closesocket`) and `socket`.

Another potential problem with this method is that some UNIX systems may restart the `connect` call automatically after the signal handler returns. In that case, the call does not return until the default TCP timeout interval has passed. All modern UNIX systems support the `sigaction` call, which can be used in place of `signal`. With `sigaction`, we can specify whether `connect` should be restarted. Some older systems, however, do not support this call, and for them using `alarm` to time out the `connect` call is more difficult.

If all we want to do is output a diagnostic and terminate, we can do so in the signal handler. Because this happens before the `connect` call is restarted, it doesn't matter whether the system supports `sigaction`. If, however, we want to take some other action, we probably have to `longjump` out of the signal handler, and this invariably introduces race conditions.

> Notice that there is a race condition even in the simple case where we terminate. Suppose the connection completes and the `connect` call returns, but before we can call `alarm` to turn off the timer, the timer fires, causing the signal handler to be called, which in turn terminates the

program:

```
alarm( 5 );
rc = connect( s, NULL, NULL );
/* timer fires here */
alarm( 0 );
```

In this case, we have terminated the program even though the connection was, in fact, successful. Our original code doesn't have this race condition because even if the timer fires between `connect` returning and the call to `alarm`, the signal handler merely returns without taking any action.

For all of these reasons, many experts believe that the proper way of timing out a `connect` call is to use `select`, as we show next.

## Using `select`

The second, more general, method of timing out a `connect` call is to make the socket nonblocking and then wait for it to complete with `select`. This approach avoids many of the difficulties that we encountered when using `alarm` for this purpose, but there are still portability problems, even among UNIX implementations, that we must accommodate.

Let's first look at the connect code itself. We begin by taking our `tcpclient.skel` code and modifying the `main` function. We show this in Figure 3.40.

*connectto1.c*

```
 1 int main( int argc, char **argv )
 2 {
 3     fd_set rdevents;
 4     fd_set wrevents;
 5     fd_set exevents;
 6     struct sockaddr_in peer;
 7     struct timeval tv;
 8     SOCKET s;
 9     int flags;
10     int rc;

11     INIT();

12     set_address( argv[ 1 ], argv[ 2 ], &peer, "tcp" );

13     s = socket( AF_INET, SOCK_STREAM, 0 );
14     if ( !isvalidsock( s ) )
15         error( 1, errno, "socket call failed" );

16     if( ( flags = fcntl( s, F_GETFL, 0 ) ) < 0 )
17         error( 1, errno, "fcntl (F_GETFL) failed" );
18     if ( fcntl( s, F_SETFL, flags | O_NONBLOCK ) < 0 )
19         error( 1, errno, "fcntl (F_SETFL) failed" );

20     if ( ( rc = connect( s, ( struct sockaddr * )&peer,
21         sizeof( peer ) ) ) && errno != EINPROGRESS )
22         error( 1, errno, "connect failed" );
```

```
23      if ( rc == 0 )              /* already connected? */
24      {
25          if ( fcntl( s, F_SETFL, flags ) < 0 )
26              error( 1, errno, "fcntl (restore flags) failed" );
27          client( s, &peer );
28          EXIT( 0 );
29      }
30      FD_ZERO( &rdevents );
31      FD_SET( s, &rdevents );
32      wrevents = rdevents;
33      exevents = rdevents;
34      tv.tv_sec = 5;
35      tv.tv_usec = 0;
36      rc = select( s + 1, &rdevents, &wrevents, &exevents, &tv );
37      if ( rc < 0 )
38          error( 1, errno, "select failed" );
39      else if ( rc == 0 )
40          error( 1, 0, "connect timed out\n" );
41      else if ( isconnected( s, &rdevents, &wrevents, &exevents ) )
42      {
43          if ( fcntl( s, F_SETFL, flags ) < 0 )
44              error( 1, errno, "fcntl (restore flags) failed" );
45          client( s, &peer );
46      }
47      else
48          error( 1, errno, "connect failed" );
49      EXIT( 0 );
50  }
```
———————————————————————————————————————————— *connectto1.c*

**Figure 3.40** Timing out connect with select

### Set Socket Nonblocking

*16–19*    We retrieve the flags for the socket, OR in the O_NONBLOCK flag, and then set the new flags.

### Initiate connect

*20–29*    We call connect to start the connection sequence. Because we marked the socket nonblocking, connect returns immediately. If the connection has already been established, as it probably is if we are connecting to ourselves, connect returns 0 and we set the socket back to its blocking state and call our client function. Normally, the connection is not established before connect returns, and it returns an EINPROGRESS error. If it returns any other error, we output a diagnostic and terminate.

### Call select

*30–36*    We do our usual setup for select, including setting a timeout for 5 seconds. We also register our interest in exception events for reasons explained later.

### Handle Return From select

*37–40*    If select returns an error or a timeout event, we output the appropriate diagnostic and terminate. We could, of course, take some other action in the event of a timeout.

*41-46*    We call `isconnected` to check whether the connection succeeded. If it did, we set the socket back to its original blocking state and call our `client` function. The `isconnected` function is shown in Figure 3.41 and Figure 3.42.

*47-48*    If we did not connect successfully, we output a diagnostic and terminate.

Unfortunately, UNIX and Winsock use different methods to indicate whether the connection was successful. That's why we abstracted the check out to a separate function. We show the UNIX version of `isconnected` first.

Under UNIX, when the connection is established the socket becomes writable. If an error occurs, the socket becomes both readable and writable. We can't rely on this to check for a successful connection, however, because `connect` could succeed and have data ready to be read before we call `select`. In this case, the socket would be both readable and writable, just as if an error had occurred. Instead, we call `getsockopt` to retrieve the error status of the socket.

*connectto1.c*

```
 1 int isconnected( SOCKET s, fd_set *rd, fd_set *wr, fd_set *ex )
 2 {
 3     int err;
 4     int len;

 5     errno = 0;            /* assume no error */
 6     if ( !FD_ISSET( s, rd ) && !FD_ISSET( s, wr ) )
 7         return 0;
 8     if ( getsockopt( s, SOL_SOCKET, SO_ERROR, &err, &len ) < 0 )
 9         return 0;
10     errno = err;          /* in case we're not connected */
11     return err == 0;
12 }
```

*connectto1.c*

**Figure 3.41** The UNIX version of `isconnected`

*5-7*    If the socket is neither readable nor writable, then the connection is not established and we return 0. We preset `errno` to zero, so the caller can determine whether the socket is just not ready (this case) or has an error condition (discussed next).

*8-11*    We call `getsockopt` to retrieve the error status of the socket. In some versions of UNIX, `getsockopt` returns -1 if the socket has an error. In this case, `errno` is set to the error. Other versions of UNIX merely return the error status of the socket and leave it to the caller to check. The idea for our code, which handles both cases, comes from Stevens [Stevens 1998].

With Winsock, errors from `connect` on a nonblocking socket are indicated by an exception event when using `select`. Note that this is unlike UNIX, in which TCP exception events always indicate the arrival of urgent data. The Windows version of `isconnected` is presented in Figure 3.42

*3-5*    Just as in the UNIX version, we check to see whether the socket is connected. If it's not, we arrange for the last error to be set to zero and return 0.

*6-8*    If there is an exception event for the socket, we return 0 otherwise we return 1.

*connectto1.c*

```
1  int isconnected( SOCKET s, fd_set *rd, fd_set *wr, fd_set *ex )
2  {
3      WSASetLastError( 0 );
4      if ( !FD_ISSET( s, rd ) && !FD_ISSET( s, wr ) )
5          return 0;
6      if ( FD_ISSET( s, ex ) )
7          return 0;
8      return 1;
9  }
```

*connectto1.c*

**Figure 3.42** The Winsock version of `isconnected`

## Summary

As we have seen, timing out a `connect` call presents a larger than usual number of portability problems. For this reason we should pay particular attention to which platform we are using when we need to do such a timeout.

Finally, we should be aware that although we can shorten the timeout interval for `connect`, there is no way to lengthen it. The methods we have examined are all ways to abort `connect` *before* TCP does. There is no general mechanism to change TCP's timeout value on a per-socket basis.

## Tip 26: Avoid Data Copying

In many network applications, especially those concerned primarily with moving data between machines, copying data from one buffer to another accounts for a majority of the processing time. In this tip we consider some ways to reduce the amount of data copying, and thus increase the performance of our applications "for free." The notion that we should avoid copying large amounts of data around in memory seems much less remarkable when we consider that it is, in fact, our standard procedure: Rather than pass the data in arrays from one function to another, we pass a pointer to the original array.

We don't normally copy a data buffer between functions in the same process, of course, but in multiprocess applications we often do transfer large chunks of data from one process to another by whatever IPC mechanism the application uses. Even within the same process, data is often copied when a message is made up of two or more pieces, and we want to combine those pieces for transmission to another process or machine. A common example of this, discussed in Tip 24, is the prepending of a header onto a message. First the header is copied into a buffer, and then the data is copied in after it, resulting in the entire message being copied.

Avoiding this copying within the same process is usually just a matter of good programming practice. If we know that we are going to prepend a header to data that we are reading into a buffer, then we should leave room for it when we do our read. That is, if we are going to prepend a header contained in `struct hdr`, then we could do our read as

```
rc = read( fd, buf + sizeof( struct hdr ),
    sizeof( buf ) - sizeof( struct hdr) );
```

We saw an example of this technique in Figure 3.9.

Another technique is to define our message packet as a structure with our data buffer as one of its elements. Then we can merely read the data into the appropriate structure field:

```
struct
{
    struct hdr header;        /* defined elsewhere */
    char data[ DATASZ ];
} packet;

rc = read( fd, packet.data, sizeof( packet.data ) );
```

We saw an example of this method in Figure 2.31. As discussed there, we must exercise care when defining such structures.

A third, very flexible, method is to use a gathering write as we discussed in Figure 3.37 (UNIX) and Figure 3.38 (Winsock). This technique allows us to combine the parts of a message when the sizes are not fixed from one message to the next.

Avoiding data copying is more difficult when there is more than one process involved. This problem is frequently encountered in UNIX applications in which the multiprocess application is a common paradigm (Figure 3.16, for example). The problem is usually more acute in this situation because most IPC methods involve copying the data from the sending process into the kernel and then from the kernel into the receiving process, so that the data is copied twice. For this reason we should, at a minimum, use one of the techniques discussed earlier to avoid any more copying than is otherwise necessary.

## Shared Memory Buffers

We can avoid virtually all data copying, even between processes, by making use of shared memory. Shared memory is a block of memory that is shared by two or more processes. Each process maps the shared memory block into a (possibly different) address in its own address space, and thereafter accesses it exactly as if it were normal user space memory.

The idea is to allocate an array of buffers in shared memory, build the message in one of these buffers, and then pass the index of the buffer to the next process using whatever IPC method is convenient. In this way, the only data that actually gets "moved" is the integer representing the buffer array index. For example, in Figure 3.43 we use TCP as our IPC mechanism to pass the integer '3' from process 1 to process 2. When process 2 receives this integer, it knows that there is data waiting for it in smbarray[ 3 ].

In Figure 3.43, the two dashed boxes represent the address spaces of processes 1 and 2, and their intersection represents the common shared memory segment that both have mapped into their address spaces. The array of buffers is in the shared memory

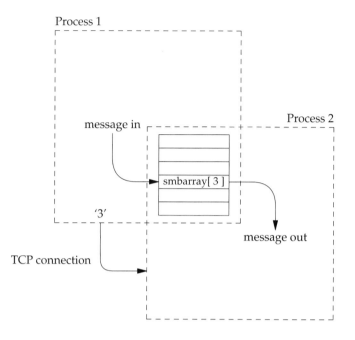

**Figure 3.43**  Passing messages in a shared memory buffer

segment and is accessible by both processes. Process 1 uses a separate IPC channel (TCP in this case) to inform process 2 that there is data ready for it, and in which array element it's located.

Although we show only two processes, the same technique works equally well for several processes. Also, process 2 can, of course, pass messages to process 1 by obtaining one of the shared memory buffers, building its message in it, and passing the index to process 1.

The only missing piece is synchronizing access to the buffers—that is, preventing two processes from obtaining the use of the same buffer at the same time. This is easily done by means of a mutex, as we demonstrate next.

### A Shared Memory Buffer System

It's easy to implement the type of shared memory buffer system just described. Most of the complexity involves obtaining and mapping the shared memory, and arranging for the synchronization of buffer access. These details are system dependent, of course, so we show both a UNIX and Windows implementation.

Before we worry about the system-dependent parts, let's look at the API and its implementation. At the user level, the system consists of five functions:

```
#include "etcp.h"

void init_smb( int init_freelist );

void *smballoc( void );

                            Returns: pointer to a shared memory buffer

void smbfree( void *smbptr );

void smbsend( SOCKET s, void *smbptr );

void *smbrecv( SOCKET s );

                            Returns: pointer to a shared memory buffer
```

Before using the system, each process calls `smb_init` to obtain and initialize the shared memory and synchronizing mutex. Exactly one of the processes must call `init_smb` with `init_freelist` set to `TRUE`.

A shared memory buffer is obtained by calling `smballoc`, which returns a pointer to the newly allocated buffer. When a process is finished with a buffer, it can return it to the system by freeing it with a call to `smbfree`.

After a process has built a message in a shared memory buffer, it can pass it to another process by calling `smbsend`. As we discussed earlier, this call merely passes an index to the buffer. A process receives a buffer from a peer by calling `smbrecv`, which returns a pointer to the just-arrived buffer.

Although our system uses TCP as the IPC method to pass buffer indices, this is not the only, or even the best, possibility. It is convenient for us because it works for both UNIX and Windows, and because we can use the machinery that we already have rather than consider other IPC methods. In a UNIX environment, UNIX domain sockets are another good possibility, as are named pipes. `SendMessage`, `QueueUserAPC`, and named pipes are other possibilities for Windows.

We begin our examination of the implementation with the `smballoc` and `smbfree` functions (Figure 3.44).

### Header Information

2–8     Buffers available for allocation are kept on a free list. While on this list, each buffer contains the index of the next buffer on the list in its first `sizeof( int )` bytes. This arrangement is captured by the `smb_t` union. At the end of the buffer array is a single integer that contains either the index of the first buffer on the free list or –1 if the free list is empty. We access this integer by referring to it as `smbarray[ NSMB ].nexti`, and use the `FREE_LIST` define as a convenient alias for it. The buffer array itself is pointed to by `smbarray`. This pointer is set to the shared memory block that each process maps to its address space. We use indices to the buffer array rather than addresses because each process may map the shared memory to a different address.

```
                                                                              smb.c
 1 #include "etcp.h"

 2 #define FREE_LIST        smbarray[ NSMB ].nexti

 3 typedef union
 4 {
 5     int nexti;
 6     char buf[ SMBUFSZ ];
 7 } smb_t;
 8 smb_t *smbarray;

 9 void *smballoc( void )
10 {
11     smb_t *bp;

12     lock_buf();
13     if ( FREE_LIST < 0 )
14         error( 1, 0, "out of shared memory buffers\n" );
15     bp = smbarray + FREE_LIST;
16     FREE_LIST  = bp->nexti;
17     unlock_buf();
18     return bp;
19 }

20 void smbfree( void *b )
21 {
22     smb_t *bp;

23     bp = b;
24     lock_buf();
25     bp->nexti = FREE_LIST;
26     FREE_LIST  = bp - smbarray;
27     unlock_buf();
28 }
```
                                                                              smb.c

**Figure 3.44** The `smballoc` and `smbfree` functions

**smballoc**

*12*       We call `lock_buf` to prohibit any other process from accessing the free list. This function is implementation dependent. We shall use SysV semaphores in the UNIX implementation, and mutexes with Windows.

*13–16*    We pop a buffer off the free list. If no buffers are available, we output a diagnostic and terminate. Returning a NULL pointer is another option here.

*17–18*    We unlock access to the free list and return a pointer to the buffer.

**smbfree**

*23–27*    After locking the free list, we place the indicated buffer on the list by placing its index at the head of the chain of free buffers. We then unlock the free list and return.

Next we look at `smbsend` and `smbrecv`. These functions simply send and receive the integer index of the buffer that is being passed from one process to another. They are easily modified to use another form of IPC, if we desire (Figure 3.45).

─────────────────────────────────────────────────────── *smb.c*

```
 1 void smbsend( SOCKET s, void *b )
 2 {
 3     int index;

 4     index = ( smb_t * )b - smbarray;
 5     if ( send( s, ( char * )&index, sizeof( index ), 0 ) < 0 )
 6         error( 1, errno, "smbsend: send failure" );
 7 }

 8 void *smbrecv( SOCKET s )
 9 {
10     int index;
11     int rc;

12     rc = readn( s, ( char * )&index, sizeof( index ) );
13     if ( rc == 0 )
14         error( 1, 0, "smbrecv: peer disconnected\n" );
15     else if ( rc != sizeof( index ) )
16         error( 1, errno, "smbrecv: readn failure" );
17     return smbarray + index;
18 }
```

─────────────────────────────────────────────────────── *smb.c*

**Figure 3.45** The `smbsend` and `smbrecv` functions

**smbsend**

*4–6*  We calculate the index of the buffer pointed to by *b* and send it to our peer process using `send`.

**smbrecv**

*12–16*  We call `readn` to read the index of the buffer being passed to us. If there is an error on the read or if we don't get the expected number of bytes, we output an error and terminate.

*17*  Otherwise, we convert the buffer index into a pointer and return it to the caller.

## A UNIX Implementation

We need two more components to complete our implementation of shared memory buffers: a way of allocating and mapping a shared memory block, and a synchronization mechanism to prevent simultaneous access to the free list. We use the SysV shared memory mechanism to handle the allocation and mapping of the shared memory. We could, as we do in the Windows implementation, use a memory-mapped file instead. For those systems that support it, POSIX shared memory is another possibility.

We use only two of the SysV shared memory system calls:

```
#include <sys/shm.h>

int shmget( key_t key, size_t size, int flags );
```

> Returns: shared memory segment ID on success, -1 on error

```
void *shmat( int segid, const void *baseaddr, int flags );
```

> Returns: base address of segment if OK, -1 on error

The `shmget` system call is used to allocate a segment of shared memory. The first parameter, *key*, is a systemwide unique integer that names the segment. We use an integer that has the ASCII representation SMBM.

> The use of a name space distinct from that of the file system is widely considered one of the major failings of the SysV IPC mechanisms. The function `ftok` can be used to map a filename to an IPC key, but this mapping is not unique. Indeed, as reported in [Stevens 1999], the standard SVR4 version of `ftok` produced a collision (that is, two filenames mapping to the same key) with a probability of approximately 75 percent.

The *size* parameter specifies the size of the segment in bytes. The kernel on many UNIX systems rounds *size* up to a multiple of the system page size. The *flags* parameter is used to specify permissions and other flags. The values `SHM_R` and `SHM_W` are used to specify read and write permissions respectively for the owner. Group and other permissions are specified by shifting these values right 3 bits (group) or 6 bits (other). Thus, group write permissions are specified as `(SHM_W >> 3)`, and other read permissions as `(SHM_R >> 6)`. If `IPC_CREAT` is ORed into the *flags* parameter, the segment is created if it doesn't already exist. If, in addition, `IPC_EXCL` is ORed into the *flags* parameter, `shmget` returns an `EEXIST` error if the segment already exists.

The `shmget` call only *creates* or *accesses* the shared memory segment. To map it to a particular process's address space, we use the `shmat` call. The *segid* parameter is the segment identifier returned by `shmget`. We can specify an address where we would like the kernel to map the segment with *baseaddr*, but this parameter is almost always specified as `NULL` to tell the kernel to select the address. The *flags* parameter is used when *baseaddr* is non-NULL to help control the rounding of the address where the segment is mapped.

As we've already mentioned, we use SysV semaphores to build a mutex for our system. Although there are some difficulties with using SysV semaphores, including the name space problem we've already discussed with respect to shared memory, they are almost universally available in today's UNIX systems, and we use them for that reason. As with shared memory, we must first allocate and then initialize the semaphore before we can begin using it. We use all three semaphore-related calls.

The `semget` call is similar to `shmget`: It allocates a semaphore and returns its ID. The *key* parameter is just like the corresponding parameter for `shmget`: It names the semaphore. With SysV IPC, semaphores are allocated in sets, and the *nsems* parameter tells how many semaphores should be in the set that we are allocating. The *flags* parameter is just like that for `shmget`.

```
#include <sys/sem.h>

int semget( key_t key, int nsems, int flags );

                              Returns: semaphore ID if OK, -1 on error

int semctl( int semid, int semnum, int cmd, ... );

                           Returns: non-negative number if OK, -1 on error

int semop( int semid, struct sembuf *oparray, size_t nops );

                                        Returns: 0 if OK, -1 on error
```

We use `semctl` to set the initial value for the semaphore. It can also be used to set and get various control values associated with the semaphore. The *semid* parameter is the semaphore ID returned by `semget`. The *semnum* parameter indicates which semaphore in the set this command refers to. Because we are allocating only a single semaphore, this value is always zero for us. The *cmd* parameter is the actual control operation that we want to perform. It may take more arguments, as indicated by the '···' in its prototype.

The `semop` call is used to increment or decrement the semaphore. When a process attempts to decrement the semaphore to a negative value, it is put to sleep until some other process increments the semaphore to a value that is equal to or greater than the amount that the process is trying to decrement it. Because we are using the semaphore as a mutex, we decrement it by one to lock the free list, and increment it by one to unlock the free list. Because we will initialize the semaphore to one, this has the effect of suspending a process that tries to lock the free list when it is already locked.

The *semid* parameter is the semaphore ID returned by `semget`. The *oparray* parameter points to an array of `sembuf` structures that specify an operation for one or more semaphores in the set. The *nops* parameter specifies the number of entries in the array pointed to by *oparray*.

The `sembuf` structure, shown here, specifies which semaphore is to be acted on (`sem_num`), how much to increment or decrement it (`sem_op`), and the two special actions flags (`sem_flg`):

```
struct sembuf {
    u_short sem_num;        /* semaphore # */
    short sem_op;           /* semaphore operation */
    short sem_flg;          /* operation flags */
};
```

The two flags that can be specified for `sem_flg` are

- `IPC_NOWAIT`—Instructs `semop` to return an `EAGAIN` error instead of putting the process to sleep if the operation would cause the value of the semaphore to become negative.

- `SEM_UNDO`—Instructs `semop` to undo the effects of any semaphore operations if the process terminates. This has the effect of releasing our mutex.

We are now in a position to examine the UNIX-centric code in our shared memory buffer system. All of the system-specific code is in the init_smb function shown in Figure 3.46.

```
                                                                      smb.c
 1 #include <sys/shm.h>
 2 #include <sys/sem.h>
 3 #define MUTEX_KEY       0x534d4253   /* SMBS */
 4 #define SM_KEY          0x534d424d   /* SMBM */
 5 #define lock_buf()      if ( semop( mutex, &lkbuf, 1 ) < 0 ) \
 6                             error( 1, errno, "semop failed" )
 7 #define unlock_buf()    if ( semop( mutex, &unlkbuf, 1 ) < 0 ) \
 8                             error( 1, errno, "semop failed" )
 9 int mutex;
10 struct sembuf lkbuf;
11 struct sembuf unlkbuf;

12 void init_smb( int init_freelist )
13 {
14     union semun arg;
15     int smid;
16     int i;
17     int rc;

18     lkbuf.sem_op = -1;
19     lkbuf.sem_flg = SEM_UNDO;
20     unlkbuf.sem_op = 1;
21     unlkbuf.sem_flg = SEM_UNDO;
22     mutex = semget( MUTEX_KEY, 1,
23         IPC_EXCL | IPC_CREAT | SEM_R | SEM_A );
24     if ( mutex >= 0 )
25     {
26         arg.val = 1;
27         rc = semctl( mutex, 0, SETVAL, arg );
28         if ( rc < 0 )
29             error( 1, errno, "semctl failed" );
30     }
31     else if ( errno == EEXIST )
32     {
33         mutex = semget( MUTEX_KEY, 1, SEM_R | SEM_A );
34         if ( mutex < 0 )
35             error( 1, errno, "semctl failed" );
36     }
37     else
38         error( 1, errno, "semctl failed" );

39     smid = shmget( SM_KEY, NSMB * sizeof( smb_t ) + sizeof( int ),
40         SHM_R | SHM_W | IPC_CREAT );
41     if ( smid < 0 )
42         error( 1, errno, "shmget failed" );
43     smbarray = ( smb_t * )shmat( smid, NULL, 0 );
44     if ( smbarray == ( void * )-1 )
45         error( 1, errno, "shmat failed" );
```

```
46      if ( init_freelist )
47      {
48          for ( i = 0; i < NSMB - 1; i++ )
49              smbarray[ i ].nexti = i + 1;
50          smbarray[ NSMB - 1 ].nexti = -1;
51          FREE_LIST = 0;
52      }
53 }
```
*―――――――――――――――― smb.c*

**Figure 3.46** The (UNIX) init_smb function

### Defines and Globals

*3-4*     We define the shared memory (SMBM) and semaphore (SMBS) keys.

*5-8*     We also define our lock and unlock primitives in terms of semaphore operations.

*9-11*    We declare variables for the semaphore that we use as a mutex.

### Allocate and Initialize Semaphore

*18-21*   We initialize the semaphore operations used for locking and unlocking the free list.

*22-38*   This code creates and initializes the semaphore. We call semget with IPC_EXCL and IPC_CREAT set in the *flags* parameter. This causes semget to create the semaphore unless it already exists. If it doesn't already exist, semget returns a semaphore ID. In this case we initialize it to one (the unlocked state). If the semaphore already exists, we call semget again without specifying IPC_EXCL and IPC_CREAT to obtain the ID of the semaphore. As pointed out in [Stevens 1999], there is a race condition here, but it doesn't affect us because our server calls init_smb before calling listen, and our client does not call it until after the connect call returns.

> [Stevens 1999] discusses this race condition and how to avoid it in the general case.

### Allocate, Attach and Initialize Shared Memory Buffers

*39-45*   We allocate and attach the shared memory segment. If the segment already exists, shmget merely returns its ID.

*46-53*   If init_smb was called with *init_freelist* set to TRUE, we push the newly allocated buffers on the free list and return.

## A Windows Implementation

Before we demonstrate our system, let's look at a Windows implementation. As we mentioned earlier, all the system-specific code is in the init_smb function. Creating a mutex is simple under Windows. We need merely call the CreateMutex function:

```
#include <windows.h>

HANDLE CreateMutex( LPSECURITY_ATTRIBUTES lpsa,
                    BOOL flnitialOwner, LPTSTR lpszMutexName );

                              Returns: A handle to the mutex if OK, NULL otherwise
```

The *lpsa* parameter is a pointer to a security structure. We shall not use this feature, so we specify NULL for it. The *fInitialOwner* parameter indicates whether the creator of the mutex should be the initial owner; that is, whether the mutex should be locked initially. The *lpszMutexName* parameter names the mutex so that other processes can also access it. If the mutex already exists, CreateMutex merely returns a handle to it.

Locking and unlocking the mutex are handled by the WaitForSingleObject and ReleaseMutex calls:

> Other calls, such as WaitForMultipleObjects can also be used to lock the mutex. In all of these calls, if the mutex is already signaled (unlocked) the call returns immediately with the mutex locked. Otherwise the thread is put to sleep until the mutex becomes signaled again.

```
#include <windows.h>

DWORD WaitForSingleObject( HANDLE hObject, DWORD dwTimeout );

                  Returns: WAIT_OBJECT_0 (0) if OK, nonzero value otherwise

BOOL ReleaseMutex( HANDLE hMutex );

                              Returns: TRUE on success, FALSE otherwise
```

The *hObject* parameter to WaitForSingleObject is the handle of the object (in our case, the mutex) for which to wait. If the object specified by *hObject* is already signaled, WaitForSingleObject puts it in the unsignaled state and returns. If the object is not signaled, it puts the calling thread to sleep until the object becomes signaled. At that time, WaitForSingleObject puts the object in the unsignaled state and wakes up the sleeping thread. The *dwTimeout* parameter specifies the time in milliseconds that the thread is willing to wait for the object to become signaled. If this timer expires before the object becomes signaled, WaitForSingleObject returns WAIT_TIMEOUT. The timeout function can be disabled by specifying INFINITE for the *dwTimeout* parameter.

When a thread is finished with the critical region protected by the mutex, it unlocks it by calling ReleaseMutex with the mutex handle specified by the *hMutex* parameter.

Under Windows, we obtain a shared memory segment by memory mapping a file into each process that needs access to the shared memory. This is similar to using the mmap system call under UNIX. To do this, we first create a file in the normal way by calling CreateFile. Once we have the file, we create a mapping of it with CreateFileMapping, and then map it into our address space with MapViewOfFile.

The *hFile* parameter to CreateFileMapping is the handle for the file to be mapped. The *lpsa* parameter is for security information, which we do not use. The *fdwProtect* parameter specifies the access rights to the memory object. It can be PAGE_READONLY, PAGE_READWRITE, or PAGE_WRITECOPY. The last choice causes the kernel to make a private copy of the data if the process writes to it. We use PAGE_READWRITE because we'll be both reading and writing the memory. There are additional flags that can be ORed into this field to control the caching of the memory

```
#include <windows.h>

HANDLE CreateFileMapping( HANDLE hFile, LPSECURITY_ATTRIBUTES lpsa,
                          DWORD fdwProtect, DWORD dwMaximumSizeHigh,
                          DWORD dwMaximumSizeLow, LPSTR lpszMapName );

                      Returns: Handle to file mapping if OK, NULL on error

LPVOID MapViewOfFile( HANDLE hFileMapObj, DWORD dwDesiredAccess,
                      DWORD dwFileOffsetHigh, DWORD dwFileOffsetLow,
                      DWORD dwBytesToMap );

                    Returns: Address at which memory mapped if OK, NULL on error
```

pages. We won't need these and therefore don't discuss them. Together, *dwMaximumSizeHigh* and *dwMaximumSizeLow* comprise a 64-bit size of the memory object. Finally, *lpszMapName* is the name of the memory object. It is provided so that other processes can access it by name.

Once created, the memory object is mapped into each process's address space with MapViewOfFile. *hFileMapObj* is the handle returned by CreateFileMapping. We again specify our desired access with *dwDesiredAccess*. This parameter can take the values FILE_MAP_WRITE (write *and* read access), FILE_MAP_READ (read-only access), FILE_MAP_ALL_ACCESS (same as FILE_MAP_WRITE), and FILE_MAP_COPY. The last value creates a private copy of the data if it is written to. The *dwFileOffsetHigh* and *dwFileOffsetLow* parameters specify the location within the file at which the mapping should begin. We specify zero for both because we want to map the entire file. The amount of memory to map is specified by *dwBytesToMap*.

For more information on using Windows mutexes and memory mapping see [Richter 1997].

We can now show the Windows version of init_smb. As we see in Figure 3.47, it is essentially the same as the UNIX version.

———————————————————————————————————————————— *smb.c*

```
 1 #define FILENAME    "./smbfile"
 2 #define lock_buf()   if ( WaitForSingleObject( mutex, INFINITE )\
 3                         != WAIT_OBJECT_0 ) \
 4                       error( 1, errno, "lock_buf failed" )
 5 #define unlock_buf() if ( !ReleaseMutex( mutex ) )\
 6                       error( 1, errno, "unlock_buf failed" )
 7 HANDLE mutex;

 8 void init_smb( int init_freelist )
 9 {
10     HANDLE hfile;
11     HANDLE hmap;
12     int i;

13     mutex = CreateMutex( NULL, FALSE, "smbmutex" );
14     if ( mutex == NULL )
15         error( 1, errno, "CreateMutex failed" );
```

```
16      hfile = CreateFile( FILENAME,
17          GENERIC_READ | GENERIC_WRITE,
18          FILE_SHARE_READ | FILE_SHARE_WRITE,
19          NULL, OPEN_ALWAYS, FILE_ATTRIBUTE_NORMAL, NULL );
20      if ( hfile == INVALID_HANDLE_VALUE )
21          error( 1, errno, "CreateFile failed" );
22      hmap = CreateFileMapping( hfile, NULL, PAGE_READWRITE,
23          0, NSMB * sizeof( smb_t ) + sizeof( int ), "smbarray" );
24      smbarray = MapViewOfFile( hmap, FILE_MAP_WRITE, 0, 0, 0 );
25      if ( smbarray == NULL )
26          error( 1, errno, "MapViewOfFile failure" );

27      if ( init_freelist )
28      {
29          for ( i = 0; i < NSMB - 1; i++ )
30              smbarray[ i ].nexti = i + 1;
31          smbarray[ NSMB - 1 ].nexti = -1;
32          FREE_LIST = 0;
33      }
34 }
```
──────────────────────────────────────────────────────── *smb.c*

**Figure 3.47** The (Windows) `init_smb` function

To try out our shared memory buffer system, we write short client (Figure 3.48) and server (Figure 3.49) programs.

──────────────────────────────────────────────────────── *smbc.c*
```
 1 #include "etcp.h"

 2 int main( int argc, char **argv )
 3 {
 4     char *bp;
 5     SOCKET s;

 6     INIT();
 7     s = tcp_client( argv[ 1 ], argv[ 2 ] );
 8     init_smb( FALSE );
 9     bp = smballoc();
10     while ( fgets( bp, SMBUFSZ, stdin ) != NULL  )
11     {
12         smbsend( s, bp );
13         bp = smballoc();
14     }
15     EXIT( 0 );
16 }
```
──────────────────────────────────────────────────────── *smbc.c*

**Figure 3.48** Client using shared memory buffer system

──────────────────────────────────────────────────────── *smbs.c*
```
 1 #include "etcp.h"

 2 int main( int argc, char **argv )
 3 {
 4     char *bp;
 5     SOCKET s;
```

```
 6      SOCKET s1;

 7      INIT();
 8      init_smb( TRUE );
 9      s = tcp_server( NULL, argv[ 1 ] );
10      s1 = accept( s, NULL, NULL );
11      if ( !isvalidsock( s1 ) )
12          error( 1, errno, "accept failure" );
13      for ( ;; )
14      {
15          bp = smbrecv( s1 );
16          fputs( bp, stdout );
17          smbfree( bp );
18      }
19      EXIT( 0 );
20  }
```
*smbs.c*

**Figure 3.49** Server using shared memory buffer system

When we run these, we get the expected results:

```
bsd: $ smbc localhost 9000    bsd: $ smbs 9000
Hello                         Hello
World!                        World!
^C                            smbs: smbrecv: peer disconnected
bsd: $                        bsd: $
```

Notice that because smbc reads each line from stdin directly into a shared memory buffer, and that because smbs writes each line to stdout directly from the shared memory buffer, there is no unnecessary data copying.

### Summary

In this tip we examined ways to avoid unnecessary data copying. In many network applications, copying data from buffer to buffer accounts for a large portion of the CPU usage.

For communications between processes, we developed a shared memory buffer system, which allows us to pass a single copy of data from one process to another. We developed versions of the system for UNIX and Windows.

## Tip 27: Zero the `sockaddr_in` Structure Before Use

Although we generally use only the three fields sin_family, sin_port, and sin_addr of the sockaddr_in structure, it has additional fields in most implementations. For example, many implementations have a sin_len field that contains the length of the structure. This field is present, for instance, in systems derived from the BSD implementations of 4.3BSD Reno and later. The Winsock implementation, on the other hand, does not have this field.

If we compare the `sockaddr_in` structures from the BSD-derived FreeBSD:

```
struct sockaddr_in {
    u_char  sin_len;
    u_char  sin_family;
    u_short sin_port;
    struct  in_addr sin_addr;
    char    sin_zero[8];
};
```

and that from the Winsock implementation:

```
struct sockaddr_in {
    short   sin_family;
    u_short sin_port;
    struct  in_addr sin_addr;
    char    sin_zero[8];
};
```

we see that one extra field that they do share, along with most implementations, is `sin_zero`. Although this field is not used (it's there to make the `sockaddr_in` structure 16 bytes long) it must nevertheless be set to zero.

> The reason for this is that some implementations do a binary compare of the address structure with the addresses associated with each interface when binding an address to a socket. This code depends on the `sin_zero` field being zero. See Section 22.7 of [Wright and Stevens 1995] for the details of this.

Because we must zero `sin_zero` anyway, it is normal practice to always zero the entire address structure before we use it. In this way, all additional fields are cleared and we avoid possible interactions with undocumented fields and their uses. Recall from Figure 2.16 that the first thing our `set_address` function does is to call `bzero` to clear the entire `sockaddr_in` structure.

## Tip 28: Don't Forget About Byte Sex

Modern computers store integer data in different ways depending on their architecture. Let's consider, for example, the 32-bit integer 305,419,896 (0x12345678). A machine could store the 4 bytes of this integer with the most significant bytes first (the so-called *big endian* format):

| 12 | 34 | 56 | 78 |
|----|----|----|----|

or with the least significant bytes first (the *little endian* format):

| 78 | 56 | 34 | 12 |
|----|----|----|----|

> The terms *little endian* and *big endian* are from [Cohen 1981], which likens the ongoing dispute over which format is "best" to the Lilliputian factions in Jonathan Swift's *Gulliver's Travels*, who waged endless wars over whether eggs should be broken on the big end or the little end.

Other storage formats have been used as well, but today virtually all machines use either the big endian format or the little endian format.

It's easy to determine the format that a given machine uses by writing a test program to see how the integer 0x12345678 is stored (Figure 3.50).

```
                                                                    ──── endian.c
 1  #include <stdio.h>
 2  #include <sys/types.h>
 3  #include "etcp.h"
 4  int main( void )
 5  {
 6      u_int32_t x = 0x12345678;    /* 305419896 */
 7      unsigned char *xp = ( char * )&x;

 8      printf( "%0x %0x %0x %0x\n",
 9          xp[ 0 ], xp[ 1 ], xp[ 2 ], xp[ 3 ] );
10      exit( 0 );
11  }
                                                                    ──── endian.c
```

**Figure 3.50** Program to test integer storage format

When we run this on the Intel-based bsd, we get

```
bsd: $ endian
78 56 34 12
bsd: $
```

verifying that it is, indeed, a little endian machine.

The particular choice of storage format is often referred to, picturesquely, as *byte sex*. This is important to us because big and little endian machines (and those using other formats for that matter) often converse with each other using the TCP/IP protocols. Because information such as source and destination addresses, port numbers, datagram lengths, window sizes, and so on, are exchanged as integers, it is imperative that all sides agree on how those integers are represented.

To avoid interoperability problems, all integral protocol data is transferred in *network byte order*, which is defined as big endian. Most of this is handled for us by the underlying protocols, but we do specify network addresses, port numbers, and occasionally other header data to TCP/IP. When we do, we must *always* specify them in network byte order.

To help us with this, there are two functions that convert data from host format to network byte order, and two functions that convert from network order to host format. The definitions presented on the next page are for POSIX. Some versions of UNIX define these functions in a header file different from netinet/in.h. The uint32_t and uint16_t data types are POSIX definitions for unsigned 32- and 16-bit integers respectively, and may not be defined in all implementations. Nevertheless, htonl and ntohl always take and return unsigned 32-bit integers, regardless of UNIX or Winsock implementation. Similarly, htons and ntohs always take and return unsigned 16-bit integers, regardless of implementation.

The 'l' and 's' at the end of the names stand for "long" and "short." This made sense when the functions were originally implemented in 4.2BSD on a 32-bit machine, because longs *were* 32

```
#include <netinet/in.h>    /* UNIX */
#include <winsock2.h>      /* Winsock */

uint32_t htonl( uint32_t host32 );

uint16_t htons( uint16_t host16 );

                              Both return: an integer in network byte order


uint32_t ntohl( uint32_t network32 );

uint16_t ntohs( uint16_t network16 );

                                 Both return: an integer in host format
```

bits and shorts *were* 16 bits. With the advent of 64-bit machines, this is no longer necessarily true, so we should be careful to remember that the 'l' functions work on 32-bit integers *not* (necessarily) longs, and that the 's' functions work on 16-bit integers *not* (necessarily) shorts. A convenient fiction is to think of the 'l' functions as working on the *longer* integer fields that occur in the protocol headers, and that the 's' functions work on the *shorter* ones.

The host-to-network functions (`htonl` and `htons`) convert an integer in host format to one in network byte order, whereas the network-to-host functions (`ntohl` and `ntohs`) go the other way. Note that on big endian machines these functions do nothing and are usually defined as macros such as

```
#define htonl(x)    (x)
```

Little endian (and other architecture) machines define them in a system-dependent way. The point is that we don't need to know or care whether our machine is big or little endian because these functions always do the "right thing."

We should also understand that these functions are only *required* for fields examined by the protocols. That is, IP, UDP, and TCP all treat the user data as a collection of bytes with no structure, and therefore don't care whether integers in the user data are in network byte order. Nonetheless, we should use the `ntoh*` and `hton*` routines on any data that we send as an aid to interoperability. Even if our application is intended to run on only one platform, when the day comes, as it surely will, that we have to port it to another, the extra effort will pay off.

The issue of data conversion between machines of different architectures is a difficult problem in general. Many engineers deal with it simply by converting everything to ASCII (or possibly EBCDIC if IBM mainframes are involved). Another way of handling the problem is the *External Data Representation* (XDR) component of Sun's *remote procedure call* (RPC) facility. XDR, which is defined in RFC 1832 [Srinivasan 1995], is a set of rules for encoding different data types as well as a language for describing the data to be encoded. Although XDR is intended to be used as part of RPC, we can also use it directly in our programs without RPC. [Stevens 1999] discusses XDR and how to use it without RPC.

Finally, we should note that the resolver functions such as `gethostbyname` and `getservbyname` (Tip 29) all return their values in network byte order. Thus code such as

```
struct servent *sp;
struct sockaddr_in *sap;

sp = getservbyname( name, protocol );
sap->sin_port = htons( sp->s_port );
```

is wrong and results in an error unless it is running on a big endian machine.

### Summary

In this tip we have seen how TCP/IP uses a standard representation, called network byte order, for integers within its protocols headers. We saw that the functions htonl, htons, ntohl, and ntohs can be used to convert integers to and from network byte order, and we mentioned that XDR is often useful for general data conversion between machines.

## Tip 29: Don't Hardcode IP Addresses or Port Numbers in Your Application

There are only two proper ways for a program to obtain an IP address or port number:

1. As command line arguments or, in the case of GUI interfaces, from a dialog box or similar mechanism

2. From one or more of the resolver functions such as gethostbyname or getservbyname

> getservbyname is not really a resolver function (that is, it is not part of the DNS client that maps names to IP addresses and vice versa), but we lump it in with them because it performs a similar service and is usually used with them.

We should never hard-code these parameters into our programs, and we should not put them in our own (private) configuration files. Both UNIX and Windows provide standard ways to get this information and we should make use of them.

The fact that many IP addresses are now assigned dynamically using the *dynamic host configuration protocol* (DHCP) provides a compelling reason to avoid specifying fixed IP addresses for our applications. Some even argue that the prevalence of DHCP and the length and complexity of IPv6 addresses mean that we shouldn't provide a numeric IP address to an application at all, but should instead provide host names exclusively, and let the application resolve them to IP addresses through calls to gethostbyname or its siblings. Even when DHCP is not in use, maintenance and network management argue strongly against hard-coding this information or putting it in nonstandard places. For example, if the network is renumbered, any application having a hard-coded address will be broken.

It is always tempting just to hard-code these values in a quick-and-dirty program so that we don't have to bother with the getXbyY and related functions. Unfortunately, once created, these quick-and-dirty programs can take on a life of their own, and sometimes even become products. One of the great advantages of our skeleton programs and the library functions derived from them (Tip 4) is that the code is already written for us, so there is no need to cut corners.

Before we go on, let's consider some of the resolver functions and how to use them. We have already seen `gethostbyname` several times:

```
#include <netdb.h>          /* UNIX */
#include <winsock2.h>       /* WinSock */

struct hostent *gethostbyname( const char *name );
```

Returns: Pointer to a `hostent` structure if OK, `NULL` with error in `h_errno` otherwise

We pass `gethostbyname` the name of a host, and it returns a pointer to a `hostent` structure:

```
struct hostent {
    char *h_name;                   /* official name of host */
    char **h_aliases;               /* alias list */
    int h_addrtype;                 /* host address type */
    int h_length;                   /* length of address */
    char **h_addr_list;             /* list of addresses from DNS */
#define h_addr h_addr_list[0]       /* first address */
};
```

The `h_name` field points to the "official" name of the host, whereas the `h_aliases` field points to a list of aliases for the official name. The `h_addrtype` field is either `AF_INET` or `AF_INET6`, depending on whether the address is an IPv4 or an IPv6 address. Likewise, `h_length` is either 4 or 16 depending on the address type. All addresses of type `h_addrtype` for the host are returned in a list pointed to by `h_addr_list`. The `h_addr` define serves as an alias for the first (possibly only) address in the list. Because `gethostbyname` returns a list of addresses, an application is able to try each address in the list until it is successful in contacting the desired host.

There are four things to keep in mind about `gethostbyname`:

1. If the host supports both IPv4 and IPv6, only one type of address is returned. Under UNIX, the type of address returned depends on the resolver option `RES_USE_INET6`, which can be set by an explicit call to `res_init`, by an environment variable, or by an option in the DNS configuration file. Under Winsock, it always returns an IPv4 address.

2. The `hostent` structure is allocated in static memory. This means that `gethostbyname` is not reentrant.

3. The pointers in the static `hostent` structure point to other static or allocated memory, and we must therefore do a *deep copy* of the structure if we wish to make a copy of it. That is, we must allocate memory for and then copy the data pointed to by the fields separately from the `hostent` structure itself.

4. As we discussed in Tip 28, the addresses pointed to by the `h_addr_list` field are already in network byte order, so we should not use `htonl` on them.

We can also map IP addresses to host names with the `gethostbyaddr` function:

```
#include <netdb.h>          /* UNIX */
#include <winsock2.h>       /* WinSock */

struct hostent *gethostbyaddr( const char *addr, int len, int type );
```

Returns: Pointer to a `hostent` structure if OK, `NULL` with error in `h_errno` otherwise

Despite having type `char*`, the *addr* parameter points to an `in_addr` (or `in6_addr` in the case of IPv6) structure. The length of this structure is given by the *len* parameter, and its type (`AF_INET` or `AF_INET6`) by *type*. Our previous remarks concerning `gethostbyname` also apply to `gethostbyaddr`.

For hosts supporting IPv6, `gethostbyname` is not really satisfactory because we cannot specify the type of address we want returned. To support IPv6 (and other) address families, the functionality of `gethostbyname` was extended by `gethostbyname2` to allow the retrieval of a specific address type:

```
#include <netdb.h>

struct host *gethostbyname2( const char *name, int af );
```

Returns: Pointer to a `hostent` structure if OK, `NULL` with error in `h_errno` otherwise

The *af* parameter is the address family, which for us is either `AF_INET` or `AF_INET6`. WinSock does not have `gethostbyname2`, but instead uses the much richer (and complicated) `WSALookupServiceNext` interface.

> IPv4/IPv6 interoperability is largely a matter of dealing with the two different types of addresses, and `gethostbyname2` provides one way of doing so. This topic is discussed at length in [Stevens 1998], which also develops an implementation of the POSIX `getaddrinfo` function. This function provides a convenient method of dealing with both types of addresses in a protocol-independent way. By using `getaddrinfo`, it is possible to write applications that work seamlessly with either IPv4 or IPv6.

Just as it makes sense to allow the system (or DNS) to convert host names to IP addresses for us, it also make sense to allow the system to manage port numbers. We have already discussed one way of doing so in Tip 18, and we want to mention another way now. In the same way that `gethostbyname` and `gethostbyaddr` translate between host names and IP addresses, `getservbyname` and `getservbyport` translate between port numbers and their symbolic names. For example, the daytime service listens for connections (TCP) or datagrams (UDP) on port 13, and we can use the service by, for instance, calling it with telnet:

```
telnet bsd 13
```

This requires, however, that we remember that the daytime service is on port 13. Fortunately, telnet also accepts the symbolic name for the service port:

```
telnet bsd daytime
```

Telnet does this mapping by calling `getservbyname`, and we can do the same in our applications. Recalling Figure 2.16, we see that, in fact, our skeleton code is already doing it. The `set_address` function first assumes that the port parameter is an ASCII integer and tries to convert it into binary. If this conversion fails, it then calls `getservbyname` to look up the symbolic port name and convert it to a port number.

The `getservbyname` call is similar to `gethostbyname`:

```
#include <netdb.h>          /* UNIX */
#include <winsock2.h>       /* WinSock */

struct servent *getservbyname( const char *name, const char *proto );
```
                    Returns: Pointer to a `servent` structure if OK, `NULL` otherwise

The *name* parameter is the name of the service we are looking up—"daytime," for example. If the *proto* parameter is not `NULL`, `getservbyname` returns a service that matches both the name and the protocol; otherwise, it returns the first service it finds that has the name *name*. The `servent` structure contains information about the service:

```
struct servent {
    char *s_name;          /* official service name */
    char **s_aliases;      /* alias list */
    int s_port;            /* port # */
    char *s_proto;         /* protocol to use */
};
```

The `s_name` and `s_aliases` fields have pointers to the official name and aliases of the service. The port number of the service is in the `s_port` field. As usual, this number is already in network byte order. The protocol (TCP or UDP) used by the service is pointed to by the `s_proto` field.

We can also map from port numbers to service name by using `getservbyport`:

```
#include <netdb.h>          /* UNIX */
#include <winsock2.h>       /* WinSock */

struct servent *getservbyport( int port, const char *proto );
```
                    Returns: Pointer to a `servent` structure if OK, `NULL` otherwise

The number of the port to look up is passed in network byte order in the *port* parameter. The *proto* parameter is as before.

From a programmatic point of view, our skeletons and the associated library solve the host and service name translation problems. They call the proper routines and we needn't worry about it any further. We do need to understand, however, how to provide the necessary information to the system so that our skeleton code can retrieve it.

The most common methods of providing this data are

- DNS
- The Network Information System (NIS) or NIS+

- The hosts and services files

DNS is a distributed database used for translating between host names and IP addresses.

> DNS is also used for routing email. When we send mail to
>
>     `jsmith@somecompany.com`
>
> DNS is used to locate the mail handler (or handlers) for `somecompany.com`. See [Albitz and Liu 1998] for more about this.

Responsibility for the entries in the database is distributed into zones (corresponding roughly to domains) and subzones. For example, `bigcompany.com` may be one zone, and it may, in turn, be broken into subzones corresponding to departments or regional offices. Each zone and subzone runs one or more DNS server that contains information about all the hosts in that (sub)zone. Other DNS servers can query the `bigcompany.com` servers to resolve names for the hosts at Bigcompany.

> DNS provides a nice example of a UDP application. Most communication with a DNS server is through short UDP transactions. The client (usually one of the resolver functions) sends a UDP datagram containing the query to a DNS server. If no answer is received within a certain time, another server is tried if one's available; otherwise, the request is reissued to the original server with the timeout value increased.

Today, the overwhelming majority of host/IP address translations are made using DNS. Even networks that are not connected to a larger WAN often use DNS because it simplifies management of IP addresses. That is, if a new host is added to the network or the IP address for an existing host is changed, only the DNS database must be updated, not the hosts files on every machine.

NIS and its successor NIS+ provide a centralized database for many types of information about the network. Besides host names and IP addresses, NIS can manage services, passwords, groups, and other network-related data. The standard resolver functions that we discussed earlier can query NIS databases. In some systems, the NIS server automatically queries DNS if it is asked to resolve a host name that it doesn't know. In other systems, the resolver functions handle this.

The advantage of NIS is that it centralizes management of network-related data and thus simplifies the administration of larger networks. Some authorities discourage the use of NIS because of potential security risks involving the password files. NIS+ addresses some of the security issues, but many feel that it is still insecure. NIS is discussed in [Brown 1994].

The final, and least desirable, standard place to put host/IP address translation information is in the hosts file on each machine. This file, which usually resides in `/etc/hosts`, contains the name, alias, and IP address of hosts on the network. Again, the standard resolver functions query the hosts file. Most systems provide a systemwide configuration item that specifies whether the host file should be consulted before or after a DNS query.

Another file, usually `/etc/services`, lists the service/port translations. Unless NIS is in use, it is common for each machine to maintain its own copy of this file.

Because the file rarely changes, this does not present the management problems that the hosts file does. We have already discussed the services file and its format in Tip 17.

The major disadvantage of using a hosts file is the obvious management problems. For a network with more than a very few hosts, these problems quickly become intractable. As a result, many authorities discourage their use altogether. [Lehey 1996], for example, says, "There is only one reason for not running DNS somewhere on your network: if you're not connected to a network."

### Summary

In this tip we are strongly advised not to hard-code addresses or port numbers into our applications. We examined several standard ways that we can make these addresses and port numbers available to our applications, and we looked at the advantages and disadvantages of each.

## Tip 30: Understand Connected UDP Sockets

In this tip we look at using `connect` with UDP. We know from Tip 1 that UDP is a connectionless protocol—that it merely transmits individually addressed datagrams—so the notion of "connect" seems out of place. Recall, however, that we have already seen one example of this in Figure 3.9, where we used `connect` in an `inetd`-launched UDP server to obtain a new (ephemeral) port for the server so that `inetd` could continue listening for datagrams on the original well-known port.

Before we discuss why we might want to use `connect` with a UDP socket, we should be clear on what "connect" really means in this context. With TCP, calling `connect` causes the exchange of initial state information between peers through the three-way handshake (Figure 3.39). Part of this state is the address and port of each peer, so one function of `connect` with TCP could be thought of as binding the address and port of the remote peer to the local socket.

> This is different from calling `bind`, whose function is to bind the *local* address and port to the socket.

With UDP, there is no shared state to exchange with our peer, so calling `connect` does not result in any network traffic. Rather, its action is entirely local; it merely binds the remote host's address and port to the local socket.

Although there may not appear to be much utility in calling `connect` for a UDP socket, we will see that in addition to some efficiency gains, it is often used to obtain functionality not otherwise available. Let's look at the reasons to connect a UDP socket first from the point of view of a sender and then from the point of view of a receiver.

The first thing we notice with a connected UDP socket is that we no longer use `sendto`, but use `send` or `write` (UNIX) instead.

> We can still use `sendto` on a connected UDP socket, but we must specify NULL for the pointer to our peer's address, and zero for its length. We can also use `sendmsg`, of course, but again we must set the `msg_name` field of the `msghdr` structure to NULL and the `msg_namelen` field to zero.

This isn't much of a gain, of course, but using `connect` actually does produce a significant increase in efficiency.

In BSD implementations, `sendto` is actually a special case of calling `connect`. When a datagram is sent with `sendto`, the kernel connects the socket temporarily, sends the datagram, and then disconnects the socket. In a study of 4.3BSD and the closely related SunOS 4.1.1, [Partridge and Pink 1993] observes that connecting and disconnecting the socket in this manner consumes nearly one third of the processing time for transmitting a UDP datagram. With the exception of improvement in the code used to locate the *protocol control block* (PCB) associated with a socket, the UDP code that they studied remains substantially unchanged in 4.4BSD and its descendants such as FreeBSD. In particular, these stacks still perform the temporary connect and disconnect. Thus, if we are going to send a series of UDP datagrams to the same peer, we may be able to improve efficiency by calling `connect` first.

Although efficiency gains, as just described, are realized in some implementations, the primary reason for a sender of UDP datagrams to connect to its peer is to receive notification of *asynchronous errors*. To understand the problem, imagine that we send a UDP datagram to a peer, but that no process is listening on the destination port. The peer's UDP returns an ICMP port-unreachable message, informing our TCP/IP stack of that fact, but unless we connect the socket, our application does not receive this notification. Let's consider why. When we call `sendto`, our message has a UDP header prepended, and is passed to the IP layer, where it is encapsulated in an IP datagram and placed on the interface output queue. After the datagram has been placed on the queue (or sent if nothing else is waiting), `sendto` returns to the application with a successful status. Sometime later (hence the term *asynchronous*), the ICMP message from our peer arrives. Although the ICMP message contains a copy of the UDP header, our stack has no record of which application sent the datagram (recall from Tip 1 that because UDP is stateless, the system forgets about the datagram once it has been sent). When, however, we connect the socket to our peer, this fact is recorded in the PCB associated with the socket, and our TCP/IP stack is able to match the copy of the UDP header with the PCB, telling it which socket to deliver the ICMP message to.

To illustrate these points we take our `udpclient` program (Figure 3.8) from Tip 17 and use it to send a datagram to a port on which no process is listening:

```
bsd: $ udpclient bsd 9000
Hello, World!
^C                                          client hangs, terminated manually
bsd: $
```

Next we modify `udpclient` by adding the lines

```
if ( connect( s, ( struct sockaddr * )&peer, sizeof( peer ) ) )
    error( 1, errno, "connect failed" );
```

right after the call to `udp_client`. If we call this `udpconn1` and run it, we get

```
bsd: $ udpconn1 bsd 9000
Hello, World!
udpconn1: sendto failed: Socket is already connected (56)
bsd: $
```

The error is due to our using `sendto` on the connected socket. What happened is that when `sendto` caused UDP to try to connect the socket temporarily, UDP found that the socket was already connected and returned the `EISCONN` error.

We fix this problem by changing the `sendto` in udpconn1 to

```
rc = send( s, buf, strlen( buf ), 0 );
```

If we call the new program udpconn2 and run it, we get

```
bsd: $ udpconn2 bsd 9000
Hello, World!
udpconn2: recvfrom failed: Connection refused (61)
bsd: $
```

This time, we get an `ECONNREFUSED` error from `recvfrom`. This error is a result of the ICMP port-unreachable error being delivered to our application.

Normally there is no reason for a receiver to connect to its peer (unless, of course, it is also going to be a sender). There is, however, one situation when it can be useful. Recall our telephone/mail analogy from Tip 1. Because TCP is a connected protocol, each side knows who its peer is and can be confident that every byte it gets is from that peer. A TCP connection is like a private phone line—there are no other parties on the line.

An application receiving UDP datagrams, on the other hand, is like a mailbox. Just as anyone can send a letter to a given mailbox, any application on any host can send our receiving application a datagram as long as it is addressed to the proper address and port.

Sometimes it is desirable to accept datagrams from only one application. A receiving application can accomplish this by connecting to its peer. Thereafter, only datagrams from that peer are delivered to the application. To see how this works, we write a UDP echo server that connects to the first client that sends it a datagram (Figure 3.51).

—————————————————————————————————————— *udpconnserv.c*

```
1 #include "etcp.h"
2 int main( int argc, char **argv )
3 {
4     struct sockaddr_in peer;
5     SOCKET s;
6     int rc;
7     int len;
8     char buf[ 120 ];

9     INIT();
10    s = udp_server( NULL, argv[ 1 ] );
11    len = sizeof( peer );
12    rc = recvfrom( s, buf, sizeof( buf ),
13        0, ( struct sockaddr * )&peer, &len );
14    if ( rc < 0 )
15        error( 1, errno, "recvfrom failed" );
```

```
16      if ( connect( s, ( struct sockaddr * )&peer, len ) )
17          error( 1, errno, "connect failed" );
18      while ( strncmp( buf, "done", 4 ) != 0 )
19      {
20          if ( send( s, buf, rc, 0 ) < 0 )
21              error( 1, errno, "send failed" );
22          rc = recv( s, buf, sizeof( buf ), 0 );
23          if ( rc < 0 )
24              error( 1, errno, "recv failed" );
25      }
26      EXIT( 0 );
27 }
```
*—————————————————————————————————————————————— udpconnserv.c*

**Figure 3.51**  A UDP echo server that connects

*9–15*    We do our standard UDP initialization and receive the first datagram, saving the sender's address and port in `peer`.

*16–17*   We connect to our peer.

*18–25*   We loop echoing datagrams until we receive a datagram containing the single word "done."

We can use `udpconn2` to experiment with `udpconnserv`. First, we start the server listening for datagrams on port 9000

```
udpconnserv 9000
```

and then we start two copies of `udpconn2` in separate windows:

```
bsd: $ udpconn2 bsd 9000    | bsd: $ udpconn2 bsd 9000
one                         | two
one                         | udpconn2: recvfrom failed:
                            |           Connection refused (61)
three                       | bsd: $
three                       |
done                        |
^C                          |
bsd: $                      |
```

In the first window we type "one," which `udpconnserv` duly echos back. Then in the second window we type "two," but `recvfrom` returns an `ECONNREFUSED` error. That's because UDP returned an ICMP port-unreachable message because our server had already connected to the first copy of `udpconn2` and was not accepting datagrams from any other address/port combination.

> Both copies of `udpconn2` have the same source address, of course, but the ephemeral ports assigned by the TCP/IP stack are different.

We type "three" in the first window to verify that udpconnserv is still operating correctly, and then type "done" to terminate the server. Finally, we manually abort the first copy of udpconn2.

As we see, not only does udpconnserv refuse to accept datagrams from any address/port other than the one to which it is connected, but it also informs other applications of that fact by an ICMP port unreachable message. Of course, the client must also connect to the server to receive the ICMP message. If we reran this last test using the original version of udpclient instead of udpconn2, we would see that the second copy of udpclient merely hangs when we type "two."

### Summary

In this tip we examined the use of connect with UDP. Although the use of connect with a connectionless protocol might not seem to make sense, we saw that it can lead to more efficient programs and is necessary if we want to receive certain error messages regarding our UDP datagrams. We also saw how we can use connect to accept datagrams from only one peer.

## Tip 31: Remember That All the World's Not C

We have used the C language for the examples and explanations throughout this text, but it is not, of course, the only choice. Many prefer to write in C++, Java, or even Pascal. In this tip, we explore the idea of using scripting languages for network programming, and give some examples in Perl.

We have seen several examples of small programs used to test or drive larger programs. In Tip 30, for example, we used udpclient, udpconn1, and udpconn2 to test the behavior of connected UDP sockets. These three programs were all simple, and were all essentially the same. In such cases it makes sense to use a scripting language. Programs written in a scripting language are easy to put together and modify because, for instance, we don't need to compile them, link them against a special library, or worry about makefiles—we simply write the script and run it.

For example, Figure 3.52 presents a minimal Perl script that implements the functionality of udpclient.

Although our purpose is not to present a Perl tutorial, it is worthwhile examining this script in a little more detail.

> The standard Perl reference is [Wall et al. 1996]. Chapter 6 discusses the networking and IPC facilities of Perl5. More information on Perl, including where to get it, can be found at <http://www.perl.com>.

### Initialization

2    This line causes Perl to make the definitions of certain constants (such as PF_INET) available to the script.

### Get Command Line Parameters

3-4    We read the host name and port number from the command line. Note that this script actually has greater functionality than the corresponding C version because it

```
                                                                    ——— pudpclient
 1  #! /usr/bin/perl5
 2  use Socket;
 3  $host = shift || 'localhost';
 4  $port = shift || 'echo';
 5  $port = getservbyname( $port, 'udp' ) if $port =~ /\D/;
 6  $peer = sockaddr_in( $port, inet_aton( $host ) );
 7  socket( S, PF_INET, SOCK_DGRAM, 0 ) || die "socket failed $!";
 8  while ( $line = <STDIN> )
 9  {
10      defined( send( S, $line, 0, $peer ) ) || die "send failed $!";
11      defined( recv( S, $line, 120, 0 ) ) || die "recv failed $!";
12      print $line;
13  }
                                                                    ——— pudpclient
```

**Figure 3.52** A Perl version of udpclient

defaults the host parameter to "localhost" and the port to "echo" if one or both is
omitted.

### Fill in the `sockaddr_in` Structure and Allocate a Socket

*5–6*    This code performs the same function as set_address from Figure 2.16 of Tip 4.
Notice how simple the code is. These two lines accept either a numeric IP address or a
host name, and similarly a numeric or symbolic port name.

*7*    We allocate a UDP socket.

### Client Loop

*8–13*    Just as in udpclient, we loop reading lines from stdin, writing them to our peer,
reading our peer's response, and writing that response to stdout.

Although the familiar networking functions sometimes take slightly different arguments and may return their results in an unexpected manner, the overall flow and feel
of Figure 3.52 is familiar and comfortable. Anyone with a basic knowledge of network
programming who obtains just a small facility with Perl can be remarkably productive
in a short time.

For comparison, Figure 3.53 shows a TCP echo server. We can connect to this server
using telnet or any other TCP application capable of acting as an echo client.

Again we see the familiar sequence of calls to the sockets API, and even if we know
no Perl at all, we can follow the flow of the program. We note two peculiarities due to
the Perl language:

1. The accept on line 11, returns TRUE if the call is successful, and returns the
   new socket in its second parameter (*S1*). This makes the for loop idiom to handle successive connections on line 11 natural.

2. Because recv returns the address of the sender (or "undefined") instead of the
   number of bytes read, we must check for an EOF by explicitly retrieving the
   length of $line (line 16). The last operator performs the same function as
   break does in C.

```
 1 #! /usr/bin/perl5
 2 use Socket;
 3 $port = shift;
 4 $port = getservbyname( $port, 'tcp' ) if $port =~ /\D/;
 5 die "Invalid port" unless $port;
 6 socket( S, PF_INET, SOCK_STREAM, 0 ) || die "socket: $!";
 7 setsockopt( S, SOL_SOCKET, SO_REUSEADDR, pack( 'l', 1 ) ) ||
 8    die "setsockopt: $!";
 9 bind( S, sockaddr_in( $port, INADDR_ANY ) ) || die "bind: $!";
10 listen( S, SOMAXCONN );
11 for( ; accept( S1, S ); close( S1 ) )
12 {
13     while ( TRUE )
14     {
15         defined( recv( S1, $line, 120, 0 ) ) || die "recv: $!";
16         last if length( $line ) == 0;
17         defined( send( S1, $line, 0 ) ) || die "send: $!";
18     }
19 }
```

**Figure 3.53** Perl version of an echo server

As we can see from these two programs, Perl, and scripting languages in general, is an excellent way to build small test programs, prototype larger systems, and build small utilities. Indeed, Perl and other scripting languages are used extensively in the development of web servers and specialized Web clients (see, for example, [Castro 1998] and [Patchett and Wright 1998]).

Besides simplicity and rapid prototyping, there are other reasons to use a scripting language. One such reason is to make use of the scripting language's special features. Perl, for example, excels at data manipulation and regular expressions, and it is often more convenient to use Perl than a conventional language such as C.

As a concrete example, let us suppose that every morning we want to check the comp.protocols.tcp-ip news group for messages about TCP or UDP. Figure 3.54 is a framework for a Perl script to automate this task. As it stands, the script is not very useful because it shows every message on the news server, even if it isn't new, and because the message selection is rather crude. We could easily modify this script to be smarter about what articles it lists, but we leave it as a framework for simplicity and so that we don't bog down in Perl minutiae. The details of the network news transfer protocol (NNTP) are discussed in RFC 977 [Kantor and Lapsley 1986].

```
 1 #! /usr/bin/perl5
 2 use Socket;
 3 $host = inet_aton( 'nntp.ix.netcom.com') || die "host: $!";
 4 $port = getservbyname( 'nntp', 'tcp' ) || die "bad port";
 5 socket( S, PF_INET, SOCK_STREAM, 0 ) || die "socket: $!";
 6 connect( S, sockaddr_in( $port, $host ) ) || die "connect: $!";
 7 select( S );
 8 $| = 1;
 9 select( STDOUT );
```

```
10 print S "group comp.protocols.tcp-ip\r\n";
11 while ( $line = <S> )
12 {
13     last if $line =~ /^211/;
14 }
15 ($rc, $total, $start, $end ) = split( /\s/, $line );
16 print S "xover $start-$end\nquit\r\n";
17 while ( $line = <S> )
18 {
19     ( $no, $sub, $auth, $date ) = split( /\t/, $line );
20     print "$no, $sub, $date\n" if $sub =~ /TCP|UDP/;
21 }
22 close( S );
```
———————————————————————————————————————— *tcpnews*

**Figure 3.54** Perl script to collect news article overviews

### Initialize and Connect to News Server

*2-6*      These lines are the Perl version of our standard TCP connect logic.

### Set Unbuffered I/O

*7-9*      In Perl, the `print` function calls the stdio library, which as we recall from Tip 17, causes the output to the socket to be buffered. These three lines turn off the buffering. Although the `select` operator appears to be some form of the `select` system call that we have studied previously, it is merely selecting the default file descriptor. Once selected, we can set output to the socket, *S*, to be unbuffered by setting the special Perl variable $ | nonzero.

> This isn't quite right. What actually happens is that `fflush` is called after every `write` or `print`. The *effect* of this is to make the output to the socket unbuffered.

Line 9 restores stdout as the default file descriptor.

### Select the `comp.protocols.tcp-ip` Group

*10-14*     We send the news server a *group* command that sets the current group to the `comp.protocols.tcp-ip` news group. The server responds to this with a line of the form

```
211 total_articles first_article# last_article# group_name
```

We search for this response at line 13, by looking for a line from the server that begins with the 211 response code. Notice how the line input operator, < · · ·>, takes care of breaking the TCP input into lines for us.

*15-16*     Once we find the response to our *group* command, we send the lines

```
xover first_article#-last_article#
quit
```

to the server. The *xover* command tells the news server to send an "overview" of each article in the given range. An overview is a tab-delimited line that contains the article number, subject, author, date and time, message ID, message ID of articles referenced by this one, number of bytes, and number of lines. The *quit* command tells the server that we have no more requests, and causes it to disconnect.

### Retrieve the Article Overviews

*17-20*    We read each overview, break it into the fields in which we are interested, and filter our output based on whether the strings "TCP" or "UDP" appear in the subject.

When we run `tcpnews`, we get

```
bsd: $ tcpnews
74179, Re: UDP multicast, Thu, 22 Jul 1999 21:06:47 GMT
74181, Re: UDP multicast, 22 Jul 1999 16:10:45 -0500
74187, Re: UDP multicast, Thu, 22 Jul 1999 23:23:00 +0200
74202, Re: NT 4.0 Server and TCP/IP, Fri, 23 Jul 1999 11:56:07 GMT
74227, New Seiko TCP/IP Chip, Thu, 22 Jul 1999 08:39:09 -0500
74267, WATTCP problems, Mon, 26 Jul 1999 13:18:14 -0500
74277, Re: New Seiko TCP/IP Chip, 26 Jul 1999 23:33:42 GMT
74305, TCP Petri Net model, Wed, 28 Jul 1999 02:27:20 +0200
bsd: $
```

We have concentrated on Perl in this tip, but there are other excellent scripting languages that can be used for networking programming. Examples include

* TCL/Expect
* Python
* JavaScript
* VB (for Windows)

All of these languages are excellent for automating simple network tasks, for prototyping, and for building quick and easy utilities or test cases. As we have seen, scripting languages are often easier to use than a conventional programming language because they handle many of the tedious networking chores for us (at a price in performance, of course). Being proficient in the use of at least one of these languages can pay large dividends in productivity.

### Summary

In this tip we explored the use of scripting languages in network programming. We saw that it often makes sense to use such languages for small utilities and test programs.

## Tip 32: Understand the Effects of Buffer Sizes

This tip presents some rules of thumb for setting TCP send and receive buffer sizes. We have already seen in Tip 7 how to set the buffer sizes with `setsockopt`. Now we want to consider what sizes we should set them to.

The first thing to observe is that the proper buffer size depends on the application. For an interactive application, such as telnet, a small buffer is desirable. There are two reasons for this:

1. The client typically sends a small amount of data to its peer and then waits for a response. Therefore, it is wasteful of system resources to allocate large amounts of buffer space to these types of connections.

2. With large buffers, user input requiring immediate response can get "stuck" behind a large amount of data. For example, if the user is listing a large file and presses the interrupt key (<CNTRL-C>, say) to abort the listing, the data in the buffers is still written to the screen. If the buffers are large, this results in a substantial delay before the listing is aborted.

Usually when we are concerned about buffer size, we want to obtain maximum data throughput. That is, the application involves bulk data transfer from one host to another, and almost all the data flows in one direction. For the rest of this tip, we consider bulk data transfer applications of this type.

The conventional advice is that for maximum throughput, the send and receive buffers should be at least as big as the *bandwidth-delay product*. As we shall see next, this is a correct but not particularly useful rule. Before discussing why, let's take a look at the bandwidth-delay product and why it's the "correct" size.

We have already encountered the round trip time, RTT, several times. This is the time that it takes a packet to travel from one host to another and back again. It accounts for the "delay" component of the bandwidth-delay product, because it measures the delay between the time that a packet is sent and an ACK for it is received by the sender. Typically the RTT is measured in milliseconds.

The other component of the bandwidth-delay product is the *bandwidth*. This is the amount of data that can be transferred per unit time on some physical medium.

> This is not technically correct, of course, but the term has long been used in this sense as a generalization of its technical meaning.

It is usually measured in bits per seconds. For example, Ethernet has a (raw) bandwidth of 10 megabits per second.

The bandwidth delay product, *BWD*, is given by

$$BWD = bandwidth \times RTT$$

If we measure the RTT in seconds, then *BWD* has the units

$$BWD = \frac{bits}{second} \times seconds$$
$$= bits$$

If we think of a communication channel between two hosts as a "pipe" (and, indeed, we often speak of them that way), then the bandwidth-delay product is the volume of the pipe in bits (Figure 3.55). It's the amount of data that can be in the network at any given time.

Now let's imagine what this pipe looks like in the steady state (that is, after slow start) during a bulk data transfer that uses all the available network bandwidth. The sender on the left side of Figure 3.56 has filled the pipe with TCP segments and must wait until segment *n* leaves the network before sending another. Because there are the

**Figure 3.55** A pipe with a capacity of *BWD* bits

same number of ACKs as data segments in the pipe, the sender can infer that segment $n$ has left the network when it receives the ACK for segment $n - 8$.

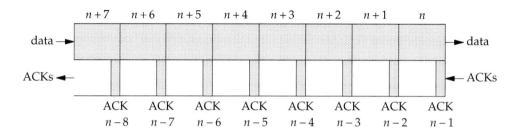

**Figure 3.56** A network at steady state

This illustrates the *self-clocking property* [Jacobson 1988] of a TCP connection in steady state. The ACKs arriving back at the sender serve as a clock that signals TCP to send another segment.

> This mechanism is often referred to as the *ACK clock*.

Notice that if this self-clocking is to work and keep the pipe full, the send window must be large enough to allow 16 ($n - 8 \cdots n + 7$) unacknowledged segments. This, in turn, means that our send buffer and our peer's receive buffer must be large enough to hold these 16 segments. In general, these buffers must hold a "pipeful" of data. That is, they must be at least as large as the bandwidth-delay product.

We remarked earlier that this rule is not particularly useful. The reason for this is that it is, in general, hard to know what the bandwidth-delay product will be. Suppose, for example, we are writing an FTP-type of application. How large should we set the send and receive buffers? First of all, we don't know, at the time we are writing the application, the type of network (and therefore its bandwidth) that will be used. Even if we query the interface at runtime to determine this, we still have to determine the delay. One could, in principle, estimate the delay with some sort of `ping`-like mechanism, but even in the unlikely event that we got a good estimate, the delay will most likely vary during the lifetime of the connection.

> One solution for this problem, proposed in [Semke et al. 1998], is to vary the buffer size dynamically during the lifetime of the connection. The authors observe that one way to view the congestion window is as an estimate for the bandwidth-delay product. By matching the buffer sizes to the congestion window (with suitable dampening and fairness restrictions), they were able to obtain excellent throughputs for simultaneous connections of varying bandwidth-delay products. Unfortunately, this solution requires changes to the kernel, and is therefore not available to the application programmer.

The normal solution is either to use the default buffer sizes or to set the buffers to a large value. Neither of these alternatives is attractive. The first can lead to reduced throughput, and the second, as related in [Semke et al. 1998], can lead to buffer exhaustion and operating system failure.

In the absence of any specific knowledge of the environment in which an application will operate, the best course of action is probably to use small buffers for interactive applications and buffers between 32K and 64K for bulk data transfers. Be aware, however, that high-speed networks require much larger buffers to make good use of the bandwidth. [Mahdavi 1997] gives some advice on tuning TCP stacks for high-performance transfers.

There is one rule that is easier to apply and that can help prevent poor performance under many implementations. [Comer and Lin 1995] describes an experiment in which two hosts were connected by a conventional 10-Mb/s Ethernet LAN and a 100-Mb/s ATM LAN. With the default buffer size of 16K, the same FTP session that achieved a 1.313-Mb/s throughput over the Ethernet LAN, dropped to 0.322 Mb/s over the faster ATM LAN.

On further investigation, the authors discovered that the buffer size, the MTU of the ATM interface, the TCP MSS, and the way the socket layer delivers data to TCP were acting to set up a Nagle/delayed ACK interaction (Tip 24).

> The MTU, or *maximum transmission unit*, is the largest frame size that a network can carry. For Ethernet the MTU is 1,500 bytes. For the ATM network described in [Comer and Lin 1995] it was 9,188 bytes.

Although these results were obtained for an ATM LAN with a specific TCP implementation (SunOS 4.1.1), they are applicable to a wide variety of networks and implementations. The critical parameters are the network's MTU and the way the socket layer delivers data to TCP, which is shared by most BSD-derived implementations.

The authors discovered a truly elegant solution to this problem. It's elegant because it involves adjusting only the send buffer size—the receiver's buffer size is immaterial. The interaction described in [Comer and Lin 1995] cannot occur if the send buffer is at least three times as large as the MSS.

> This works by forcing the receiver to send a window update, and hence an ACK, thereby preventing the delayed ACK and its interaction with the sender's Nagle algorithm. The reason for the window update depends on whether the receiver's buffer is less than or at least as large as three times the MSS, but in either case the update is sent.

For this reason, noninteractive applications should always set their send buffers to at least $3 \times MSS$. Recall from Tip 7 that this must be done *before* calling `listen` or `connect`.

## Summary

The performance of TCP is very sensitive to the sizes of its send and receive buffers. (See Tip 36 for a particularly startling example of this.) In this tip we saw that the optimum buffer size for efficient bulk data transfer is given by the bandwidth-delay product, but that this observation has limited practical application.

Although it is hard to apply the bandwidth-delay rule, there is a rule that is easy to apply and that we should always observe. We should always make our send buffer at least three times as large as the MSS.

# 4

# *Tools and Resources*

### Tip 33: Become Familiar with the `ping` Utility

One of the most fundamental and useful tools for debugging networks and the applications that run on them is the `ping` utility. Its primary function is to verify connectivity between two hosts. As such, it is an invaluable tool for debugging network problems.

Before we go on, we should clear up a couple of misunderstandings about `ping`. First, according to the author Mike Muuss, "ping" does *not* stand for packet internet groper, but was named for the sound that submarine sonar makes. The history of the `ping` program and its development is recounted on Muuss' *The Story of the Ping Program* page at <http://ftp.arl.mil/~mike/ping.html>, where there is also a copy of the source code.

Second, `ping` does not use TCP or UDP, and therefore has no well-known port associated with it. Rather, `ping` uses the ICMP echo function to probe a peer's connectivity. Recall from Tip 14 that although ICMP messages are carried in IP datagrams, they are not considered a separate protocol on top of IP, but as a part of the IP protocol.

> RFC 792 [Postel 1981] states on page 1, "ICMP, uses the basic support of IP as if it were a higher level protocol, however, ICMP is actually an integral part of IP, and must be implemented by every IP module."

Thus, a `ping` packet has the form shown in Figure 4.1. The ICMP portion of the message, shown in Figure 4.2, consists of the 8-byte ICMP header and $n$ bytes of optional data.

Popular values for $n$, the number of extra data bytes included in the `ping` packet, are 56 (UNIX) and 32 (Windows), but this number can be changed with the `-s` (UNIX) or `-l` (Windows) option.

| IP header | ICMP echo request/reply |
|---|---|
| 20 bytes | $8 + n$ bytes |

**Figure 4.1** The format of a `ping` packet

Some versions of `ping` allow the user to specify the values of the extra data or even to specify that they should be pseudorandom. By default, most versions just use rotating data for the extra bytes.

> Specifying particular data patterns is sometimes useful when troubleshooting data-dependent problems.

The UNIX version of `ping` puts a time stamp (a `timeval` structure) in the first 8 bytes of the extra data (providing that there are at least that many extra bytes, of course). When `ping` receives the echo response, it uses the time stamp to compute the RTT. The Windows version of `ping` does not appear to do this (based on an examination of the `tcpdump` output), but the sample `ping` application that comes with Visual C++ does.

| 0                          7 8 | 15 16                              31 |
|---|---|
| type<br>(reply = 0, request = 8) | code<br>(0) | checksum |
| identifier | sequence number |
| optional data | |

**Figure 4.2** The ICMP echo request/response packet

Because the `identifier` and `sequence number` fields are not used by the ICMP echo request/response messages, `ping` uses them to identify the ICMP responses that are returned. Because ICMP datagrams have no port associated with them, they are delivered to every process that has an open raw socket specifying the ICMP protocol (Tip 40). Therefore, `ping` puts its process ID in the `identifier` field so that each instance of `ping` is able to identify its own responses when they come back. We can think of this use of the `identifier` field as a substitute for a port number.

Similarly, `ping` puts an increasing counter in the `sequence number` field to tie an echo reply to an echo request. It is this number that `ping` reports as `icmp_seq`.

Usually when we are having problems communicating with a peer, the first thing we try is to ping the host with which we are trying to communicate. For example, suppose we are trying to telnet to host A, but the connection times out. This could be because there is a network problem between us and host A, it could be because host A is down, or it could be that there is a problem with its TCP stack or telnet server.

We first verify that we are able to reach host A by pinging it. If the ping succeeds, we know that there are probably no network problems and that something is wrong on host A itself. If we are unable to ping host A, we can try to ping the nearest router to see whether we can at least reach the boundary of our local network segment. If this succeeds, we might want to invoke traceroute (Tip 35) to see how far along the path from our host to host A we can get. Often this helps pinpoint the problem router, or at least suggests where the problem may lie.

Because ping operates at the IP layer, it does not depend on TCP or UDP being configured properly. Thus it is sometimes useful to ping ourselves to verify that our networking software is installed correctly. At the very lowest level, we can ping our loopback address, localhost (127.0.0.1), to see whether we have any networking functionality at all. If this succeeds, we can ping one or more of our network interfaces to ensure that they are configured correctly.

Let's try pinging the host netcom4.netcom.com, which is ten hops away (Figure 4.3).

```
bsd: $ ping netcom4.netcom.com
PING netcom4.netcom.com (199.183.9.104): 56 data bytes
64 bytes from 199.183.9.104: icmp_seq=0 ttl=245 time=598.554 ms
64 bytes from 199.183.9.104: icmp_seq=1 ttl=245 time=550.081 ms
64 bytes from 199.183.9.104: icmp_seq=2 ttl=245 time=590.079 ms
64 bytes from 199.183.9.104: icmp_seq=3 ttl=245 time=530.114 ms
64 bytes from 199.183.9.104: icmp_seq=5 ttl=245 time=480.137 ms
64 bytes from 199.183.9.104: icmp_seq=6 ttl=245 time=540.081 ms
64 bytes from 199.183.9.104: icmp_seq=7 ttl=245 time=580.084 ms
64 bytes from 199.183.9.104: icmp_seq=8 ttl=245 time=490.078 ms
64 bytes from 199.183.9.104: icmp_seq=9 ttl=245 time=560.090 ms
64 bytes from 199.183.9.104: icmp_seq=10 ttl=245 time=490.090 ms
^C                                              ping terminated manually
--- netcom4.netcom.com ping statistics ---
12 packets transmitted, 10 packets received, 16% packet loss
round-trip min/avg/max/stddev = 480.137/540.939/598.554/40.871 ms
bsd: $
```

**Figure 4.3** A short ping run

There are a number of things to notice about this. First the RTT for the pings is pretty consistently about 500 ms. Indeed, we see from the last line that the RTT ranged from 480.137 ms to 598.554 ms with a standard deviation of 40.871 ms. This run is too short to draw any conclusions, but a longer run of approximately 2 minutes shows similar results, so we can conclude that the load on the network is fairly constant. RTTs that fluctuate are usually an indication of varying network load. During times of greater load, the router queues are longer so the RTT is greater. When the load lessens, the queue lengths shorten and so does the RTT.

The next thing to notice about Figure 4.3 is that the ICMP echo request with sequence number 4 was not returned. This indicates that either the request or the reply was dropped by one of the intermediate routers. We see on the summary line that 12 requests (0–11) were sent, but only ten were received. One of the missing replies is sequence number 4. The other is sequence number 11, and is probably due to our terminating the ping run before it could be returned.

## Summary

The ping utility is one of our most basic tests for network connectivity. Because it requires only the lower level networking services to operate, it is often useful in verifying connectivity even when higher level services such as TCP or an application layer service, such as telnet, is not working

Using ping, it is often possible to infer network conditions by observing the values of and variance in the RTT of the replies, and by noticing lost responses.

## Tip 34: Learn to Use `tcpdump` or a Similar Tool

One of the most useful tools at our disposal for debugging network applications or troubleshooting network problems is a *sniffer* or network analyzer. Traditionally, sniffers were expensive hardware devices, but modern workstations are more than able to perform their function as just another process.

Today, sniffer programs are available for most network-aware operating systems. Sometimes, the operating system provides a proprietary sniffer (the Solaris snoop or the AIX iptrace/ipreport programs, for example), and sometimes third-party programs such as tcpdump are used.

Furthermore, sniffers have evolved from strictly diagnostic tools to a more general role as research and educational tools. For example, sniffers are routinely used by researchers to study network dynamics and interactions. In [Stevens 1994, Stevens 1996], Stevens shows how to use tcpdump to study and understand the TCP/IP protocols. By watching the actual data that a protocol sends, we come to a deeper understanding of how the protocols work in practice and can also see when a particular implementation is not performing according to specification.

In this tip we concentrate on tcpdump. As we have already mentioned, there are other software-based network sniffers, some of them with arguably better output, but tcpdump has the advantage of running on virtually every UNIX system and on Windows machines as well. Because tcpdump is available as source code, it can be adapted for special purposes or ported to new environments as needed.

The source distribution for tcpdump is available at:

```
<http://www-nrg.ee.lbl.gov/nrg.html>
```

Source and binaries for the Windows version, WinDump, are available at

```
<http://netgroup-serv.polito.it/windump>
```

## How `tcpdump` Works

Before we go on, let's take a look at how `tcpdump` works, and where in the protocol stack packets are intercepted. This is worthwhile because it is a frequent cause of confusion. Like most sniffers, `tcpdump` has two components: a kernel component to capture and possibly filter packets from the network, and a user space component to handle user interface, formatting, and filtering if it's not done in the kernel.

The user space component of `tcpdump` uses `libpcap` (the packet capture library) to communicate with the kernel component. This library, which is useful in its own right, abstracts the system-dependent details of communicating with the link layer. For example, on BSD-based systems, `libpcap` talks to the *BSD packet filter* (BPF) [McCanne and Jacobson 1993]. BPF examines each packet passing through the link layer and matches it against a user-specified filter. If the filter selects the packet, a copy of the packet is placed in a kernel buffer for the application associated with that filter. When the buffer fills up or when a user-specified timer expires, the contents of the buffer are delivered to the application through `libpcap`.

This is illustrated in Figure 4.4, which shows `tcpdump` and another (unspecified) program reading raw network packets from BPF and a third conventional TCP/IP application reading data from the TCP/IP stack as usual.

> Although we show both `tcpdump` and the other program using `libpcap`, it is possible to talk directly to BPF or any of the other interfaces that we discuss later. The advantage of `libpcap` is that it gives us a system-independent means of accessing raw packets. The library currently supports BPF, the data link provider interface (DLPI), SunOS NIT, streams-based NIT, Linux `SOCK_PACKET` sockets, the `snoop` interface (IRIX), and the Stanford `enet` interface. A Windows version of `libpcap` is available with the `WinDump` distribution.

Notice that BPF intercepts the network packets at the device driver level—that is, as soon as they come in off the wire. This is *not* the same as reading from a *raw socket*. In the raw socket case, IP datagrams are processed by the IP layer and are then passed directly to the application without first passing through the transport (TCP/UDP) layer (see Tip 40).

After version 2.0, the `WinDump` architecture is very similar to that used by BSD systems. `WinDump` uses a special Network Device Interface Specification (NDIS) driver that provides a BPF-compatible filter and interface. In the `WinDump` architecture, the NDIS driver is actually a part of the protocol stack, but functionally it looks the same as Figure 4.4, with "BPF" replaced by "NDIS Packet Driver."

Other operating systems behave a little differently. SVR4-derived systems use the DLPI [Unix International 1991] to provide access to raw packets. DLPI is a protocol-independent, STREAMS-based [Ritchie 1984] interface to the link layer. We can access the link layer directly through DLPI, but for efficiency reasons we usually push the `pfmod` and `bufmod` STREAMS modules onto the stream. The `bufmod` module provides message buffering and increases efficiency by limiting the number of context switches required to deliver data.

> This is similar to reading a buffer full of data from a socket rather than a byte at a time.

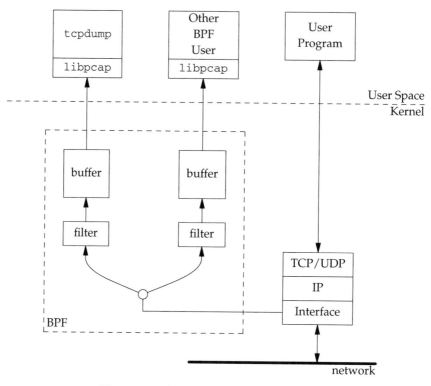

**Figure 4.4** Capturing packets with BPF

The pfmod module is a filter similar to that provided by BPF. Because this filter is incompatible with the BPF filter, tcpdump does not push this module onto the stream, but does the filtering in user space instead. This is not as efficient as the BPF architecture because every packet must be passed to user space regardless of whether tcpdump is interested in it.

This is illustrated in Figure 4.5, which shows tcpdump without pfmod and another application that is also receiving raw packets, but which is using the kernel filter.

Again, we show the applications using libpcap, but as with BPF this is not necessary. We could use the getmsg and putmsg functions to send and receive messages directly to and from the stream. [Rago 1993] is an excellent source of information about STREAMS programming, DLPI, and the use of the getmsg and putmsg system calls. A more concise discussion can be found in Chapter 33 of [Stevens 1998].

Finally, there is the Linux architecture. Under Linux, access to raw network packets is through the SOCK_PACKET socket interface. To use this simple and elegant interface, we merely open a SOCK_PACKET socket, bind the required interface, enable promiscuous mode, and read from it.

> Starting with the 2.2 version of the Linux kernel, a slightly different interface is available and recommended, but the current version of libpcap still uses the interface described here.

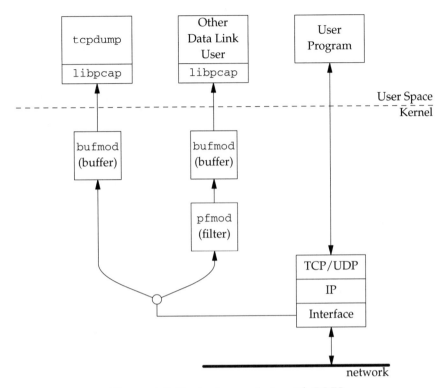

**Figure 4.5** Capturing packets with DLPI

For example,

```
s = socket( AF_INET, SOCK_PACKET, htons( ETH_P_ALL ) );
```

opens a socket that gives us access to all Ethernet packets. We can also specify `ETH_P_IP` (IP packets), `ETH_P_IPV6` (IPv6 packets), or `ETH_P_ARP` (ARP packets) as the third parameter. We can think of this interface as similar to raw sockets (`SOCK_RAW`) except that it provides access to the link layer instead of the network (IP) layer.

Unfortunately, although this interface is simple and convenient, it's not very efficient. There is no kernel buffering other than the normal socket buffers, so each packet is delivered to the application as it becomes available. There is also no kernel filtering (other than by the `ETH_P_*` parameter), so filtering must be done at the application level, which means that every packet must be delivered to the application.

## Using `tcpdump`

The first step in using `tcpdump` is to get permission. Because sniffers present obvious security risks, the default configuration of `tcpdump` requires root privileges.

> This does not apply in the Windows environment. Once the NDIS packet capture driver is installed, `WinDump` can be used by anyone.

In many situations it is convenient to make `tcpdump` available to all users without the need to give them root privileges. The way to do this varies with the version of UNIX, and is documented in each system's `tcpdump` man pages. In most cases it involves either making the network interface readable by everyone or installing `tcp-dump` as a setuid application.

The simplest invocation of `tcpdump` is without any command line arguments at all. This causes `tcpdump` to capture and list all packets on the network. It is usually more useful, however, to specify a filter so that we see only the packets in which we're interested and don't get distracted by the others. For example, if we only want to see packets to or from host bsd, we would call `tcpdump` as

```
tcpdump host bsd
```

If we are interested in packets between hosts bsd and sparc, we would use the filter

```
host bsd and host sparc
```

or the abbreviation

```
host bsd and sparc
```

The filter language is quite rich and can be used to filter on attributes such as

- Protocol
- Source and/or destination host
- Source and/or destination network
- Source and/or destination Ethernet address
- Source and/or destination port
- Size of the packet
- Whether the packet was broadcast or multicast (either IP or Ethernet)
- Whether the packet used a specified host as a gateway

In addition, specific bits or bytes in the protocol headers can be tested. For example, to capture only TCP segments that have the urgent bit set, we would use the filter

```
tcp[ 13 ] & 16
```

To understand this last example, we must know that bit 4 of the fourteenth byte of the TCP header is the urgent bit.

Because we can use the Boolean operators **and** (or '&&'), **or** (or '||'), and **not** (or '!') to combine the simple predicates that we showed earlier, we can specify arbitrarily complex filters. As a final example, the following filter captures ICMP packets that come from an external network:

```
icmp and not src net localnet
```

See the `tcpdump` man page for other examples with complex filters.

## `tcpdump` Output

The output from `tcpdump` is protocol dependent. We consider a few examples to get a feel for the output of the most common protocols. The `tcpdump` documentation covers the various outputs in detail.

The first example is a network trace of a Simple Mail Transfer Protocol (SMTP) session—that is, of sending an email. The output in Figure 4.6 appears exactly as produced by `tcpdump` except that we have added a line number in italics at the beginning of each line, have removed the domain name from host bsd, and have wrapped long lines to fit on the page.

To generate this trace, we sent email to a user at `gte.net`. That is, the address of the email was of the form `user@gte.net`.

Lines 1–4 are concerned with finding the address of the SMTP server for `gte.net`. They are examples of the output generated by `tcpdump` for DNS queries and responses. In line 1, bsd queries the name server of its ISP (`ns1.ix.netcom.com`) for the name or names of the mail server at `gte.net`. The first field gives the time stamp of the packet (12:54:32.920881). Because bsd provides a timer with microsecond resolution, six decimal places are shown. Next, we see that this packet is from port 1067 on bsd to port 53 (domain) on host ns1. Finally, we see information about the data in the packet. The first field (45801) is a query number that the resolver functions on bsd use to match the response to the query. The '+' indicates that the resolver wants the DNS server to query other servers if it doesn't have the answer. The 'MX?' indicates that this is a request for a mail exchange record for the network named in the next field (`gte.net`). The '(25)' means the query was 25 bytes long.

Line 2 is the response to the query in line 1. The number 45801 is the number of the query that this response is for. The next three slash-delimited fields are the number of answer records, the number of name server (authority) records, and the number of other records. The '(371)' tells us that there are 371 bytes in the response. Finally, the '(DF)' indicates that the response has the "Don't Fragment" bit set in the IP header. These first two lines illustrate the use of DNS to locate mail handlers that we hinted at in Tip 29.

Whereas the first two lines discovered the name of a mail handler for `gte.net`, the next two look up its IP address. The 'A?' in line 3 indicates that this is a request for the IP address of `mtapop2.gte.net`, one of GTE's mail servers.

Lines 5–28 show the details of the actual SMTP transfer. The three-way handshake between bsd and mtapop2 starts on line 5 and completes on line 7. The first field after the time stamp and hosts is the *flags* field. The 'S' on line 5 indicates that the SYN flag is set. Other possible flags are 'F' (FIN flag), 'U' (URG flag), 'P' (PUSH flag), 'R' (RST flag) and '.' (no flag). Next come the first and "last" sequence numbers followed by the number of data bytes in parentheses. These fields can be a little confusing because the "last" sequence number is usually the first unused sequence number except when there is no data. The best way to think of these fields is that the first sequence number in the segment (either the SYN or data) is given as the first number, and the second number is the first sequence number plus the number of bytes of data in the segment. Notice that

```
 1 12:54:32.920881 bsd.1067 > ns1.ix.netcom.com.domain:
                   45801+ MX? gte.net. (25)
 2 12:54:33.254981 ns1.ix.netcom.com.domain > bsd.1067:
                   45801 5/4/9 (371) (DF)
 3 12:54:33.256127 bsd.1068 > ns1.ix.netcom.com.domain:
                   45802+ A? mtapop2.gte.net. (33)
 4 12:54:33.534962 ns1.ix.netcom.com.domain > bsd.1068:
                   45802 1/4/4 (202) (DF)
 5 12:54:33.535737 bsd.1059 > mtapop2.gte.net.smtp:
                   S 585494507:585494507(0) win 16384
                   <mss 1460,nop,wscale 0,nop,nop,
                   timestamp 6112 0> (DF)
 6 12:54:33.784963 mtapop2.gte.net.smtp > bsd.1059:
                   S 1257159392:1257159392(0) ack 585494508 win 49152
                   <mss 1460,nop,wscale 0,nop,nop,
                   timestamp 7853753 6112> (DF)
 7 12:54:33.785012 bsd.1059 > mtapop2.gte.net.smtp:
                   . ack 1 win 17376 <nop,nop,
                   timestamp 6112 7853753> (DF)
 8 12:54:34.235066 mtapop2.gte.net.smtp > bsd.1059:
                   P 1:109(108) ack 1 win 49152
                   <nop,nop,timestamp 7853754 6112> (DF)
 9 12:54:34.235277 bsd.1059 > mtapop2.gte.net.smtp:
                   P 1:19(18) ack 109 win 17376
                   <nop,nop,timestamp 6113 7853754> (DF)

                   14 lines deleted

24 12:54:36.675105 bsd.1059 > mtapop2.gte.net.smtp:
                   F 663:663(0) ack 486 win 17376
                   <nop,nop,timestamp 6118 7853758> (DF)
25 12:54:36.685080 mtapop2.gte.net.smtp > bsd.1059:
                   F 486:486(0) ack 663 win 49152
                   <nop,nop,timestamp 7853758 6117> (DF)
26 12:54:36.685126 bsd.1059 > mtapop2.gte.net.smtp:
                   . ack 487 win 17376
                   <nop,nop,timestamp 6118 7853758> (DF)
27 12:54:36.934985 mtapop2.gte.net.smtp > bsd.1059:
                   F 486:486(0) ack 664 win 49152
                   <nop,nop,timestamp 7853759 6118> (DF)
28 12:54:36.935020 bsd.1059 > mtapop2.gte.net.smtp:
                   . ack 487 win 17376
                   <nop,nop,timestamp 6118 7853759> (DF)
```

**Figure 4.6** An SMTP trace showing DNS and TCP output

the default behavior is to show the actual sequence numbers for the SYN segments and to show (easier to track) offsets for subsequent segments. This behavior can be changed with the -S command line option.

All but the initial SYN will contain an *ACK* field indicating the sequence number that the sender expects next from its peer. This field comes next (in the form ack *nnn*), and again, by default, is given as an offset except for the SYN segments.

After the *ACK* field comes the *window* field. This is the amount of data that the peer application is willing to accept. It is usually taken as reflecting the amount of buffer space available for the connection at the peer.

Finally, any TCP options present in the segment are given between the angle brackets (< and >). The main TCP options are discussed in RFC 793 [Postel 1981b], and RFC 1323 [Jacobson et al. 1992]. There is also a discussion of them in [Stevens 1994], and a complete list is available at

<http://www.isi.edu/in-notes/iana/assignments/tcp-parameters>.

Lines 8–23 show the conversation between `sendmail` on bsd and the SMTP server on mtapop2. Most of these lines are omitted. Lines 24–28 are the connection tear-down. First bsd sends a FIN in line 24 followed by a FIN from mtapop2 on line 25. Note that mtapop2 resends its FIN on line 27, indicating that it did not receive the ACK from bsd for its first FIN. This underscores the importance of the TIME-WAIT state as discussed in Tip 22.

Next we look at the output generated by UDP datagrams. To do this we use `udphelloc` (Tip 4) to send a single NULL byte to the daytime port of a server in the `netcom.com` domain:

```
bsd: $ udphelloc netcom4.netcom.com daytime
Thu Sep 16 15:11:49 1999
bsd: $
```

The host netcom4 returns its notion of the date and time as another UDP datagram. The `tcpdump` output is

```
18:12:23.130009 bsd.1127 > netcom4.netcom.com.daytime: udp 1
18:12:23.389284 netcom4.netcom.com.daytime > bsd.1127: udp 26
```

These lines tell us that bsd sent a 1-byte UDP datagram to netcom4, and that netcom4 responded with a 26-byte datagram.

The output from ICMP packets is similar. Here is a trace of a single `ping` from bsd to netcom4:

```
1 06:21:28.690390 bsd > netcom4.netcom.com: icmp: echo request
2 06:21:29.400433 netcom4.netcom.com > bsd: icmp: echo reply
```

The `icmp:` tells us that this is an ICMP datagram, and the following text tells us what type of ICMP datagram it is.

One of the shortcomings of `tcpdump` is its support for data display. Often it is useful, while debugging a network application, to see what data is actually being sent. We can capture this data using the `-s` and `-x` command line switches, but the display is in hex only. The `-x` switch tells `tcpdump` to output the contents of the packet in hex. The `-s` switch tells how much of the packet to capture. By default, `tcpdump` only captures the first 68 (96 for SunOS's NIT) bytes—enough to retrieve the header information for most protocols. Let's repeat the previous UDP example, but capture the data also:

```
tcpdump -x -s 100 -1
```

After removing the DNS traffic and removing the domain from bsd we get

```
1 12:57:53.299924 bsd.1053 > netcom4.netcom.com.daytime: udp 1
                  4500 001d 03d4 0000 4011 17a1 c7b7 c684
                  c7b7 0968 041d 000d 0009 9c56 00
2 12:57:53.558921 netcom4.netcom.com.daytime > bsd.1053: udp 26
                  4500 0036 f0c8 0000 3611 3493 c7b7 0968
                  c7b7 c684 000d 041d 0022 765a 5375 6e20
                  5365 7020 3139 2030 393a 3537 3a34 3220
                  3139 3939 0a0d
```

The last byte of the first packet is the NULL byte that udphelloc sends to netcom4. The last 26 bytes of the second packet are the answer. If we are looking for specific data, this output is tedious to interpret.

Historically, the authors of tcpdump have been reluctant to provide an ASCII interpretation of the data because they felt it would make it easier for the technically unsophisticated malfeasant to snoop passwords. Many feel that the proliferation of tools for snooping passwords has rendered this reluctance beside the point, and there are indications that future versions of tcpdump may provide this capability.

In the meantime, writing filters for tcpdump to provide ASCII output is a common exercise for network programmers, and there are several available on the Internet. In that spirit, here is another. The Perl script in Figure 4.7 calls tcpdump, pipes its output to the script, and formats the data in ASCII.

_____ *tcpd*

```
 1 #! /usr/bin/perl5
 2 $tcpdump = "/usr/sbin/tcpdump";
 3 open( TCPD, "$tcpdump @ARGV |" ) ||
 4     die "couldn't start tcpdump: \$!\\n";
 5 $| = 1;
 6 while ( <TCPD> )
 7 {
 8     if ( /^\t/ )
 9     {
10         chop;
11         $str = $_;
12         $str =~ tr / \t//d;
13         $str = pack "H*" , $str;
14         $str =~ tr/\x0-\x1f\x7f-\xff/./;
15         printf "\t%-40s\t%s\n", substr( $_, 4 ), $str;
16     }
17     else
18     {
19         print;
20     }
21 }
```

_____ *tcpd*

**Figure 4.7** Perl script to filter tcpdump output

If we repeat the last example using tcpd instead of tcpdump, we get

```
1 12:58:56.428052 bsd.1056 > netcom4.netcom.com.daytime: udp 1
                  4500 001d 03d7 0000 4011 179e c7b7 c684    E.......@.......
                  c7b7 0968 0420 000d 0009 9c53 00           ...h. .....S.
```

```
2 12:58:56.717128 netcom4.netcom.com.daytime > bsd.1056: udp 26
    4500 0036 10f1 0000 3611 146b c7b7 0968    E..6....6..k...h
    c7b7 c684 000d 0420 0022 7256 5375 6e20    ....... ."rVSun
    5365 7020 3139 2030 393a 3538 3a34 3620    Sep 19 09:58:46
    3139 3939 0a0d                             1999..
```

## Summary

tcpdump is an indispensable tool for understanding what is happening on a network. Seeing what is actually being sent or received "on the wire" often renders hard-to-find bugs in our applications trivial to identify and fix. It also serves an important role as a research tool for studying network dynamics and as a pedagogical tool, as exemplified by Stevens' *TCP/IP Illustrated* series, for understanding the operation of network protocols.

## Tip 35: Learn to Use traceroute

The traceroute utility is an important and useful tool for debugging routing problems, studying traffic patterns on the Internet, or just exploring network topology. Like many of the other common networking tools, traceroute was developed at the Lawrence Berkeley Laboratory of the University of California.

> In comments in the source code, Van Jacobson, the author of traceroute, says, "I was trying to find a routing problem and this code sort-of popped out after 48 hours without sleep."

The idea behind traceroute is simple: It tries to determine the network path between two hosts by forcing each intermediate router to send an ICMP error message to the originating host. We look at the exact mechanism in a moment, but first let's look at a couple of runs and the information they provide. First we trace the route between bsd and a computer at the University of South Florida in Tampa (Figure 4.8). As usual, we have wrapped some of the lines so that they fit on the page.

```
bsd: $ traceroute ziggy.usf.edu
traceroute to ziggy.usf.edu (131.247.1.40), 30 hops max, 40 byte packets
 1  tam-fl-pm8.netcom.net (163.179.44.15)
                128.960 ms  139.230 ms   129.483 ms
 2  tam-fl-gw1.netcom.net (163.179.44.254)
                139.436 ms  129.226 ms   129.570 ms
 3  h1-0.mig-fl-gw1.netcom.net (165.236.144.110)
                279.582 ms  199.325 ms   289.611 ms
 4  a5-0-0-7.was-dc-gw1.netcom.net (163.179.235.121)
                179.505 ms  229.543 ms   179.422 ms
 5  h1-0.mae-east.netcom.net (163.179.220.182)
                189.258 ms  179.211 ms   169.605 ms
 6  sl-mae-e-f0-0.sprintlink.net (192.41.177.241)
                189.999 ms  179.399 ms   189.472 ms
 7  sl-bb4-dc-1-0-0.sprintlink.net (144.228.10.41)
                180.048 ms  179.388 ms   179.562 ms
```

```
 8   sl-bb10-rly-2-3.sprintlink.net (144.232.7.153)
                      199.433 ms   179.390 ms   179.468 ms
 9   sl-bb11-rly-9-0.sprintlink.net (144.232.0.46)
                      199.259 ms   189.315 ms   179.459 ms
10   sl-bb10-orl-1-0.sprintlink.net (144.232.9.62)
                      189.987 ms   199.508 ms   219.252 ms
11   sl-gw3-orl-4-0-0.sprintlink.net (144.232.2.154)
                      219.307 ms   209.382 ms   209.502 ms
12   sl-usf-1-0-0.sprintlink.net (144.232.154.14)
                      209.518 ms   199.288 ms   219.495 ms
13   131.247.254.36 (131.247.254.36)   209.318 ms   199.281 ms   219.588 ms
14   ziggy.usf.edu (131.247.1.40)   209.591 ms  *   210.159 ms
```

**Figure 4.8** A `traceroute` to `ziggy.usf.edu`

The number to the left of each line in Figure 4.8 is the hop number. Following that is the name of the host or router at that hop followed by its IP address. If the name is not available, `traceroute` merely prints its IP address. There is an example of this at hop 13. As we shall see, by default the host or router at each hop is probed three times, and the three numbers following the IP address are the RTTs for those probes. If a probe does not elicit a response, or if the response is lost, a '*' is printed in place of the time.

Although `ziggy.usf.edu` is across town from bsd, it is 14 hops away on the Internet. If we follow the path we see that it travels through two routers in Tampa belonging to the `netcom.net` network (the ISP that bsd uses for its Internet connection), through two more Netcom routers, and then to the `netcom.net` router at MAE-EAST (hop 5) in the Washington, DC, area. MAE-EAST is a major network exchange point where ISPs exchange Internet traffic. We see the path leaving MAE-EAST at hop 6 on the `sprintlink.net` network. From the Sprintlink MAE-EAST router we travel back down the east coast until we reach the `usf.edu` domain at hop 13. Finally we reach ziggy at hop 14.

As an interesting comparison, let's see how far away UCLA is from bsd. Geographically, of course, UCLA is across the country in Los Angeles, California. When we do a `traceroute` to the host panther at UCLA, we get the results in Figure 4.9.

```
bsd: $ traceroute panther.cs.ucla.edu
traceroute to panther.cs.ucla.edu (131.179.128.25),
                    30 hops max, 40 byte packets
 1   tam-fl-pm8.netcom.net (163.179.44.15)
                      148.957 ms   129.049 ms   129.585 ms
 2   tam-fl-gw1.netcom.net (163.179.44.254)
                      139.435 ms   139.258 ms   139.434 ms
 3   h1-0.mig-fl-gw1.netcom.net (165.236.144.110)
                      139.538 ms   149.202 ms   139.488 ms
 4   a5-0-0-7.was-dc-gw1.netcom.net (163.179.235.121)
                      189.535 ms   179.496 ms   168.699 ms
 5   h2-0.mae-east.netcom.net (163.179.136.10)
                      180.040 ms   189.308 ms   169.479 ms
 6   cpe3-fddi-0.washington.cw.net (192.41.177.180)
                      179.186 ms   179.368 ms   179.631 ms
```

```
  7   core5-hssi6-0-0.Washington.cw.net (204.70.1.21)
                        199.268 ms   179.537 ms   189.694 ms
  8   corerouter2.Bloomington.cw.net (204.70.9.148)
                        239.441 ms   239.560 ms   239.417 ms
  9   bordercore3.Bloomington.cw.net (166.48.180.1)
                        239.322 ms   239.348 ms   249.302 ms
 10   ucla-internet-t-3.Bloomington.cw.net (166.48.181.254)
                        249.989 ms   249.384 ms   249.662 ms
 11   cbn5-t3-1.cbn.ucla.edu (169.232.1.34)
                        258.756 ms   259.370 ms   249.487 ms
 12   131.179.9.6 (131.179.9.6)   249.457 ms   259.238 ms   249.666 ms
 13   Panther.CS.UCLA.EDU (131.179.128.25)   259.256 ms   259.184 ms   *
bsd: $
```

**Figure 4.9** A `traceroute` to `panther.cs.ucla.edu`

This time we see that the path is only 13 hops, and that it reaches the `ucla.edu` domain in 11. Thus bsd is topologically closer to UCLA than it is to the University of South Florida.

> Chapman University, also near Los Angeles, is only nine hops away from bsd. That's because
> `chapman.edu`, like bsd, connects to the Internet through the `netcom.net` network, and traf-
> fic is carried completely on the `netcom.net` backbone.

## How It Works

Now let's see how `traceroute` works. Recall from Tip 22 that every IP datagram has a *TTL* field, which is decremented by one at every router. When a datagram with a TTL of one (or zero) reaches a router, it is discarded and an ICMP "time exceeded in transit" error message is returned to the sender.

The `traceroute` utility takes advantage of this by first sending a UDP datagram to the destination with the TTL set to one. When the UDP datagram reaches the first hop, the router notices that the TTL is set to one, discards the datagram, and sends the ICMP message back to the originator. The IP address of the first hop is now known (from the ICMP message source address), and `traceroute` looks up its name using `gethostbyaddr`. To get the identity of the next hop, `traceroute` repeats this procedure, but sets the TTL to two. When this datagram reaches the first hop, its TTL is decremented to one and it is forwarded to the next hop, which, on seeing the TTL of one, discards the datagram, and returns an ICMP message. By repeating this process with ever-increasing TTLs, `traceroute` is able to build up knowledge of the path between the originator and the destination.

When a datagram with an initial *TTL* field that is large enough finally makes it to the destination, its *TTL* field will be one, but because it is not being forwarded, the TCP/IP stack tries to deliver it to a waiting application. However, `traceroute` sends the UDP datagrams with a destination port that is unlikely to be in use, so the destination host returns an ICMP "port unreachable" error message. When `traceroute` receives this message, it knows that it has found the destination, and the trace is terminated.

Because UDP is an unreliable protocol (Tip 1), the possibility exists for datagrams to be lost. Therefore, `traceroute` probes each router or host multiple times. That is, several UDP datagrams are sent for each value of TTL. By default, `traceroute` probes each hop three times, but this can be changed with the -q flag.

Similarly, `traceroute` must make a decision about how long to wait for the ICMP message to come back for each probe. By default, it waits for 5 seconds, but this can be changed with the -w flag. If an ICMP message is not received within this interval, a '*' is printed in place of the RTT value.

Several things can go wrong with this process. Obviously, `traceroute` depends on routers to properly discard IP datagrams with a TTL value of one *and* to send the "time exceeded in transit" ICMP message. Unfortunately, some routers don't send time-exceeded messages, and for these hops only asterisks are printed. Other routers send the time-exceeded message, but send it with a TTL of whatever value remains in the incoming datagram. Because for routers this value is zero, it is discarded by the next hop along the reverse path (unless it happens at hop 1, of course). The effect of this is the same as if the router had not sent the ICMP message at all, so this case also results in only asterisks being printed.

Some routers erroneously forward datagrams with a TTL of zero. When this happens, the next-hop router, say router $N + 1$, discards the datagram and returns the ICMP "time exceeded in transit" message. When the next round of probes arrive, router $N + 1$ receives a datagram with a TTL of one and returns the ICMP error message as usual. This results in router $N + 1$ appearing in two hops—once as a result of the error in the previous hop's router and once as a result of a legitimate TTL discard. This situation is illustrated in Figure 4.10, and an apparent instance of it is shown in hops 5 and 6 of Figure 4.11.

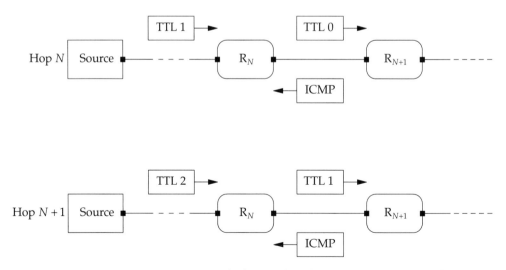

**Figure 4.10** Router $N$ erroneously forwards a datagram with a TTL of zero

```
bsd: $ traceroute syrup.hill.com
traceroute to syrup.hill.com (208.162.106.3),
                     30 hops max, 40 byte packets
 1  tam-fl-pm5.netcom.net (163.179.44.11)
                     129.120 ms   139.263 ms   129.603 ms
 2  tam-fl-gw1.netcom.net (163.179.44.254)
                     129.584 ms   129.328 ms   149.578 ms
 3  h1-0.mig-fl-gw1.netcom.net (165.236.144.110)
                     219.595 ms   229.306 ms   209.602 ms
 4  a5-0-0-7.was-dc-gw1.netcom.net (163.179.235.121)
                     179.248 ms   179.521 ms   179.694 ms
 5  h2-0.mae-east.netcom.net (163.179.136.10)
                     179.274 ms   179.325 ms   179.623 ms
 6  h2-0.mae-east.netcom.net (163.179.136.10)
                     169.443 ms   199.318 ms   179.601 ms
 7  cpe3-fddi-0.washington.cw.net (192.41.177.180) 189.529 ms
                     core6-serial5-1-0.Washington.cw.net (204.70.1.221)
                     209.496 ms   209.247 ms
 8  bordercore2.Boston.cw.net (166.48.64.1)
                     209.486 ms   209.332 ms   209.598 ms
 9  hill-associatesinc-internet.Boston.cw.net (166.48.67.54)
                     229.602 ms   219.510 ms   *
10  syrup.hill.com (208.162.106.3)  239.744 ms   239.348 ms   219.607 ms
bsd: $
```

**Figure 4.11** A `traceroute` with duplicate hops

Figure 4.11 shows another interesting phenomenon. At hop 7, we see the route change after the first probe. This could be because the router at hop 6 is performing some sort of load balancing, or it could be that cpe3-fddi-0.washington.cw.net went offline after the first probe of hop 7, and core6-serial5-1-0.Washington.cw.net was used instead.

Another problem, unfortunately increasingly common, that `traceroute` can encounter is routers that block ICMP messages indiscriminately. Some organizations, in the mistaken belief that any ICMP message is dangerous, block them all. Such behavior can render `traceroute` useless because when a router that does this is encountered, it acts as a black hole as far as `traceroute` is concerned. No information beyond that router is ever returned because it will discard both the "time exceeded in transit" and "port unreachable" ICMP messages.

Another problem with `traceroute` of which we should be aware is asymmetry in routes. When we run `traceroute`, we get a path from the source to the destination, but it tells us nothing about the path a datagram would take from the destination to the source. Although one might think that they would nearly always be the same, [Paxson 1997] found that 49 percent of the routes studied showed an asymmetry in which the paths to and from the destination visited at least one different city.

> By using the -s option to specify a loose source routing through the destination back to the source, it is theoretically possible to obtain a path to and from a destination, but as Jacobson

points out in comments in the `traceroute` source code, so many routers fail to handle source routing correctly, that the technique is essentially worthless. See Chapter 8 of [Stevens 1994] for an explanation of the method and an example of its successful application.

Elsewhere, Paxson points out that we can expect asymmetric routes to increase due to *hot potato routing* [Paxson 1995].

> In hot potato routing, host A located (say) on the east coast of the United States sends a datagram to host B located (say) on the west coast. Host A connects to the Internet through ISP 1, whereas host B connects via ISP 2. Suppose that both ISP 1 and ISP 2 both have cross-country backbones. Because the backbone bandwidth is a scarce commodity, ISP 1 attempts to deliver the datagram to ISP 2 on the east coast (at MAE-EAST, say) so that it is carried on ISP 2's backbone. Similarly, when host B replies, ISP 2 attempts to deliver the reply to ISP 1 on the west coast, resulting in an asymmetric path.

## Windows `TRACERT`

We have been describing the UNIX version of `traceroute`. A very similar tool, `TRACERT` is available for the various versions of the Windows operating system. `TRACERT` works similarly to `traceroute`, except that instead of probing with UDP datagrams, it probes with ICMP echo requests (`pings`). This results in the destination host returning an ICMP echo response instead of a port unreachable. The intermediate routers still return the "time exceeded in transit" message of course.

> Recent versions of `traceroute` have an option (`-I`) that mimics this behavior. The latest version of `traceroute` is available at `<ftp://ftp.ee.lbl.gov/traceroute.tar.Z>`.

This change was presumably made out of a concern that UDP datagrams are frequently filtered by routers, whereas the ICMP echo request/response used by `ping` is less likely to be. Ironically, the original `traceroute` also used echo requests to probe the routers, but was changed to use UDP datagrams because many routers strictly adhered to the RFC 792 [Postel 1981] injunction that ICMP should not respond to an ICMP message with another ICMP message [Jacobson 1999]. RFC 1122 [Braden 1989] now says that an ICMP message should not be sent in response to an ICMP *error* message, but `TRACERT` still has problems with older routers.

RFC 1393 [Malkin 1993] proposed adding an IP option and separate ICMP message to provide reliable `traceroute` services (plus other useful information), but because it required changes in the routers and hosts, the method was not deployed.

## Summary

The `traceroute` utility is a very useful tool for diagnosing network problems, studying network routing, or exploring network topology. As we have seen, the "shape" of the Internet is often surprising, and this can lead to surprising effects in our applications. By using `traceroute` we are often able to discover the network anomalies that lead to problems with our applications.

The `traceroute` and `TRACERT` utilities both work by sending datagrams to the destination host with increasing TTL values, and by watching for ICMP time exceeded in transit messages from the intermediate routers. They differ in that `traceroute` sends UDP datagrams, whereas `TRACERT` sends ICMP echo requests messages.

## Tip 36: Learn to Use `ttcp`

Often it is useful to have a utility that can send arbitrary amounts of data to another machine (or even the same machine) using TCP or UDP, and to collect statistics about the transfer. We have already built several little programs that do this, but now we want to consider a ready-made tool with this functionality. We can use such a tool to drive our own application or to obtain information about the performance of a particular TCP/IP stack or network. Such information can be vital during the prototyping and design stage of a project.

The tool that we will study is `ttcp`, a public domain program from the U.S. Army Ballistics Research Laboratory (BRL) that was written by Mike Muuss (author of the `ping` utility) and Terry Slattery. The utility is widely available on the Internet. The version that we are using, which was modified by John Lin to report some additional statistics, is available by anonymous FTP from `gwen.cs.purdue.edu` in the `/pub/lin` directory. A version without Lin's modifications is available by anonymous FTP from `ftp.sgi.com` in directory `sgi/src/ttcp`. The latter version comes with a man page.

As we shall see, `ttcp` has several options that allow us to control the amount of data sent, the size of individual writes and reads, the size of socket send and receive buffers, whether the Nagle algorithm should be disabled, and even buffer alignment in memory. Figure 4.12 shows the usage summary output by `ttcp`.

```
Usage: ttcp -t [-options] host [ < in ]
       ttcp -r [-options > out]
Common options:
    -l ## length of bufs read from or written to
          network (default 8192)
    -u use UDP instead of TCP
    -p ## port number to send to or listen at (default 5001)
    -s   -t: source a pattern to network
         -r: sink (discard) all data from network
    -A align the start of buffers to this modulus (default 16384)
    -O start buffers at this offset from the modulus (default 0)
    -v verbose: print more statistics
    -d set SO_DEBUG socket option
    -b ## set socket buffer size (if supported)
    -f X format for rate: k,K = kilo{bit,byte}; m,M = mega;
                          g,G = giga
Options specific to -t:
    -n## number of source bufs written to network (default 2048)
    -D don't buffer TCP writes (sets TCP_NODELAY socket option)
Options specific to -r:
    -B for -s, only output full blocks as specified by -l (for TAR)
    -T "touch": access each byte as it's read
```

**Figure 4.12** `ttcp` usage summary

As an example, let's experiment a little with the socket send buffer size. First, we run a test with the default size to get a baseline. In one window we start an instance of `ttcp` that acts as a data sink:

```
bsd: $ ttcp -rsv
```

and in another we start a data source:

```
bsd: $ ttcp -tsv bsd
ttcp-t: buflen=8192, nbuf=2048, align=16384/0, port=5013  tcp -> bsd
ttcp-t: socket
ttcp-t: connect
ttcp-t: 16777216 bytes in 1.341030 real seconds
        = 12217.474628 KB/sec (95.449021 Mb/sec)
ttcp-t: 16777216 bytes in 0.00 CPU seconds
        = 16384000.000000 KB/cpu sec
ttcp-t: 2048 I/O calls, msec/call = 0.67, calls/sec = 1527.18
ttcp-t: buffer address 0x8050000
bsd: $
```

As we see, `ttcp` provides us with performance figures for the transfer. It took about 1.3 seconds to transfer 16 MB.

> Similar statistics are printed by the receiving process, but because they provide essentially the same information, we have not shown them.

We also monitored the transfer with `tcpdump`. A typical line from the dump is

```
13:05:44.084576 bsd.1061 > bsd.5013: . 1:1449(1448)
                ack 1 win 17376 <nop,nop,timestamp 11306 11306> (DF)
```

from which we see that TCP is sending 1,448-byte segments.

Now let's set the output buffer size for our data source to 1,448 bytes and rerun the experiment. We leave the data sink the same:

```
bsd: $ ttcp -tsvb 1448 bsd
ttcp-t: socket
ttcp-t: sndbuf
ttcp-t: connect
ttcp-t: buflen=8192, nbuf=2048, align=16384/0, port=5013,
        sockbufsize=1448  tcp -> bsd
ttcp-t: 16777216 bytes in 2457.246699 real seconds
        = 6.667625 KB/sec (0.052091 Mb/sec)
ttcp-t: 16777216 bytes in 0.00 CPU seconds
        = 16384000.000000 KB/cpu sec
ttcp-t: 2048 I/O calls, msec/call = 1228.62, calls/sec = 0.83
ttcp-t: buffer address 0x8050000
```

This time the transfer took almost 41 minutes to complete. What happened here? The first thing we notice is that although it took more than 40 minutes of wall-clock time, the actual CPU time used was too small to measure. Whatever's happening, we aren't spending the time in a CPU-intensive operation.

Next we look at the `tcpdump` output for this run. Four typical lines are shown in Figure 4.13.

```
16:03:57.168093 bsd.1187 > bsd.5013: P 8193:9641(1448)
                ack 1 win 17376 <nop,nop,timestamp 44802 44802> (DF)
16:03:57.368034 bsd.5013 > bsd.1187: . ack 9641 win 17376
                <nop,nop,timestamp 44802 44802> (DF)
16:03:57.368071 bsd.1187 > bsd.5013: P 9641:11089(1448)
                ack 1 win 17376 <nop,nop,timestamp 44802 44802> (DF)
16:03:57.568038 bsd.5013 > bsd.1187: . ack 11089 win 17376
                <nop,nop,timestamp 44802 44802> (DF)
```

**Figure 4.13** Typical `tcpdump` output for `ttcp -tsvb 1448 bsd`

We notice right away that the time between segments is almost exactly 200 ms, and we immediately become suspicious that we are seeing a Nagle algorithm/delayed ACK interaction (Tip 24). Indeed, we see that it is the ACKs that are being delayed.

We can test our hypothesis by turning off the Nagle algorithm with the `-D` option. When we rerun our experiment with the Nagle algorithm disabled

```
bsd: $ ttcp -tsvDb 1448 bsd
ttcp-t: buflen=8192, nbuf=2048, align=16384/0, port=5013,
        sockbufsize=1448 tcp -> bsd
ttcp-t: socket
ttcp-t: sndbuf
ttcp-t: connect
ttcp-t: nodelay
ttcp-t: 16777216 bytes in 2457.396882 real seconds
        = 6.667218 KB/sec (0.052088 Mb/sec)
ttcp-t: 16777216 bytes in 0.00 CPU seconds
        = 16384000.000000 KB/cpu sec
ttcp-t: 2048 I/O calls, msec/call = 1228.70, calls/sec = 0.83
ttcp-t: buffer address 0x8050000
```

we discover that it makes no difference—the results are the same.

> We might view this as a cautionary tale about the dangers of jumping to conclusions. A moment's thought about the matter should make it clear that the Nagle algorithm was not involved because we are sending *full-size* segments. Indeed, that was one of the points of our baseline run: to discover the MSS.

In Tip 39, we will study tools that allow us to trace system calls through the kernel. In that tip, we will revisit this example, and discover that the writes that `ttcp` makes do not return for approximately 1.2 seconds. We also see an indication of this in the `ttcp` output that shows each I/O call taking approximately 1,228 ms. Because, as we discussed in Tip 15, TCP write operations do not usually block unless the send buffer fills up, we can now understand what's happening. When `ttcp` writes 8,192 bytes, the kernel copies the first 1,448 bytes to the socket buffer and then blocks the process because there is no more room. TCP sends these bytes as a single segment but can't send more because there is no more unsent data in the send buffer.

> We can see this happening in Figure 4.13 because the PSH flag is set for each segment sent, and BSD-derived stacks set the PSH flag only when the current transmission empties the send buffer.

Because the data sink makes no response to received data, the delayed ACK mechanism comes into play and the ACK is not returned until the 200-ms timer fires.

In the baseline run, TCP is able to keep sending full-length segments because the socket buffer is large enough (16K on bsd) to hold several. A similar kernel trace for the baseline run shows that, in that case, the writes return in about 0.3 ms.

What we have actually shown here is the importance of keeping the send buffer size at least as large as our peer's receive buffer. Although the receiver is willing to accept more data, the sender's output buffer is full with the last segment sent, and the sender can't release that data until it knows, by receipt of an ACK, that its peer has received it. Because a single segment is small in comparison with the 16K receive buffer, its receipt does not trigger a window update (Tip 15), so the ACK is delayed 200 ms. See Tip 32 for more about buffer sizes.

The point of this exercise, though, was not to demonstrate a particular fact about the relative sizes of the send and receive buffers, but to show how we can use `ttcp` to test the effects of setting various TCP connection parameters. We also saw how we can bring together data from the `ttcp` statistics, `tcpdump`, and kernel system call traces to understand the observed behavior.

Before leaving `ttcp`, we should mention that it can also be used to provide a "network pipe" between hosts. For example, here is one way of copying a directory hierarchy from host A to host B. On host B we enter the command

```
ttcp -rB | tar -xpf -
```

and on host A the command

```
tar -cf - directory | ttcp -t A
```

We can extend our network pipe across several machines by using

```
ttcp -r | ttcp -t next_hop
```

on the intermediate machines.

## Summary

We have seen how to use `ttcp` to experiment with various TCP connection parameters. As we mentioned, `ttcp` can also be used to test our own applications by providing a TCP or UDP data source or sink. Finally, we have seen how we can use `ttcp` to provide a network pipe between two or more machines.

## Tip 37: Learn to Use `lsof`

A frequent problem in network programming (and non-network programming for that matter) is determining which process has a file or socket open. This can be especially important in networking because, as we saw in Tip 16, some other process holding a socket open will prevent a FIN from being sent when the process actually using the socket exits or otherwise closes it.

Although it might seem odd that some other process would be holding a socket open, it can occur easily, especially in a UNIX environment. What usually happens is that one process accepts a connection and starts another process to handle the work for that connection. This is what `inetd` (Tip 17) does, for example. If the process accepting the connection fails to close the socket after starting the child process, the reference count of the socket will be two, so that when the child closes the socket, the connection remains open and no FIN is sent.

The problem can also occur the other way around. Suppose the host of the client talking to the child process crashes and the child hangs as a result. We discussed this type of situation in Tip 10. If the process accepting connections terminates, it is not able to restart (unless it has specified `SO_REUSEADDR`—see Tip 23) because the local port is already bound to the child process.

In these cases and others, it is necessary to determine which process or processes still have the socket open. The `netstat` utility (Tip 38) tells us that some process is using a particular port or address, but it doesn't tell us which process. Some UNIX systems have the `fstat` utility to do this, but it is not available on all systems. Fortunately, Victor Abell's public domain `lsof` program is available for a wide variety of UNIX systems.

> The `lsof` distribution is available by anonymous FTP from `vic.cc.purdue.edu` in the `pub/tools/unix/lsof` directory.

`lsof` is extraordinarily flexible—its man page is 26 typeset pages—and can provide a large variety of information about open files. As with `tcpdump`, the fact that it provides a single common interface for several UNIX dialects is a big advantage.

Let's look at a few of its features that are useful in networking. Its man page contains a wealth of information about its use in more general settings.

Suppose we do a `netstat -af inet` (Tip 38) and we notice that some process is listening on port 6000 as shown in the following partial output:

```
Active Internet connections (including servers)
Proto Recv-Q Send-Q  Local Address     Foreign Address        (state)
tcp        0      0  *.6000            *.*                    LISTEN
```

Port 6000 is not in the "well-known port" range (Tip 18), so we might wonder what server is listening for connections on it. As we have already noted, the `netstat` output is silent on this—it merely tells us that some process is listening on that port. Fortunately, the question is easily answered with lsof:

```
bsd# lsof -i TCP:6000
COMMAND    PID USER FD   TYPE     DEVICE SIZE/OFF NODE NAME
XF86_Mach 253 root  0u inet 0xf5d98840      0t0  TCP *:6000 (LISTEN)
bsd#
```

The first thing to notice is that we ran `lsof` as root. That's because the version of `lsof` that we're using is configured to list files belonging only to the user unless the user is root. This is a security feature that can be disabled when the utility is compiled. Next we notice that the process was started by root with the command `XF86_Mach`. This is the X-server that runs on our host.

The `-i TCP:6000` tells `lsof` to look for open "inet" TCP sockets that are bound to port 6000. We could ask for all TCP sockets with `-i TCP` or all TCP/UDP sockets with `-i`.

Next, suppose we run another `netstat` and discover that someone has an FTP connection to `vic.cc.purdue.edu`:

```
Active Internet connections
Proto Recv-Q Send-Q Local Address Foreign Address      (state)
tcp      0      0 bsd.1124     vic.cc.purdue.edu.ftp  ESTABLISHED
```

We can discover which user this is with lsof:

```
bsd# lsof -i @vic.cc.purdue.edu
COMMAND PID USER   FD   TYPE     DEVICE SIZE/OFF NODE NAME
ftp     450  jcs   3u  inet 0xf5d99f00     0t0  TCP bsd:1124->
    vic.cc.purdue.edu:ftp (ESTABLISHED)
bsd#
```

As usual, we have removed the domain name from bsd, and have wrapped the `lsof` output for formatting reasons. We see from the output that user jcs has the FTP connection open.

We should emphasize that `lsof`, whose name, after all, stands for list open files, can only provide information about files that are actually *open*. This means, in particular, that it can't give us any information about TCP connections that are in the TIME-WAIT state (Tip 22) because there is no open socket or file associated with such a connection.

### Summary

We have seen how we can use the `lsof` utility to answer a variety of questions about open files. Although we have concentrated on its application to networking, `lsof` can provide information about a variety of open file types. Unfortunately, `lsof` is only available on UNIX systems; there is no Windows version.

## Tip 38: Learn to Use `netstat`

The kernel maintains a number of useful statistics about network-related objects that we can query with `netstat`. There are four types of information available.

### Active Sockets

First, we can get information about active sockets. Although `netstat` can provide information on several types of sockets, we are only interested in those that are concerned with inet domain and UNIX domain sockets; that is, those sockets with `AF_INET` and `AF_LOCAL` (or `AF_UNIX`) domains. We can list all types of sockets, or we can choose the type of socket to list by specifying an address family with the `-f` option.

By default, those servers with a socket bound to `INADDR_ANY` are not listed, but this can be changed by specifying the `-a` option. For example, if we were interested in

TCP/UDP sockets, we could call `netstat` as

```
bsd: $ netstat -f inet
Active Internet connections
Proto Recv-Q Send-Q  Local Address          Foreign Address      (state)
tcp        0      0  localhost.domain       *.*                  LISTEN
tcp        0      0  bsd.domain             *.*                  LISTEN
udp        0      0  localhost.domain       *.*
udp        0      0  bsd.domain             *.*
bsd: $
```

This output shows only the domain name server (`named`) that runs on bsd. If we ask for all servers, we get

```
bsd: $ netstat -af inet
Active Internet connections (including servers)
Proto Recv-Q Send-Q  Local Address          Foreign Address      (state)
tcp        0      0  *.6000                 *.*                  LISTEN
tcp        0      0  *.smtp                 *.*                  LISTEN
tcp        0      0  *.printer              *.*                  LISTEN
tcp        0      0  *.rlnum                *.*                  LISTEN
tcp        0      0  *.tcpmux               *.*                  LISTEN
tcp        0      0  *.chargen              *.*                  LISTEN
tcp        0      0  *.discard              *.*                  LISTEN
tcp        0      0  *.echo                 *.*                  LISTEN
tcp        0      0  *.time                 *.*                  LISTEN
tcp        0      0  *.daytime              *.*                  LISTEN
tcp        0      0  *.finger               *.*                  LISTEN
tcp        0      0  *.login                *.*                  LISTEN
tcp        0      0  *.cmd                  *.*                  LISTEN
tcp        0      0  *.telnet               *.*                  LISTEN
tcp        0      0  *.ftp                  *.*                  LISTEN
tcp        0      0  *.1022                 *.*                  LISTEN
tcp        0      0  *.2049                 *.*                  LISTEN
tcp        0      0  *.1023                 *.*                  LISTEN
tcp        0      0  *.sunrpc               *.*                  LISTEN
tcp        0      0  localhost.domain       *.*                  LISTEN
tcp        0      0  bsd.domain             *.*                  LISTEN
udp        0      0  *.udpecho              *.*
udp        0      0  *.chargen              *.*
udp        0      0  *.discard              *.*
udp        0      0  *.echo                 *.*
udp        0      0  *.time                 *.*
udp        0      0  *.daytime              *.*
udp        0      0  *.ntalk                *.*
udp        0      0  *.biff                 *.*
udp        0      0  *.1011                 *.*
udp        0      0  *.nfsd                 *.*
udp        0      0  *.1023                 *.*
udp        0      0  *.sunrpc               *.*
udp        0      0  *.1024                 *.*
udp        0      0  localhost.domain       *.*
udp        0      0  bsd.domain             *.*
udp        0      0  *.syslog               *.*
bsd: $
```

If we were to run `lsof` (Tip 37), we would see majority of these "servers" are, in fact, `inetd` (Tip 17) listening for connections or datagrams to the standard services. The "LISTEN" under the state column for TCP connections means that the server is waiting for a client to connect.

If we telnet to the echo server

```
bsd: $ telnet bsd echo
```

we see that we now have an ESTABLISHED connection:

```
Proto Recv-Q Send-Q  Local Address      Foreign Address    (state)
tcp       0      0    bsd.echo           bsd.1035           ESTABLISHED
tcp       0      0    bsd.1035           bsd.echo           ESTABLISHED
tcp       0      0    *.echo             *.*                LISTEN
```

We have deleted those lines not concerned with the echo server from the output. Notice that because we connected to the same machine, the connection appears twice in the `netstat` listing—once for the client and once for the server. Also notice that `inetd` is still listening for additional connections to the echo server.

> This last point deserves a little discussion. Although our `telnet` client has connected to port 7 (the echo port), and is, in fact, using port 7 as its destination port, the host is still listening for connections on port 7. This is OK because TCP identifies connections by the 4-tuple consisting of the local IP address and port and the remote IP address and port as discussed in Tip 23. As we see, `inetd` is listening at the "wildcard" address (INADDR_ANY) as indicated by the asterisk, whereas the IP address for the connection is "bsd." If we were to start another telnet connection with the echo server, we would have two more entries that look exactly like the first two except that the source port for the client would be different from 1035.

If we now terminate our client and run `netstat` again, we get

```
Proto Recv-Q Send-Q  Local Address      Foreign Address    (state)
tcp       0      0    bsd.1035           bsd.echo           TIME_WAIT
```

This shows the client's side of the connection in the TIME-WAIT state, as we discussed in Tip 22. The other possible states can also occur in the state column. See RFC 793 [Postel 1981b] for information concerning TCP connection states.

## Interfaces

The second type of data that we can get from `netstat` is information concerning interfaces. We have already seen an example of this in Tip 7. We obtain the basic interface information by using the `-i` option:

```
bsd: $ netstat -i
Name  Mtu    Network        Address              Ipkts Ierrs  Opkts Oerrs  Coll
ed0   1500   <Link>         00.00.c0.54.53.73    40841     0   5793     0     0
ed0   1500   172.30         bsd                  40841     0   5793     0     0
tun0* 1500   <Link>                                397     0    451     0     0
tun0* 1500   205.184.142    205.184.142.171        397     0    451     0     0
sl0*  552    <Link>                                  0     0      0     0     0
lo0   16384  <Link>                                353     0    353     0     0
lo0   16384  127            localhost             353     0    353     0     0
```

We see from this that bsd has four interfaces configured. The first, ed0, is the Ethernet LAN adaptor. As we see, it is on the private (RFC 1918 [Rekhter, Moskowitz et al. 1996]) network 172.30.0.0. The 00.00.c0.54.73 in the first entry is the medium access control (MAC) address of the Ethernet card. There have been 40,841 input packets, 5,793 output packets, no errors, and no collisions. As we discussed in Tip 7, the MTU is 1,500, the most an Ethernet can accommodate.

The tun0 interface is a dialup Point-to-Point Protocol (PPP) link. It is on the 205.184.142.0 network. It also has a 1,500-byte MTU.

The sl0 interface is for the Serial Line Internet Protocol (SLIP; RFC 1055 [Romkey 1988]), another, older, point-to-point protocol. This interface is not used on bsd.

Finally, there is the loopback interface, lo0. We have already discussed it several times.

We can also specify the -b and/or -d options in conjunction with the -i option to list the number of bytes in and out of the interface, and the number of dropped packets.

## Routing Table

The next piece of information available from netstat is the routing table. We use the -n option to request numbers instead of names for IP addresses so that we can see the actual networks involved.

```
bsd: $ netstat -rn
Routing tables

Internet:
Destination     Gateway           Flags   Refs   Use    Netif Expire
default         163.179.44.41     UGSc    2      0      tun0
127.0.0.1       127.0.0.1         UH      1      34     lo0
163.179.44.41   205.184.142.171   UH      3      0      tun0
172.30          link#1            UC      0      0      ed0
172.30.0.1      0:0:c0:54:53:73   UHLW    0      132    lo0
bsd: $
```

**Figure 4.14** Routing table output from netstat

The interfaces and connections reported in Figure 4.14 are shown in Figure 4.15. The lo0 interface is not shown because it is contained completely within the bsd host.

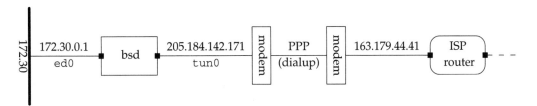

**Figure 4.15** Interfaces and hosts reported in Figure 4.14

Before we look at the individual entries of this output, let's discuss the meaning of the columns. The first column identifies the destination of the route. It could be a specific host, a network, or a default route.

There are several flags that can appear in the *Flags* field, many of which are implementation dependent. We shall consider only

U—The route is "UP."

H—This is a route to a host. If this flag is not present, the route is to a network (or possibly a subnetwork if CIDR (Tip 2) is not in use).

G—The route is indirect. That is, the destination is not connected directly but must be reached through an intermediate router or gateway (hence G).

It is easy to mistakenly think of the H and G flags as opposite sides of the same thing: The route is either to a host (H) or to an intermediate gateway (G). This is *not* correct. The H flag tells us that the address in the first column is the complete IP address of a host. The absence of the H indicates that the address in the first column does not contain the host ID portion—that it is the address of a network. The G flag tells us whether the address in the first column is reachable directly from this host or whether we must go through an intermediate gateway.

It is perfectly possible for a route to have both the G and H flags set. Consider the two networks shown in Figure 4.16, for example. Hosts H1 and H2 are connected to the Ethernet network 172.20. H3 is connected to H2 through a PPP connection with network 198.168.2.

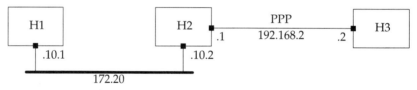

**Figure 4.16** H2 acting as a gateway to H3

The route to H3 would appear in H1's routing table as

```
Destination     Gateway          Flags    Refs    Use    Netif Expire
192.168.2.2     172.20.10.2      UGH       0       0     ed0
```

The H flag is set because 192.168.2.2 is a complete host address. The G flag is set because H1 does not have a direct connection to H3, but must go through H2 (172.20.10.2) to reach it. Notice that in Figure 4.14, the route to 163.179.44.41 does not have the G flag set because 163.179.44.41 is connected directly to the tun0 interface (205.184.142.171) of bsd.

In Figure 2.9, there would be no entry in H1's routing table for H3. Rather, there would be an entry for the 190.50.2 subnetwork—that's the point of subnetting: to reduce routing table size. The routing entry in H1 for this subnetwork would be

```
Destination      Gateway            Flags   Refs   Use   Netif Expire
190.50.2         190.50.1.4         UG         0     0   ed0
```

The H flag is not set because 190.50.2 is the address of a subnetwork, not of a host. The G flag is set because H3 is not connected directly to H1. Datagrams to H3 from H1 must go through the router R1 (190.50.1.4).

The meaning of the *Gateway* field depends on whether the G flag is set. When the route is indirect (the G flag is set), the *Gateway* field is the IP address of the next hop (the "gateway"). When the G flag is not set, the *Gateway* field contains information on how to reach the directly connected destination. In many implementations, this is always the IP address of the interface to which the destination is directly connected. In BSD-derived implementations, it could also be the link layer MAC address as shown in the last line of Figure 4.14. In this case the L flag is set.

The *Refs* field tells us the reference count for this route. That is, how many active uses there are of the route.

The *Use* field tells us how many packets have been sent using that route, and the *Netif* field is the name of the associated interface. This interface is the same object that we obtained information about with the `-i` option.

Now that we've looked at what the fields in the output of `netstat -rn` mean, we can, finally, examine the entries of Figure 4.14.

The first line in Figure 4.14 is the *default route*. This is the where IP datagrams are sent if the routing table doesn't contain a more specific route. For example, if we `ping` netcom4.netcom.com, we get

```
bsd: $ ping netcom4.netcom.com
PING netcom4.netcom.com (199.183.9.104): 56 data bytes
64 bytes from 199.183.9.104: icmp_seq=0 ttl=248 time=268.604 ms
...
```

Because there is no route to 199.183.9.104 or to any network containing that host, the ICMP echo requests (Tip 33) are sent to the default route. According to the first line of the `netstat` output, the gateway for this route is 163.179.44.41, so the datagram must be sent there. Line 3 of Figure 4.14 shows us that there is a direct route to 163.179.44.41 and that datagrams to it should be sent out the interface that has IP address 205.184.142.171.

Line 2 of the output is the route for the loopback address (127.0.0.1). Because this is a host address, the H flag is set. Because it is directly connected, the G flag is not set, and the *Gateway* field tells us the IP address of the interface (`lo0`).

Line 4 of Figure 4.14 is the route to the local Ethernet. Because bsd is a BSD-derived system, the *Gateway* field is designated as Link#1. Other systems would simply put the IP address (172.30.0.1) of the interface connected to the LAN

## Protocol Statistics

The last class of information available from `netstat` is protocol statistics. If we specify the `-s` option, `netstat` provides information on the IP, ICMP, IGMP, UDP, and TCP protocols. If we are only interested in one protocol, we can specify it with the `-p` option. To get statistics concerning UDP, for instance, we would use

```
bsd: $ netstat -sp udp
udp:
    82 datagrams received
    0 with incomplete header
    0 with bad data length field
    0 with bad checksum
    1 dropped due to no socket
    0 broadcast/multicast datagrams dropped due to no socket
    0 dropped due to full socket buffers
    0 not for hashed pcb
    81 delivered
    82 datagrams output
bsd: $
```

We can suppress statistics with no occurrences by doubling the `s` option:

```
bsd: $ netstat -ssp udp
udp:
    82 datagrams received
    1 dropped due to no socket
    81 delivered
    82 datagrams output
bsd: $
```

It is a sobering and worthwhile exercise to examine the TCP statistics occasionally. On bsd, `netstat` reports 45 different TCP statistics. Here are the nonzero statistics collected by invoking `netstat` with the `-ssp tcp` options:

```
tcp:
    446 packets sent
        190 data packets (40474 bytes)
        213 ack-only packets (166 delayed)
        18 window update packets
        32 control packets
    405 packets received
        193 acks (for 40488 bytes)
        12 duplicate acks
        302 packets (211353 bytes) received in-sequence
        10 completely duplicate packets (4380 bytes)
        22 out-of-order packets (16114 bytes)
        2 window update packets
    20 connection requests
    2 connection accepts
    13 connections established (including accepts)
    22 connections closed (including 0 drops)
        3 connections updated cached RTT on close
        3 connections updated cached RTT variance on close
    2 embryonic connections dropped
    193 segments updated rtt (of 201 attempts)
    31 correct ACK header predictions
    180 correct data packet header predictions
```

These statistics were collected after bsd was rebooted and then used to send and receive a few email messages and to read some news groups. If we had any illusions that events such as out-of-order or duplicate segments are unlikely or rare, these statistics should dispel them. For example, of 405 packets received, 10 were duplicates and 22 were out of order.

> [Bennett et al. 1999] shows why the reordering of packets is not necessarily pathological behavior, and why we can expect to see more of it in the future.

### Windows `netstat`

We have been discussing the UNIX family of `netstat` utilities. The Windows environment also has a `netstat`, which provides many of the same options and data. The output although similar is, in general, not as comprehensive but still provides much useful information.

### Summary

We have examined the `netstat` utility and some of the information about network objects that it provides. We have seen that `netstat` can tell us about active sockets, the networking interfaces configured on the system, the routing table, and protocol statistics.

Although this tip was long and contained a great deal of information, this reflects the utility itself. `netstat` provides information about many aspects of the networking subsystem, and as such has many different kinds of output.

## Tip 39: Learn to Use Your System's Call Trace Facility

It is sometimes useful, when debugging network applications, to be able to trace system calls through the kernel. We have already seen an example of this in Tip 36, and we will revisit that example shortly.

Most operating systems provide some way of tracing system calls. In the BSD world it is `ktrace`, in the SVR4 (and Solaris) world it is `truss`, and with Linux it is `strace`.

These utilities are similar, so we demonstrate their use with `ktrace`. A glance at the man pages for `truss` or `strace` should be enough to allow us to carry the same techniques over to the other environments.

### A Premature Termination

Our first example is based on an early version of the `shutdownc` program (Figure 3.2) that we developed in Tip 16. The idea behind `badclient` is the same as that behind `shutdownc`: We accept input from stdin until we get an EOF. At that point, we call `shutdown` to send our peer a FIN, and then continue to read input from our peer until we receive an EOF on the connection indicating our peer has also finished sending data. The badclient program is shown in Figure 4.17.

———————————————————————————————— *badclient.c*

```
 1 #include "etcp.h"
 2 int main( int argc, char **argv )
 3 {
 4     SOCKET s;
 5     fd_set readmask;
 6     fd_set allreads;
 7     int rc;
 8     int len;
 9     char lin[ 1024 ];
10     char lout[ 1024 ];
11     INIT();
12     s = tcp_client( argv[ optind ], argv[ optind + 1 ] );
13     FD_ZERO( &allreads );
14     FD_SET( 0, &allreads );
15     FD_SET( s, &allreads );
16     for ( ;; )
17     {
18         readmask = allreads;
19         rc = select( s + 1, &readmask, NULL, NULL, NULL );
20         if ( rc <= 0 )
21             error( 1, errno, "bad select return (%d)", rc );
22         if ( FD_ISSET( s, &readmask ) )
23         {
24             rc = recv( s, lin, sizeof( lin ) - 1, 0 );
25             if ( rc < 0 )
26                 error( 1, errno, "recv error" );
27             if ( rc == 0 )
28                 error( 1, 0, "server disconnected\n" );
29             lin[ rc ] = '\0';
30             if ( fputs( lin, stdout ) )
31                 error( 1, errno, "fputs failed" );
32         }
33         if ( FD_ISSET( 0, &readmask ) )
34         {
35             if ( fgets( lout, sizeof( lout ), stdin ) == NULL )
36             {
37                 if ( shutdown( s, 1 ) )
38                     error( 1, errno, "shutdown failed" );
39             }
40             else
41             {
42                 len = strlen( lout );
43                 rc = send( s, lout, len, 0 );
44                 if ( rc < 0 )
45                     error( 1, errno, "send error" );
46             }
47         }
48     }
49 }
```

———————————————————————————————— *badclient.c*

**Figure 4.17**  An incorrect echo client

*22-32*    If `select` has indicated that we have a read event on our connection, we try to read the data. If we get an EOF, our peer is through sending data, so we terminate. Otherwise, we write the data that we just read to stdout.

*33-47*    If `select` has indicated that we have a read event on stdin, we call `fgets` to read the data. If `fgets` returns `NULL`, indicating an error or EOF, we call `shutdown` to inform our peer that we are through sending data. Otherwise, we send the data to our peer.

Now lets see what happens when we run `badclient`. We use `tcpecho` (Figure 3.3) as our server for this experiment. Recall from Tip 16 that we can specify the number of seconds that `tcpecho` should delay before echoing its response. We set this delay to 30 seconds. After we start `badclient`, we type in "hello," followed immediately by a <CNTRL-D> to serve as an EOF to `fgets`:

```
bsd: $ tcpecho 9000 30               bsd: $ badclient bsd 9000
                     30 seconds later  hello
tcpecho: recv failed:                ^D
    Connection reset by peer (54)    badclient: server disconnected
bsd: $                               bsd: $
```

As we see, `badclient` terminates immediately, complaining that `tcpecho` disconnected. But `tcpecho` is still running and remains sleeping until the 30-second delay is up. At that time, it gets a "Connection reset by peer" on its read.

These are surprising results. We were expecting to see `tcpecho` echo (and have `badclient` print) the "hello" after 30 seconds and then terminate when it got an EOF on its next read. Instead, `badclient` terminates immediately and `tcpecho` gets a read error.

A reasonable first step in diagnosing this problem is to use `tcpdump` (Tip 34) to see what the two programs are sending back and forth. We show the `tcpdump` output in Figure 4.18. We have removed the connection setup phase and wrapped the lines to fit on the page.

```
1 18:39:48.535212 bsd.2027 > bsd.9000:
    P 1:7(6) ack 1 win 17376 <nop,nop,timestamp 742414 742400> (DF)
2 18:39:48.546773 bsd.9000 > bsd.2027:
    . ack 7 win 17376 <nop,nop,timestamp 742414 742414> (DF)
3 18:39:49.413285 bsd.2027 > bsd.9000:
    F 7:7(0) ack 1 win 17376 <nop,nop,timestamp 742415 742414> (DF)
4 18:39:49.413311 bsd.9000 > bsd.2027:
    . ack 8 win 17376 <nop,nop,timestamp 742415 742415> (DF)
5 18:40:18.537119 bsd.9000 > bsd.2027:
    P 1:7(6) ack 8 win 17376 <nop,nop,timestamp 742474 742415> (DF)
6 18:40:18.537180 bsd.2027 > bsd.9000:
    R 2059690956:2059690956(0) win 0
```

**Figure 4.18** `tcpdump` output from `badclient`

Strangely enough, everything looks normal except for the last line. We see `badclient` send the "hello" to `tcpecho` at line 1, and we see the FIN resulting from shutdown about a second later at line 3. tcpecho responds to both of these with the expected ACKs at lines 2 and 4. Thirty seconds after badclient sends "hello," we see tcpecho send it back at line 5, but instead of responding with an ACK, the badclient side of the connection returns an RST (line 6) that results in the "Connection reset by peer" error in tcpecho. The RST is because badclient has already terminated, but why did it do so? The tcpdump output gives no clue.

The tcpdump output does tell us that tcpecho did nothing to cause its peer to terminate early, so the problem must lie entirely within badclient. It's time to see what's going on inside badclient, and one way to do that is to see what system calls it's making.

To that end, we rerun our experiment, but we invoke badclient as

bsd: $ **ktrace badclient bsd 9000**

This runs badclient as before, but also produces a trace of the system calls that it makes. By default, the results of this trace are written to the file ktrace.out. To print the results of the trace, we run kdump. We show the result of this in Figure 4.19, where we have removed several preliminary calls that deal with starting the application and with connection setup.

```
 1 4692 badclient CALL  read(0,0x804e000,0x10000)
 2 4692 badclient GIO   fd 0 read 6 bytes
   "hello
   "
 3 4692 badclient RET   read 6
 4 4692 badclient CALL  sendto(0x3,0xefbfce68,0x6,0,0,0)
 5 4692 badclient GIO   fd 3 wrote 6 bytes
   "hello
   "
 6 4692 badclient RET   sendto 6
 7 4692 badclient CALL  select(0x4,0xefbfd6f0,0,0,0)
 8 4692 badclient RET   select 1
 9 4692 badclient CALL  read(0,0x804e000,0x10000)
10 4692 badclient GIO   fd 0 read 0 bytes
   " "
11 4692 badclient RET   read 0
12 4692 badclient CALL  shutdown(0x3,0x1)
13 4692 badclient RET   shutdown 0
14 4692 badclient CALL  select(0x4,0xefbfd6f0,0,0,0)
15 4692 badclient RET   select 1
16 4692 badclient CALL  shutdown(0x3,0x1)
17 4692 badclient RET   shutdown 0
18 4692 badclient CALL  select(0x4,0xefbfd6f0,0,0,0)
19 4692 badclient RET   select 2
20 4692 badclient CALL  recvfrom(0x3,0xefbfd268,0x3ff,0,0,0)
21 4692 badclient GIO   fd 3 read 0 bytes
   " "
22 4692 badclient RET   recvfrom 0
23 4692 badclient CALL  write(0x2,0xefbfc6f4,0xb)
24 4692 badclient GIO   fd 2 wrote 11 bytes
   "badclient: "
25 4692 badclient RET   write 11/0xb
```

```
26 4692 badclient CALL   write(0x2,0xefbfc700,0x14)
27 4692 badclient GIO    fd 2 wrote 20 bytes
   "server disconnected
   "
28 4692 badclient RET    write 20/0x14
29 4692 badclient CALL   exit(0x1)
```

**Figure 4.19** Results of running `ktrace` on `badclient`

The first two entries in each line are the process ID and name of the program executing. In line 1, we see the call to `read` with the fd set to zero (stdin). In line 2, 6 bytes
are read (the "GIO" stands for general I/O), and that "hello\n" was read. Line 3
shows the call to `read` returning 6, the number of bytes read. Similarly, lines 4–6 show
`badclient` writing this to fd 3, the socket connected to `tcpecho`. Next lines 7 and 8
show `select` returning 1, meaning that a single event is ready. In lines 9–11 we see
`badclient` reading the EOF on stdin, and calling `shutdown` as a result in lines 12 and
13.

So far, everything is just what we expected, but there is a surprise in lines 14–17:
`select` returns a single event and `shutdown` is called again. Checking Figure 4.17, we
see that this can only happen if descriptor 0 becomes ready. There is no call to `read`, as
we might expect, because `fgets` marked the stream at EOF when we typed the
<CNTRL-D>, so it just returns without actually calling `read`.

> We can follow this in, for example, the sample implementation of `fgets` (by way of `getc`) in
> [Kernighan and Ritchie 1988].

In lines 18 and 19 `select` returns with an event ready on both stdin and the socket.
Lines 20–22 show `recvfrom` returning 0 (an EOF), and the rest of the trace shows
`badclient` writing its error message and terminating.

It is now clear what happened: `select` returned with stdin ready for reading in
line 15 because we failed to call `FD_CLR` for stdin after our first `shutdown`. The subsequent (second) call to `shutdown` caused TCP to close the connection.

> We can see this on page 1014 of [Wright and Stevens 1995], where `tcp_usrclosed` is called as
> a result of the `shutdown`. If `shutdown` has already been called, the connection is in the FIN-
> WAIT-2 state, and `tcp_usrclosed` calls `soisdisconnected` at line 444 on page 1021. This
> call will completely closes the socket and causes `select` to return with a read event, which is
> the EOF.

Because the connection closed, `recvfrom` returned 0, indicating an EOF, and
`badclient` output its "server disconnected" diagnostic and terminated.

The key to understanding what was happening in this example was the second call
to `shutdown`. Once we saw that, we merely needed to ask ourselves how it happened,
and from there it was easy to discover the missing `FD_CLR`.

## Bad `ttcp` Performance

The next example is a continuation of one begun in Tip 36. Recall that when, in that
example, we set the socket send buffer to the size of the connection MSS, the time to
transmit 16 MB went from 1.3 seconds for the default buffer size to almost 41 minutes.

We show some representative `ktrace` results from that experiment in Figure 4.20. We invoked `kdump` as

```
kdump -R -m -1
```

to print the relative times between entries and to inhibit printing the 8 KB of data associated with each write.

```
12512 ttcp       0.000023 CALL   write(0x3,0x8050000,0x2000)
12512 ttcp       1.199605 GIO    fd 3 wrote 8192 bytes
      " "
12512 ttcp       0.000446 RET    write 8192/0x2000
12512 ttcp       0.000022 CALL   write(0x3,0x8050000,0x2000)
12512 ttcp       1.199574 GIO    fd 3 wrote 8192 bytes
      " "
12512 ttcp       0.000442 RET    write 8192/0x2000
12512 ttcp       0.000023 CALL   write(0x3,0x8050000,0x2000)
12512 ttcp       1.199514 GIO    fd 3 wrote 8192 bytes
      " "
12512 ttcp       0.000432 RET    write 8192/0x2000
```

**Figure 4.20** Representative `ktrace` results for `ttcp -tsvb 1448 bsd`

Notice the time for each write is pretty consistently 1.2 seconds. For comparison, the results of the baseline run are shown in Figure 4.21. There, we see that although there is more variance in the times, they average well below 0.5 ms.

```
12601 ttcp       0.000033 CALL   write(0x3,0x8050000,0x2000)
12601 ttcp       0.000279 GIO    fd 3 wrote 8192 bytes
      " "
12601 ttcp       0.000360 RET    write 8192/0x2000
12601 ttcp       0.000033 CALL   write(0x3,0x8050000,0x2000)
12601 ttcp       0.000527 GIO    fd 3 wrote 8192 bytes
      " "
12601 ttcp       0.000499 RET    write 8192/0x2000
12601 ttcp       0.000032 CALL   write(0x3,0x8050000,0x2000)
12601 ttcp       0.000282 GIO    fd 3 wrote 8192 bytes
      " "
12601 ttcp       0.000403 RET    write 8192/0x2000
```

**Figure 4.21** Representative `ktrace` results for `ttcp -tsv bsd`

The long times for the GIO entries in Figure 4.20 compared with the much shorter GIO times in Figure 4.21 led us to the conclusion, in Tip 36, that our writes were blocking in the kernel, and from there we were able to understand the exact mechanism that was causing the large transmit time.

## Summary

We have seen how we can use a system call trace in two ways. In the first example we were able to discover the error in our application by seeing what system calls it was making. In the second example, it was not the call itself that was of interest, but the amount of time that it took to complete.

As we have seen before in our discussions of other tools, it is often the combination of information gathered by several tools that enable us to understand an anomalous behavior in our applications. Call tracing utilities such as `ktrace`, `truss`, and `strace` are just one more weapon that the network programmer can bring to bear in understanding the behavior of an application.

## Tip 40: Build and Use a Tool to Capture ICMP Messages

It is occasionally useful to be able to monitor ICMP messages. We can always use `tcpdump` or some other line monitor to do this, but sometimes a lighter weight tool is more appropriate. Using `tcpdump` has performance and security implications that merely listening for ICMP messages does not.

In the first place, using a line monitor such as `tcpdump` usually means placing the network interface into promiscuous mode. This places a burden on the CPU because every Ethernet packet on the wire will cause an interrupt, regardless of whether the packet is addressed to the host running the line monitor.

Second, many organizations limit or even proscribe the use of line monitors because of their potential for eavesdropping and sniffing of passwords. Reading ICMP messages does not pose these security risks and so is more apt to be acceptable in such organizations.

In this tip we develop a tool that lets us monitor ICMP messages without the disadvantages associated with using a line monitor. This also gives us an opportunity to study the use of raw sockets, something we have not looked at before.

Recall from Tip 33 that ICMP messages are carried within IP datagrams. Although the contents of an ICMP message vary depending on its type, we are concerned only with the `icmp_type` and `icmp_code` fields shown in Figure 4.22 except when we deal with ICMP unreachable messages.

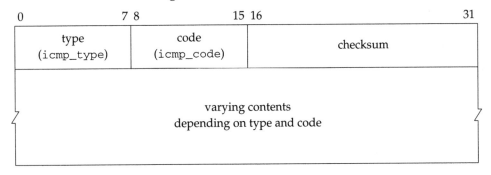

**Figure 4.22** A generic ICMP message

There is often confusion about raw sockets and their capabilities. Raw sockets can not be used to intercept TCP segments or UDP datagrams because these are never passed to a raw socket. Nor will a raw socket necessarily receive every type of ICMP message. In BSD-derived systems, for example, ICMP echo requests, time stamp requests, and address mask requests are handled entirely within the kernel, and are not made available to raw sockets. In general, raw sockets receive any IP datagram with a protocol unknown to the kernel, most ICMP messages, and all IGMP messages.

The other important point is that the *entire* IP datagram, header and all, is passed to the raw socket. As we shall see, our application code must arrange to "step over" this IP header.

## Reading the ICMP Messages

We begin with the includes and main function of our tool (Figure 4.23).

```
                                                                              ─── icmp.c
 1 #include <sys/types.h>
 2 #include <netinet/in_systm.h>
 3 #include <netinet/in.h>
 4 #include <netinet/ip.h>
 5 #include <netinet/ip_icmp.h>
 6 #include <netinet/udp.h>
 7 #include "etcp.h"

 8 int main( int argc, char **argv )
 9 {
10     SOCKET s;
11     struct protoent *pp;
12     int rc;
13     char icmpdg[ 1024 ];

14     INIT();
15     pp = getprotobyname( "icmp" );
16     if ( pp == NULL )
17         error( 1, errno, "getprotobyname failed" );
18     s = socket( AF_INET, SOCK_RAW, pp->p_proto );
19     if ( !isvalidsock( s ) )
20         error( 1, errno, "socket failed" );

21     for ( ;; )
22     {
23         rc = recvfrom( s, icmpdg, sizeof( icmpdg ), 0,
24             NULL, NULL );
25         if ( rc < 0 )
26             error( 1, errno, "recvfrom failed" );
27         print_dg( icmpdg, rc );
28     }
29 }
                                                                              ─── icmp.c
```

**Figure 4.23**  `main` function of `icmp`

### Open a Raw Socket

*15–20*    Because we are using a raw socket, we must specify the protocol we are interested in. The call to `getprotobyname` returns a structure containing the protocol number of

ICMP. Notice that we specify SOCK_RAW instead of SOCK_STREAM or SOCK_DGRAM as we have previously.

### Event Loop

*21-28*   We read each IP datagram using recvfrom just as we would a UDP datagram. We call print_dg to print the ICMP messages as they're received.

## Printing the ICMP Messages

Next we consider formatting and printing the ICMP messages. This is done by the print_dg function shown in Figure 4.25. The buffer passed to print_dg has the structure shown in Figure 4.24.

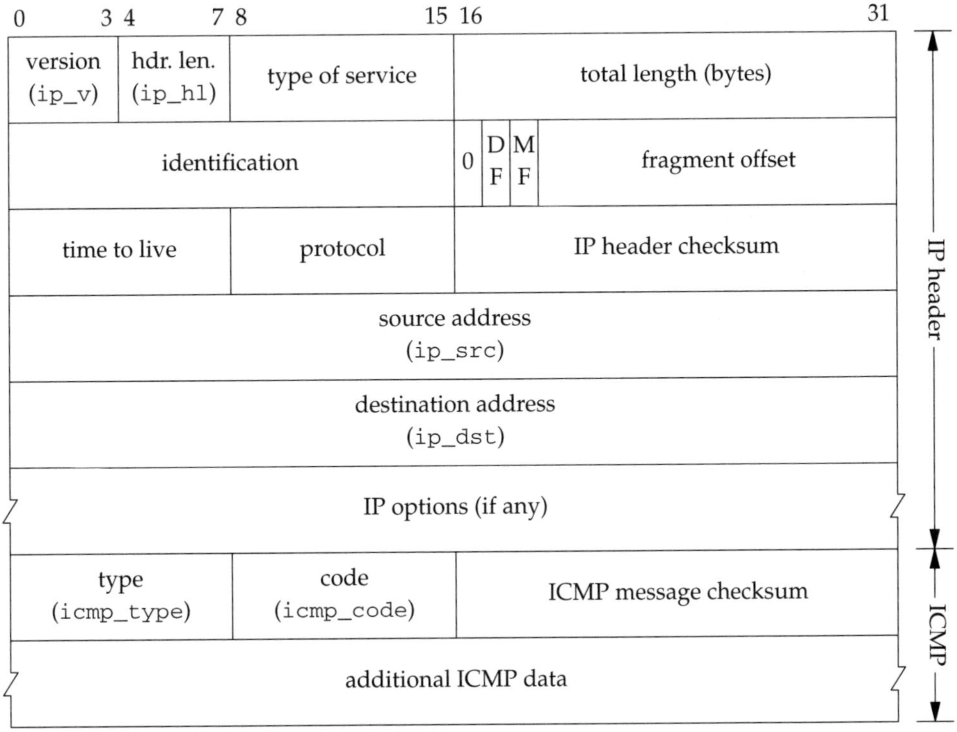

DF = Don't Fragment flag
MF = More Fragments flag

**Figure 4.24** The ICMP message passed to print_dg

As shown in Figure 4.24, the buffer contains an IP header followed by the ICMP message itself. The names of the fields referenced by the code are typeset in Courier.

*icmp.c*

```
 1 static void print_dg( char *dg, int len )
 2 {
 3     struct ip *ip;
 4     struct icmp *icmp;
 5     struct hostent *hp;
 6     char *hname;
 7     int hl;
 8     static char *redirect_code[] =
 9     {
10         "network", "host",
11         "type-of-service and network", "type-of-service and host"
12     };
13     static char *timexceed_code[] =
14     {
15         "transit", "reassembly"
16     };
17     static char *param_code[] =
18     {
19         "IP header bad", "Required option missing"
20     };
21
22     ip = ( struct ip * )dg;
23     if ( ip->ip_v != 4 )
24     {
25         error( 0, 0, "IP datagram not version 4\n" );
26         return;
27     }
28     hl = ip->ip_hl << 2;        /* IP header length in bytes */
29     if ( len < hl + ICMP_MINLEN )
30     {
31         error( 0, 0, "short datagram (%d bytes) from %s\n",
32             len, inet_ntoa( ip->ip_src ) );
33         return;
34     }
35     hp = gethostbyaddr( ( char * )&ip->ip_src, 4, AF_INET );
36     if ( hp == NULL )
37         hname = "";
38     else
39         hname = hp->h_name;
40     icmp = ( struct icmp * )( dg + hl );  /* ICMP packet */
41     printf( "ICMP %s (%d) from %s (%s)\n",
42         get_type( icmp->icmp_type ),
43         icmp->icmp_type, hname, inet_ntoa( ip->ip_src ) );
44     if ( icmp->icmp_type == ICMP_UNREACH )
45         print_unreachable( icmp );
46     else if ( icmp->icmp_type == ICMP_REDIRECT )
47         printf( "\tRedirect for %s\n", icmp->icmp_code <= 3 ?
48             redirect_code[ icmp->icmp_code ] : "Illegal code" );
49     else if ( icmp->icmp_type == ICMP_TIMXCEED )
50         printf( "\tTTL == 0 during %s\n", icmp->icmp_code <= 1 ?
            timexceed_code[ icmp->icmp_code ] : "Illegal code" );
```

```
51      else if ( icmp->icmp_type == ICMP_PARAMPROB )
52          printf( "\t%s\n", icmp->icmp_code <= 1 ?
53              param_code[ icmp->icmp_code ] : "Illegal code" );
54 }
```
*———————————————————————————— icmp.c*

**Figure 4.25** The `print_dg` function

### Get Pointer to IP Header and Check for Valid Packet

*21*      We first set `ip`, a `struct ip` pointer, to the datagram that we just read.

*22–26*      The `ip_v` field is the version of this IP datagram. If this is not an IPv4 datagram, we output an error message and return.

*27–33*      The `ip_hl` field contains the length of the header in 32-bit words. We multiply that by four to get the length in bytes and save the result in `hl`. Next we check the datagram to ensure that the ICMP message is at least as big as the minimum legal size.

### Get the Sender's Host Name

*34–38*      We use the source address of the ICMP message to look up the host name of its sender. If `gethostbyaddr` returns `NULL`, we set `hname` to the empty string; otherwise, we set it to the host's name.

### Step Over the IP Header and Print Sender and Type

*39–42*      We set our `struct icmp` pointer, `icmp`, to the first byte after the IP header. We use this pointer to obtain the ICMP message type (`icmp_type`) and print the type and sender's address and host name. We call `get_type` to get an ASCII representation of the ICMP type. The `get_type` function is shown in Figure 4.26.

### Print Type-Specific Information

*43–44*      If this is one of the ICMP unreachable messages, we call `print_unreachable`, shown later in Figure 4.29, to print more information.

*45–47*      If this is a redirect message, we obtain the type of redirect from the `icmp_code` field and print it.

*48–50*      If this is a time-exceeded message, we examine the `imcp_code` field to determine whether the message timed out in transit or reassembly, and print the result.

*51–53*      If this ICMP message reports a parameter problem, we obtain the type of problem from the `icmp_code` field and print it.

The `get_type` function is straightforward. We merely check that the type code is legal and return a pointer to the appropriate string (Figure 4.26).

*———————————————————————————— icmp.c*
```
1 static char *get_type( unsigned icmptype )
2 {
3      static char *type[] =
4      {
5          "Echo Reply",                          /* 0 */
6          "ICMP Type 1",                         /* 1 */
7          "ICMP Type 2",                         /* 2 */
```

```
 8              "Destination Unreachable",          /* 3 */
 9              "Source Quench",                    /* 4 */
10              "Redirect",                         /* 5 */
11              "ICMP Type 6",                      /* 6 */
12              "ICMP Type 7",                      /* 7 */
13              "Echo Request",                     /* 8 */
14              "Router Advertisement",             /* 9 */
15              "Router Solicitation",              /* 10 */
16              "Time Exceeded",                    /* 11 */
17              "Parameter Problem",                /* 12 */
18              "Timestamp Request",                /* 13 */
19              "Timestamp Reply",                  /* 14 */
20              "Information Request",              /* 15 */
21              "Information Reply",                /* 16 */
22              "Address Mask Request",             /* 17 */
23              "Address Mask Reply"                /* 18 */
24      };

25      if ( icmptype < ( sizeof( type ) / sizeof( type[ 0 ] ) ) )
26          return type[ icmptype ];
27      return "UNKNOWN";
28 }
```
                                                                            —— icmp.c

**Figure 4.26** The get_type function

The last function is print_unreachable. ICMP unreachable messages return the IP header and first 8 bytes of the IP datagram of the message that caused the unreachable error to be generated. This allows us to determine the addresses and port numbers of the sender and intended recipient of the undeliverable message.

The structure of the IP datagram read from the raw socket for an ICMP unreachable message is shown in Figure 4.27. The portion that print_dg has already processed is shaded, and is not passed into print_unreachable. The print_unreachable input variable icmp and local variables ip and udp are also shown.

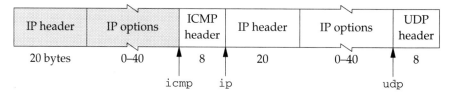

**Figure 4.27** ICMP unreachable message

Our print_unreachable function extracts information from the header and the first 8 bytes of the included IP datagram. Although we label those first 8 bytes as a UDP header, they could just as well be the first first 8 bytes of a TCP header: The port numbers are in the same place in both headers. The format of the UDP header is shown in Figure 4.28.

| 0 | 15 | 16 | 31 |
|---|---|---|---|
| source port number<br>(uh_sport) | | destination port number<br>(uh_dport) | |
| UDP datagram length | | checksum | |

**Figure 4.28**  UDP header

The code is shown in Figure 4.29.

*—————————————————————————————————————— icmp.c*
```
 1 static void print_unreachable( struct icmp *icmp )
 2 {
 3     struct ip *ip;
 4     struct udphdr *udp;
 5     char laddr[ 15 + 1 ];
 6     static char *unreach[] =
 7     {
 8         "Network unreachable",              /* 0 */
 9         "Host unreachable",                 /* 1 */
10         "Protocol unreachable",             /* 2 */
11         "Port unreachable",                 /* 3 */
12         "Fragmentation needed, DF bit set", /* 4 */
13         "Source route failed",              /* 5 */
14         "Destination network unknown",      /* 6 */
15         "Destination host unknown",         /* 7 */
16         "Source host isolated",             /* 8 */
17         "Dest. network admin. prohibited",  /* 9 */
18         "Dest. host admin. prohibited",     /* 10 */
19         "Network unreachable for TOS",      /* 11 */
20         "Host unreachable for TOS",         /* 12 */
21         "Communication admin. prohibited",  /* 13 */
22         "Host precedence violation",        /* 14 */
23         "Precedence cutoff in effect"       /* 15 */
24     };
25     ip = ( struct ip * )( ( char * )icmp + 8 );
26     udp = ( struct udphdr * )( ( char * )ip + ( ip->ip_hl << 2 ) );
27     strcpy( laddr, inet_ntoa( ip->ip_src ) );
28     printf( "\t%s\n\tSrc: %s.%d, Dest: %s.%d\n",
29         icmp->icmp_code < ( sizeof( unreach ) /
30             sizeof( unreach[ 0 ] ) )?
31             unreach[ icmp->icmp_code ] : "Illegal code",
32         laddr, ntohs( udp->uh_sport ),
33         inet_ntoa( ip->ip_dst ), ntohs( udp->uh_dport ) );
34 }
```
*—————————————————————————————————————— icmp.c*

**Figure 4.29**  The `print_unreachable` function

### Set Up Pointers and Get Source Address

*25-26*    We start by setting the `ip` and `udp` pointers to the IP header and the first 8 bytes of the IP datagram payload respectively.

*27*    We copy the source address out of the IP header and into the local variable `laddr`.

### Print Addresses, Ports, and Type

*28-33*    We print the source and destination addresses and ports as well the specific type of unreachable message.

As an example of `icmp`'s use, here are the last few ICMP messages generated as a result of the `traceroute` (Tip 35):

```
traceroute -q 1 netcom4.netcom.com
```

The `-q 1` option tells `traceroute` to send each probe only once instead of the default three times:

```
ICMP Time Exceeded (11) from h1-0.mig-fl-gw1.icg.net (165.236.144.110)
    TTL == 0 during transit
ICMP Time Exceeded (11) from s10-0-0.dfw-tx-gw1.icg.net (165.236.32.74)
    TTL == 0 during transit
ICMP Time Exceeded (11) from dfw-tx-gw2.icg.net (163.179.1.133)
    TTL == 0 during transit
ICMP Destination Unreachable (3) from netcom4.netcom.com (199.183.9.104)
    Port unreachable
    Src: 205.184.142.71.45935, Dest: 199.183.9.104.33441
```

We normally wouldn't bother running `icmp` to monitor `traceroute`, of course, but it can be very useful when troubleshooting connectivity problems.

## Summary

In this tip we developed a tool to capture and print ICMP messages. Such a tool can be helpful in diagnosing network and router problems.

While developing `icmp`, we explored the use of raw sockets and examined the header formats for IP and UDP datagrams, and for ICMP messages.

## Tip 41: Read Stevens

One of the frequently asked questions in the network programming-related news groups is: "What book should I read to learn about TCP/IP?" The overwhelming majority of answers mention a book by Rich Stevens.

We have referenced Stevens' books often in this text, but now we want to take a closer look at them. For the network programmer, Stevens wrote two sets of books: the *TCP/IP Illustrated* series in three volumes, and the *UNIX Network Programming* series in two volumes. The focus and purpose of the two series is different, so we discuss them separately.

## The *TCP/IP Illustrated* Series

As suggested by the title, *TCP/IP Illustrated* is a direct demonstration of how the common TCP/IP protocols and programs work. As we have already mentioned in Tip 13, the primary vehicle used for this is `tcpdump`. By writing and running small test programs and then watching the resulting network traffic with `tcpdump`, Stevens leads us to a deepening understanding and appreciation of how the protocols work in practice.

By using a variety of systems, Stevens shows how differing implementations of the same protocol often lead to subtly different behavior. More importantly, we also learn how to devise, run, and interpret our own experiments, so we can answer questions that come up in our own work.

Because each volume of the series addresses the TCP/IP protocol suite in a different way, it is useful to give a brief description of each.

### Volume 1: The Protocols

This volume discusses the classical TCP/IP protocols and how they relate to each other. The book starts with the link layer protocols such as Ethernet, SLIP, and PPP. From there the discussion moves up to ARP and the Reverse Address Resolution Protocol (RARP), and how they act as glue between the link layer and the IP layer.

Several chapters are devoted to the IP protocol and its relationship to ICMP and routing. Applications such as `ping` and `traceroute` that operate at the IP level are also discussed.

Next, UDP and related issues such as broadcasting and IGMP are discussed. Protocols that are based primarily on UDP, such as DNS, the Trivial File Transfer Protocol (TFTP), and the Bootstrap Protocol (BOOTP) are also covered.

Eight chapters are devoted to TCP and its operations. This is followed by several more chapters that discuss the common TCP applications such as telnet, rlogin, FTP, SMTP (email), and NFS.

Anyone finishing this volume will have an excellent knowledge of the classical TCP/IP protocols and the applications based on them.

### Volume 2: The Implementation

The second volume, written with Gary Wright, is an almost line-by-line exegesis of the 4.4BSD networking code. Because the BSD networking code is widely considered the reference implementation, this volume is indispensable to anyone who wants to see and understand how to implement the basic TCP/IP protocols.

The book covers the implementation of several link layer protocols (Ethernet, SLIP, and the loopback interface), the IP protocol, routing, ICMP, IGMP and multicasting, the socket layer, UDP, TCP, and a few other related areas. Because the actual code is presented in the book, the reader gains an appreciation for the tradeoffs and problems involved in implementing a significant networking system.

### Volume 3: TCP for Transactions, HTTP, NNTP, and the UNIX Domain Protocols

The third volume is a continuation of both volumes 1 and 2. It begins with a description of T/TCP and how it operates. This description is very much in the style of volume 1. Next the implementation of T/TCP is given, this time in the style of volume 2.

In the second part, two very popular application protocols, the Hypertext Transfer Protocol (HTTP) and the Network News Transfer Protocol (NNTP) are covered. These protocols are the basis of the World Wide Web and the Usenet New Groups respectively.

Finally, Stevens covers UNIX domain sockets and their implementation. This is really a continuation of volume 2, but was omitted from that volume due to size constraints.

## The *UNIX Network Programming* Series

*UNIX Network Programming* approaches TCP/IP from the point of view of an application programmer. The focus in this series is not TCP/IP itself, but rather how to use it to build network applications.

### Volume 1: Networking APIs: Sockets and XTI

Every practicing network programmer should have this book. The volume covers TCP/IP programming in great detail using both the sockets and XTI APIs. Besides the normal topics in client-server programming, Stevens covers multicasting, routing sockets, nonblocking I/O, IPv6 and its interoperability with IPv4 applications, raw sockets, programming at the link level, and UNIX domain sockets.

The book includes an especially useful chapter that compares client-server design models. There are also useful appendices covering virtual networks and debugging techniques.

### Volume 2: Interprocess Communications

This volume covers IPC in exhaustive detail. In addition to the traditional UNIX pipes and FIFOs, and the SysV message queues, semaphores, and shared memory, the book discusses the more modern POSIX IPC methods.

There is an excellent introduction to POSIX threads and their use with synchronization objects such as mutexes, condition variables, and read-write locks. For those who like to know how things work, Stevens gives implementations for several of the synchronization primitives and for POSIX message queues.

The book concludes with chapters on RPC and Solaris Doors.

A third volume covering applications was planned, but sadly Stevens passed away before he could complete it. Some of the material planned for this volume is available in the first edition of *UNIX Network Programming* [Stevens 1990].

## Tip 42: Read Code

Beginning network programmers often ask their experienced colleagues how they learned their craft and the seemingly staggering amount of material that every journey-man network programmer knows. We come to knowledge and understanding in many ways, of course, but one of the most valuable, and underused, is reading code from the masters.

Fortunately for us, the burgeoning open-source movement makes this easier than ever. Reading and studying some of the high-quality code available provides two distinct benefits:

1. Most obviously, we can see how the masters approached and solved particular problems. We can take their techniques and apply them to our own problems, modifying and adapting them in the process. As we do this, the techniques evolve and become our own. Someday, someone else will read *our* code and wonder how we ever came to devise such a clever technique.

2. Not as obvious, but in some ways more important, is that we learn there is no magic. Beginning programmers sometimes believe that operating system code, or the code that implements networking protocols is deep and unknowable—that it is a magic spell cast by wizards and that mere mortals must not tamper with it. By reading this code, we come to understand that it's just good (and mostly standard) engineering, and that we can also do it.

In short, by reading code we learn that the deep and mysterious are largely just a matter of standard techniques, and we learn what those techniques are and how to apply them ourselves. Reading code isn't easy. It requires concentration and focus, but the rewards are well worth the effort.

There are several sources of good code to read, but it's easier if we have some help in the form of a narrative, so let's begin with some books. Lions' *A Commentary on the UNIX Operating System* [Lions 1977], has long been an underground favorite. Recently, due to the efforts of several people, including Dennis Ritchie, and the generosity of SCO, current owner of the UNIX code base, this book has become available to the public.

> Originally, the book was available only to holders of a UNIX source license, but Xeroxed copies (of Xeroxed copies) made their way through the UNIX underground and were a prized possession of many early UNIX programmers.

The book presents the code for a very early release (version 6) of the UNIX operating system, which had no networking component other than support for time shared TTY terminals. Nonetheless, it is well worth our while to study this code, even if we have no interest in UNIX, as a wonderful example of software engineering by masters of their craft.

Another excellent book on operating systems that includes source code is *Operating Systems: Design and Implementation* [Tanenbaum and Woodhull 1997]. This book describes the MINIX operating system. Although the networking code is not described in the book, it is available on the accompanying CDROM.

For those more interested in networking there is *TCP/IP Illustrated, Volume 2* [Wright and Stevens 1995]. We have already discussed this book in Tip 41, and noted that anyone interested in the implementation of TCP/IP and networking techniques in general should study it closely.

Because *TCP/IP Illustrated, Volume 2* discusses the BSD networking code on which several current open-source systems (FreeBSD, OpenBSD, NetBSD) are based, it provides an excellent laboratory manual for those who want to experiment with the code. The original 4.4BSD Lite code is available from the Walnut Creek CDROM FTP server (`<ftp://ftp.cdrom.com/pub/4.4BSD-Lite>`).

*Internetworking with TCP/IP Volume II* [Comer and Stevens 1999] presents another TCP/IP stack. As with *TCP/IP Illustrated, Volume 2*, this book provides a complete explanation of the working of the code. The code itself is available for download and use.

There are many other sources of good code to read, although most don't come with handy books to ease the way. A good place to start is one of the open-source UNIX/Linux projects. All of these projects make the source code available on CDROM and by FTP.

The Free Software Foundation's GNU project has source code for reimplementations of most of the standard UNIX utilities, and is another excellent source of code worthy of study.

Information about these projects can be found at

- FreeBSD's home page

      `<http://www.freebsd.org>`

- GNU project

      `<http://www.gnu.org>`

- Linux Kernel Archives

      `<http://www.kernel.org>`

- NetBSD's home page

      `<http://www.netbsd.org>`

- OpenBSD's home page

      `<http://www.openbsd.org>`

All of these sources have an abundance of network-related code and are worth studying even for those whose interests don't include UNIX.

## Summary

One of the best, and most enjoyable, ways of learning about network programming (or any other type of programming for that matter) is to read code written by those who have already mastered the material. Until recently, it was difficult to get access to the source code for operating systems and their networking subsystems. With the advent of the open source movement, this is no longer the case. Code for several TCP/IP stacks and the associated utilities (telnet, FTP, `inetd`, and so forth) are available from the BSD and Linux operating system projects. We have discussed some of these sources, and many more can be found on the Web.

The four books that we mentioned are particularly worthy of mention because they provide commentary along with the code.

# Tip 43: Visit the RFC Editor's Page

We have mentioned previously that "specifications" for the TCP/IP suite and related Internet architectural matters are contained in a series of documents called *Requests for Comments* (RFCs). Actually, the RFCs, which date back to 1969, are much more than a set of protocol specifications. They are probably best viewed as a set of working papers that discuss many different aspects of computer communications and networking. Not all of the RFCs deal with technical matters; some are merely humorous observations, parodies, or poems, and still others opinions. As of late 1999 there are a little more than 2,700 RFC numbers assigned, although some of these are for RFCs that were never issued.

Although not every RFC specifies an Internet standard, every "Internet Standard" is published as an RFC. Members of this subseries of the RFCs are given an additional "label" of the form "STDxxxx." The current list of standards and the status of RFCs that are on their way to becoming Internet Standards are listed in STD0001.

We should not conclude, however, that RFCs not mentioned in STD0001 are without technical merit. Some of these RFCs describe ideas or protocols that are still in development or undergoing research. Others are merely informational, or report the deliberations of one of the many working groups chartered by the IETF.

### Getting RFCs

There are several ways to get a copy of an RFC, but the easiest is to visit the RFC editor's page at `<http://www.rfc-editor.org>`. This Web page provides a forms-based download facility that makes retrieval easy. There is also a key word search to help in locating the appropriate RFC if its number is not known. Also available from the same form are the STDs, FYIs (For Your Information), and BCPs (Best Current Practices) subseries of RFCs.

The RFCs are also available by FTP from `ftp.isi.edu` in directory `in-notes/`, as well as from several other FTP archive sites.

Those without Web or FTP access can request copies of an RFC by email. Complete instructions for ordering RFCs by email as well as a list of FTP sites can be obtained by sending email to `RFC-INFO@ISI.EDU` with a message body of

```
help: ways_to_get_rfcs
```

For any of these methods, the first thing to retrieve is the current index of RFCs (`rfc-index.txt`). Once published, RFCs are never changed, so the information in an RFC can be modified only by issuing a superseding RFC. For each RFC, the index indicates whether there is a superseding RFC and if so, what it is. The index also indicates any RFCs that update but do not replace the RFC in an entry.

Finally, the RFCs are available on CDROM from various distributors. Walnut Creek CDROM (`<http://www.cdrom.com>`) and InfoMagic (`<http://www.info-magic.com>`) both offer CDROMs that contain the RFCs as well as other documents concerning the Internet. Such CDROMs cannot claim to have a complete set of RFCs for very long of course, but because the RFCs themselves do not change, they become out of date only in the sense that they do not contain the latest RFCs.

## Tip 44: Frequent the News Groups

One of the most valuable places on the Internet to get advice and information about network programming is in the Usenet news groups. There are news groups that cover virtually every aspect of networking from cabling (`comp.dcom.cabling`) to the Network Time Protocol (`comp.protocols.time.ntp`).

An excellent news group that covers TCP/IP issues and programming is `comp.protocols.tcp-ip`. Just a few minutes a day spent reading the postings to this group can yield all sorts of useful information, tips, and techniques. Topics range from how to connect a Windows machine to the Internet to the finest technical points about the TCP/IP protocols, their implementation, and their behavior.

When first starting, the sheer number of networking news groups (at least 70) can be intimidating. It's probably best to start with `comp.protocols.tcp-ip` and perhaps one of the operating system-specific groups such as `comp.os.linux.network-ing` or `comp.os.ms-windows.programmer.tools.winsock`. The postings we see in these groups will suggest other more specialized news groups that may also interest us or prove useful.

Paradoxically, one of the best ways to learn from the news groups is to answer questions. By taking our knowledge of a specific area and organizing it well enough to explain to others, we come to a deeper understanding of the material ourselves. The minimal effort required to compose a 50- or 100-word reply to a posting can pay off handsomely in our own knowledge.

An excellent introduction to the Usenet news groups is available at the Usenet Info Center (`<http://metalab.unc.edu/usenet-i>`). This site contains articles on the history, use, and practices of Usenet as well as summaries of most of the news groups, including the average number of messages per day, the average number of readers, its moderator (if any), where it's archived (if anywhere), and pointers to FAQs associated with each group.

The Usenet Info Center also has a search facility to help find news groups covering particular topics. This is another valuable resource we can use to locate news groups that discuss areas in which we are interested.

As suggested earlier, many news groups have an FAQ, and it's a good idea to read it before posting a question. If we ask a question that's covered in the FAQ, chances are we'll be referred to it anyway, and we may also get a scolding for being too lazy to do our homework before posting.

## Other News Group-Related Resources

Before leaving the subject of news groups, we should mention two other valuable resources connected with them. The first is Deja News (`<http://www.deja.com>`).

> In May 1999 Deja News changed its name from Deja News to Deja.com. This was, they say, both because they were already familiarly referred to as "Deja" and because they expanded their focus and range of services. In this tip, we mention only the original Usenet news group archiving and retrieval services.

The site archives messages from approximately 45,000 discussion forums including the Usenet news groups and their own Deja Community Discussions groups. Deja.com reports that approximately two thirds of these are from the Usenet news groups. As of late 1999, Deja.com had archived messages back to March 1995.

Deja's Power Search facility allows us to search a particular news group, group of news groups, or even all news groups by keyword, subject, author, or date range. This provides a powerful research tool when we're trying to solve a particular problem or get an answer to a particular question.

The second valuable resource is Uri Raz's *TCP/IP Resources List*, which is posted to `comp.protocols.tcp-ip` and some of the more specific news groups every two weeks. This list is an excellent starting point when trying to locate either specific information or a broader, more general overview of TCP/IP and its programming APIs.

Topics that the list provides pointers for include books on TCP/IP and networking, online resources such as the IETF pages and where to find FAQs, online books and magazines, TCP/IP tutorials, information sources about IPv6, the home pages for many of the popular networking books, publishers' home pages, GNU and open-source OS home pages, search engines and their use, and news groups related to networking.

The latest version of the list is available from the Web at

```
<http://www.private.org.il/tcpip_rl.html>
<http://www.best.com/~mphunter/tcpip_resources.html>
```

or via FTP from

```
<ftp://rtfm.mit.edu/pub/usenet-by-group/news.answers/internet/tcp-ip/
    resource-list>
<ftp://rtfm.mit.edu/pub/usenet-by-hierarchy/comp/protocols/tcp-ip/
    TCP_IP_Resources_List>
```

One of the things that makes the TCP/IP Resources List exceptionally valuable is that its author keeps it up to date. This is important because Web links are especially volatile and can quickly become stale.

# Appendix A

# Miscellaneous UNIX Code

## The `etcp.h` Header

Almost all of our example programs start by including the `etcp.h` header file
(Figure A.1). This file contains the other includes that we generally need, including
`skel.h` (Figure 2.14) as well as a few other defines, typedefs, and prototypes.

——————————————————————————————————————————————— *etcp.h*

```
 1 #ifndef __ETCP_H__
 2 #define __ETCP_H__

 3 /* Include standard headers */

 4 #include <errno.h>
 5 #include <stdlib.h>
 6 #include <unistd.h>
 7 #include <stdio.h>
 8 #include <stdarg.h>
 9 #include <string.h>
10 #include <netdb.h>
11 #include <signal.h>
12 #include <fcntl.h>
13 #include <sys/socket.h>
14 #include <sys/wait.h>
15 #include <sys/time.h>
16 #include <sys/resource.h>
17 #include <sys/stat.h>
18 #include <netinet/in.h>
19 #include <arpa/inet.h>
20 #include "skel.h"
```

```
21 #define TRUE           1
22 #define FALSE          0
23 #define NLISTEN        5        /* max waiting connections */
24 #define NSMB           5        /* number shared memory bufs */
25 #define SMBUFSZ        256      /* size of shared memory buf */

26 extern char *program_name;      /* for error */

27 #ifdef __SVR4
28 #define bzero(b,n)  memset( ( b ), 0, ( n ) )
29 #endif

30 typedef void ( *tofunc_t )( void * );

31 void error( int, int, char*, ... );
32 int readn( int, char *, size_t );
33 int readvrec( int, char *, size_t );
34 int readcrlf( int, char *, size_t );
35 int readline( int, char *, size_t );
36 int tcp_server( char *, char * );
37 int tcp_client( char *, char * );
38 int udp_server( char *, char * );
39 int udp_client( char *, char *, struct sockaddr_in * );
40 int tselect( int, fd_set *, fd_set *, fd_set *);
41 unsigned int timeout( tofunc_t, void *, int );
42 void untimeout( unsigned int );
43 void init_smb( int );
44 void *smballoc( void );
45 void smbfree( void * );
46 void smbsend( SOCKET, void * );
47 void *smbrecv( SOCKET );
48 #endif  /* __ETCP_H__ */
```
———————————————————————————————————————————————————— *etcp.h*

**Figure A.1**  The etcp.h header

## The daemon Function

The daemon function that we use in tcpmux is a standard BSD library routine. For SVR4 systems, we supply the version presented in Figure A.2.

———————————————————————————————————————————————————— *library/daemon.c*
```
 1 int daemon( int nocd, int noclose )
 2 {
 3     struct rlimit rlim;
 4     pid_t pid;
 5     int i;

 6     umask( 0 );      /* clear file creation mask */

 7     /* Get max files that can be open */

 8     if ( getrlimit( RLIMIT_NOFILE, &rlim ) < 0 )
 9         error( 1, errno, "getrlimit failed" );
```

```
10       /* Become session leader, losing controlling terminal */
11       pid = fork();
12       if ( pid < 0 )
13           return -1;
14       if ( pid != 0 )
15           exit( 0 );
16       setsid();

17       /* ... and make sure we don't aquire another */
18       signal( SIGHUP, SIG_IGN );
19       pid = fork();
20       if ( pid < 0 )
21           return -1;
22       if ( pid != 0 )
23           exit( 0 );

24       /* Change to root directory unless asked not to */
25       if ( !nocd )
26           chdir( "/" );

27       /*
28        * Unless asked not to, close all files.
29        * Then dup stdin, stdout, and stderr
30        * onto /dev/null.
31        */
32       if ( !noclose )
33       {
34 #if 0   /* change to 1 to close all files */
35           if ( rlim.rlim_max == RLIM_INFINITY )
36               rlim.rlim_max = 1024;
37           for ( i = 0; i < rlim.rlim_max; i++ )
38               close( i );
39 #endif
40           i = open( "/dev/null", O_RDWR );
41           if ( i < 0 )
42               return -1;
43           dup2( i, 0 );
44           dup2( i, 1 );
45           dup2( i, 2 );
46           if ( i > 2 )
47               close( i );
48       }
49       return 0;
50 }
```

*library/daemon.c*

**Figure A.2** The `daemon` function

## The `signal` Function

As we discussed in the text, some versions of UNIX implement the `signal` function using unreliable signal semantics. On these systems we should use the `sigaction` function to get the reliable signal semantics. As an aid to portability, we reimplement signal using sigaction (Figure A.3).

———————————————————————————————————————————— *library/signal.c*

```
 1 typedef void sighndlr_t( int );
 2 sighndlr_t *signal( int sig, sighndlr_t *hndlr )
 3 {
 4     struct sigaction act;
 5     struct sigaction xact;

 6     act.sa_handler = hndlr;
 7     act.sa_flags = 0;
 8     sigemptyset( &act.sa_mask );
 9     if ( sigaction( sig, &act, &xact ) < 0 )
10         return SIG_ERR;
11     return xact.sa_handler;
12 }
```

———————————————————————————————————————————— *library/signal.c*

**Figure A.3** The signal function

# *Appendix B*

# *Miscellaneous Windows Code*

## The `skel.h` Header

When compiling the example programs under Windows, we can use the same `etcp.h` as we do for UNIX (see Figure A.1). All of the system-dependent information is in the `skel.h` header file. The Windows version is shown in Figure B.1

*——— skel.h*

```
 1 #ifndef __SKEL_H__
 2 #define __SKEL_H__

 3 /* Winsock version */

 4 #include <windows.h>
 5 #include <winsock2.h>

 6 struct timezone
 7 {
 8     long tz_minuteswest;
 9     long tz_dsttime;
10 };
11 typedef unsigned int u_int32_t;

12 #define EMSGSIZE       WSAEMSGSIZE
13 #define INIT()         init( argv );
14 #define EXIT(s)        do { WSACleanup(); exit( ( s ) ); } \
15                        while ( 0 )
16 #define CLOSE(s)       if ( closesocket( s ) ) \
17                            error( 1, errno, "close failed" )
18 #define errno          ( GetLastError() )
19 #define set_errno(e)   SetLastError( ( e ) )
```

```
20 #define isvalidsock(s)   ( ( s ) != SOCKET_ERROR )
21 #define bzero(b,n)        memset( ( b ), 0, ( n ) )
22 #define sleep(t)          Sleep( ( t ) * 1000 )
23 #define WINDOWS

24 #endif   /* __SKEL_H__ */
```
———————————————————————————————————————————————————— *skel.h*

**Figure B.1**  The Windows version of `skel.h`

## Windows Compatibility Routines

Figure B.2 shows various routines that we used in our example code but that are not provided by Windows.

———————————————————————————————————————— *library/wincompat.c*
```
 1 #include <sys/timeb.h>
 2 #include "etcp.h"
 3 #include <winsock2.h>

 4 #define MINBSDSOCKERR        ( WSAEWOULDBLOCK )
 5 #define MAXBSDSOCKERR        ( MINBSDSOCKERR + \
 6                              ( sizeof( bsdsocketerrs ) / \
 7                              sizeof( bsdsocketerrs[ 0 ] ) ) ) )

 8 extern int sys_nerr;
 9 extern char *sys_errlist[];
10 extern char *program_name;
11 static char *bsdsocketerrs[] =
12 {
13     "Resource temporarily unavailable",
14     "Operation now in progress",
15     "Operation already in progress",
16     "Socket operation on non-socket",
17     "Destination address required",
18     "Message too long",
19     "Protocol wrong type for socket",
20     "Bad protocol option",
21     "Protocol not supported",
22     "Socket type not supported",
23     "Operation not supported",
24     "Protocol family not supported",
25     "Address family not supported by protocol family",
26     "Address already in use",
27     "Can't assign requested address",
28     "Network is down",
29     "Network is unreachable",
30     "Network dropped connection on reset",
31     "Software caused connection abort",
```

```
32      "Connection reset by peer",
33      "No buffer space available",
34      "Socket is already connected",
35      "Socket is not connected",
36      "Cannot send after socket shutdown",
37      "Too many references: can't splice",
38      "Connection timed out",
39      "Connection refused",
40      "Too many levels of symbolic links",
41      "File name too long",
42      "Host is down",
43      "No route to host"
44 };

45 void init( char **argv )
46 {
47      WSADATA wsadata;

48      ( program_name = strrchr( argv[ 0 ], '\\' ) ) ?
49          program_name++ : ( program_name = argv[ 0 ] );
50      WSAStartup( MAKEWORD( 2, 2 ), &wsadata );
51 }

52 /* inet_aton - version of inet_aton for SVr4 and Windows */
53 int inet_aton( char *cp, struct in_addr *pin )
54 {
55      int rc;

56      rc = inet_addr( cp );
57      if ( rc == -1 && strcmp( cp, "255.255.255.255" ) )
58          return 0;
59      pin->s_addr = rc;
60      return 1;
61 }

62 /* gettimeofday - for tselect */
63 int gettimeofday( struct timeval *tvp, struct timezone *tzp )
64 {
65      struct _timeb tb;

66      _ftime( &tb );
67      if ( tvp )
68      {
69          tvp->tv_sec = tb.time;
70          tvp->tv_usec = tb.millitm * 1000;
71      }
72      if ( tzp )
73      {
74          tzp->tz_minuteswest = tb.timezone;
75          tzp->tz_dsttime = tb.dstflag;
76      }
77 }
```

```
78 /* strerror - version to include Winsock errors */
79 char *strerror( int err )
80 {
81     if ( err >= 0 && err < sys_nerr )
82         return sys_errlist[ err ];
83     else if ( err >= MINBSDSOCKERR && err < MAXBSDSOCKERR )
84         return bsdsocketerrs[ err - MINBSDSOCKERR ];
85     else if ( err == WSASYSNOTREADY )
86         return "Network subsystem is unusable";
87     else if ( err == WSAVERNOTSUPPORTED )
88         return "This version of Winsock not supported";
89     else if ( err == WSANOTINITIALISED )
90         return "Winsock not initialized";
91     else
92         return "Unknown error";
93 }
```
*———— library/wincompat.c*

**Figure B.2**  The Windows compatibility routines

# Bibliography

Albitz, P. and Liu, C. 1998. *DNS and BIND, 3rd Edition.* O'Reilly & Associates, Sebastopol, Calif.

Baker, F., ed. 1995. "Requirements for IP Version 4 Routers," RFC 1812 (June).

Banga, G. and Mogul, J. C. 1998. "Scalable Kernel Performance for Internet Servers Under Realistic Loads," *Proceedings of the 1998 USENIX Annual Technical Conference*, New Orleans, LA.

> http://www.cs.rice.edu/~gaurav/my_papers/usenix98.ps

Bennett, J. C. R., Partridge, C., and Shectman, N. 1999. "Packet Reordering Is Not Pathological Network Behavior," *IEEE/ACM Transactions on Networking*, vol. 7, no. 6, pp. 789–798 (Dec.).

Braden, R. T. 1985. "Towards a Transport Service for Transaction Processing Applications," RFC 955 (Sept.).

Braden, R. T. 1992a. "Extending TCP for Transactions—Concepts," RFC 1379 (Nov.).

Braden, R. T. 1992b. "TIME-WAIT Assassination Hazards in TCP," RFC 1337 (May).

Braden, R. T. 1994. "T/TCP—TCP Extensions for Transactions, Functional Specification," RFC 1644 (July).

Braden, R. T., ed. 1989. "Requirements for Internet Hosts—Communication Layers," RFC 1122 (Oct.).

Brown, C. 1994. *UNIX Distributed Programming.* Prentice Hall, Englewood Cliffs, N.J.

Castro, E. 1998. *Perl and CGI for the World Wide Web: Visual QuickStart Guide.* Peachpit Press, Berkeley, Calif.

Clark, D. D. 1982. "Window and Acknowledgement Strategy in TCP," RFC 813 (July).

Cohen, D. 1981. "On Holy Wars and a Plea for Peace," *IEEE Computer Magazine*, vol. 14, pp. 48–54 (Oct.).

Comer, D. E. 1995. *Internetworking with TCP/IP Volume I: Principles, Protocols, and Architecture, Third Edition.* Prentice Hall, Englewood Cliffs, N.J.

Comer, D. E. and Lin, J. C. 1995. "TCP Buffering and Performance Over an ATM Network," *Journal of Internetworking: Research and Experience*, vol. 6, no. 1, pp. 1–13 (Mar.).

    `ftp://gwen.cs.purdue.edu/pub/lin/TCP.atm.ps.Z`

Comer, D. E. and Stevens, D. L. 1999. *Internetworking with TCP/IP Volume II: Design, Implementation, and Internals, Third Edition.* Prentice Hall, Englewood Cliffs, N.J.

Fuller, V., Li, T., Yu, J., and Varadhan, K. 1993. "Classless Inter-Domain Routing (CIDR): An Address Assignment," RFC 1519 (Sept.).

Gallatin, A., Chase, J., and Yocum, K. 1999. "Trapeze/IP: TCP/IP at Near-Gigabit Speeds," *1999 Usenix Technical Conference (Freenix track)*, Monterey, Calif.

    `http://www.cs.duke.edu/ari/publications/tcpgig.ps`

Haverlock, P. 2000. Private communication.

Hinden, R. M. 1993. "Applicability Statement for the Implementation of Classless Inter-Domain Routing (CIDR)," RFC 1517 (Sept.).

Huitema, C. 1995. *Routing in the Internet.* Prentice Hall, Englewood Cliffs, N.J.

International Standards Organization 1984. "OSI—Basic Reference Model," ISO 7498, International Standards Organization, Geneva.

Jacobson, V. 1988. "Congestion Avoidance and Control," *Proc. of SIGCOMM '88*, vol. 18, no. 4, pp. 314–329 (Aug.).

    `http://www-nrg.ee.lbl.gov/nrg.html`

Jacobson, V. 1999. "Re: Traceroute History: Why UDP?," Message-ID <79m7m4$reh$1 @dog.ee.lbl.gov>, Usenet, comp.protocols.tcp-ip (Feb.).

    `http://www.kohala.com/start/vanj99Feb08.txt`

Jacobson, V., Braden, R. T., and Borman, D. 1992. "TCP Extensions for High Performance," RFC 1323 (May).

Jain, B. N. and Agrawala, A. K. 1993. *Open Systems Interconnection: Its Architecture and Protocols, Revised Edition.* McGraw-Hill, N.Y.

Kacker, M. 1998. Private communication.

Kacker, M. 1999. Private communication.

Kantor, B. and Lapsley, P. 1986. "Network News Transfer Protocol," RFC 977 (Feb.).

Kernighan, B. W. and Pike, R. 1999. *The Practice of Programming.* Addison-Wesley, Reading, Mass.

Kernighan, B. W. and Ritchie, D. M. 1988. *The C Programming Language, Second Edition.* Prentice Hall, Englewood Cliffs, N.J.

Knuth, D. E. 1998. *The Art of Computer Programming, Volume 2, Seminumerical Algorithms, Third Edition.* Addison-Wesley, Reading, Mass.

Lehey, G. 1996. *The Complete FreeBSD.* Walnut Creek CDROM, Walnut Creek, Calif.

Lions, J. 1977. *Lions' Commentary on UNIX 6th Edition with Source Code.* Peer-to-Peer Communications, San Jose, Calif.

Lotter, M. K. 1988. "TCP Port Service Multiplexer (TCPMUX)," RFC 1078 (Nov.).

Mahdavi, J. 1997. "Enabling High Performance Data Transfers on Hosts: (Notes for Users and System Administrators)," Technical Note (Dec.).

    `http://www.psc.edu/networking/perf_tune.html`

Malkin, G. 1993. "Traceroute Using an IP Option," RFC 1393 (Jan.).

McCanne, S. and Jacobson, V. 1993. "The BSD Packet Filter: A New Architecture for User-Level Packet Capture," *Proceedings of the 1993 Winter USENIX Conference*, pp. 259–269, San Diego, Calif.

    ftp://ftp.ee.lbl.gov/papers/bpf-usenix93.ps.Z

Miller, B. P., Koski, D., Lee, C. P., Maganty, V., Murthy, R., Natarajan, A., and Steidl, J. 1995. "Fuzz Revisited: A Re-examination of the Reliability of UNIX Utilities and Services," CS-TR-95-1268, University of Wisconsin (Apr.).

    ftp://grilled.cs.wisc.edu/technical_papers/fuzz-revisited.ps.Z

Minshall, G., Saito, Y., Mogul, J. C., and Verghese, B. 1999. "Application Performance Pitfalls and TCP's Nagle Algorithm," ACM SIGMETRICS Workshop on Internet Server Performance, Atlanta, Ga..

    http://www.cc.gatech.edu/fac/Ellen.Zegura/wisp99/papers/minshall.ps

Mogul, J. and Postel, J. B. 1985. "Internet Standard Subnetting Procedure," RFC 950 (Aug.).

Nagle, J. 1984. "Congestion Control in IP/TCP Internetworks," RFC 896 (Jan.).

Oliver, M. 2000. Private communication.

Padlipsky, M. A. 1982. "A Perspective on the ARPANET Reference Model," RFC 871 (Sept.).

Partridge, C. 1993. "Jacobson on TCP in 30 Instructions," Message-ID <1993Sep8.213239.28992 @sics.se>, Usenet, comp.protocols.tcp-ip Newsgroup (Sept.).

    http://www-nrg.ee.lbl.gov/nrg-email.html

Partridge, C. and Pink, S. 1993. "A Faster UDP," *IEEE/ACM Transactions on Networking*, vol. 1, no. 4, pp. 427–440 (Aug.).

    http://www.ir.bbn.com/~craig/udp.ps

Patchett, C. and Wright, M. 1998. *The CGI/Perl Cookbook*. John Wiley & Sons, N.Y.

Paxson, V. 1995. "Re: Traceroute and TTL," Message-ID <48407@dog.ee.lbl.gov>, Usenet, comp.protocols.tcp-ip (Sept.).

    ftp://ftp.ee.lbl.gov/email/paxson.95sep29.txt

Paxson, V. 1997. "End-to-End Routing Behavior in the Internet," *IEEE/ACM Transactions on Networking*, vol. 5, no. 5, pp. 601–615 (Oct.).

    ftp://ftp.ee.lbl.gov/papers/vp-routing-TON.ps.Z

Plummer, W. W. 1978. "TCP Checksum Function Design," IEN 45 (June). Reprinted as an appendix to RFC 1071.

Postel, J. B. 1981. "Internet Control Message Protocol," RFC 792 (Sept.).

Postel, J. B., ed. 1981a. "Internet Protocol," RFC 791 (Sept.).

Postel, J. B., ed. 1981b. "Transmission Control Protocol," RFC 793 (Sept.).

Quinn, B. and Shute, D. 1996. *Windows Sockets Network Programming*. Addison-Wesley, Reading, Mass.

Rago, S. A. 1993. *UNIX System V Network Programming*. Addison-Wesley, Reading, Mass.

Rago, S. A. 1996. "Re: Sockets vs TLI," Message-ID <50pcds$jl8@prologic.plc.com>, Usenet, comp.protocols.tcp-ip (Oct.).

Rekhter, Y. and Li, T. 1993. "An Architecture for IP Address Allocation with CIDR," RFC 1518 (Sept.).

Rekhter, Y., Moskowitz, R. G., Karrenberg, D., Groot, G. J. de, and Lear, E. 1996. "Address Allocation of Private Internets," RFC 1918 (Feb.).

Reynolds, J. K. and Postel, J. B. 1985. "File Transfer Protocol (FTP)," RFC 959 (Oct.).

Richter, J. 1997. *Advanced Windows, Third Edition*. Microsoft Press, Redmond, Wash.

Ritchie, D. M. 1984. "A Stream Input-Output System," *AT&T Bell Laboratories Technical Journal*, vol. 63, no. No. 8 Part 2, pp. 1897–1910 (Oct.).

    `http://cm.bell-labs.com/cm/cs/who/dmr/st.ps`

Romkey, J. L. 1988. "A Nonstandard for Transmission of IP Datagrams Over Serial Lines: SLIP," RFC 1055 (June).

Saltzer, J. H., Reed, D. P., and Clark, D. D. 1984. "End-to-End Arguments in System Design," *ACM Transactions in Computer Science*, vol. 2, no. 4, pp. 277–288 (Nov.).

    `http://web.mit.edu/Saltzer/www/publications`

Sedgewick, R. 1998. *Algorithms in C, Third Edition, Parts 1–4*. Addison-Wesley, Reading, Mass.

Semke, J., Mahdavi, J., and Mathis, M. 1998. "Automatic TCP Buffer Tuning," *Computer Communications Review*, vol. 28, no. 4, pp. 315–323 (Oct.).

    `http://www.psc.edu/networking/ftp/papers/autotune-sigcomm98.ps`

Srinivasan, R. 1995. "XDR: External Data Representation Standard," RFC 1832 (Aug.).

Stevens, W. R. 1990. *UNIX Network Programming*. Prentice Hall, Englewood Cliffs, N.J.

Stevens, W. R. 1994. *TCP/IP Illustrated, Volume 1: The Protocols*. Addison-Wesley, Reading, Mass.

Stevens, W. R. 1996. *TCP/IP Illustrated, Volume 3: TCP for Transactions, HTTP, NNTP, and the UNIX Domain Protocols*. Addison-Wesley, Reading, Mass.

Stevens, W. R. 1998. *UNIX Network Programming, Volume 1, Second Edition, Networking APIs: Sockets and XTI*. Prentice Hall, Upper Saddle River, N.J.

Stevens, W. R. 1999. *UNIX Network Programming, Volume 2, Second Edition, Interprocess Communications*. Prentice Hall, Upper Saddle River, N.J.

Stone, J., Greenwald, M., Partridge, C., and Hughes, J. 1998. "Performance of Checksums and CRC's Over Real Data," *IEEE/ACM Transactions on Networking*, vol. 6, no. 5, pp. 529–543 (Oct.).

Tanenbaum, A. S. 1996. *Computer Networks, Third Edition*. Prentice Hall, Englewood Cliffs, N.J.

Tanenbaum, A. S. and Woodhull, A. S. 1997. *Operating Systems: Design and Implementation, Second Edition*. Prentice Hall, Upper Saddle River, N.J.

Torek, C. 1994. "Re: Delay in Re-Using TCP/IP Port," Message-ID <199501010028.QAA16863 @elf.bsdi.com>, Usenet, comp.unix.wizards (Dec.).

    `http://www.kohala.com/start/torek.94dec31.txt`

Unix International 1991. "Data Link Provider Interface Specification," Revision 2.0.0, Unix International, Parsippany, N.J. (Aug.).

    `http://www.whitefang.com/rin/docs/dlpi.ps`
    The latest version of the DLPI specification (Version 2) is available from The Open Group at
    `http://www.opengroup.org/publications/catalog/c811.htm`

Varghese, G. and Lauck, A. 1997. "Hashed and Hierarchical Timing Wheels: Efficient Data Structures for Implementing a Timer Facility," *IEEE/ACM Transactions on Networking*, vol. 5, no. 6, pp. 824–834 (Dec.).

    `http://www.ccrc.wustl.edu/~varghese/PAPERS/twheel.ps.Z`

Wall, L., Christiansen, T., and Schwartz, R. L. 1996. *Programming Perl, Second Edition*. O'Reilly & Associates, Sebastopol, Calif.

WinSock Group 1997. "Windows Sockets 2 Application Programming Interface," Revision 2.2.1, The Winsock Group (May).

`http://www.stardust.com/wsresource/winsock2/ws2docs.html`

Wright, G. R. and Stevens, W. R. 1995. *TCP/IP Illustrated, Volume 2: The Implementation.* Addison-Wesley, Reading, Mass.

# Index

2MSL (two maximum segment life-
    times), 165–166, 171

Abell, V., 243
abortive release, 119
`accept` function, 12–13, 35, 43, 87, 128,
    213
    definition of, 12
ACK
    clock, 218
    delayed, 175–180, 219, 241–242
acknowledgment/retry mechanism, 18
active close, 166–167, 171–172
address
    broadcast, 28–29
    classfull, 21–32
    hierarchical, 31–32
    loopback, 10, 22, 223, 249
    physical, 23–27
    private IP, 32–34
Address Resolution Protocol, *see* ARP

`AF_INET` constant, 7–8, 39, 204–205, 244
`AF_INET6` constant, 204–205
`AF_LOCAL` constant, 7, 244
`AF_UNIX` constant, 7, 244
Agrawala, A. K., 71, 107
`alarm` function, 182–183
Albaugh, T., xiv
Albitx, P., 207
algorithm, Nagle, 4, 104, 114–116,
    173–180, 219, 239, 241
`allocate_timer` function, 151
answer record, 229
application skeleton, 35–47
applications, console, 2
ARP (Address Resolution Protocol), 24,
    227, 265
    hack, 24
    promiscuous, 24
    proxy, 24
assassination, TIME-WAIT, 167–169
asymmetric routing, 237–238
asynchronous error, 209

# Addison-Wesley Professional

# How to Register Your Book

## Register this Book

Visit: **http://www.aw.com/cseng/register**
Enter the ISBN*
Then you will receive:

- Notices and reminders about upcoming author appearances, tradeshows, and online chats with special guests
- Advanced notice of forthcoming editions of your book
- Book recommendations
- Notification about special contests and promotions throughout the year

*The ISBN can be found on the copyright page of the book

## Visit our Web site

http://www.aw.com/cseng

When you think you've read enough, there's always more content for you at Addison-Wesley's web site. Our web site contains a directory of complete product information including:

- Chapters
- Exclusive author interviews
- Links to authors' pages
- Tables of contents
- Source code

You can also discover what tradeshows and conferences Addison-Wesley will be attending, read what others are saying about our titles, and find out where and when you can meet our authors and have them sign your book.

We encourage you to patronize the many fine retailers who stock Addison-Wesley titles. Visit our online directory to find stores near you.

## Contact Us via Email

**cepubprof@awl.com**
Ask general questions about our books.
Sign up for our electronic mailing lists.
Submit corrections for our web site.

**cepubeditors@awl.com**
Submit a book proposal.
Send errata for a book.

**cepubpublicity@awl.com**
Request a review copy for a member of the media interested in reviewing new titles.

**registration@awl.com**
Request information about book registration.

**Addison-Wesley Professional**
**One Jacob Way, Reading, Massachusetts 01867 USA**
**TEL 781-944-3700 • FAX 781-942-3076**